Turn Your Eyes Toward Texas

NUMBER THIRTY

Centennial Series

of the Association of Former Students,

Texas A&M University

Turn Your Eyes Toward Texas

PIONEERS SAM AND MARY MAVERICK

•

Paula Mitchell Marks

TEXAS A&M UNIVERSITY PRESS

COLLEGE STATION

The paper used in this book meets the minimum requirements
of the American National Standard for Permanence
of Paper for Printed Library Materials, Z39.48-1984.
Binding materials have been chosen for durability.

Library of Congress Cataloging-in-Publication Data

Marks, Paula Mitchell, 1951–
    Turn your eyes toward Texas : pioneers Sam and
Mary Maverick / Paula Mitchell Marks.
        p.   cm. – (Centennial series of the Associa-
tion of Former Students, Texas A&M University ;
no. 30)
    Based on thesis (Ph. D.)–University of Texas at
Austin.
    Bibliography: p.
    Includes index.
    ISBN 0-89096-380-0 : $27.50
    1. San Antonio (Tex.)–Biography.   2. Maverick,
Samuel Augustus, 1803-1870.   3. Maverick, Mary
Adams.   4. Pioneers–Texas–San Antonio–
Biography.   5. Frontier and pioneer life–Texas.
I. Title.   II. Series.
F394.S2M365   1989
976.4'351'00992–dc19
[B19]   88-27573
                                              CIP

To my parents,
who taught me to love learning,
and to my husband, Alan,
who encouraged me to follow that love

Contents

Illustrations

ix

Preface

MARY MAVERICK'S PUBLISHED MEMOIRS first drew me into the story of the pioneer life she shared with her husband in frontier Texas. I had found many nineteenth-century American pioneer women's accounts to be disappointing models of Victorian rectitude; a mother who had given birth in a covered wagon in the middle of the prairie would fail even to mention the event. By contrast, Mary Maverick's memoirs had a freshness, an immediacy of detail, a relative frankness that brought me closer to her frontier experience.

If the memoirs did this, the diaries from which she had drawn her manuscript proved even more invaluable. I will never forget the thrill I felt on first opening at random one of her still-extant diaries in the Barker Texas History Center and reading, "Wednesday Dec 30th [1846] and no husband and rumours of Indians at Austin My God oh how many times in this miserable existence have I been reduced to the brink of despair."

Here in all its emotional intensity was the real frontier experience of a literate, observant frontier woman. I knew I had to write about her. At the same time, however, I found that her husband, Samuel Augustus Maverick, also deserved full treatment as a significant and often overlooked Texas public figure of the Republic and early statehood eras.

Thus, what follows is a dual biography recapturing the lives of both the Mavericks as played out against the backdrop of Texas history, 1835–70. Based on the materials available, it is to a great extent a record of the public life of Sam Maverick and the private life of Mary Maverick. Thirty years ago, historians would have considered Sam Maver-

xi

ick's public career of far more importance than the story of his wife's traditional life at home. Today, social historians will be far more interested in Mary's rich record of her emotional life than in her husband's empire building. I have worked from the premise that public and private lives are equally worthy of study and that both individuals' stories deserve to be told.

From the storming of Béxar during the Texas revolution to the state's secession from the United States twenty-five years later, Sam Maverick played a dizzying variety of roles, including delegate from the Alamo garrison to the independence convention, frontier minuteman, Republic congressman, West Texas explorer and land speculator, six-term state legislator, railroad promoter, and Union supporter-turned-Texas–secession commissioner. His extensive land speculation and his limited foray into cattle ranching were carried into the realm of Texas myth by his contemporaries, with his name becoming indelibly linked with the Texas cattle industry and extrapolated as a synonym for a person who behaves independently.

He married Mary Adams in Alabama in August, 1836, and brought her to the Texas frontier in January, 1838. She became the chronicler, the family record keeper, and from the diaries and correspondence she so carefully saved comes a sense of the daily struggles and uncertainties faced by all those who chose to make their home "in wilderness," as Mary would phrase it forty years after her June, 1838, arrival in the small Mexican settlement of San Antonio de Béxar.

Near the end of her life, she prepared her memoirs and had six copies printed for her family. Granddaughter Rena Maverick Green directed the publishing of the manuscript in 1921, and in 1952 she included it in *Samuel Maverick, Texan, 1803–1870: A Collection of Letters, Journals and Memoirs*. Drawing on family papers now in the Barker Texas History Center at the University of Texas at Austin, Green outlined the couple's lives through their correspondence and diaries.

Historians have mined Green's work for information on life in early Texas, but little has been done with the Mavericks themselves. Green's effort, useful as it is, does not constitute a full biography of the two and their lives on the Texas frontier. Working almost exclusively from the family papers, Green chose to focus on the dramatic events of the early years—Maverick's participation in the Texas revolution and the couple's attempts to establish a permanent home in the Republic during the volatile 1830s and 1840s.

I have tried to present a more complete picture, both a social history of the couple and a reasonably full account of Sam Maverick's political and business activities, in order to help readers better understand the roles the Mavericks played in Texas history and the pioneer era in which they lived. The couple and their contemporaries on the far Texas frontier existed for years under the threat of Mexican invasion and for decades under the menace of Indian raids. They lived with great political instability, as Texas underwent one reincarnation after another: from Mexican province to independent republic, republic to state in the Union, Union to Confederate state, and finally state in the Union once more, suffering through the harshness and confusion of the Civil War and Reconstruction.

The Mavericks can be viewed to an extent as representative of a certain high socioeconomic class of Texas pioneers, antebellum southerners carrying their own culture southwestward. However, in rejecting the plantation life they had both known since childhood and selecting Mexican San Antonio as their home, they charted a different course from many of their fellow emigrants who extended southern plantation culture to Texas.

Thus, as real, complex human beings, the two do not fit any categories. Sam Maverick came to the Texas frontier at thirty-one, with his character already firmly molded. He was a prudent, rational lawyer who nonetheless delighted in adventure and thrived on hardship, a reserved man who nonetheless could pour forth in fervent eloquence when contemplating his "Mary-love," the lands of West Texas, or the destiny of Texas itself. He disdained the fortunes of the world and possessed a strong sense of public duty whetted by a Jeffersonian and Jacksonian belief in democratic equality. At the same time, he was a highly acquisitive businessman building an empire when land ownership was the surest measure of wealth and status.

Sam Maverick's "land-loving fury," as he himself termed it, may seem excessive to the modern reader, and indeed, he engaged in land speculation with an ardor and persistence that would bear psychological study. Yet for his time, his enthusiastic purchasing activities do not appear far out of the ordinary. American political and financial leaders were engaging in large-scale land speculation with fervor and sweeping vision as the nation expanded westward. Sam Maverick's personal empire building resulted not only from his training and natural inclinations but also from the heady times in which he lived.

Mary Maverick was just nineteen when she crossed the Sabine with her husband and baby, and her character would develop through adversity and spiritual struggle. She would move from being an untried girl buoyed by youth, high spirits, and love to a mature woman whose strength was built on hard-won religious faith. During a time when woman's sphere was narrowly defined and feminists such as Susan B. Anthony were beginning to speak out against women's secondary status, Mary Maverick followed a conventional path as wife and mother, pouring most of her energies into nurturing her family. But she read, she thought, and she explored the spiritual questions that held prime importance for her.

The church was for her, as for many nineteenth-century women, a first step outside the domestic sphere. As her frontier community developed and her children matured, women's role in the culture as a whole began to expand, with the justification that the world was only "a large home" in need of women's moral and spiritual involvement. Thus, Mary was eventually able to follow her interests and convictions into other public roles socially acceptable for women, such as historic preservation. Always, she possessed a sense of history, both in the making and in memory.

This, then, is her history and that of her husband as they joined the exodus to the West and met the difficult demands of life on a Texas frontier developing slowly and painfully.

In using family correspondence and other nineteenth-century sources in these pages, I have in some cases corrected spelling and altered punctuation for clarity's sake. As almost all family letters and journals quoted in the text are to be found in the Maverick Family Papers, Barker Texas History Center, Austin, I have often omitted a note after a dated quotation, trusting that the reader will understand the source to be the Barker Center collection. The reader may find references to "substance copies" puzzling; it is a term that both Sam Maverick and his father used to refer to copies of correspondence they made for themselves containing the "substance" of their missives.

Acknowledgments

BEFORE I BEGAN WORKING on a project of this scope, I would look at an acknowledgment page and wonder how so many people could become involved in an author's research and writing effort. Now I know. Not only did a number of people help answer research and writing questions, but their support and enthusiasm nourished me through a difficult endeavor.

Among those who provided assistance in South Carolina, special thanks go to Hurley E. Badders and Donna Roper of the Pendleton District Historical and Recreational Commission, to independent researcher Rita Horton McDavid of Columbia, and to Myrtle Riggins, who kindly opened the doors of the second Montpelier to me. In Alabama, independent researcher Maggie H. Sudduth of Tuscaloosa and Darrell A. Russel of the Natchez Trace Genealogical Society, Florence, were particularly helpful.

I am indebted to the staffs at a number of libraries, especially those at the Daughters of the Republic of Texas Library in San Antonio, the Barker Texas History Center in Austin, and the Texas State Library Archives Section in Austin. At the Barker Center, the cheerful assistance of Ralph Elder, Bill Richter, Bevery McFarland, John Slate, and Larry Landis made my hours there both pleasant and profitable. Michael Green at the State Archives was equally helpful.

Quotations from the Zenas R. Bliss Papers are used courtesy of Ben E. Pingenot. Quotations from the Alice Clow Papers and the Maverick Family Papers appear with the permission of the Barker Texas History Center.

Members of the Maverick family provided support and assistance.

Special thanks go to the late Mary Vance Green, whose interest in an accurate picture of her great-grandparents continued until her death. Thanks also are due Rowena Fenstermaker, Bebe Fenstermaker, Carey Rote, and Emily Wells. Rowena Fenstermaker, Rena Maverick Green's daughter, granted permission to reprint photographs and quote materials from her mother's books. My gratitude to Ellen Maverick Dickson simply cannot be expressed; her acceptance and enthusiasm buoyed my efforts from the beginning.

Records clerks at various federal, state, county, and city offices were also accommodating. Among them, John O. Leal, archivist and deputy clerk at the Bexar County Courthouse, deserves special mention.

Members of my dissertation committee also provided invaluable assistance through their research suggestions and careful reading of the manuscript. Thanks are due supervising professor William Goetzmann and committee members Thomas Cutrer, Don Graham, Elspeth Rostow, and John Sunder. I am also indebted to William Green for his perusal of the manuscript.

Finally, my thanks to Alan, to Glenna and Ivan, and to Carrie, who shared her mother with a computer.

Turn Your Eyes Toward Texas

Squire Sam

*". . . yet the idea of independence is the thing; by one's own industry,
no matter how small or how great; and to trust in the providence
of God is a kingdom of itself."*
—Samuel Maverick of South Carolina
to his grandson in Texas, July 4, 1846

ON AN APRIL DAY IN 1835, Samuel Augustus Maverick stepped out of
a dinghy at the mouth of the Brazos River, gateway to the Texas frontier. Behind him at anchor floated the brig *Henry*, which had transported Maverick and thirty-seven other adventurers westward from
New Orleans. Before him stood the rude port community of Velasco,
established in 1821 by empresario Stephen F. Austin's first colonists.
Austin's father, Moses, had won from the Mexican government permission to settle emigrants from the United States in this vast territory
claimed by Mexico as part of its state of Coahuila-y-Texas. Now the
son and a handful of other empresarios held title to huge tracts of
Texas land, generating American interest in this southwestern frontier.

Maverick was thirty-one years old that spring day when he arrived
on Texas soil, a lean man just under six feet tall, with a grave manner
and the bearing of a gentleman from the East.[1] The Yale-educated lawyer was looking for land, lots of land. He was also looking for a more
satisfying life than he had yet found in his years of ranging along the
Eastern Seaboard and through the Deep South. In Texas, he would
find what he sought; here he was to build a fabled empire of land and
participate in some of the most stirring and significant events in the
shaping of the Republic and state.

He had moved westward gradually as part of a great southern exodus, an eddying stream of restless humanity flowing from the Carolinas, Georgia, and Tennessee through Alabama, Mississippi, Arkan-

sas, and Louisiana. In their quest for fertile soil and other favorable economic conditions, emigrants would often settle briefly in one of the states through which the stream of humanity flowed, then rejoin it on its westward journey.

Maverick himself arrived in Texas after limited residences in Georgia and Alabama, but for the first thirty years of his life, South Carolina claimed his allegiance. He was born the first child of Charleston businessman Samuel Maverick and Elizabeth Anderson Maverick at their summer home in Pendleton District, South Carolina, on July 23, 1803. Only months before, Pres. Thomas Jefferson had doubled the young nation's size with the Louisiana Purchase, instigating an era of western exploration in which Samuel Augustus Maverick would take an active part.

Pendleton was as far west as many South Carolinians cared to go. The village in the rolling, wooded hills near the state's western tip served primarily as a summer refuge for wealthy planters escaping the muggy, disease-ridden coastal plains, or "Low Country." One established year-round resident was maternal grandfather, Robert Anderson, a native Virginian of Scotch-Irish descent whose twenty-one hundred–acre Westville plantation bordered the Seneca River west of the village.

Anderson, or "Old Thunder Gusty" as the Cherokees called him, was one of Pendleton District's most influential pioneers, having served as surveyor, Indian fighter, Revolutionary War leader, magistrate, and state militia brigadier general. He had helped draft South Carolina's first constitution, served repeatedly in the state legislature, and amassed landholdings along most of the streams of Pendleton district.[2]

The general was to die when his grandson was only nine, but the parallels in their frontier activities are striking. Samuel Augustus Maverick would follow in his grandfather's footsteps, surveying and buying land on a new frontier and serving Texas in the same capacities in which his grandfather served South Carolina. He was also to share the older man's egalitarian democratic sentiments, expressed when Anderson was sixty-three and Samuel Augustus barely a year old. Asserting that all of his public involvement had been motivated by a desire for the country's good, Anderson proclaimed, "I am for all mankind, the poor equal with the rich, enjoying equal rights in every respect both civil and religious."[3]

In the antebellum southern mind, equal rights did not extend to

Indians or slaves, however, and an anonymous visitor near the end of Anderson's life came upon him penning a six hundred–page vindication of slavery. The guest found the general, suffering from gout and attended by a granddaughter, to be "a religious and devout good man" who was getting fine cotton yields from "some of his best lands."[4]

Samuel Augustus moved in his grandfather's presence only sporadically for the first seven years of the boy's life, as the Maverick family lived primarily in Charleston before they settled on Pendleton as their home in 1810. When the old man died in 1813, his son Robert assumed his place in the community, taking over the plantation and most of the slaves. Samuel Augustus received one slave in his grandfather's will.[5] He also received another bequest — a legacy of frontier activity and public service that must have appealed to him greatly, as he gravitated toward similar pursuits.

His legacy from his father was altogether different but just as valuable. The elder Samuel Maverick was a shrewd and successful Charleston businessman who inculcated in his son the self-made man's values of industry, individual initiative, and financial prudence, as well as a stoic's faith in God's providence. Samuel sometimes became uncomfortably aware of the paradoxes inherent in his teachings, for he encouraged his son's acquisitive instincts at the same time as he counseled against material wealth as a road to happiness. Neither father nor son was ever able to reconcile his desire for more with his understanding of the fleeting nature of earthly gain, but this did not stop both from building far-flung land empires.

The Mavericks belonged to an old Charleston family that could trace its origins in the New World to 1624, when Samuel Maverick of England arrived in New England. This first Samuel Maverick embodied the term "maverick" long before a venture by Samuel Augustus led to its coining, for as a royalist in a Puritan family, he clashed with his Puritan neighbors in both political and religious matters. Massachusetts Bay Colony governor John Winthrop called him an "estimable man" possessing "substance and worth," but he was denied any position of public authority within the Puritan community.[6]

Members of this Maverick's immediate family emigrated to Barbados, then to Charleston, where Samuel Augustus' grandfather "Captain" Samuel, who owned fifteen ships, married Lydia Turpin, daughter of another Charleston shipowner. The union in December, 1772 produced firstborn son Samuel, the father of Samuel Augustus.[7]

Young Samuel's early experiences molded him into a man preoccupied with health and filled with an entrepreneurial spirit. Although Lydia bore five more children, one was stillborn and the others fell victim to the yellow fever that periodically swept the Carolina Low Country. In addition, Captain Samuel had lost all five children of a previous marriage. Thus, Samuel was the only one of his father's eleven offspring to grow to adulthood, and the knowledge of the fearsome odds against staying healthy on the coast would eventually lead him to pepper his letters with admonitions to his own children not to endanger their health by choosing sickly climates. "Of what use," he would later write to Samuel Augustus, "is all the lands in Texas or the figures on a Bank book to a dead man?"[8]

At the same time, Captain Samuel would encourage his son in the business goals that led the younger man to the Texas frontier. Samuel's experiences as a child during the Revolutionary War had whetted his appetite for a life of entrepreneurial enterprise. His father had been captured by the British while participating in the defense of Charleston. Freed from a British prison ship before Charleston's fall, Captain Samuel took the boy and Lydia along with Lydia's parents, Joseph and Mary Brown Turpin, and her brother, William Turpin, to Providence, Rhode Island, where the Turpins, who had Quaker origins, were known as shipbuilders.[9]

In Rhode Island, the continental money that Samuel's father had sold out for in Charleston depreciated, the former prisoner's health declined as a result of injuries suffered on the prison ship, and the family's outlook seemed bleak. However, for young Samuel the time in Rhode Island was an exciting period in which, as he later made clear in letters to his children and grandchildren, he absorbed the lessons that made possible his later successes. He received little formal education, a deficiency that he felt strongly enough to send his children to fine eastern schools. But his practical education began in Rhode Island when his grandfather Joseph Turpin's sister came to visit the family and made a skillet of molasses candy, giving it to the boy to sell.

Over sixty years later, Samuel would write to his nine-year-old grandson in Texas about this first enterprise: "I went into the street and soon sold it at a copper a stick and run home with the money delighted with the grand discovery." Buying sugar with the coppers he had earned, the boy learned from his great-aunt how to make the candy. Soon he had developed a street business in which he easily doubled his money.

He experienced a minor setback when another street vendor sold him a cheap pair of "sleeve buttons set with beautiful red cut glass," claiming the pewter buttons were silver. But it was all part of his education, for "it induced me to look better in future to my bargains."[10]

Shortly after the war's end, Captain Samuel died, and the rest of the family returned to Charleston. Young Samuel's mentor became his uncle, William Turpin, who with a partner quickly built up the Charleston mercantile firm of Wadsworth and Turpin. Employed as a shop boy, Samuel was allowed a corner of the establishment to market items not stocked by the firm, and here he built a trade selling grease for wagon wheels. One day a friend of Grandfather Joseph Turpin was visiting the family at home and proposed to "carry a venture" for the boy on a voyage to France. Samuel obtained five French crowns and ordered a list of luxuries—ostrich feathers, ladies' fans, umbrellas—selling them when they arrived for more than double the cost. Soon the firm of Wadsworth and Turpin had become the firm of Wadsworth, Turpin and Maverick.[11]

In 1793, while Samuel was launching his business career, his mother remarried. Her new husband was none other than Gen. Robert Anderson of Pendleton, who brought to the union five children, four under the age of eighteen, with the youngest being nine-year-old Elizabeth. Lydia joined her new family at Pendleton while Samuel stayed in Charleston and in the decade between his twentieth and thirtieth birthdays, 1792 to 1802, made a fortune importing goods from England, Holland, Germany, Cuba, and France. He also traded in slaves and cotton. Years later, he remembered "when the first parcel of cotton we shipped to Liverpool in small bags" caused difficulty because the recipients "could not separate the seed from the cotton without an immense deal of trouble."[12]

Despite his delight in independent enterprise, his entrepreneurial spirit was beginning to be subdued by "mercantile miscarriages," "sad accidents in trade" that he hints at occasionally in later family correspondence. His mother's pastoral home in the rolling foothills of the Blue Ridge Mountains near Pendleton began to have many attractions.

Even before Lydia's marriage to General Anderson, Samuel Maverick had cast his eye toward the relatively healthy South Carolina "Up Country." Before Pendleton District was formed out of old Ninety-Six District in 1789, Samuel as a boy of fifteen had received a land grant of 126 acres in the district, and his uncle William also owned land in

Samuel Maverick of South Carolina, from a painting attributed to Samuel Morse.

the area.[13] Now Samuel established a summer home on acreage about three miles north of Pendleton, building a traditional southern plantation house with tall columns and iron balconies.[14] He named it Montpelier, after the French estate abandoned by the family of his paternal grandmother, Catherine Coyer Maverick. The elderly lady died in

8

Charleston only three years before Samuel's marriage, and he was sufficiently proud of his French heritage to display a Coyer coat of arms in his new home.[15]

In October, 1802, Maverick wed his nineteen-year-old stepsister Elizabeth Anderson. Lydia Turpin Maverick Anderson lived to see her son and stepdaughter united, but she died before the birth of grandson Samuel Augustus Maverick in July of the following year.

As a child, Samuel Augustus came to know two worlds: the bustling urban environment of a Charleston recovered from the devastation of the Revolutionary War, and the relaxed plantation life of Pendleton District. Charleston was the seaport trading hub of a growing cotton and rice kingdom; at the factors' counting houses on the bay, so the story went, furniture was painted blue to accentuate the whiteness of these two cash crops. Ships, brigs, and schooners sailed into the bay laden with luxuries, from puncheons of Barbados rum to silk ribbons, from Havana chocolate to "rich figured Florentines for gentlemen's waistcoats."[16] Retail stores on Elliott, Tradd, and Broad streets did a brisk business, as wealthy Charlestonians arrived and departed in their expensive carriages. The return of the planters to the city each January signaled the advent of balls, assemblies, concerts, and highly popular races at the Washington Course.

However, the infectious yellow fever periodically crept into the city. Beginning with fever, chills, and prostration, it produced jaundice and, all too often, internal hemorrhage, coma, and death. Charleston's yellow fever outbreaks were terrifying in their sweep and intensity, as the elder Samuel Maverick knew all too well. By the time he started his own family, he had seen not only the yellow fever deaths of his siblings in the city, but also those of his grandfather Turpin and an uncle, Lydia and William's brother Joseph.

When Samuel Augustus was almost two, Elizabeth gave birth to a daughter, Ann Caroline. Eighteen months later, a son, Robert, arrived but lived less than a day, victim of his mother's recent fall from a carriage. A fourth child, Sam's sister Mary Elizabeth, was born in Charleston in December, 1807. On September 2, 1809, four-year-old Ann Caroline died in a yellow fever outbreak. The anguish of the loss and his own poor health caused her father to determine to remove permanently to Montpelier in the more salubrious climate of Pendleton, and this the family did in 1810.[17]

At first, with his family safely established in a better climate near

Elizabeth's relatives, Samuel continued to try to divide his time between Charleston and Pendleton. But he soon developed a passion for horticulture, eagerly tending to a wide array of fruits and vegetables while overseeing the production of cotton by the family slaves. Gradually, he began to enter into some small business operations in the Pendleton area and to withdraw from his Charleston ventures. A friend, writing to him in early 1812, expressed surprise at Maverick's decision to live "in the woods," but concluded that "health is before wealth" and "you have taken care to get wealth enough."[18]

One last child was born to Samuel and Elizabeth at Pendleton— Lydia Ann, eleven years younger than Samuel Augustus. The family settled into a comfortable existence at Montpelier, and Samuel began to accumulate more land in the district. The Mavericks moved in the elite society surrounding Pendleton, where many plantation owners kept summer or year-round homes. However, many of the neighbors were "old money" aristocrats who looked with slight disfavor at Samuel Maverick's mercantile aggressiveness. He entered into a partnership to own and operate the largest mill in the district, and in the Pendleton *Messenger* he advertised "Farms, and Houses and Lots in the village to Rent and Lands to Lease, on reasonable terms."[19]

Samuel's name is conspicuous by its absence on the list of members of the Pendleton Farmers Society, an influential group made up of the premier names in Pendleton affairs and formed in 1815 with his brother-in-law Robert Anderson as a charter member; nor does his name appear on the rolls of other organizations involving the prominent men of the community.[20] Still, Samuel Maverick was by no means an outcast for his business activities; visitors to Pendleton spoke of moving easily between the Maverick estate and the estates of the other gentry, and Samuel was appointed one of two wardens at St. Paul's Episcopal Church upon its completion in 1822.[21]

By this time, he was a widower, Elizabeth having died "after a painful illness of four months" on September 28, 1818, when Samuel Augustus was fifteen, Mary Elizabeth ten, and Lydia four. The effect of the life and death of Elizabeth Anderson Maverick on her son Samuel Augustus is difficult to gauge, as references to her in family correspondence are brief and factual. Thus, she joins the many phantom women of history who are remembered only by date of birth, number of children, and date of death.[22]

The record is equally mute on Samuel Augustus' early life growing

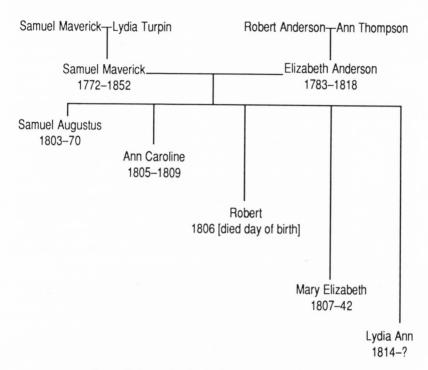

Samuel Maverick–Elizabeth Anderson family tree.

up at Montpelier. Most accounts state that he was educated at home. A long-lived boys' academy was not established at Pendleton until he was in college, but other efforts at group education were made during his childhood, for General Anderson was a trustee of the Hopewell Academy just outside Pendleton in 1807. Whether Samuel Augustus attended an academy or was tutored at home, it is likely that his studies resembled those of Hopewell, which reported instruction in original composition, Latin and Greek authors, public speaking, English grammar, and geography.[23]

He grew into "a serious young man, mature beyond his years," absorbing his father's maxims concerning a prudent, businesslike approach to living.[24] Samuel was fond of quoting Uncle William Turpin, now living in New York City—don't keep all your eggs in one basket, sell when everyone wants to purchase, and purchase when things are under their intrinsic value.[25] He transmitted to his son his sound business sense, his love of horticulture, and his growing lust for more land.

At the same, Uncle Robert Anderson carried on General Anderson's life of public involvement and public duty, providing a second model for the young man's emulation. On the Texas frontier, Samuel Augustus was to combine the Maverick talent for business enterprise with the Anderson attention to public duty.

But it would take a number of years for Samuel Augustus to find his way westward. He first moved northward, departing in 1822, at age eighteen, for Ripton, Connecticut, where he spent the summer preparing under a tutor for September entrance into Yale University's sophomore class. Graduation exercises were held then as the fall term commenced, so the newcomer matriculated at New Haven as ninety-four young men received diplomas.[26] That autumn, all of Yale was mourning the loss of mathematics and natural philosophy professor Alexander Metcalf Fisher, who had just perished in the shipwreck of the packet boat *Albion* off the Irish coast. Maverick was to recall the incident with some anxiety thirty-four years later when he placed his own son aboard the steamer *Atlantic* bound for Liverpool.[27]

He kept a journal during his college years, only the first page of which survives. In the terse, precise prose that was to mark his style in later journals, he noted, "Sophomore class which I entered contains 105 students. Total undergraduates 373. Presdt. Jeremiah Day."[28]

The young southerner, known as "Gus" to his family but as "Sam" to his classmates, was entering an institution already more than one hundred years old and steeped in authoritarian religious tradition. When Day had assumed the presidency five years earlier, the school was still governed according to "the ideas of an aristocratic Federalism and a demanding Puritanism."[29] Day carried on the religious tradition by upholding Puritan virtues of duty and discipline and by viewing the institution as standing *in loco parentis*, molding the students' characters as well as their minds. On Sundays, students were still required to attend morning and evening prayers, as well as two worship services.

At the same time, however, Yale was becoming more secular as the church's hold on life in New England weakened and as national democratic spirit grew. The liberalization was evident in the textbooks considered essential at the university throughout the first half of the nineteenth century, Archdeacon of Carlisle William Paley's treatises combining Christian faith with rational Enlightenment thought.[30]

If Yale was becoming more secular, it did not mean any withdrawal from the heavy emphasis on character building. On the contrary, the needs of a new democratic nation and an Enlightenment view of human progress dictated that character development remain at the core of the university's program. American political and educational leaders shared a "post-Revolutionary consciousness" that the United States was undertaking a "great, though risky, experiment in government" requiring careful grooming of future public leaders.[31] Paley stressed civic duty, and Yale educators continued to encourage mental and moral discipline in their charges.

Maverick's attention to character development after leaving college, his sense of public duty, his Enlightenment concern for order and reason, his belief in a unified republic with opportunity for those of different backgrounds and beliefs – all were nurtured at Yale. Perhaps his interest in landownership was nurtured there, too, for in Paley's text he could read a reasoned defense of large private holdings. Paley acknowledged great inequality of property to be an evil, "abstractly considered," but pointed out that through buying and selling men were "incited to industry," rendering the object of their industry "secure and valuable."[32]

A typical student's day during Maverick's three years at the institution included classes in mathematics and natural science as well as in classical subjects such as logic, rhetoric, and moral philosophy. During leisure hours, students' impromptu outdoor activities included football, sailing, swimming, and hiking the countryside. At night, despite the stringent rules, young men often shared a bottle of wine while playing cards or backgammon in their dormitory rooms.[33]

New Haven itself was described by a traveler shortly before Maverick's arrival as a tranquil, picturesque, and pious city of between eight and ten thousand, where college students were well behaved, and where everyone from youngest to oldest went to church.[34] It was an idealistic picture, of course; at least one student uprising occurred during Maverick's stay. Yet students who could not submit to the constricting rules tended to disappear quietly, with approximately half of each class falling away before graduation.[35]

The traveler's peaceful view of the environment is reinforced by entries in Maverick's memory book from his senior year, a compendium of conventional poetry and eloquent good wishes penned by his classmates, three of whom directed their addresses to "Squire Sam." The specifics of the students' experiences together are lost in their attempts to adopt an elegant, elegiac tone, but what emerges is an easy, untroubled camaraderie and respect. One bitter note was sounded by a malcontent who cited jealousies, animosities, malice, and unrestrained ambitions among his classmates, which "will ever embitter my recollections of the past." However, he concluded, "none of the unhappy occurrences which have disturbed my feelings can I associate with the remembrance of your name. Such a classmate I shall ever esteem and respect."[36]

Maverick graduated in the fall of 1825 and returned to Pendleton.[37] Seventeen-year-old Mary Elizabeth had married a cousin, Joseph Turpin Weyman, in Charleston in March of the year, so only Samuel and ten-year-old Lydia remained at home, along with a retinue of house and field slaves. Samuel was eagerly cultivating his orchards and vineyard, with his greatest passion the growing of the grape. It had led him into correspondence with Thomas Jefferson in 1822 on the problems involved. Three years later, he told a summer visitor enjoying his homemade wine that he thought wine could be "as lucrative a commodity as cotton" in the region.[38] Though his conjectures were overly optimistic, he passed on to his son the same enthusiasm; when Sam Maverick attended the legislature at Austin in the 1850s, his letters home to San Antonio would be laced with frequent instructions on the care of his beloved grapevines.

Shortly after Maverick's Yale graduation, a letter from a college friend encouraged him to attend a New York ball, concluding, "As you are a great admirer of the fair sex, I doubt not but that you will be gratified in seeing some of the beauty of the City & of the Country."[39] However, if any serious romance entered Sam Maverick's life during his adolescence or early adulthood, the record does not show it. He now began a long, solitary business apprenticeship under his father, who had continued his enterprises around Pendleton and extended his land empire to other South Carolina districts, to Georgia, and to Alabama.

Samuel soon started deeding land to his firstborn; records show that he gave lots in Pendleton and in Tuscaloosa, Alabama, to Sam in 1825 and in 1826 began giving him tracts in the district. Sam himself began to enter into the real estate spirit, making his first district purchase with half a lot in Pendleton on February 4, 1826.[40] The passion for land speculation was to label son as well as father "mercenary" in the eyes of some of their neighbors, but many prominent citizens of the era indulged in large-scale speculation, and both Mavericks continued to enjoy good standing in the community.[41] The son joined the Pendleton Farmers Society shortly after his return from Yale and witnessed the arrival in the community of John C. Calhoun, who had received an honorary degree from the school when Maverick entered and was now U.S. vice-president. Up-Country native Calhoun and his family settled at Fort Hill Plantation near Pendleton and began attending St. Paul's Episcopal Church, where the Mavericks worshiped.

An 1826 notebook Sam Maverick kept shows a lively interest in everything from politics to wine making. Sandwiched in with scraps of news and medical treatments for rheumatism and even jokes is the first reference that shows Maverick's mind was turning to Texas. Meticulously providing a subject heading for each entry, he noted, "(Growth, U.S.) Austin's grant in Texas, Mexico is becoming settled very fast."

Maverick also recorded pithy quotations that reflected his interest in an enlightened democratic government and in character building. One entry defines precedent as "the inclined plane down which all governments has [sic] slid into monarchy and corruption." Others provide maxims for personal living: "The most empty vessels are always the most noisy," he wrote, and followed it with "The most strong bodies (when struck) yield the least noise." The extent of the elder Samuel's influence on his son can be measured in part by the fact that the son recorded his father's words on the hereafter in the journal, too: "'Eternity,' says Saml Maverick, 'is one unending day lighted up by the presence of God.'"[42]

In 1827 the younger Maverick spent three months in Alabama and Tennessee on business for his father. A notebook in which he took geographical, botanical, and business notes reveals that he was developing a careful business sense, as well as an eye for the agricultural and mineral potential of land. He also showed great interest in democratic government and the future of the young United States, copying or composing in his journal an address on the importance of American democratic principles of civil liberty, religious toleration, and government based on "the good of the governed."[43]

Back in South Carolina, he continued filling paper booklets with terse bits of information and observations. A March, 1828, diary covering a visit to Charleston included an assessment of court painter David's painting of the coronation of Napoleon, which the young man viewed with his sister and cousins at the Academy of Fine Arts. "If he is not indeed flattered," wrote Maverick, "it must stand as the most perfect model of a man of genius." He recorded with approval the lack of "striking passion or enterprise" on the emperor's face, concluding that "it was the habit of the man to conceal and rather to surprise the world with the rapid execution of what no one believed he had ever conceived much less pondered on."[44] The power and restraint of the figure held a fascination for the young man who was beginning to seek an avenue for his own ambitions and for whom self-discipline was a strong part of his nature and training.

In 1828 Pendleton District was split into Anderson and Pickens districts, the former named in honor of Maverick's grandfather. As Pendleton was not centrally located in the new Anderson District, the town of Anderson was founded as seat of district government on land originally granted to William Turpin and a partner. Samuel Maverick bought Anderson lots at the first auction, and his son began extending his own holdings by making his first purchase of acreage, one hundred acres on Twenty-Three Mile Creek east of Montpelier, and following that quickly with the acquisition of a tract in Alabama.[45]

It was well and good to be a landholder, but the younger Maverick had still not settled on a profession. In 1828, he traveled to Winchester, Virgina, and began studying law under noted jurist Henry St. George Tucker, who in 1803 had produced the essential legal tome for any aspiring American lawyer by adapting Sir William Blackstone's *Commentaries* on English common law for American usage. Tucker, a former U.S. congressional representative, Virginia senator, and judge superior of district chancery courts, provided another public service role model for a conscientious student.

Most aspiring lawyers of the time still studied under experienced lawyers or in private technical schools rather than in universities. Private law school lecturer David Daggett had begun teaching law at Yale during Maverick's time there but followed the university tradition of treating the subject as part of a genteel citizen's liberal education. Thus, many future lawyers read for their profession in law offices, and they already had a significant literature for self-study, as leading lawyers had been attempting to provide a complete inventory of legal principles over the preceding quarter decade.[46]

As the younger Maverick commenced his law studies, his father continued his horticultural interests, prevailing on his neighbor Calhoun to forward to John Quincy Adams a request for assistance from

U.S. agents abroad in obtaining grapevines from China. In his transmittal letter, Calhoun called Samuel "a worthy and respectable citizen, who has devoted much of his attention to the cultivation of the vine."[47]

The Mavericks and Calhouns, from all appearances, enjoyed a benign social relationship, but their political differences ran deep. While the younger Maverick was in Virginia, his father kept him apprised of the volatile political situation swirling around Calhoun and other leaders in South Carolina. The U.S. Congress had recently passed the "Tariff of Abominations," a protective tariff placed on manufactured goods. The move enraged many southerners, as it helped the industrial North but seemed to hinder the agricultural South, particularly in its cotton trade with England. The Virginia legislature declared the tariff unconstitutional; in South Carolina, the legislature issued "South Carolina Exposition and Protest," anonymously authored by Calhoun and asserting the state's constitutional right to nullify the tariff.

Among the Maverick neighbors and acquaintances were vehement cries of agreement. Already the whole state was straining toward secession and war. On Christmas Day, 1828, Samuel wrote to his son, "Our members are just returning from the Legislature, where they went labouring under that most dreadful malady, the Tariff fever, but [I] am happy that they appear to be on the mend." Then he added prophetically, "But I fear like the small pox, those that had it in the natural way, may retain the pits."

As the issue smoldered, the younger Maverick completed his law studies in Virginia and became licensed to practice in that state on March 26, 1829, in Frederick County.[48] He then returned to South Carolina and, a few weeks later, on May 6, in Columbia, received his license to practice in his home state. Traveling to Charleston, he bought "Law Books and Groceries," then returned with his uncle Robert Anderson to Pendleton, where he took lodging at a public house and established a law practice. "A public notice," read the ad signed by Samuel A. Maverick in the Pendleton *Messenger* of August 26, 1829. "The subscriber has commenced, at the Village of Pendleton, the PRACTICE OF LAW: and will attend to business in the Courts of Law and Equity for Anderson and Pickens, and the other Court Houses on the Western Circuit."

It was a small practice, "very small," as the new lawyer wryly conceded, particularly since government functions had moved to the new district seat of Anderson.[49] Pendleton remained a pleasant village, boasting a post office, two churches, primary and secondary schools, a newspaper and printing office, a farmers' hall, about forty homes, and a variety of shops and taverns clustered around a picturesque village green. But as pleasant as it was, Pendleton did not offer much to a young man of ambition. Maverick decided to run for the South Carolina legislature in the state elections of 1830 on a strong, and unpopular, antinullification platform. He advocated a peaceful, gradual approach to the tariff problem through established federal channels, and did so with clarity and logic.

However, the campaign proved difficult, with all the inflamed rhetoric breaking forth on the main issue. "On the 17th Inst. at the Barbecue, I with others spoke on the subject of the Tariff and the means South Carolina ought to use to oppose it," he wrote in an undated address to voters that survives among his papers. "I attempted to make a very full avowal of my views, to the end that those who entertained different opinions might have an opportunity to oppose my election on the fair ground of political difference. In these respects it seems that I stood alone."[50]

He placed ninth in a field of thirteen candidates, accumulating 1,628 votes to the winner's 2,386.[51] It was certainly not a disastrous political beginning, but popular feeling in the state continued to run counter to the convictions of both Maverick men. Most South Carolinians applauded Calhoun's response to President Jackson's toast on April 6, 1830. "Our Federal Union," proclaimed the president, "It must be preserved," and the vice-president replied, "The Union—next to our liberty most dear."

Sam Maverick opposed all talk of nullification, but he apparently maintained good relations with those disagreeing with his unionist views, as he helped host a Pendleton dinner in honor of Calhoun in April, 1831, and he continued to participate in community life, serving as warden of St. Paul's in 1832.[52]

Meanwhile, the nullification controversy was heating to a point at which political differences could not be ignored. In 1832, Henry Clay pushed through yet another tariff act, and an incensed South Carolina convention responded by passing an Ordinance of Nullification, proclaiming a state's right to veto federal action.

Drafts of letters and of Pendleton Anti-Nullification Committee materials among Sam Maverick's papers show that he threw himself whole-

heartedly into this hottest debate of the day, lashing out against the
"cup of delusion" handed the South Carolina populace by its leaders.
"There is no liberty without union, no union without liberty," he wrote
in one letter. "I hesitate not one moment to say that it is a question
whether or not we shall abandon our original frame of government.
. . . Let violence once into our system and so peculiar is our polity that
it cannot but destroy us."[53]

Maverick penned a report of the Pendleton Anti-Nullification Committee, which promised to cooperate with any constitutional and peaceful plan, including the calling of a southern convention to improve
tariff policy. It repudiated the nationally divisive imposition of state
vetoes and endorsed Andrew Jackson in his re-election bid.[54]

The Pendleton lawyer also wrote a lengthy, judicious letter to the
Pendleton *Messenger* further outlining the antinullification position.
He conceded that the tariff laws were unconstitutional, but only in the
sense that they violated the equitable spirit of the Constitution. He
also conceded that the laws were injurious to the South, but felt that
"the Tariff is represented to be ten-fold more oppressive than it really
is." He saw it as a temporary evil, one that "must be expected at times
to result in every republican govt. where the majority must rule & ought
to rule." He advocated change through normal government action and
through a natural process of public opinion swinging in the South's
favor. The state and federal governments, he argued, must remain co-
equal, neither one gaining ascendancy at the expense of the other.[55]

According to an oft-repeated story in the Maverick canon, the young
lawyer used not only his pen but also his sword after his father was
heckled while answering Calhoun's arguments at a public meeting. As
the story goes, Sam Maverick sprang to his father's defense, challenging the heckler to a duel, then nursing the adversary back to health
after wounding him.[56] The biographical sketch of Maverick on file at
Yale University takes the tale one step farther by identifying the wounded
duelist as Calhoun himself.

Whether or not Sam Maverick entered this dramatically into the
fray, his pro-Union stand was clearly costing him any immediate political future in the state. Ironically, thirty years later, tired of fighting
for unity between North and South, Maverick would cast his vote for
Texas secession. But in 1832 the secession and nullification issue was
blocking his political ambitions. Sam Maverick was almost thirty years
old and still casting about for some life work beyond his meager law

practice. At his father's suggestion, he determined to devote some time to managing family holdings in the Deep South.[57]

By mid-February, 1833, he had temporarily located in the Cherokee Nation, northern Georgia, where his journal indicates that he engaged in land management and business dealings across the South. According to one later account, he also tried to run a gold mine, which proved unprofitable.[58] Gold had been discovered in the northern Georgia hills in 1829, spurring a continuing rush of eager miners who helped to accomplish what Georgia officials had been trying to do for years—force the Cherokees out. With the tacit approval of Pres. Andrew Jackson, whose harsh Indian removal policy matched their own, Georgia political leaders continued to intimidate the Indians and make questionable treaties with them.

Maverick would comment on the situation on a return visit the following year, writing that "people are selling out here; the whole nation is drooping under the ruthless barbarity of Georgia. Her motto for years has in practice been 'Might is Right.'"[59] He could not have been unaware, however, that in locating in the Cherokee Nation he had been an agent of such change.

During his son's months in Georgia, the elder Samuel repeatedly wrote cautioning against going into debt or trusting others in financial dealings. His urgings were intensified by his own financial difficulties brought on by an agent placing Maverick money into the Bank of the United States, a monopoly that Andrew Jackson was determined to topple by depositing federal funds in state banks. Financial problems caused Samuel to recall the hard lessons he had learned in trade in Charleston, and he cautioned his son on April 10, 1833, to "become your own banker and keep the key in your own pocket and the knowledge of the amount in your own mind," to avoid those who would "have your money by begging, borrowing or stealing, by flattery or cursing." Later, he would write that great wealth was a curse, always "attended by troubles and dangers that even poverty is clear of."[60]

Indeed, between pressing money matters and the continuing nullification stalemate, with Jackson signing a Force Bill to enforce the tariff statute, Samuel began to "fear the fates are against us," as he wrote his son in the April 10 letter. Nonetheless, he encouraged his eldest to bear up under the inevitable "lashings of experience," advising him to not be discouraged but to "push on and do the best you can."

The younger Maverick returned to Pendleton late in the year and witnessed his sister Lydia's marriage at St. Paul's to his old Yale school-mate William Van Wyck of New York City. Lydia had been attending a school for young women in New York, and the coy, high-spirited letter to her brother that survives from this period, written to him in Georgia in March, reveals a warm relationship. Commenting on her Uncle William Turpin's unsuccessful attempts to link her affections with those of a distant relative, she vowed herself mindful of her brother's "wise precepts" outlined in a previous letter and promised, "I can never forget my dear Brother that 'You and I are one person in our relations of Brother and Sister.'"[61]

After the wedding, Maverick prepared to relocate to a plantation given to him by his father on the Tennessee River, fourteen miles from the town of Florence in Lauderdale County, Alabama. The planta-tion was part of Colbert's Reserve, a ten thousand–acre expanse on the river's north side, which had been given in treaty to half-breed Chickasaw leaders George and Levi Colbert in 1816, the year before Alabama gained statehood. The reserve had quickly passed from their hands to those of planters and land speculators. In 1820, the elder Maverick had bought the Tennessee River site, probably with a specu-lative eye on the fact that it lay beside that vital southern artery, the Natchez Trace.[62] At the time of his purchase, cotton plantations al-ready dotted the area, and the next year Florence itself was described by one visitor as a promising place "patronized by the wealthiest gen-tlemen in the state," with a "bold, enterprising, and industrious" citi-zenry and with river traffic "pouring every necessary and every luxury into its lap."[63]

On January 24, 1835, Sam Maverick departed Pendleton, this time with forty-five slaves belonging to the Maverick family, a wagon, carriage, twenty horses, and $644.50 in cash.[64] The entourage encoun-tered the usual troubles shared by travelers of the day—difficulties find-ing river fords and repairing wagon wheels. Later hints in Maverick's correspondence and in his family's indicate that he intensely disliked the business of supervising slaves—he was to call himself a "recreant governor of negrodom"—so the full responsibility that he took over his coterie of workers in coordinating the move must have proved par-ticularly taxing.[65] If he found it distasteful, however, he nonetheless remained a product of his culture, an antebellum slaveholder tacitly accepting and participating in the slave system until its demise.

On February 20, Maverick and his workers reached his land on the

Tennessee River. As Maverick plunged into plantation management, his father back in Pendleton sent regular reports on the nullification tempest, writing on April 8, "They go on cooking until they will have a devilish dish of it I fear . . . they want (I fear) disunion."

He also feared the physical consequences on his son of a summer spent along an Alabama riverbank. "You are at your own discretion in everything but *one*," he wrote in the same letter, "that is you must not on any account attempt to live in Colberts reserve in the summer or in any other sickly place."

Adding to Samuel's worry born of grim experience with other relatives was his knowledge of Sam's tendency toward digestive problems, then called dyspepsia. Years later, Mary Adams Maverick would write to a son who had provoked her husband's wrath by announcing he wanted to be a doctor, "As to your Pa's answer about studying medicine did you never hear how he & his father always hated these 'licensed murderers' and how a quack once turned your Pa grey & nearly dead calomelizeing [sic] for chills & left him a dyspeptic for life."66

Now, in the spring of 1834, Samuel repeatedly urged his son against staying in an unhealthy place. "Arrange w/respect to the people [slaves] as well as you can, instantly," he wrote on May 20, "and let no consideration of money or advantage or anything else induce you to risque a summer in that Quarter, or stay there a single moment longer . . . flee to the mountains, remember that life is all we have and our duty to ourselves and to one another is to preserve it. Eternity lasts forever."

Sam Maverick's replies are lost, but he chose to remain in the Low Country his father so feared. Records show that he did not leave until the end of August, when he embarked on a trip to New York to visit with Lydia and William Van Wyck. At thirty-one, he was quietly rebelling against his father's well-meant dicta and was moving toward the independence Samuel so lauded.

By the New Year, 1835, the younger Maverick had returned to his Lauderdale County land, this time accompanied by his other sister, the widowed Mary Elizabeth Maverick Weyman, and her three small children, Elizabeth, Augustus, and Joseph. Mary Elizabeth's husband of nine years, Joseph Turpin Weyman, had arrived destitute at Pendleton in early 1834, and Samuel tried to help by offering him several farms. However, before the young man could make a new start, he became ill with dysentery and fever. After lingering for more than two months, he died at Montpelier.[67]

Mary Elizabeth chose to migrate to northwestern Alabama with her older brother and settled on her own farm near his property. Now Samuel had two children and three grandchildren in the Low Country, and he resumed his appeals for them to consider their health above all things. The news that Sam had been unwell brought an instruction to Mary Elizabeth on January 14, 1835, that both attend to health so that "no consideration whatever will induce either SAM or yourself to remain a single day in a sickly place or expose your health on a/c of any earthly matter." To his son Samuel wrote, "For my sake for yr sister's sake for yr own sake for God's sake stay no longer in Colberts reserve or in any sickly place."

In that same month, the childless Uncle William Turpin died in New York, leaving Samuel various properties and deeding to Sam and Lydia jointly a house on King Street in Charleston.[68] For Samuel, an era had closed with the death of a man who had been both close relative and business mentor, and he renewed his efforts to ensure the welfare of those representatives of the future, his children. To Sam he wrote on March 9, "It will not do for you to risque your life another summer at Colberts reserve, I have written you before and write you now, that if you think proper to settle on any tract [of] land that I own in Alabama or Carolina to do so without further ceremony." He added ominously, "The second & third summer after timber is killed it becomes more sickly than it is the first summer."

Sam Maverick was ready to move, but not back to South Carolina or to another location in Alabama. He found himself unsuited to a life of plantation management. First, there was his dislike for the duties of slave supervision. According to one account, he was lenient with his charges and they fought among themselves until, in frustration, Maverick "ran in amongst them with a stick and whacked them right and left."[69] In truth, Maverick simply did not like telling anyone what to do; his solitary nature and democratic principles made the task unpleasant, and he would later refuse to dictate choices to his wife or children.

Then, his hidden adventurous streak rebelled against the slow, fixed nature of plantation life. Trips to Tuscaloosa and New Orleans on business for his father did not provide the kind of challenge and solitary independence he craved. As his subsequent actions prove, he was eager to start amassing his own land empire. In New Orleans he had listened to animated talk of what was going on in the Mexican territory of Texas. American empresario Stephen F. Austin might be locked away in a Mexican prison by officials grown wary of the colonists and their democratic ideas of government, but settlers and adventurers were still following their dreams from the New Orleans harbor to the scattered communities of Texas. On March 16, 1835, Sam Maverick abruptly left Alabama to join them.

The Road to Independence

We cut our cables, launch into the world,
And fondly dream each wind and star our friends;
All in some daring enterprise embark'd,
But where is he can fathom its event?

—Lines recorded by a classmate
in Maverick's memory book from Yale University, 1825

THE TEXAS that spread out before Sam Maverick when he stepped ashore at the mouth of the Brazos in April, 1835, was only sparsely settled, primarily by contentious colonists from the American South who were about to explode under Mexican rule. The communities of Stephen F. Austin's settlers stretched northward along the river to Washington-on-the-Brazos, about two hundred miles from the port of Velasco, where Maverick had disembarked. Most of these communities boasted a few families and single men living in log cabins with earth or rude puncheon floors. The dirt streets were muddy in wet weather, dusty in dry, and dangerous at night, as tree stumps still jutted from the roadways.[1]

The settlers had been drawn to this forested river region because they needed wood to build their houses, to make their tools and furniture, to warm their bodies. They also carried with them a farmer's appreciation for the fertile woodland soil, a hunter's appreciation for woodland game, and an affinity for wooded pastoral landscapes. Some of the Texians, as they called themselves, had moved out onto the southeastern coastal plains to establish farms and plantations, but all, out of necessity and preference, remained as close as possible to trees and water.[2]

Austin's original settlement on the Brazos, San Felipe de Austin, remained the center of American activity in Texas with between two and three thousand inhabitants. The five principal settlements in Austin's colony—San Felipe, Columbia, Matagorda, Gonzales, and Mina (later renamed Bastrop) together boasted approximately eight thousand residents.[3]

Only three Texas communities predated Anglo-American settlement: Nacogdoches to the east, La Bahía to the south, and San Antonio to the northwest. Nacogdoches had served as a center for various filibustering attempts to wrest the territory from Spain before Mexican independence in 1821; by the time independence was won, the community had been virtually wiped out by Spanish troops. However, by the spring of 1835, Anglo-American emigrants had resurrected the town and dominated both it and La Bahía, rechristened Goliad. Mexicans continued to predominate in San Antonio de Béxar, then called simply "Béxar" or "Béjar," long Mexico's northwesternmost outpost and the most substantial settlement in the territory.

Few Mexicans had settled in Texas during the periods of Spanish and Mexican rule, and now, even with the influx of Anglo-American settlers and adventurers, the population remained small. Mexican law required a citizenry of eighty thousand, excluding roving Indians, for Texas to become a Mexican state. Instead, the territory was simply a province of the vast state of Coahuila-y-Texas. When Sam Maverick arrived, the population probably did not exceed thirty thousand.[4]

Among that number were Anglo-Americans such as Erastus "Deaf" Smith, who had been surveying the territory for years. Smith had discovered lead and silver deposits by pushing northwest of the settlements into the Central Texas Hill Country west of where Austin now stands. Maverick immediately began searching out such knowledgeable rovers. At Velasco, he talked with Byrd Lockhart, a Texian since 1826 and municipal land surveyor since 1831. Lockhart warned that counterfeit land grants were proliferating. Since Mexico had begun offering vacant lands at public auction the year before, thousands of leagues had been granted to Mexican and American promoters, and land scrip had been selling wildly in both Texas and the United States. The whole ownership question seemed hopelessly snarled, but Lockhart advised that "the governor at Bexar *keeps record* and can tell the genuine."[5]

The governor needed superhuman powers to do so, for knotty problems with land grants predated Mexico's latest attempt to fill its coffers and settle its empty territory. The first Texas grant had been issued by Spain to a San Antonio settler in 1727, and the European nation

First page of Samuel Augustus Maverick's 1835 diary of his initial journey to Texas. *From Maverick Family Papers, Barker Texas History Center, Austin.*

went on to grant ten thousand leagues of Texas land, mostly to cattlemen, before Mexico gained its independence. A league equaled 4,428
acres, and many Spanish grants were made for four leagues, "a league
to each wind" from the cattlemen's dwellings, which were spread along
the Rio Grande.

After independence, the Mexican government began allowing large
tracts to empresarios, who in turn granted land to their colonists. Then
in 1828 Mexico began selling parcels of up to eleven leagues to its citizens. This practice quickly led to abuse; for example, James Bowie, who
married the daughter of Béxar resident Juan Martín Veramendi, bought
sixteen eleven-league grants from Mexican citizens. Then came the
act allowing public auction of vacant land, followed by a law permit-
ting sale of unauctioned acreage at minimum price. Finally, only a few
weeks before Maverick's arrival, the Mexican government authorized
the governor to sell lands, and he was selling vast tracts to American
speculators in exchange for their promise to provide frontier militias.[6]

All of this created great confusion over land claims, and as an aspiring land baron, Maverick had his work cut out for him in discovering who owned title to what and how he, Maverick, could get it. He
was not interested in empresario contracts, the success of which de-
pended on the empresario's performing some near-impossible job such
as settling hundreds of emigrants on the far frontier. Land was cheap,
and, thanks to his father's fortune and his own business management,
he had the financial means to buy it and wait for someone else to want
it. He came to Texas with a few thousand dollars in hand, perhaps
in part from his January sale in Alabama of eight slaves for almost
three thousand dollars.[7]

He moved carefully at first, having absorbed the philosophy his father outlined in a letter to a distressed Weyman relative. Drawing a
spiral marked with a zero in the middle and with increments of ten
on each succeeding curve, the elder Maverick had written, "Here is
the road leading from nothing (o) to hundreds of thousands of knowledge, comfort or money & requiring constant attention on our part
to live & act within our means." He added, "The other end of this
road leads from hundreds of thousands to misery & want, requiring
no exertion, no calculation about tomorrow; like a whirlpool it inevitably draws in all who are not aware of its constant tendency."[8]

For a few months, Sam Maverick wandered. His journal shows that
he first cast his eye toward coastal property that might prove valuable

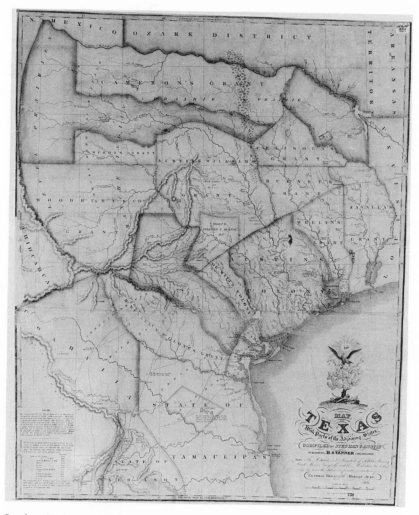

Stephen F. Austin's 1835 map of Texas showing how Texas land was apportioned at the time of Samuel Augustus Maverick's arrival. *From Barker Texas History Center Map Collection, Austin.*

for commerce and settlement—sites that looked promising as future port communities. Taking the *Henry* upriver to Brazoria, forty miles inland, he spent the month of May on horseback exploring westward, working his way back down to the coast and stopping at Matagorda on shoaly, muddy Matagorda Bay. Here he found a settlement of "20

29

or more families, 4 stores & one new Tavern" on such low ground that drift logs lay on the community's higher elevations. "All the hopes this place has," he wrote, "is its location at the mouth of the Colorado, and near Caney [Creek] and the Colorado lands."⁹

He found the area "sickly country and too low," but pressed westward along the coast, stopping to visit with Austin colonist Thomas Marshall Duke on his Caney Creek league. Duke had served in the Convention of 1833, a meeting of colonial delegates convened to draw up a list of petitions to the Mexican government. He had also acted as *alcalde*, a Mexican position loosely combining the duties of a mayor and judge. Here discussion naturally turned to the uncertain future of Texas, with Maverick noting in his journal, "talked about cession to England or United States."

Maverick continued his travels close to the bay, reaching the inner Lavaca Bay and the higher land at Cox's Point at the mouth of the Lavaca River. Thomas Cox, another Austin colonist, lived on the league granted him by the empresario, and here Maverick arranged his first Texas land purchase; with a fellow *Henry* passenger, Pleasant B. Cocke, he agreed to buy half of Cox's league on May 20, 1835.¹⁰ This would give him, for sixteen hundred dollars, over one thousand acres of Texas land. "Might lay my quarter of a league on the marsh," he mused in his journal, "& secure the ferry which would be worth 1 or 2 thousand dollars a year."

The deal required a trip to San Felipe to make it official, so Maverick now turned to the northeast, reaching the heart of Austin's colonies in early June and sealing the purchase from Cox on the fourteenth. San Felipe, perched on the Brazos riverbank and flanked by heavily timbered river bottoms to the east and a great expanse of prairie to the west, became Maverick's base of operations for the summer as he ranged up and down the river. It was a summer of discontent and disturbance across the settlements, with political events so forboding that they would soon bring a halt to such mundane activities as the buying of land.

In San Felipe, no one could escape the escalating tension between the Texians and the Mexican government that controlled Texas. American residents of the territory were confused by Mexican president Santa Anna, whose posture as an enlightened liberal had won their support. Now he was revealing himself to be an autocratic ruler, dispensing with democratic reforms and stifling dissent across the Mexican nation.

In Mexico City, the government had remained in constant flux since the country had won independence from Spain. Most of the authorities who paraded through the revolving doors of government saw the emigrants from the United States only as a necessary evil, necessary because Spanish and Mexican efforts to colonize Texas and subdue the Indian population had failed, evil because there was always the danger that the colonizers would try to wrest control of the territory from Mexico, despite the United States' renunciation of all claim to it in 1819.

Actually, the U.S. government honored the treaty, and most colonists were loyal to the Mexican government, under whose auspices they had been allowed to settle. However, a basic problem existed in relations between Mexican officials and Texian emigrants. In the former's experience, when a group assembled politically and called for reform, it was a direct challenge to the existing power structure and would be followed by revolt. To the colonists, peaceful assembly and petition were simply the way in which a democratic people made known to their government their wants and needs.

Thus, the Anglo-American settlers had become frustrated, the government suspicious. The authorities were beginning to have more reason for suspicion, for Maverick arrived with a tide of newcomers who felt no allegiance to their neighbor to the south. Most of the settlers who had arrived before 1830 had agreed to certain conditions, such as a nominal conversion to Catholicism. For them, the crucial issue now was whether Santa Anna would honor the liberal Mexican Constitution of 1824, which guaranteed certain democratic rights. For those who had slipped in illegally after the ban on emigration in 1830, and for those who had streamed in since the ban was lifted in 1833, the issue was how to rid the settlements of Mexican rule and pave the way for Texas to become independent or join the United States.

Santa Anna was not one to tolerate the slightest dissension, much less outright defiance. Even as Maverick began his journeys in Texas, the dictator's brother-in-law, Gen. Martín Perfecto de Cós, was eyeing the obstreperous occupants of Texas from across the border. Cós was in Coahuila subduing the unruly government there; why not teach Mexico's northern subjects a lesson as well?

In addition to the threat from Mexico, many colonists saw danger in the actions of such Americans as William Barret "Buck" Travis, like Maverick a young lawyer from South Carolina who had migrated through Alabama to Texas. While Maverick was at San Felipe, Travis took about two dozen men and a small brass cannon and captured the community of Anáhuac on Galveston Bay from the Mexican garrison there. This aggressive action angered many of the colonists, but when General Cós, his army massed below the Rio Grande, demanded that the colonists turn over Travis and others, even peace advocates refused.

At about the same time, the suspicious Cós detained the Mexican governor of Texas, Agustín Viesca, and Texian merchant and colonizer Ben Milam as they were returning to Texas from Monclova, the new capital of Coahuila-y-Texas. Maverick turned from his land matters to write in his journal, "reports of arrest of Gov. & Milam—of invasion—usurpation" and recorded meetings of July 4 and 5 resolving to "rescue the Gov. & bring him to Texas." However, the furor over the incident died down as Milam and Viesca escaped and joined Texians at Goliad.

Maverick's reporting of the political unrest in his journal intruded only slightly on his land notes. He resumed his travels in early July, pushing up the Brazos to the rambling cottonwood-log mansion of Leonard Groce on a bluff overlooking the river northeast of Washington. Groce had inherited his home, Bernardo Plantation, from his father, Jared, a wealthy Alabamian who moved family, slaves, livestock, wagons, and equipment to Texas in 1821. Now the younger Groce was building a modest Texas land empire.[11]

From Groce's, Maverick proceeded to Washington, where raw clearings and piles of burning oak, hickory, and pecan branches attested to the settlers' determination to carve a town from the heavily wooded region. Then he returned to San Felipe and began a slow tour downriver, making his way back to the coast, where he continued his journal musings on which bays were best for vessels and town sites. Regretfully, he noted that Live Oak Point was held as private property by empresario James Power "& can't be bought but will become the most considerable place in that bay."

He noted the cost of entering leagues of land in Austin's grant and the grant adjoining it to the southwest, Martín DeLeón's, but more and more his attention turned inland. Empresarios had already gained tentative control of lands stretching all the way to present San Patricio County bordering the southern coast, to the Pecos River in the west, and to the headwaters of the Trinity and Sabine rivers in the north. However, from Béxar stretched a long finger of unclaimed territory to the southeast and a large chunk of unassigned territory to the west.

After a severe attack of malaria, then identified as bilious fever, sent him shaking with chills back to San Felipe in early August, Maverick determined to push westward to Gonzales, a community laid out by Byrd Lockhart, and to the westernmost settlement of Béxar.

He was drawn in this direction by the fact that, as Lockhart pointed out, authority for land claims lay at Béxar, by the promise of improved health in the higher-lying climate, by the knowledge that no empresario claimed the lands around the Mexican community, and by enticing stories of mineral wealth in the uncharted areas beyond. He had talked to Deaf Smith or to a third party about Smith's silver finds, for in his journal he noted that the explorer had found a small silver vein "thick [as] a knife blade" in the bed of the Llano River near its mouth far north of Béxar in Comanche country.

A recovering Maverick departed San Felipe as the town eagerly awaited the arrival of Stephen F. Austin, liberated from his Mexican captivity. Long the most moderate and cautious of Mexican subjects, Austin had written one intemperate letter and had been detained by the authorities for a year and a half on suspicion of inciting rebellion. What would he advocate in this time of crisis—war or peace? Citizens of the settlements began planning a general convention at Washington-on-the-Brazos for October.

Maverick was already in the Gonzales area, west of San Felipe on the road to Béxar, when a weary but determined Austin arrived in the Brazos River colonies. Their founder had seen firsthand the type of repressive reforms Santa Anna was instituting and could no longer practice accommodation. On September 19, he issued a call to arms.

Two events significant to Sam Maverick's fortunes preceded the call: on September 8, he arrived in the Mexican stronghold in Texas, San Antonio de Béxar; and on September 16, General Cós began moving troops across the Rio Grande. According to legend, when Maverick entered the San Antonio River valley, he built his first campfire on the site of his future home, under a giant pecan tree just northwest of the deserted Alamo mission, where he was soon to participate in one of the most memorable events of Texas history.[12] His journal entry simply states, "Arrived on 8th Sept.," but by all accounts, Maverick immediately fell in love with San Antonio de Béxar, and the record of his long association with the city certainly bears this out. Something in him responded strongly to the pleasantly foreign antiquity of its Spanish churches and homes, to the great sweep of prairie to the west as well as the gradually rising slopes to the north. San Antonio was to be the scene of the most dramatic events of his life, of his greatest happiness and despair, and the lands beyond were to be his joy, his solace, and his passion.

The first governor of Texas, Domingo de Terán, explored the San Antonio River valley and named the river in 1691; eighteen years later, Franciscan friars pronounced the well-watered valley an ideal town site. They discovered and named San Pedro Creek, "full of water and very well wooded."[13] For generations, Indians had come to enjoy the two streams, the creek and the river winding under vine-draped trees bordered by herbs and ferns.

Nine years after the Franciscan friars' visit, one returned to establish the Mission San Antonio de Valero, which would be relocated and become known as the Alamo. At the same time, a new governor established the Villa de Béjar, earliest San Antonio community. A second mission soon joined the first, and in 1722 the Fort of San Antonio de Béxar was erected on the site of the present Military Plaza for a small military garrison. The Spanish population of Béxar during the 1720s has been estimated as about two hundred, with about six hundred Coahuiltecan Indians occupying the two missions.

In 1731 a band of Canary Islanders was sent to populate the site. The Alamo mission had already been moved to its present location on the east side of the river, and the newcomers chose to settle around the presidio on the river's west side. At the same time, three additional missions were moved to the banks of the river from other parts of Texas.

The industrious friars, with the help of their Indian converts, led the way in developing the surrounding farm and ranch lands. Lipan Apaches often wreaked havoc on their efforts, but in 1849 the Apaches entered into a peace treaty with the residents. For a brief time during the eighteenth century the embryonic city flourished as a ranch and farm center. However, the Indian converts dwindled, in large part as a result of diseases brought in by the Spaniards, and the Comanches swept southward to disrupt farming and ranching activities. By 1780 the Spanish citizens who resided in Béxar were petitioning for permission to abandon their settlement effort. In short, the community had failed to remain a strong mission outpost, nor had it become the strong frontier colony Spanish authorities sought.[14]

Despite all this, Béxar continued to be a community and military outpost of some substance. With Mexico's independence from Spain, more Mexicans had trickled northward to the town. When Maverick arrived, he found between one and two thousand inhabitants, a colorful mixture of aristocratic old Spanish families, gaily attired "*rancheros*" who spent most of their time in the saddle, a lower class of mixed Spanish and Indian blood called "mestizos," and a few merchants and land speculators from the United States.[15]

Despite the rudeness of most of its adobe and mud-and-post homes, and despite its exposure to Comanche depredations, San Antonio presented a refreshing view to the dusty traveler. Water gushed from San Pedro Springs and gurgled softly through the city's *acequias*, or artificial watercourses. The river, too, looped languidly through town, its banks lined with cypresses. During the long growing season, fruits and flowers blossomed around every house.

The flat-roofed structures of mortar and stone or adobe also possessed an exotic novelty for travelers from the United States, as did the picturesque churches with their iron crosses, carved wooden doors, and colorfully painted wooden icons. The town was laid out in a grid pattern, particularly pronounced near the center, which was dominated by the Main and Military plazas. The Church of San Fernando sat on the west side of the Main Plaza, and the stone houses of prominent families surrounded the square. *Rancheros* lived in sparsely furnished one-room homes farther down the narrow streets and alleyways. The mestizos often lived in *jacales*, makeshift dwellings of posts, mud, and thatch.[16]

The rhythms of Béxar, too, were new and strange. The streets teemed with activity in the morning, then quieted during the siesta period after lunch. As the afternoons drew to a close, residents would bathe in the river, take coffee, and smoke corn-shuck cigarettes. Before day turned to dusk, women would visit or shop or ride about town while men indulged their passion for fine horses by riding out onto the prairies. In the evenings, the fandango places would spring to life with calico-clad Mexican girls and brightly dressed men. Horse races, cockfights, and gambling often provided diversion.[17]

Leisurely living, horse races, and fandangos interested Maverick less than did the business opportunities Béxar offered. His father's training, his Puritan and Quaker heritage, his own acquisitive instincts, and the ascetic tendencies that would become more apparent in subsequent years kept his mind fixed on the work at hand—possible means of acquiring money and land. He considered merchandising, in which he dabbled from time to time with his father's encouragement, periodically buying goods and placing them for sale with an agent in New Orleans. In fact, his journal shows he had left nine hundred dollars' worth of "goods and groceries" for sale in the city on his departure for Texas. Now he recorded in his journal advice from another American resident of Béxar, Lancelott Smithers, on items that would find a ready market there, including "calicos cheap & deep colours sky blues. orange pink waist ribbons. Spanish books & maps a few Amc Hats & boots."[18]

Maverick also considered using his legal training. American lawyer Thomas Jefferson Chambers, who had studied law in Mexico and had been appointed superior judge of the Texas judicial court the year before, had advised him that summer on the practice of law in Mexican Texas, with Maverick noting in his journal the names of authors of Spanish legal tomes.[19]

However, land remained the strongest lure, and when Maverick found a room in the lodging of John W. Smith, he also found a knowledgeable adviser on the subject. Smith, married to Mexican citizen María de Jesús Curbelo, had been a resident of the city for five years and moved easily between the Mexican inhabitants and the American newcomers. He knew what land was desirable, what land was available, and whom to contact to obtain it. Maverick's journal contains recurring references to Smith's information on land matters. Fifteen days after arriving in Béxar, the newcomer reached a bargain with two Mexican residents for a large tract on Cibolo Creek southeast of the city, bordering the road to Goliad, and he followed this two days later with a second purchase.[20]

As he bought, the rift was growing between Maverick's own countrymen and the Mexican government. At September's end, Mexican cavalry rode out of Béxar's garrison bound for Gonzales, their mission to retrieve a cannon that had been given the settlers a few years before for protection against Indians. The defiant settlers, supported by armed Texians slipping into Gonzales from other frontier communities, emblazoned a banner with the taunt "COME AND TAKE IT" and fired the first shot of the Texas revolution.

After a brief skirmish, the cavalry returned to San Antonio. Garrison commander Domingo de Ugartechea, who had maintained a friendly attitude toward the colonists, both tried to enlist Stephen Austin's help in settling matters peaceably and set out to retrieve the cannon himself. The imminent arrival of Cós and his army, however, caused Ugartechea to return and await the direction of his superiors.[21]

Maverick could no longer concentrate on land matters. On October 8, he picked up his journal to note three events: his landlord's return from Gonzales with the colonists' "final resolution" refusing to relinquish the cannon, the news that more armed Texians were pouring into that defiant town, and the arrival of General Cós in San Antonio. The troops Cós brought with him swelled the number of soldiers in San Antonio to eight hundred.

Maverick attended mass with some of these soldiers three days later and learned that about sixty Americans had taken control of Goliad, killing one Mexican. No sooner had the Béxar garrison and residents absorbed this information than "great flurry and excitement" were caused, Maverick noted, by news that "great crowds of Americans" were moving along the road toward their city. Smith and other private citizens were quickly pressed into service mounting cannon, as both the presidio west of the river and the Alamo east of the river were fortified.[22]

October fifteenth was the date appointed for the colonists' convention at Washington-on-the-Brazos, and Maverick duly recorded the fact in his diary, along with the news, "Americans on the march from Gonzales." Strange and exciting times had arrived. Only the day before, a comet had been sighted flaming across the western horizon.[23] Now the whole territory of Texas was poised for an earthquake, and Maverick had found his way to the epicenter. The ragtag, buckskin-clad Texian army was coming, some striding along in moccasins, some riding American horses, Spanish ponies, half-wild mustangs, or lowly mules.[24]

As he contemplated the looming confrontation, Cós looked unhappily at the Anglo-Americans residing in Béxar itself. On October 16, a guard was placed at John Smith's door. Smith, Maverick, and another boarder named A. C. Holmes were forbidden to leave the city. The siege of Béxar was about to begin, and before it was over, Sam Maverick would cast his lot firmly with his rebellious countrymen.

3

The Siege of Béxar

The quartel in the Alamo is very strongly fortified, and the streets to the plaza here well guarded, and all trees, grass, fences and other lurking places and barricades removed and being removed in order to see the Americans when they come up.

—Sam Maverick's 1835 journal, November 3 entry

As CÓS TIGHTENED HIS HOLD on the city, the tents and huts of the Texian forces began to dot the adjoining cornfields. Arriving from the settlements to the east, the colonists at first camped south of town, but within a few weeks most of them had moved to a position within half a mile north of the Mexican stronghold, at a mill on the west side of the river where the millrace provided a natural breastwork.[1]

Cós meanwhile divided his forces between the Alamo mission east of the river and the town to the west, where Mexican troops began heavily fortifying the two principal plazas. As they erected breastworks in the streets and positioned cannon on the roof of San Fernando Cathedral, many Mexican residents fled the city and gathered on ranches a few miles to the south.

In the midst of this activity, Smith, Maverick, and Holmes made repeated unsuccessful appeals for release. Maverick turned more often to his journal now, not to record land observations but to note facts and rumors concerning the standoff between Mexican troops and the Anglo-Americans camped outside the city. He was guardedly optimistic about the latter's chances, at one point stating that the Mexican picket guards had erroneously reported the Texian force coming with ladders to scale the walls. "Poh!" he wrote, "No need of ladders."[2]

At first, the three detainees considered themselves in little danger from their captors. Maverick did remove his $1,023 in silver money from Holmes' trunk and hid it under a trapdoor in his bedroom, along with

some of Smith's funds.[3] The captives could communicate with the besieging forces through both official and unofficial channels. On October 18, Maverick recorded, "Courier with communications from Cós
to Austin, and my note to Austin." Cós, of course, was communicating with Stephen F. Austin; Maverick's note was probably to Brazoria
merchant William Austin, with whom he also corresponded secretly.[4]

The secret communications would be of much greater use than official ones to the Texians, and Smith and his boarders began sending
missives by Mexican residents of San Antonio who favored the Texian
cause.[5] Out in the American camp, an old friend of Maverick's was
leading a group of volunteers from Nacogdoches, and the two South
Carolinians quickly sent greetings to each other.

Thomas Jefferson Rusk, who was to become one of the most influ-
ential figures of the revolution and early Texas government, had known
Maverick from childhood. They were born the same year in Pendleton
District, and Rusk's father had built the Old Stone Church outside
Pendleton where Maverick's Presbyterian Anderson relatives worshiped.
Rusk, with the aid of John C. Calhoun, had settled on a legal career
earlier than had Maverick and had departed his home state in 1825
to practice law in Georgia. He arrived in Texas in 1832.[6]

In addition to corresponding with Rusk and William Austin, Maverick made cautious reference to other communications, and he is believed to have been in touch with Ben Milam and San Antonio native
Juan Seguín, a tireless Mexican advocate of independence.[7] Not only
were Maverick and his friends receiving information secretly from the
colonists' camp, but they could relay information picked up daily from
the Mexican officers, soldiers, and residents of Béxar. The captives were
not placed in isolation. Thus, Maverick's siege diary provides a generally faithful eyewitness record of the events that followed.[8]

As the number of frontiersmen stationed outside the city multiplied,
Cós attempted to treat with Austin by offering to meet with him and
two or three others if the latter would disperse his army. The offer,
Maverick wrote, was read aloud "at the beat of the drum at the four
corners of the public square." But Austin, weary of conciliatory measures, replied curtly that he had not come to treat but to fight. The
response provoked Cós to declare, "I want no more communications.
Let the damn rascals come."[9]

Actually, the Texians seemed to pose a paltry threat to Santa Anna's
centralist government. For one thing, they appeared in hopeless dis-

array. Despite his bold resolve, Austin was a diplomat, not a general; his army was composed of fiercely independent frontiersmen, not disciplined troops. As Hermann Ehrenberg later recalled, men lined up for roll call as the mood suited them, often refusing to leave a warm rug in a tent or a sizzling strip of meat by the fire, and their makeshift dwellings were scattered about with no attempt at regimentation.[10] Accounts of the siege reveal that various leaders would give orders for attack, then have them countermanded; at one point Austin ordered an attack and was ignored. Most of the men with military training, professionals such as Sam Houston, had stayed away, advising against the march on Béxar.

Despite these negatives, the Texians by October 24 had forced Cós into a state of siege. The frontiersmen might have their troubles with military discipline, but they were a deadly lot nonetheless. Such men as the legendary James Bowie, a former Béxar resident who sent his compliments to the town on October 21, could throw themselves into a fight with cunning and courage. The Texians, who often had had to hunt game for their livelihood, were superior marksmen. This fact was not lost on Cós' troops, as lack of adequate provisions in town quickly forced them to rely on stealthy foraging parties into the surrounding countryside.

On October 25, Maverick reported in his journal a letter from Austin stating that the colonists had not taken the city at once because four or five hundred more were on their way to participate, and the presence of all was desired to decide the next move. "It is expected," Maverick wrote, "that a resolution will be taken by all or most to march on to Matamoros, and from thence to any quarter thought to be best." Already, the Texians were planning to march below the Rio Grande; such a scheme would soon prove almost fatal to their revolution.

The goal of his countrymen, Maverick noted in the same entry, was "to concert measures for giving general, united & effective support to the Constitution of 1824, and to put down Centralism." This objective echoes the sentiments of the long-established colonists who were not attempting to break away from Mexico but to return to a republican system under their adopted country. As volunteer reinforcements from the United States began to arrive, they too rallied around the return-to-the-constitution issue and flew the Mexican flag that represented republican principles.

All watched hopefully as Mexican general José Antonio Mexía challenged Santa Anna's rule by directing an expedition against Tampico on Mexico's Gulf Coast, planning to rouse the eastern Mexican states to insurrection. He had the support of Texian leaders, although many felt Matamoros a better target. Maverick's diary shows that Austin made sure Cós was aware of the threat posed by Mexía and the colonists combined.

However, it would be naïve to suppose that many of the Texians and their U.S. supporters were acting to keep Texas a Mexican territory, however noble they found the tenets of the 1824 Constitution. Ever since the first filibusters from the United States had pushed into Texas, Anglo-Americans had eyed the territory with the idea of wresting it first from Spain, then from Mexico. Participants in the revolution could conclude with little reluctance that no return to democratic principles was possible as long as Mexico controlled Texas. They knew that the American government would remain officially disapproving of any efforts to link Texas to the United States, but they also knew that there was strong popular sentiment in the states for extending the American frontier. Consciously or unconsciously, Texians and volunteers from the United States held the attitude that would be articulated and given the name "Manifest Destiny" in an 1845 *Democratic Review* article: U.S. emigrants had a right and a duty to extend the republic westward.[11]

With or without the presence of empire-hungry Americans, the Mexican government was having tremendous troubles in administering its far-flung northern provinces, which extended through New Mexico and present-day Arizona to the provinces of Baja (Lower) and Alta (Upper) California. In addition, Mexico claimed the lands that now make up Nevada and Utah, as well as parts of present-day Colorado and Wyoming. The Spaniards had established missions and small trading communities in their New Mexico, Baja, and Alta provinces, but as in Texas, the missions had faded and ranchers and residents of the communities chafed under changeable, ineffective management from afar. Mexican inhabitants of Baja California had already flirted with insurrection; New Mexico farmers and Pueblo Indians would band together in 1837 in the temporarily successful Chimayó Rebellion. In Alta California nine years later, opportunistic Americans would stage the Bear Flag Rebellion, trying to establish an independent republic just as such efforts were superseded by a treaty annexing Upper California to the United States.

In Texas in 1836, some Mexican residents and many disgruntled Anglo-Americans were banding together in revolution. However, the latter demonstrated an ethnocentric sense of superiority toward Mexicans. One observer reported from San Felipe in early 1835 that "the North Americans look on the Mexicans as more contemptable than a troop of slaves, & treat those who live among them accordingly. There are none but the lower class in the colony. . . . They are receding to the interior as the Americans approach & will either acquire our habits or leave us."[12] It was not as easy to look down on the many cultured Mexicans living in San Antonio, but Anglo-American newcomers often managed to do so. To Maverick's credit, he was later to speak out forcefully against such prejudice.

However, he shared his countrymen's lack of respect for the professional Mexican soldiers at Béxar, as his comment on ladders shows. Maverick and his fellows recognized that, although the Mexican troops were an efficient fighting force, they were out of their element hemmed in in the city.

The captives could not have complete confidence in a Texian victory—far from it. Maverick's spirits often shifted as the days stretched into weeks and even months. Near the end of October, he was able to report the Texians victorious in an engagement at the Concepción mission south of town. Bowie and the ill-starred James Fannin had successfully fought off infantry and artillery sent from the city by Cós; Maverick figured at least eighty Mexicans "put past duty." On the heels of this news came word of more Americans arriving at Austin's camp, and the Texian forces spread to three campsites surrounding the city.

However, Maverick looked on with dismay as the Mexican troops redoubled their efforts to fortify Béxar. Seven cannon, including an eighteen-pounder, were mounted in the Alamo mission; cannon also dominated both city plazas. Streets to the plazas were well guarded, and the Mexican soldiers stripped areas of trees, fences, and long grass so that they could see the enemy approaching.

Austin had again rejected Cós' advice to disperse and "make [his] representations peaceably to the Government"; he instead promised that "he would have a fight and if Cós would not come out he would go into the town."[13] But Maverick wrote gloomily on November 3, "The place could much easier have been taken with 200 men after the affair of Gonzales than it can now with 1500 men."

Word of a Texian attack finally reached the captives. It was planned for the evening of the fourth. At the same time, Maverick and his fellow prisoners heard disturbing tales of quarrels in the besieging camp, particularly between Stephen F. Austin and Bowie. On November 5, after a night passed without any sign of attack, Maverick wrote, "From the effect of a number of little reports, stories and conjectures, our house is in great dejection this morning; have been drooping some days. I still have confidence." This confidence was bolstered the next day by a report of four or five hundred reinforcements sweeping into the Texian camp on autumn's first norther with cannon and provisions. More men and cannon followed, including, Maverick noted on November 10, "one requiring six yoke [of oxen] to haul. Suppose an 18 pounder."

This may well be a reference to the twelve-pounder that Joseph Field reported was eagerly awaited with much "vexatious delay" by the Texians. But the weapon proved a disappointment, for after a hard night's work positioning it on the west bank of the river within 250 yards of the Alamo, the men cannonaded for two days and "accomplished nothing but the tumbling of a few rocks from the top of the walls."[14]

Meanwhile, the composition of the besieging army was changing. Maverick recorded on November 11 news from William Austin that the troops were "900 strong," but "some who were obliged" had gone home while others, including "some from New Orleans" were on their way. During the month, volunteers from the United States would replace many Texian colonists who had only signed on for a two-month hitch after the fall harvest and were beginning to think about spring planting. The new recruits were not settlers but adventurers—some idealistic, and some simply spoiling for a fight.

The fight was long in coming, and nerves frayed on both sides during November as food and clothing became precious commodities for both armies and as northers whistled in to plummet temperatures. Maverick discovered just how explosive the situation was on the evening of the eleventh, when a harried Mexican captain almost shot Smith and his boarders. Two guns had been fired close to Smith's house during an evening of cannonading and musket firing, and the captain claimed that he had been shot at by the Anglo-Americans in the house. He entered with four soldiers, muskets cocked and bayonets ready, accusing the residents and demanding to know if any from the enemy camp were ensconced on the premises.

Smith and the women in the house vehemently denied that the

home harbored any riflemen, but the captain remained enraged. Only the quick action of a Mexican neighbor, Alejandro Vidal, rescued Maverick and his friends.[15] Hearing the commotion, Vidal appeared and asserted that he had been firing at Anglo-Americans across the river. It was a lie, but Maverick soon realized that the falsehood had saved his life, and he wrote in his journal, "It was certainly a fine specimen of Centralism . . . [I] felt that [the captain's] was an idle bravado and that we were safe. On a full explanation, however, I saw we were very near being shot through a mistake. Dm [sic] such a government."

The indignant captives went to Colonel Ugartechea and repeated their demand that they be allowed to leave town. Ugartechea in turn went to Cós, who refused the request but promised protection, giving them leave to "shoot down the rascals" if "the like insult is offered again." Maverick found the commander's advice "kind assurance" but "impracticable and useless."[16] The incident left him more aware of the precariousness of his position and even more eager for some action on the part of the Texians.

Still November dragged on, each day punctuated by the boom of cannon from the Alamo and from the American camp. On the fifteenth, Maverick wrote in his journal, "I am engaged in making a plan," and the next day brought a cryptic entry, "Sent my project to [blank] at 9 o'clock." Rena Maverick Green, in *Samuel Maverick, Texan, 1803–1870*, conjectures that the plan was sent to Milam and contained a scheme for attacking from house to house, as the invaders finally did.[17] Given the context and the secrecy, it seems reasonable to assume that Maverick's missive was an attack plan of some sort.

By the seventeenth, an air of expectancy hung about the city. The Mexicans were anticipating the arrival of a few hundred reinforcements under Ugartechea, who had departed Béxar, and Maverick wrote, "Not a sound. The wind hardly blows. All gaiety again in town. Officers riding about on their pampered and mettlesome steeds." By evening, the relaxed attitude changed to watchfulness, for an attack was expected before the reinforcements could arrive. The captive reported the sudden "very uncommon caution" exercised "in challenging citizens as they passed Musquiz's corner [an entrance to Main Plaza], and (what they never did before) making them tell what business they were upon, etc."

No attack materialized, however, and the days continued with occasional skirmishing between the Anglo-Americans and small parties of Mexican troops sent from the fort. The prized cannons had proved of little use to either—with a flash of dry humor, Maverick wrote on November 16 that one Texian ball had entered the city and "knock[ed] down a woman's hen house—dreadful!!" Despite the lack of much real damage, both sides kept up their bombardment. On November 22, Maverick noted, "One hundred guns at least fired through the day; say seventy from the Alamo and a cannon placed on W. side of the river, and thirty by the Americans."

Meanwhile, the weather was getting colder, with frigid northers pushing the temperature in the normally mild climate to below freezing. Maverick and his companions awoke the morning of the twenty-third to find water in their house "froze over as thick as a dinner plate." The harsh cold seemed to quiet the American camp, but Maverick surmised that they might be occupied with Ugartechea and the reinforcements marching from the south.

Actually, major changes were taking place among the Texian forces. While the city had been under siege, a makeshift colonists' government had not been idle. The anticipated October 15 meeting had turned into a "Permanent Council," erroneously named, since it only lasted until November 3. But the Permanent Council was replaced by the November Consultation, which met through November 14. In creating a provisional government, the consultation appointed Stephen F. Austin a commissioner to the United States, his mission to raise support for the Texian cause. Thus, on November 25, Austin left the siege camp; the troops elected in his place Col. Edward Burleson, commander of a Gonzales regiment.

The empresario departed on the heels of most of his original army. Their term of service over and the end of the siege nowhere in sight, the Texians had elected to return to families and warm firesides. By some estimates, including Maverick's, the army had at one time totaled two thousand. Now it mustered at a few hundred, primarily young men from the southern states who had scented excitement and moved westward alone or in companies such as the New Orleans Greys.

By early December, U.S. volunteers clearly outnumbered the remaining Texians. Both the newcomers and the long-term besiegers were determined to fight—the newcomers because they had not traveled so far and so long simply to disperse, the remaining Texians because they were ready to commit to Texas freedom and see the conflict through. The "Grass Fight" of November 26, in which the Americans emerged victorious from a skirmish with Mexican soldiers foraging for hay, only whetted many fighting appetites.

Finally, events began to move more quickly. On December 1, Cós relented and allowed Maverick and Smith to leave the city, "Smith having promised for us that we would go soon to the United States," Maverick noted in his December 1 diary entry.[18] The two removed to the ranch of staunch independence supporter José Antonio Navarro, ten miles to the south.

The liberated captives made their way to the American camp the following day amidst "great cannonading" from both sides. Here Maverick found a number of familiar faces. Rusk had departed, but such Texians as Thomas Cox, Byrd Lockhart, and Deaf Smith remained.

Maverick had preferred examining land to plunging into the political turmoil of the summer, but two and a half months as a captive and a developing love affair with San Antonio and its surrounding lands had turned him into an advocate for action. He and Smith arrived urging attack. With firsthand knowledge of the state of affairs in Béxar, they now felt sure that it could be taken. But on reaching camp they found a cautious set of officers, who were about to abandon the siege altogether, and a grumbling army estimated at only three to seven hundred.

The newcomers attempted to galvanize the officers to action against Cós' weary, hemmed-in troops. Maverick and Smith argued convincingly for a strong offensive, and Maverick reported, "After a great many objections being urged and answered by our offering to head the divisions etc., it is finally agreed to make the attack by taking: 1st Veramendi's; 2nd La Garza's; and 3d Cardena's houses."[19]

At last the impatient volunteers could load their rifles and sharpen their knives in anticipation of a real fight. However, the next day, December 2, Maverick had to note in his journal that the great offensive had failed to materialize because the two colonels had said "they were not ready." It was also reported that the enemy knew of the impending attack.[20] Like his colonels, Burleson remained hesitant. Times did not seem auspicious for the rebels. Even as the besiegers deliberated, General Mexía was landing his defeated army at the mouth of the Brazos, his Tampico expedition a complete failure.

Burleson called together the increasingly dispirited troops and recommended that they retreat beyond the Guadalupe, camp, and wait for spring reinforcements from the states.[21] Most of the listeners met his suggestion with deep disgust. Between 250 and 300 of them left the camp on the morning of the fourth, cursing the officers as they went. So many departed that Burleson called the remaining volunteers together and begged that some remain to accompany the cannon to Goliad. Maverick and Smith watched the scene with dismay. "All day," Maverick wrote, "we get more and more dejected." But then Ben Milam, an unsuccessful colonizer who had probably been a Texian longer than anyone present, fanned a spark that ignited the remaining men.

Versions of what happened to fire the army's remnants differ slightly. Most agree that near sunset a Mexican deserter appeared and assured Burleson within hearing of the troops that the demoralized garrison of San Antonio could be taken. Encouraged by adjutant general Col. Frank Johnson, Milam raised a call for volunteers. According to legend, he cried, "Who will go with old Ben Milam into San Antonio?" and over two hundred men responded.

Milam's dramatic cry may be an embellishment on history, but those who were at the siege did credit Milam with rallying the troops. Maverick recorded in his diary for December 4 that two deserters arrived almost simultaneously, one bearing dispatches from Cós to Ugartechea, and that Milam turned their arrival to account through his "animating manner and untiring zeal." "An impulse is given and received," wrote Maverick, "the men fall into ranks to see if we are strong enough." He reported 250 volunteers for an early-morning attack.[22]

The men rolled from their warm rugs at two the next morning, as yet another bitter norther swept through their cactus-ringed camp. But enthusiasm ran high; volunteers now numbered over three hundred. Two detachments were marching into Béxar, one under Milam, with Maverick guiding, and one under Johnson, guided by Smith. The columns filed out into the cornfields before dawn. When they had traversed half the distance to the city, a small artillery detachment left behind began shelling the Alamo, creating a diversion so that the troops could enter Béxar and work their way, building by building, to the heavily fortified central plazas. The Mexicans responded with rocket fire and the sky was lit with explosions.

Maverick's diary entry for the day reads, "Attack made, myself going with Col. Milam at the head of the right division. Johnson commanded the left." But he recorded no more during the storming; for five days, he and his comrades used all of their energies in a deadly, confusing warfare.

On that first morning, they made their way through gardens and along the bare ground near the river to the city's outer ring of fortresslike houses. Many paused on reaching the safety of a building to stare curiously at the thick-walled structure, so new and foreign to their eyes. With his three months' knowledge of the city, Maverick remained intent on his personal mission: to direct Milam safely along Acequia Street to the De la Garza house in the heart of Béxar.

The Mexican garrison quickly became aware of the intruders, of course, and the plaza and Alamo batteries "poured forth continuous volleys of shot."[23] The attackers dug trenches between the buildings that they held, cut openings in adobe house walls, and peppered Mexican batteries with rifle fire. At the same time, they continued their slow progress toward the center of town. Often, they did not know whether the blue-coated Mexican troops or their own comrades held the next building on their route. Fighting intensified as darkness closed in on that first day. The assault forces suffered parched throats, but a trip to the river for water could cost a man his life.

On the morning of the second day, the southerners and Texians who made up the invading army peered from windows to see a dark red flag flying from the roof of the central church. Cós was announcing that he would give no quarter.

They responded by pushing onward, taking house after house. With crowbars, they would attack the soft stone, pour rifle fire into the hole they had created, then climb in and move from room to room, rifles ready. Sometimes opposing soldiers would occupy rooms of the same house, until the Mexicans fled under the invaders' fusillade or fell in hand-to-hand combat. By evening, the siege force held whole blocks of houses and had connected them with trenches. They also held the De la Garza house.

However, on the third day, they lost their commander. Ben Milam took a bullet in the head and died a hero. He had lived long enough to scent victory, to see both the De la Garza home and Johnson's first objective, the Veramendi house, taken. In fact, he was standing in the yard of the latter, the home of James Bowie's father-in-law, when the bullet pierced his brain.

Years later, Sam Maverick would tell his children the story of how he caught Milam as the commander fell. His son George recalled standing at the Veramendi house with his father as Maverick pointed to the southeast corner and told him, "There Ben Milam was shot—as

he staggered back I caught him in my arms." Pointing toward Veramendi Street, he continued, "There during the fight I helped to cut
off a man's shattered leg, and we saved his life."[24]

The man was Thomas William Ward, a member of the New Orleans
Greys who was to have a distinguished career in Texas, despite numerous mishaps. Sixteen years after the siege, Maverick would hold Ward
up as an exemplary model for another son, writing, "Col. Ward is a
particular old comrade of mine whose left leg I assisted in cutting off,
after it had been smashed by a cannon ball in the street opposite La
Garza's in December 1835." Maverick remembered that Ward "begged
me to hand him a pistol to end his unhappy life, when we were in
the old mill several days after losing his leg & when our situation was
unpleasant. But he repented of this; and ever after bears up against
misfortune with a brave heart."[25]

By some accounts, Ward's leg was buried with Ben Milam and an
English artilleryman in the courtyard of the Veramendi house, with
a dirge provided by "the loud, monotonous boom of the enemy's cannon."[26] Now Johnson and Maj. Robert Morris of the New Orleans Greys
took over, and their frontier army prepared to push into Main Plaza
itself, where the central church housed the Mexicans' powder magazine.

On the fourth day, Ugartechea returned with five hundred reinforcements, but the Anglo-Americans pressed onward, infiltrating the
buildings of the central city. The fifth day dawned clear and mild, but
the sun shone on "blackened tree-stumps, battered walls, smoldering
ash heaps," as heavy artillery fire continued from both sides.[27] Cós tried
a last ruse, sending five or six hundred soldiers marching toward the
American camp in hopes of drawing the invaders from Béxar. But the
invaders simply watched from their fortifications, knowing that now
they had the upper hand.

That night at nine, the Mexicans mounted an offensive, pouring
artillery fire into the American strongholds. The barrage nearly leveled the walls, but the Mexicans failed to press the advantage. They
had learned too well how deadly their foe could be with rifle or Bowie
knife. Now the invaders rose from behind their leveled walls and
penetrated to the very heart of the Mexican defenses. In the darkness,
they captured key positions around Main Plaza and seized the cannon
that had inflicted the most damage.

Cós knew he was beaten. On the morning of the sixth day, a white
flag flew over the Alamo ruins; a force of no more than 350 had de-

feated a firmly entrenched garrison of more than 1,100. Maverick accompanied Burleson, Johnson, and Morris to the surrender ceremony. He could now face the Mexican officers not as a captive but as a victor. He had chosen to remain and fight, and in so doing, he had more firmly committed himself to the future of an independent Anglo-Texas.

He returned to his diary to make two final entries. The first, dated December 10, states simply, "White flag of surrender sent us." The second, marking the beginning of 1836, reports, "Men set out for La Bahia [Goliad] to rendezvous for an attack on Matamoros." Insurrection had become full-fledged revolution, and Maverick would soon find himself in the midst of events even more dramatic—and more fateful—than the storming of Béxar.

4

The Alamo, Independence, and Retreat

[We] do hereby resolve and declare, that our political connection with the Mexican nation has forever ended, and that the people of Texas do now constitute a free, sovereign, and independent republic.
—Texas Declaration of Independence

TWO DAYS AFTER the surrender, Cós led his troops out of San Antonio de Béxar, having pledged never again to take up arms against the colonists and their allies. Mexican residents who had fled Béxar began filtering back, and most of the Texian forces remained in town, awaiting decisions as to their next move from the provisional governor and council appointed by the November Consultation.

Through December, then, the volunteers from the States who had fought their way into Béxar with crowbars and rifle butts leisurely roamed the city, succumbing to the slow-paced life-style of its inhabitants. They visited in the Mexican homes and smoked corn-shuck cigarettes with their hosts, then attended evening fandangos in tallow-lit rooms where violinists played Mexican airs. When the hour grew late, many of the Americans would cross the river and bed down in the eighty-year-old Alamo mission, which they had shelled only weeks before.[1]

Maverick's activities during this interlude and during the crucial revolutionary months following remain clouded, as no account by Maverick himself, other than a few stray remarks, has been uncovered, and neither records of the period nor the public and private records of his later life render more than tantalizing bits of information. Because the revolution was so poorly reported and documented, it is difficult to track individual participants. What can be established by piecing the fragments together is that Maverick stayed in San Antonio, continued his land-buying quest, became a member of the garrison, was elected by garrison members as a delegate to the independence convention at Washington-on-the-Brazos, and departed the Alamo for the convention during the final siege of the fort, only days before it fell.

On December 15, he received a receipt from Texian commander Burleson stating that the provisional government would pay him ninety dollars for his horse, which was "pressed, used and is found to be lost, in the service of the public army."[2] Military rolls do not show that Maverick himself joined the army, but he and Smith later received bounty land certificates normally given for three months' service. Smith's certificate clearly specified December, 1835, to March, 1836, thus covering the period from the siege of Béxar until the fall of the Alamo.[3]

This period was one of great uncertainty in the territory, with another clash inevitable. However, Maverick began to buy land again, either in ignorance or in defiance of the provisional government's November decision to void all land sales transacted after August 20, 1835. Since many land offices ignored the edict, speculators could continue to transact business. On Christmas Day, Maverick purchased a tract from a Mexican couple and followed this with three purchases in January—one from Smithers, two from Mexican citizens. He was still buying on February 16, only a week before Santa Anna's troops appeared and hemmed in the American garrison.[4] In these purchases, made in the face of tremendous political uncertainty, the intensity of Maverick's zeal for Texas land acquisition first becomes evident. Most of the rest of his life would be spent accumulating Texas acreage in spite of shifting land laws and precarious political situations.

As Maverick began his speculative Texas career, the political situation was approaching chaos. On January 3, the provisional council authorized a military campaign against Matamoros, to be led by Béxar siege veteran Frank Johnson and James Grant, a former resident of Mexico who had been lobbying for the attack. Provisional governor Henry Smith vehemently opposed the expedition; so did Sam Houston, the commander-in-chief of the army appointed by the provisional government. Johnson wavered, and another siege veteran, James Fannin, was appointed in his place. Then Johnson decided to go and was reappointed.

Undaunted by Johnson's reappointment, Fannin established a force at Goliad, fifty miles southeast of San Antonio, and began making his own plans for an attack on Matamoros. Grant and Johnson teamed up at Refugio, a few miles farther south. Most of the veterans in San Antonio now migrated to both sites, eager for more action. Each force was operating independently of the other and paid no attention to the wishes of Houston. Grant and Johnson helped themselves to most of the rich storehouse of Alamo armaments—cannon, powder, muskets, cartridges, cannonballs, musketballs—captured in the December siege.

The government that had created this confusion further exacerbated the situation by unraveling. Smith and the council wrangled until the council dissolved on January 17. Smith tried to keep running Texas revolutionary affairs but had only limited support. Meanwhile, Santa Anna, furious at Cós' Béxar defeat, was pushing his army northward, determined to crush revolt in Texas once and for all.

In Béxar, residents were apprehensive. Lt. Col. James C. Neill, who had commanded an artillery company during the siege of Béxar and now commanded the Alamo garrison, had written to the governor and council on January 14, "There can exist but little doubt that the enemy is advancing on this post, from the number of families leaving town today." These included the pregnant wife of John W. Smith, whom Smith was sending to New Orleans.[5]

On the same day the council dissolved, the commander-in-chief without an army, Sam Houston, dispatched James Bowie to the Alamo with a small band in response to Neill's plea for reinforcements and to determine whether the site should be abandoned now that most of the troops had moved south.

Bowie found Neill commanding only 104 men, most of whom had been in Texas less time than had Maverick. Like Maverick, many had moved westward in the eddying stream of humanity from the southeastern states. They were a curious mixture of educated professional men, young adventurers, and seasoned frontiersmen. Some of the Texians whose names appeared in Maverick's journal in connection with land matters now remained after the first siege or would return to fight— John W. Smith, Byrd Lockhart, Albert Martin of Gonzales.[6] Some men had remained at the Alamo intending to return to the States; others were intent on the conflict with Mexico but lacked relish for the Matamoros plan. Maverick already identified himself as a Béxar resident, if his signing of the declaration of independence a month later is any indication, for he firmly wrote "from Bexar" while the other delegates simply signed their names.[7]

He was elected on February 1 to attend the convention, scheduled for exactly a month later at Washington-on-the-Brazos. It had looked as if the Alamo would go unrepresented at this key meeting, for the civilians of San Antonio had elected four Mexican envoys—Lorenzo

de Zavala, José Francisco Ruiz, José Antonio Navarro, and Juan Seguín
—and excluded the American men of the garrison from voting, judging them transients rather than residents. The Alamo occupants responded by holding their own delegate election, and they chose two
South Carolinians, Maverick and a member of Bowie's band, James
Butler Bonham.

The two knew each other, for Bonham had established a law practice in Pendleton the same year that Maverick hung out his shingle,
and both had practiced there before removing to Alabama—Maverick
to Lauderdale County and Bonham to Montgomery. There the parallels ended, however, for Bonham had been a zealous states' rights advocate and Calhoun supporter. An impetuous idealist, he apparently
preferred action to deliberation, so declined the delegate position. Thus
Jesse Badgett, who had arrived from Louisiana in early December, became the second delegate.[8] On February 5, garrison members petitioned the convention to seat Maverick and Badgett.[9]

One of the petition signers was another recent arrival, Lt. Col. William Barret Travis, the Anáhuac firebrand who had been in the center
of political turmoil the previous summer. There is no evidence that
his path had crossed Maverick's in South Carolina; however, the two
may well have met the previous summer, for the former's name is included in a brief list of names and addresses Maverick noted in his
diary in 1835.[10] Travis had been recruiting at San Felipe for Houston's
army when orders had come from former Governor Smith to proceed
to Béxar.

Neill readied to return to the States on February 11, and passed the
command to Travis, but the garrison voted and overruled Neill, placing celebrated frontiersman Bowie in charge. Both Bowie and Travis
agreed that Mexican troops would invade Texas and that San Antonio
would be a key point of conflict. Travis estimated that the earliest Santa
Anna's forces could be expected would be the middle of March.

He was more prescient than most of the other Texians and volunteers, but he was wrong. Meeting the defeated Cós and his troops, Santa
Anna had ordered them to turn around, and by mid-February, when
Maverick was making his last Texas land purchase for two years, the
whole army was poised on the Rio Grande near Laredo.

Meanwhile, a man with a legend to rival Bowie's had entered the
Alamo. On the same day Neill relinquished command, David Crockett, a skilled border rover and former Tennessee congressman, rode

into the mission-turned-fort with twelve Tennessee riflemen. Their addition brought the total at the fort to approximately 150, when a force of 1,000 was considered necessary for defense.[11]

Delegate Badgett left on or shortly after February 17.[12] He was seated at the convention without debate over his credentials on March 1. Thus, he missed the storm that soon swirled around the Alamo walls. Maverick stayed until he almost became one of the Alamo martyrs. The die was cast for most of the defenders when Bowie wrote former Governor Smith on February 2 resolving to "die in these ditches [rather] than give them up to the enemy."[13]

The first real hint of trouble came on February 19, when a friendly Mexican assured the defenders that he had personally seen thousands of troops pouring across the Rio Grande. Because the city was vibrating with rumors, garrison members counted this as just one more.

On the evening of the twenty-second, rumor became reality. A messenger brought word that advance Mexican forces were camped a mere eight miles south of Béxar. Only a rainstorm had kept them from taking the garrison completely unaware. The ominous news was confirmed the following morning, when remaining Mexican residents of Béxar, warned in advance, began a hurried exodus from the city.

Bowie and Travis immediately sent physician John Sutherland and John W. Smith on a scouting mission. The commanders then pulled all their men into the Alamo and prepared for a siege. They did not act a moment too soon, for the scouts quickly returned with news of smartly equipped cavalry lined up between the chaparral and mesquite bushes only a short distance south of town.

The Alamo commanded a view of the city, and by two in the afternoon, Maverick and his fellows could see the blue-coated Mexican troops spreading through Béxar. Santa Anna demanded the garrison's surrender and was answered with a cannon shot. The siege of Béxar participants who had remained now found themselves the ones under siege, as Mexican artillery units began bombarding the Alamo's stone walls.

Travis, who received the command from an ailing Bowie the day after the Mexican vanguard appeared, was determined to follow through on Bowie's vow to die in the ditches rather than escape or commit suicide by surrendering to Santa Anna's blood-red flag. He immediately sat down and penned his romantic, defiant war cry to his "Fellow Citizens and Compatriots," vowing emphatically, "*I shall never surrender or retreat.*"[14]

Even as Travis wrote, Mexican cavalry regiments and infantry bat-
talions continued to stream into the city. The light artillery Santa Anna's troops had managed to drag from Mexico was having as little effect on the Alamo walls as the Texians' guns had had in December.
However, as the Mexican numbers swelled, they were able to move the
weapons closer, despite sniper fire from the trapped Texians. By dawn
on February 25, batteries had been seated just three hundred yards south
and a thousand yards southwest of the mission, and the invaders ringed
three sides of the structure.

Maverick and his comrades could only hope for reinforcements. They
had a number of cannon but little powder. Even worse, they were trapped
in an old mission that served poorly as a fortress. Travis dispatched
messengers, Sutherland and Smith to Gonzales to alert the colonies
to the predicament, Bonham to Fannin at Goliad. With five hundred
men, Fannin commanded most of what was left of the Texian army,
but he vacillated. Meanwhile, Johnson's troops were being defeated at
San Patricio by Mexican reinforcements bound for Béxar, and Grant
was soon to face the same fate. By February 28, the Alamo defenders
were almost completely boxed in. Nine Mexican batteries were trained
on their makeshift fortifications, the walls were dissolving under the
steady punishment, and Santa Anna's troops were nightly extending
their entrenchments toward the mission.

Nonetheless, Texian couriers managed to come and go almost at
will throughout the siege; Maverick could have left at almost any time.
Instead, he remained to see the only help that would arrive slip in the
gates on the day the convention started—thirty-two settlers from Gonzales guided by two emissaries from the fort, Smith and Gonzales resident Albert Martin. Their number was certainly too few to be of much
help, but they provided a great morale boost to the embattled garrison.

While the other convention delegates were congregating in an un-
finished frame building at Washington, Maverick still moved in the
din of the Alamo bombardment, sharing the privation and tension
of the defenders. Why he waited so long remains open to conjecture.
He may have been one of the twenty to thirty men on sick call within
the mission, a victim again of the bilious fever.[15] Or Travis may have
held him as long as possible in hopes of using him as a messenger as
well as a delegate. The commander was using Mexican delegate Seguín
as an emissary to find reinforcements, and Seguín did not make it to
the convention at all. Perhaps Maverick intended to stay, then changed

his mind. Jane Maverick McMillan has logically suggested that Travis and Maverick could not be sure that Badgett had arrived to cast the Alamo vote for independence, possibly leading Maverick to become convinced that he must attend for the garrison to have a vote.[16]

Maverick finally departed on March 2, the day other delegates were signing the independence declaration and only one day before the Alamo defenders looked with dull certainty at the fact that no further help could arrive in time. His children would later recall one of his Alamo stories—that of Travis leaning his head against their father's horse and urging Maverick to get the convention to send reinforcements.[17]

Years later, Maverick would make a brief reference to his departure when he sought to get permission to build his home on the northwest corner of Alamo Plaza. "I have a desire to reside on this particular spot," he wrote to a San Antonio military commander in 1847, "a foolish prejudice no doubt as I was almost a solitary escape[e] from the Alamo massacre having been sent by those unfortunate men" to represent them in the independence convention.[18]

One story from this confused period of the Alamo's final days places Maverick and Smith on a hill overlooking the mission with Bonham on March 3. According to contemporary historian John Henry Brown, the three were returning to the mission and "reached the heights overlooking San Antonio" only to discover that the fall was now inevitable. Maverick and Smith argued that it was hopeless to go forward, while Bonham in a grand gesture spurred his horse toward the failing garrison and chose to become one of the martyrs.[19]

Other historians dispute this account, placing Smith inside the Alamo walls at this point and conjecturing that Bonham had only one companion, Ben Highsmith. What evidence we have indicates that Maverick was on his way to the convention and Smith was about to be dispatched when Bonham made his famous ride.

Although Brown was wrong in placing Maverick on the hillside with Bonham, historian Samuel E. Asbury's assessment of the character of the men in Brown's story has the ring of truth. Asbury characterizes Bonham and Travis as having "the stuff of which heroes are made" rather than "the stuff . . . for statesmen and generals." Maverick, Smith, and Sam Houston, on the other hand, he characterizes as being brave in a practical way, as being "out to win the war and reap the fruits of winning the war."[20]

Winning and reaping the fruits must have appeared a remote possibility to Maverick as he journeyed the 150 miles eastward to Washington. His progress was delayed by the rain and mud that made traveling in early Texas a torturous affair, and thus Smith was apparently able to catch up with him and share Travis' final missive.[21]

The two arrived in Washington on Saturday, March 5, after the convention had adjourned until Monday. "A rare [town] to hold a national convention in," William Fairfax Gray had written three weeks earlier. "They will have to leave it promptly to avoid starvation." Both food and housing were scarce. The other Béxar representatives—Badgett, de Zavala, Ruiz, and Navarro—were sharing a rented carpenter's shop with Gray at a daily rate of $1.25 each.[22]

The missive Smith brought was so urgent that convention president Ellis called a special session on Sunday morning. "We have contended for ten days against an enemy whose numbers are variously estimated from fifteen hundred to six thousand men," Travis had written, urging that the convention "hasten on reinforcements, ammunitions and provisions to our aid so soon as possible."[23]

At 10 A.M. on Sunday morning the delegates gathered to hear this last appeal. On motion of fellow Alamo delegate Badgett, Maverick was presented and took his seat.[24] As he did so and as the letter was read, the Alamo defenders lay dead within its walls. Santa Anna's final onslaught had started just after midnight, and by 9 A.M. every defender, 187 in all, had been killed.[25] Mexican lieutenant José Enrique de la Peña recorded in his diary that 7 of the garrison members, including Crockett, had survived only to be captured and executed by Santa Anna's order.[26]

Maverick and his fellow delegates remained ignorant of the carnage. News of the debacle did not even reach Gonzales until March 11, when a Mexican informant arrived and was followed by the noncombatant survivors, a few women and children and a black slave. Delegate Sam Houston had arrived in Gonzales to raise reinforcements and received the grim news.

Meanwhile, the convention turned to the business of creating a constitution for the Republic of Texas. Maverick joined three other late-comers—S. Rhoads Fisher, John W. Moore, and John W. Bowers—in signing the independence declaration on March 7. Fellow delegates later remembered Maverick as a diplomatic, cautious, and attentive representative, "a man of determined will, unyielding when advocat-

ing what he believed to be right, and uncompromising in favor of a
definite programme of separation from Mexico." Delegate William Menefee recalled that Maverick emphasized the need to cultivate U.S. sentiment toward the Texian cause, drawing parallels between the American revolution and the one in progress, and declaring, "Let our acts
prove to the world that we are sincere patriots and we need not fear
the results."[27]

As the constitution took shape, Maverick voted with the majority
on most points. However, he did make a motion that met quick defeat
—to strike Section 15, which, from the state of the document at the
time, probably referred to Section 15 of the draft General Provisions,
a sweeping rejection of various land claims from purchases made through
the Coahuila-y-Texas legislature to all lands "the locations of which
were unauthorized by law."[28]

The convention continued to hammer out the land issue, with both
positive and negative results for a speculator lately arrived on the scene
such as Maverick. The body followed the lead of the November Consultation in invalidating all surveys conducted and titles awarded after
August 20 of the previous year. This meant that Maverick's Béxar purchases were all invalid. Even worse, his later correspondence indicates
that he had engaged in a bit of speculative risk taking by picking up
certificates for ten leagues granted by an Edward R. Guild.[29] All of his
purchases—over five leagues in specific tracts and ten in certificates with
which to locate a claim—were in jeopardy except the quarter league
at Cox's Point, bought before the ban.

In overturning the massive eleven-league claims made by a few individuals under Mexican acts of 1834 and 1835, however, the convention was opening new land opportunities for others. It also tried to
bring some much-needed control to land matters by creating a General Land Office and rejecting any future surveys or titles not approved
by the government. Finally, the delegates voted to authorize land grants
for citizens residing in the territory on March 2, the date of the declaration of independence. Every head of a family would receive a certificate to locate a league and a smaller land unit of 177 acres called a labor; every single man seventeen or older, a certificate for one-third of
a league.

Land was clearly a major concern of the convention, for large-scale
speculation had caused much confusion and resentment in the colonies. Of course, there were other pressing issues as well. One was the

Indian problem, as settlers petitioned the convention for relief from Indian depredation. Maverick was appointed to a committee on Indian affairs to study and report on a letter received on the subject. The problem was to last much longer than any of the delegates could have imagined.

All of this was overshadowed for the moment, however, by the current state of affairs with Mexico. On March 13, Gray wrote, "No intelligence yet from the Alamo. The anxiety begins to be intense." The next day, a rumor spread that Travis had repulsed the Mexican attack, but this was quickly followed by the stark truth. Everyone was horrified —and edgy at the thought of where Santa Anna might turn next. Delegates became "impatient of debate," and the convention almost fell into disarray, as the chair could exercise little control over members determined to speak at once or to shout questions.[30]

On March 16, the convention managed to complete the constitution and elect an interim government. Maverick voted with the majority for fellow delegate and old friend Thomas Jefferson Rusk for secretary of war, and David Burnett became interim president.[31] Everyone was anxious to disperse. Rumors were flying through the colonies about Mexico's next move, and Sam Houston was training six hundred recruits at Burnam's Crossing on the Colorado. The siege of Béxar and the Alamo had been but a prelude to a concerted war effort on the part of the Texians.

The town of Washington itself was in a panic; families and storekeepers were packing up and moving eastward to escape Santa Anna. Gray reported that he went to pick up some laundry he had left with a woman and found her gone, his clothes "washed and neatly tied up."[32]

As the convention dispersed, Maverick was suffering an attack of chills and fever that, he later wrote to Rusk, "grew worse than any case I ever saw" and caused him "to lay some days over the river near Washington." He then turned eastward, traveling with a Mr. Roberts (probably Nacogdoches delegate John S. Roberts) to "the neighborhood of Nacogdoches where I remained sick 2 or 3 weeks."[33]

While Maverick lay ill in eastern Texas, events moved quickly onward. Fannin abandoned the fortress at Goliad for the open plains on March 19, and immediately ran into trouble from a Mexican force under José Urrea, which forced Fannin's surrender. On Palm Sunday, March 27, the American commander and most of his force were summarily executed on orders of Santa Anna, who was so confident now that he began a destructive sweep toward the eastern border of Texas, the Sabine River, instructing his troops to burn every settlement, plantation, and home in their path.

The result was the Runaway Scrape of 1836, when terrified settlers fled eastward in early April by whatever means possible, abandoning homes, storehouses, livestock, and growing gardens. Maverick reported to Rusk, "I was at Nacog[doche]s when the families all left it & when it was reported, at a distance, that it was taken by Indians and Mexicans."[34] The letter does not make clear whether Maverick stayed in Texas long enough to hear of Houston's victory over Santa Anna at the battle of San Jacinto. After reporting that he was at Nacogdoches during the Runaway Scrape, Maverick stated that he took a ferry "20 or 30 miles above Gaines" and left the territory. Meanwhile, Houston on April 21 staged a successful surprise attack on the Mexican army on the coastal plains east of Houston at San Jacinto in the decisive struggle of the revolution.

Maverick's untimely departure reflected not only ill health but also urgency in family affairs. He had left Alabama abruptly more than a year before, causing his father to write dryly to Mary Elizabeth that "as I am informed by yr letter . . . that he was gone to Texas you will please inform me if he left any word respecting the cotton."[35]

Mary Elizabeth was not faring well in handling family business, and her brother had apparently notified her in January or early February that he was safe and promised to return soon, for Samuel wrote to his daughter on March 14, "I join you in thanks to *Almighty God* for a continuance of his kindness to us in sparing your brother, yours 13th ulto [last month] gave me some hope, but that of the 23rd has overflowed me with joy inexpressible. . . . I hope Sam Augt will be with you ere this reaches you or soon after." The elder Maverick also hinted at a need for immediate action to save the family's considerable Tuscaloosa property "and all our lands from being sold for taxes or any other way."[36]

The decision to leave Texas at this juncture must have been galling to Sam Maverick, who had helped to write a constitution barring persons "who shall leave the country for the purpose of evading a participation in the present struggle, or shall refuse to participate in it" from citizenship and land rights.[37] He had participated fully in the struggle until his departure from the convention, and when he returned to the Texas frontier he would exhibit a relish for hardship and danger, as well as a strong sense of public duty. In April of 1836, however, it looked bad to leave, and he knew it.

This may explain why he spoke so little of his participation in the revolution that even his own sister Lydia, visiting the Alamo years later, seemed oblivious to the fact that Maverick had been one of its defenders.[38] Naturally reticent and introspective, Maverick was even more so on the subject of the Alamo and the fight for independence. When he returned to San Antonio, he was to enjoy a reputation as a particularly honorable man, even among those differing politically from him. Yet he apparently felt a sense of guilt at having survived the Alamo slaughter, as he would later feel a sense of guilt at being released from a Mexican prison when other Texans were not. Further, he was conscious of having failed to participate in the final conflict.

Undeniably, the revolutionary events had great meaning to him, for Maverick did indeed eventually build his house bordering the site of the Alamo massacre, and it was at his urging that a veteran of San Jacinto penned his memories of that battle.[39] Maverick was acutely conscious of the "brave blood and bitter tears" that were, he later mused, "ever wanted as the only true & patent cement for the institutions of Liberty."[40] But at the moment of victory, sick and dispirited, he turned away from the struggle. It would take him more than a year and a half to return, spirit and health renewed and with a young family to share in the struggles to come.

5

"Turn Those Sweet Eyes toward Bejar"

*I blame myself also, that you, my love, should have to bear the
thousand petty annoyances of our unsettled mode of living. But
amidst all, I have a little redeeming consolation in the Knowledge
that my efforts are bent in the direction in which we both wish to
go. I still hope every thing, and fear nothing.*

—Sam Maverick to his wife, February 26, 1838

THE MONTH OF MAY, 1836, found Sam Maverick in Tuscaloosa, where
he promptly fell in love. Aside from the brief reference to his appreciation of the fairer sex made by a college friend, one can look in vain
among Maverick's early papers for evidence of affairs of the heart. His
Texas journals include romantic-sounding names of Spanish women,
but the women's names, like the men's, were recorded in relation to
his real passion, the buying of land. Only once did he make a wry note
on the pursuit of romance in his 1835 journal, commenting, "Texas
over[run] with bachelors; the old tom cat Dr. Sanchez is a fine specimen of that kind of animal."[1]

The distant amusement of the entry reflects the cooly logical, re-
strained personality of its writer, who possessed, said one longtime friend,
a "gravity and sedateness beyond his years."[2] Yet a chance encounter
with Mary Ann Adams while riding on a country road near Tuscaloosa unleashed a floodgate of warmth, affection, and playfulness in
Maverick's nature. She was his "Mary-love," and though their marriage was to be bittersweet, there can be no mistaking the deep regard
each held for the other through both the pleasant and the harrowing
years ahead. Almost twenty years after their first meeting, Maverick
would stop before boarding a ship in New Orleans to dash off an impromptu will giving all property to his wife, concluding, "Like the Roman Catholics in regard to another Mary I have full faith in this one."[3]

Mary Ann Adams was only eighteen when the couple met, an auburn-haired girl of imposing size. She measured six feet tall, and a plaster cast of her hand that survives, part of one finger missing because of a childhood accident, shows her to be a large-boned woman.[4] Portraits made of her in middle and old age show a broad face with regular features.

She had not been without admirers; one timid suitor's letters are retained in the Maverick Family Papers, and there are hints of other suitors. A cousin wrote years later while visiting Tuscumbia, Alabama, of talking with "Judge Nove" who "used to be a beaux of yours did he not cousin Mary?"[5]

However, within three months of thirty-three-year-old Sam Maverick's appearance, Mary Ann Adams had become Mary Adams Maverick at her widowed mother's plantation near Tuscaloosa, with a minister from Tuscaloosa's Christ's Episcopal Church officiating. Despite the age gap, the couple's family backgrounds paralleled in many respects. Like her husband's, Mary's ancestors included French Huguenots and American patriots from the Eastern seaboard. Like his, her family was Episcopalian, and like him, she had early lost a parent and had grown to maturity in antebellum plantation culture.

On her mother's side, Mary could trace her heritage through a distinguished Virginia line to Huguenot William Lewis. The most prominent family member, Mary's great-grandfather Andrew Lewis, served as a brigadier general during the Revolution. His son William married Lucy Madison, cousin of Pres. James Madison, and from this union was born Mary's mother, Agatha Strother Lewis. In 1811 Agatha wed fellow Virginian Robert Lewis Adams, son of Massachusetts native Robert Adams and Mary Lynch, whose family founded Lynchburg, Virginia.[6]

At first, Mary's parents remained in Virginia near their families, settling on the James River, where William made a living exporting flour and tobacco. When the War of 1812 brought economic hardship, William departed alone for Alabama. He bought a plantation near the fledgling settlement of Tuscaloosa, then traveled to Mobile to purchase supplies. Here, according to his daughter's later account, he saw Andrew Jackson's call for volunteers to defend New Orleans, raised a company, and participated in the Battle of New Orleans.[7] In 1816 he brought Agatha to the Alabama frontier, settling across the Warrior River from

Tuscaloosa at Northport and practicing law in Tuscaloosa with Ezekiel Pickins of South Carolina.[8]

Mary later stated that her father secured an appointment from Pres. Andrew Jackson as Indian agent for the Creek and Cherokee country and died while serving in this capacity in 1827; however, Jackson did not become chief executive until 1828, and Adams' name is not listed among the Creek and Cherokee agents of the era. Instead, William L. Adams was serving as an agent of the federal Treasury Department in Alabama in early 1827, a position that could involve handling disbursements to the Creeks and Cherokees spread across the northeastern and central eastern portions of the state.[9] In a February, 1827, report as agent of the Treasury Department, he evaluated the chances for success of a French colony growing olive trees in Alabama, concluding, "I feel confident in the belief that the tree will not succeed in this climate."[10]

Two months later, Adams made out his will, specifying that his estate "be and remain undivided and entire in the free and full enjoyment of my beloved wife Agatha L. Adams and my several children."[11] The eldest child, Lucy, born before the move to Alabama, had died young, but the couple had six surviving offspring, all under twelve. Mary, born March 16, 1818, in Tuscaloosa, had followed her brothers William and George, and had been followed in turn by Andrew, Robert, and Elizabeth.[12]

William Lewis Adams died two months after completing the will. The loss had a devastating effect on the family; Mary would later attribute George's dissipation and early death to the loss of "his best friend & adviser our father while yet a child," and Mary herself continued in mid-life to suffer over the absence of a man "ever very gentle and fond to me."[13]

She could draw little sustenance from her harried mother, though the two maintained an affectionate correspondence after Mary's marriage. Agatha was ill-suited to handle a growing family and plantation alone, and she was susceptible to depression. Years later, sister Elizabeth would warn Mary not to "let unavailing sorrow prey too much upon your mind," as it would "throw a shadow over your home and even affect the dispositions of your children to a degree from which they will not recover. This I know as you do, from our own home."[14]

Significantly, when Mary herself edited and reshaped her diary for

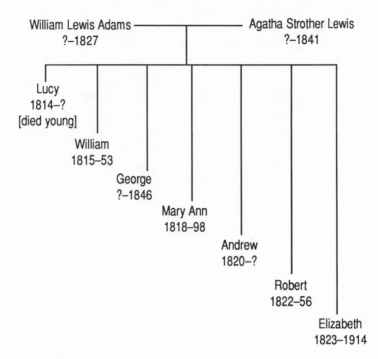

William Lewis Adams — Agatha Strother Lewis
?–1827 ?–1841

Lucy
1814–?
[died young]

William
1815–53

George
?–1846

Mary Ann
1818–98

Andrew
1820–?

Robert
1822–56

Elizabeth
1823–1914

William Lewis Adams–Agatha Strother Lewis family tree.

publication near the end of her life, deleting much painful material, she still included for publication a bleak, thoughtful assessment of Agatha's character and circumstances. "My mother had a sorrowful widowed life," Mary wrote, "for she was not always successful in managing business or in governing her boys. She blamed herself for her want of success as she called it, and she seldom smiled and never appeared to enjoy life. She was a devoted mother, but probably too strict with her children, and she was an humble, faithful Christian."[15]

William had emphasized in his will that the children were to "be educated in a manner Suitable and Convenient," and Mary was eventually sent across the river to Tuscaloosa to board and attend school.[16] Many years later, she remembered that the separation temporarily made her feel homesick and unloved by her mother. But there were numerous friends in Tuscaloosa, including the minister of Christ's Episcopal Church and his wife, in whose home she often visited.[17]

Tuscaloosa was still a raw, new town in many ways, having been in-

corporated the year after Mary's birth. However, when it was designated the state capital in 1826, the community began to take on an
air of cultivated solidity, only heightened by its selection as home of
the University of Alabama the following year. A "permanent" capitol
was completed in 1829 on town lots obtained by the government from
Samuel Maverick and two other lot holders, and in 1831 the university
opened its doors.[18]

When Mary and her school friends were old enough to partake of
the social life of the city, they would visit the capitol and listen to the
governor and senators speak.[19] Mary moved in a social set that included
the governor's son and other children of influential state residents, but
the record of her words and actions over the years shows that she had
little interest in status seeking and distrusted the enticements of city
life. On a trip to New Orleans with Maverick shortly after their marriage, she would write her mother about meeting two young women
who were "beautiful, accomplished, wealthy, flattered and caressed and
still possess[ing] heart and sensibility, things I consider rare indeed in
a City."[20]

The writer possessed heart and sensibility and a fair degree of optimism, confiding to her mother on September 8, 1839, that "my temperament leads me to the sunny side of life." Actually, Mary had a
brooding, introspective side and would walk many shadowy paths ahead,
struggling with a sense of her own inadequacies in relation to the idealized portrait of a Christian wife and mother that dominated perceptions of woman's role in her era. But in these early years, she still had
the natural optimism, the sense of invincibility and of unlimited possibilities, common to youth.

The Mavericks honeymooned among Alabama friends and relatives,
including Mary's old school friend E. A. Shortridge Lewis in Talladega
Springs, Mary's Uncle John and Aunt Ann Bradley in Tuscumbia, and
Sam's sister Mary Elizabeth in Florence. About the time of their visit,
Mary Elizabeth, too, married, choosing as her second husband Joseph
Thompson, one of five brothers from North Carolina who had been
among the earliest settlers of Colbert's Reserve.

Returning to Tuscaloosa with his bride in October, Sam Maverick
paused to write to Thomas Jefferson Rusk. Rusk had continued to perform with distinction in Texas, participating in the Battle of San Jacinto and serving through the months Maverick had been away as
brigadier general in command of the Texas Army. "I have not taken

my pen for the purpose of trespassing on the rights of the historian, in alluding to the great events in which you have been so enviably employed," Maverick began. "Your friend knows all: and his bosom, which was ever warmed with love, now glows with admiration."[21]

He was understandably diffident about his own movements, but he gave a reasonably full accounting and announced, "My dear friend I have got married—to Miss Mary Adams near this place." His chief concern in writing, however, was to get Texas land news. Asking Rusk to consider him "as your client for some time to come," Maverick eagerly inquired what actions the new Texas Congress might be taking that would affect his shaky Texas land purchases. If his purchases could be considered valid, he wanted to know whether he would have to locate within a short time and whether he could do so as soon as a new land office opened. "I may not, perhaps expect to see a publication of the Constitution & acts of Texas," he wrote, "and therefore I pray you to write me, and give me the true force of the denunciation against the large grants, &c."

Maverick was also concerned specifically about the one Texas purchase to which he held clear title, the quarter league on Cox's Point, "which I consider a site for a future city." He feared that neighboring quarter-league owner Pleasant Cocke and half-league owner George Sutherland would try to "get an order of court and manage to divide me out [of] that part which is suitable for the town."

Despite his pointed, eager questions, Maverick showed an uncharacteristic lassitude. Reporting that he had not yet recovered his health, he wrote that Alabama did not agree with him. "I am very bilious & have very bad digestion," he explained. "I long to get back to Texas, but not the Brazos in particular. I am in a very torpid inert state of body & mind; and do not feel able to leave my wife if I can help it."

One factor in Maverick's reluctance to return to Texas was probably the knowledge or suspicion that his wife was already two-months pregnant. However, his extended illness and inertia may have in part resulted from psychological pressures brought on by the fact that he had turned away, willingly or not, from the Republic at a crucial point in its history and having done so, could not see his way back. On a more mundane level, he may simply have been waiting at a safe distance for affairs in Texas to stabilize, but his subsequent pattern of actively exposing himself to frontier hazards undercuts this supposition. Once he returned to the Texas frontier, he was never healthier than when in the surveying camp, enduring dangers and privations that made most of his fellow surveyors actually prone to illness.[22]

However, he was not back in Texas yet. He did burn one bridge as the new year of 1837 began, selling his Lauderdale County plantation.[23] In January he went west as far as New Orleans, taking Mary with him. Maverick and his father continued sporadic mercantile activities through an agent there when they found an attractive price on goods. But the port city also lured him because in it he could gain more immediate news of Texas than he could in Alabama. Mary wrote her mother shortly after arriving in the city that "Mr. Maverick has learned all that possibly can be heard from there, thinks it the most propitious time for speculators and would gladly go himself if it were not for the necessity of leaving me." She reported that recent Texas travelers brought favorable reports of a country "settl[ing] down to peace and tranquility."[24]

This assessment betrayed a certain amount of wishful thinking, for Texas affairs were still far from stable. For diplomatic reasons, President Jackson had even refused to recognize the struggling Republic at this point, much less heed the postrevolutionary vote of Texas residents to make it a state in the union. Pres. Sam Houston was following a conservative fiscal course, but the Republic's debt was nonetheless mounting rapidly while the Mexican and Indian threats remained serious. The General Land Office the independence convention had sought to create had not yet come into existence, and without it, no legally sanctioned land purchases could take place. So land affairs remained confused and tentative.

Still, many emigrants were hurrying toward Texas, eager to claim a share of its future. One such hopeful adventurer was Mary's oldest brother, William, who soon arrived in New Orleans bound for Texas. By letter, Mary hastened to relieve any anxiety her mother might feel by reassuring her about William's chances for safety and success and adding, "He promises in event of the country being again disturbed by war not to join the army." Her husband, Mary reported, "shrinks from persuading another to do what *might* in the end prove disadvantageous," but he was encouraging William, "for he believes the opportunity so great he can soon render himself independent with one tenth of the labour and drudgery it would require at home."[25]

William departed from San Antonio, but the Mavericks remained in the booming port city, where Mary enjoyed such novelties as a ride on the newly constructed Pontchartrain steam railroad. In early March, they were back at her home outside Tuscaloosa, but did not stay long, this time turning eastward to Pendleton. According to family tradition, the elder Samuel had let it be known that "I will not believe that you did not perish [in the Alamo] until I see you with my own eyes."[26] Finally, with his first child on the way, Sam Maverick gave in to his father's wishes and arrived to a joyful reception at Montpelier on March 19.

Samuel immediately began urging his son and daughter-in-law to stay. To his disappointment, none of his three children had settled near him. Mary Elizabeth was in Alabama expecting the birth of the first child of her new union. Lydia and William Van Wyck were settled in New York City with their two-year-old, Samuel Maverick Van Wyck. Sam, the firstborn son and heir, had proven hard to keep up with. Now Samuel, who was divesting himself of some of his business interests and devoting even more time to horticulture, offered his son Montpelier—"mills, vineyards, orchards, lands, and shops," or a neighboring plantation. But it was "all in vain," Mary later wrote, "for my husband dreamed constantly of Texas, and said: 'We must go back.'"[27]

Still they delayed, detained by Samuel's "sad and afflicted" look at every mention of their going and by the birth of a son, who arrived on May 14, 1837. Samuel grew particularly attached to his new grandchild, and as the summer months passed, the family remained at Montpelier, where Maverick could get only piecemeal news from Texas. Pendleton residents had mourned the death of Bonham in the Alamo and now proudly followed the accomplishments of Rusk and of Barnard Bee, a friend of the elder Maverick's who had joined Rusk after the revolution and served in the interim government.

The Pendleton *Messenger* reported what news it could garner from Texas, announcing on June 16, "Emigrants are now entitled to 640 acres of land, if single men, and 1280, if married" and editorializing that "with such inducements, all who value their interests, should avail themselves of it." But the news could be frightening, too. Less than a month later the paper reported that a passenger on the schooner *Byron* from Galveston had brought word of massacres by Comanche Indians near Washington-on-the-Brazos and in the town of Nashville, Texas. The article carried exaggerated accounts of the number of Indian raiders, stating, "They can, it is said, bring fifteen thousand well armed warriors into the field. The number now engaged in devastating the frontiers of Texas, is about 5,000, led on, it is said, by painted white men."[28]

Sam Maverick delayed, but he did not waver. He maintained a vital interest in the newly democratic Texas nation, and his land hunger had been fueled by his glimpse of the broad western vistas for which San Antonio was the gateway. Finally, in October, he, Mary, and the baby set out with a small retinue of slaves: nurse Rachel, a gift from Mary's mother; wagon driver Wiley, a Maverick retainer; cook Jinny Anderson, Maverick's former nurse; and Jinny's four children. Mary later wrote that Samuel traveled with them half a day, delaying the parting, and "it was a sad sight to witness his grief when he at last parted with his son. My heart ached for the dear old man."[29]

When the entourage crossed the Tugaloo River, which forms part of the boundary between South Carolina and Georgia, they stopped to christen the five-month-old baby, adding another Samuel Maverick to the lineage. Informed by letter of the christening, his grandfather at Pendleton wrote, "With great pleasure I have filled up a blank record in the old bible with the old family word of Samuel," adding, "[May he] hand down the name of Samuel to the end of time."[30]

Once more, the Mavericks stopped at Tuscaloosa, this time to make preparations for settling in Texas. Here they learned that not only had William found San Antonio to his liking, but he had returned to Alabama to raise capital and was setting up a store in a rented room on Bexar's Main Plaza.

By the time the couple set off for Texas on December 7, Agatha Adams had been persuaded to allow another brother, the sickly fifteen-year-old Robert, to accompany them, and he brought his own manservant, Uncle Jim. Agatha added two adult male slaves, Griffin and Granville, to the traveling party for her daughter, bringing the number bound for Texas to fourteen. Mary, the baby, and Rachel were to ride in a roomy carriage, while a large Kentucky wagon would carry Jinny and her children, as well as camping supplies.

Like Samuel Maverick in Pendleton, Agatha reluctantly watched her children migrating westward to unknown lands. When the day came for parting, Agatha ran after the party "for one more embrace" and then cried prophetically, "Oh, Mary, I will never see you again on Earth."[31]

After this wrenching parting, the travelers turned southwest, crossing the Father of Waters a few miles above Natchez, then proceeding in a leisurely manner along a standard emigrant trail to Alexandria, Louisiana, and westward across the thin, muddy Sabine, reaching Texas soil about New Year's Day, 1838.

They paused for carriage repairs in San Augustine, a rude strip of log cabins, then pressed onward through Nacogdoches to stop at the home of John Durst, an old settler who had tracked Mexican troop movements during the revolution and was now serving as a member of the Second Congress of the Republic. Here, too, Maverick was able to confer with Rusk, also serving in the Congress. Two concerns were uppermost in Maverick's mind: where to locate his family, and how to pick up where he had left off in land speculation.

Much ground remained to be covered to get to the central settlements of the Republic and find at least a temporary home. Through intermittent rains, the Maverick entourage journeyed across sparsely settled countryside, wagon wheels sinking deep into the pervasive muck that passed for roads in early Texas. Their route led them to Washington, still the uppermost settlement on the Brazos, and farther westward to the Colorado River.

After crossing the Colorado at Columbia, they neared the Gulf Coast and faced a "bleak, desolate, swamp-prairie" that Mary remembered vividly many years later. The animals sloshed through cold, knee-deep water, and when the party stopped for the night, Mary's mattress floated in water. The wagons repeatedly became mired, and a blustering norther descended on the travelers. Their provisions were running out by the time they reached a homestead on the Navidad River, after taking four days to journey fourteen miles.

Through the whole experience, however, Mary reported her husband's optimism unflagging, commenting, "Mr. Maverick kept cheerful all the while and was not a bit discouraged that we could see—said that water was better than mud to pull in."[32] Indeed, on the frontier, Maverick would come to thrive on physical hardship and new surroundings to the point that after a forced march into Mexico as a prisoner a few years later, he could write to a friend, "If I had not known how unhappy my family was, I could have enjoyed the trip."[33]

The journey from Tuscaloosa ended temporarily for all but Maverick himself on February 4, when the entourage arrived at a common stop for wayfarers, Spring Hill on the Navidad. The home of George Sutherland, it was located in a stand of timber adjacent to what one traveler described as a beautiful prairie. Here, despite Maverick's earlier suspicions toward Sutherland concerning the Cox's Point land, Mary and the others remained for four months while Maverick traveled onward alone.

At Spring Hill, Mary was imbued with a large dose of Texas na-
tionalism. Sutherland had served at San Jacinto and provided supplies
to the Texas Army. His wife, Fannie, was the sister of William Menefee, with whom Maverick served at the independence convention, and
the Sutherlands had lost a nineteen-year-old son at the Alamo. Other
boarders, too, had participated in the revolution, and she listened to
their stories, as well as to those Mrs. Sutherland and the other pioneer
women told of the Runaway Scrape following the Alamo's fall. She
attended a San Jacinto ball at Texana with Mrs. Sutherland's nephew
John Menefee, one of the veterans of the engagement, and his sister
Fannie. All around her were people who talked with pride and determination about their destiny as Texians.

Meanwhile, her husband rode onward to Cox's Point, thinking of
locating his family there if San Antonio still echoed with rumors of
Mexican invasion. But his chief destination was Bexar, his chief impetus the desire to plunge once more into Texas land speculation.

He was not alone. The Panic of 1837 had not yet clouded the hopes
of Texas entrepreneurs, and that year had seen a frenzy of land speculation in the new Republic, despite the fact that laws for handling land
transactions had yet to be passed. Headright holders were already having to move outside the settlements to locate claims. The First Congress of the Republic had voted in accord with the independence convention on December 22, 1836, to establish a General Land Office. But
President Houston procrastinated in establishing one even after a second congressional mandate in June, 1837.

Finally, in December, 1837, as the Mavericks were journeying to Texas,
the legislature passed a new law providing for a General Land Office,
county surveyors, and county boards of land commissioners to study
the validity of claims. In San Antonio, the first meeting of the Board
of Land Commissioners for Bexar County was called to order on January 25, 1838. Maverick arrived in Bexar four weeks later, finding the
city "putting on a neglected & ruinous appearance," yet still "strikingly
pretty and oriental in its look."[34]

He immediately began buying individual headright certificates. His
working capital included money from lands he had sold in Tuscaloosa
and Florence. It is likely that Samuel, too, had provided funds, as he
shared his son's interest, and his later letters indicate that he was for-
warding money for land and taxes.

Maverick also set out to convince the board of the validity of the purchases he had made during the fall and winter of 1835–36. On the Cibolo Creek property, his first Bexar purchase, he found three settlers, including, he reported, "a man in high office" whom it would prove troublesome to remove. But then, this was to be only one small part of his empire. Four days after his arrival, he wrote to Mary, "I am looking out for good locations for 5 other Leagues and shall probably buy some more."[35]

He discovered that the furious speculation of the year before had been particularly intense in Bexar, where over half a million acres had changed hands in 1837.[36] Maverick's old compatriot John W. Smith had become clerk of the Bexar County Court, established in April, 1837, and he had seen to it that each land transaction was as official as possible, and therefore likely to stand up under the scrutiny of a land board when one was created.

Most of the transactions involved the "league and a labor" granted under the constitution to all heads of households residing in Texas on March 2, 1836. This provision of the document Maverick had helped to create gave many Mexican residents of Bexar County landownership rights they had never expected. Since Maverick had last transacted a land deal in Bexar, other enterprising Anglo-Americans had begun bargaining with the Mexican residents for their headrights. As one historian has pointed out, "Nothing was actually being sold but a Constitutional right, one which at that time due to the closing of the land offices [they] could not exercise."[37] The successful speculator was buying in a headright the opportunity to claim over forty-five hundred acres of unclaimed land of his choosing.

At the center of all this activity, Smith acted not only as county clerk but as buyer and agent, for he was advertising his services for "the purchase, sale, and location of land in the western part of Texas" in the Houston *Telegraph and Texas Register*.[38] Maverick, too, began acting both in his own behalf and as an agent, helping citizens establish headright claims, then buying them up.[39] He received his own headright on March 2, after Smith and three others testified that the applicant had participated in the revolution.[40]

Maverick hoped that now that a board of commissioners had been formed, some of the land certificates granted in his absence would be thrown out, for, he complained to his wife on March 13, "all the artful & unprincipled speculators of the country seem to have got the start & made application for nearly all the favourite spots of vacant land."

However, he clearly brimmed with unabashed excitement at the challenge before him, describing San Antonio to Mary with the fervor of a promoter. "This is the only place in Texas," he wrote in the same letter, "where there is plenty to eat, & every body in good spirits. I shall not praise the sky, climate, soil etc. I have done it before & I do not wish you to anticipate too much for Earth to furnish." Yet he could not resist further rhapsodies, asserting that most Texans east of the Guadalupe River secretly wished to escape their unhealthy environment for "the blessed clime of the west."

In the midst of his excitement, however, Maverick expressed a deep longing for his wife and sounded a continuing note of self-reproach for the way his choices affected her. "Two weeks, this day, have elapsed since I left you," he had written in late February, "and my bosom tells me it is an age." When the two weeks dragged into two months, he again noted the time as "an age of misery." The uncertainties of the frontier life he was asking Mary to share sometimes bedeviled him — the difficult travel, the unsettled living, the waiting and wondering. Despite possessing a restless, adventurous spirit, Maverick had a paradoxical longing for stability and a genuine concern for his wife's wishes. "Oh! how I long for repose from this rambling adventurous life, and to settle down in the sweet, *delicious* comforts of home," he wrote, but consoled himself with "the Knowledge that my efforts are bent in the direction in which we both wish to go."[41]

As their time apart lengthened, Maverick thanked his wife for her "generosity, confidence, and good spirits," begged her forgiveness for his long absence, and berated himself for the distance he had led her from a romantic ideal. "That sweet home of ours," he wrote on March 31, "that delightful garden, that Eden of Love and Content which our good angels promised to our united & confident hearts! Where are they? How easy for me to procure them all; and yet they are still unattained. Any quiet cottage would fill all our wishes, behold we are wanderers! *wanderers* merely because *I* was a wanderer." In his less poetic moments, he knew well enough, as did his wife, that "any quiet cottage" would *not* suffice, that he was happiest surveying and dealing in lands on the edge of settled Texas.

Still, such a life was fraught with uncertainties, and not just those accompanying any speculative business. Ever since Sam Houston had vanquished Santa Anna at San Jacinto, rumors of another Mexican invasion had drifted into Bexar. In truth, Mexico, racked by its own internal problems and by the threat of aggression from France, posed little threat yet. But United States–Mexican relations were poor. The U.S. government had now recognized the Texas Republic; Mexico had not, nor had it recognized Texan land claims. All concerned knew that future hostilities were likely to occur, and Maverick had to think about possible consequences. If the United States should declare war against its southern neighbor, then he wished Mary to join him in San Antonio. If Mexico tried once more to invade Texas, they would both have to return to Alabama. "But my dear," he wrote, "I beg you to turn those sweet eyes toward Bejar rather than towards Mothers."[42]

The extent of Maverick's concern for his wife's wishes is revealed in his most optimistic letter from San Antonio during this separation, one overflowing with happy pronouncements about the city he so enthusiastically reclaimed as his own. He wanted her to be there with him, but, he wrote, "I do not propose any such important step, beloved, without leaving it all to you. If your heart, tired of Texas for the present (or altogether), should beat for Mother's or Father's or any other place, I shall be ready in a short time to accompany you withersoever thou listeth. I am ready to do all to repay you for the sweet smiles you gave me in the midst of our greatest toils & fatigues."[43]

Perhaps Maverick made the offer feeling secure that his wife would not pull him from the Texas scene, but the couple's relationship over the years reinforces Carl Degler's thesis that many nineteenth-century marriages were more egalitarian than historians have supposed. Maverick would frequently express confidence in his wife's decision-making abilities and encourage her interests, as she encouraged his.[44]

Mary Adams Maverick possessed her own share of adventurous curiosity, and her letters and diaries show that she felt a tremendous devotion toward her husband. Thus, she readily chose to turn her eyes toward Bexar, not counting or yet knowing the cost. On June 2, 1838, after Maverick had made a quick trip to Mobile and New Orleans to buy housekeeping provisions, she joined him on the road to Bexar.

6

"A Family of Adventurers"

*We find ourselves a family of adventurers, as far West as it is
possible for Americans to go under the present circumstances, and
yet I can find nothing to regret—but the distance which separates
us from so many near and dear friends.*

—Mary Adams Maverick in a letter to her mother, August 25, 1838

THE MAVERICKS had their most difficult journey ahead of them when
they departed Spring Hill for San Antonio. Their northerly route led
them through another sparsely settled region, with a broken wagon
wheel and the chills that struck brother Robert, Griffin, and Jinny
slowing the party. When they found one frontier dwelling, it was inhabited primarily by fleas.

Such problems and irritations paled, though, beside a visit from a
Tonkawa Indian war party. The Maverick entourage had camped while
having the wagon wheel fixed and was making preparations to move
on in late afternoon when seventeen Tonkawas, bison hunters who
ranged through Central Texas, began filtering into the camp.

Mary Maverick had seen Indians before, of course, but not like
these. Civilized Creeks and Cherokees had occupied eastern Alabama
lands during her maturing years, and in the summer of 1836 they and
other members of the Five Civilized Tribes had camped throughout
the Tuscaloosa area, having been pushed farther west by Pres. Andrew
Jackson's Indian removal policy. In Texas at Spring Hill, Mary had encountered Sam Houston's Indian peace negotiator, old Cherokee Chief
Bowles, whose desire to dance with the ladies and half-Indian, half-
civilized garb she regarded with amused ethnocentrism.

These Tonkawas had nothing of the "civilized" about them. Fresh
from a battle with the Comanches, painted and well armed, they "dis-
played in triumph two scalps, one hand, and several pieces of putrid

flesh from various parts of the human body," Mary would remember. The Indians appeared interested in two things—the party's horses and one-year-old Sammy. Mary held him up for their inspection but steadfastly refused to let them hold him, believing, she would write, "that they, being cannibals, would like to eat my baby and kill us all and carry off our horses."[1] No passive stereotype of a nineteenth-century lady, she also made sure the Indians could see her pistol and bowie knife.

Maverick and the other men continued coolly readying for travel while Jinny, who was to prove equally unperturbed in further Indian encounters, complained mightily about not getting to fix supper. As the party quietly moved out, the Indians followed through a bright moonlit night. Finally, about midnight, the Tonkawas began to drop away; by the time the travelers reached the banks of the Cibolo and made camp, only two Indians remained.

In later years, Mary Maverick was to complain to her diary that though she had tried to be a good slave owner, she could not "see that *one* loves me or cares consistently to please me."[2] She was forgetting one by then long dead—her man Griffin, who stationed himself in front of her tent with gun and ax and called to the two remaining intruders, "Come this way if you dare, you devils, and I'll make hash out of you!"[3]

The Indians slipped away without incident, and the Maverick party continued toward the relative safety of San Antonio, now traveling up the San Antonio River valley and passing by the *ranchos* of various well-established Mexican Texans. Finally, on June 15, 1838, twenty-year-old Mary viewed the new El Dorado that had so captured her husband.

Anglo-American travelers often paused at a distance to admire this "white town" rising oasislike from the valley floor. They often found, as Maverick had, an oriental beauty, or a European one imparting the flavor of "the dilapidated cities of old Spain."[4] Jon Winfield Scott Dancy, viewing it about two months after the Mavericks arrived, commented that the town reminded him of "one of the old fortified towns of antiquity," and added, "all that Washington Irving ever wrote about the silver windings of the Xenil in the valley of Granada is equalled if not surpassed by the S.A. river."[5]

Up close, however, the impoverished agricultural community lost some of its glamour. Elizabeth Riddle Canterbury, recalling her arrival

Sketched by W. Bisse

W. Bissett's pre-1841 sketch of San Antonio reveals the rude state of the town as the Mavericks first knew it. *From Francis Moore, Jr., Map and Description of Texas (1840).*

in 1841, reported that "the houses I saw all around me were so low and dingy looking with their flat roofs and dirt chimneys, where there were any, that the entire place had the appearance to me of being visited by fire." An 1845 visitor found the town picturesque, but described the houses as "low, squatty, unprepossessing adobe buildings with flat roofs of mud or a cement composition, or frail and aboriginal jacals with thatched roofs if any at all" and remembered "but one so-called bridge across the river."[6]

In fact, during the entire Republic period, San Antonio was, in one historian's words, "nearly desolate," a far-western frontier; many Mexican families elected to move away from the constant Indian and Mexican threats and few American families moved in.[7] Although the Houston *Telegraph and Texas Register* reported six thousand emigrants entering the Republic at one Sabine ferry crossing alone during the summer and fall of 1837, such emigrants went primarily to existing Anglo-American settlements east and south of Bexar.

By many accounts, Mary Maverick was the first female of U.S. origin actually to settle in the city, and the cover of her memoirs identifies her as "San Antonio's First American Woman." Yet Mary herself mentioned a predecessor in a letter to her mother, a "very fine American lady" married to an Irishman. The woman soon died of whooping cough. Thus, "Our only society are Mexicans; two Irish families live in town but they are no society, such home people."[8] Most of the Anglo-Americans in the community were single male adventurers drawn there by land speculation and by chances of trade with Mexico.

The Mavericks established their first real home in the city house of Don José Cassiano, a wealthy rancher who had rented a front room to brother William for his store and who now gave the family temporary lodging.[9] The house fronted on San Antonio's Main Plaza, affording an opportunity for the newcomers to absorb the colorful diversity of San Antonio life. The plaza that had during the revolution served as a strategic battleground for Mexican and revolutionary forces once again bustled with townspeople, travelers, and peddlers of *cigaritos*, sweetmeats, and chile. Comanches and Mescalero and Lipan Apaches often appeared to trade hides and game, and English mingled with Spanish and Indian tongues in a confusing medley. Animals — horses, donkeys, dogs, and oxen pulling carts — added to the general mêlée during the busy hours of the day. At night, wagon drivers would camp on the plaza, and a fandango house anchoring one corner of the square would reverberate with music and laughter.

If Mary Maverick experienced any dismay with her new surroundings, her letters and memoirs do not show it. Her husband's passion for the area imbued her with a dream of its future as well, and she refused to be discouraged by the lack of Anglo-American families. She wrote her mother in August of 1838, "I can find nothing to regret — but the distance which separates us from so many near and dear friends."

Yet that first summer brought many harbingers of troubles that would plague those determined enough to settle on this far frontier. Barely had the Mavericks become established in the Cassiano house when Comanches staged two nighttime raids into the city, killing two Mexicans and a German and kidnapping a child. Swift Comanche horsemen commanded the central plateaus and high plains of Texas, and

This view of Military Plaza, San Antonio, showing the Mexican flavor of the community, was drawn by Arthur Schott, engraved by James D. Smillie, and included in William H. Emory, *Report on the United States and Mexican Boundary Survey* (1857).

San Antonio lay exposed on the edge of their broad range. Nor could the settlers long forget the hostile Mexican presence to the south. In July, rumors once more began circulating of Mexican invasion and of a Mexican alliance with the Comanches.

Sam Maverick was confident things would settle down sooner or later, and when they did, he planned to have large amounts of land to sell to new waves of emigrants he was sure would come from the United States and Europe. The General Land Office upheld the numerous claims made in Maverick's absence in 1837, but he soon found little opportunity had been lost. Plenty of certificates remained to be had, and plenty of land remained around Bexar and farther west on which to locate claims. After bringing his wife to the settlement, Maverick continued laying the basis for his land empire by buying up tracts and certificates from the primarily Mexican population of Bexar.

The result of such transactions, of course, was that land rights passed rapidly from San Antonio natives, often poor and illiterate, to Anglo-American speculators, a fact that smacks of exploitation. However, as John Bost Pitts has pointed out in his study on San Antonio headright speculation, many Mexicans were only too glad to dispose of headrights they had not ever expected to receive and had little interest in locating. Everything on the Texas frontier was a gamble at this point, and Mexican San Antonio was a gambling town.[10] Anglo-American speculators were offering large sums of money, a commodity much needed by many residents of the war-ravaged agricultural settlement, and the new Republic seemed shaky at best. The Mexican army might march northward again any day and force the speculators out, leaving the residents with a tidy profit from nonexistent land claims.

More ominously for the Mexican residents, the intolerance exhibited by some Anglo-Americans across the Republic toward Mexicans might grow and eventually lessen the latter's opportunities under this new system. Why not pocket the cash now? So Mexicans sold and Anglo-Americans bought. Many Anglo-Americans, too, sold, with a casualness that is hard to imagine today. Noah Smithwick, who received three land certificates for just over two years' ranger service, later related, "No one cared anything for land those days. I gave one of my certificates for 1,280 acres for a horse which the Indians relieved me of in less than a week."[11]

Pres. Sam Houston noted with alarm the ways in which land claims were being bartered, particularly in Bexar County, which then comprised a huge chunk of Central and Southwestern Texas. In an address to the Texas Congress in May of 1838, as the Mavericks prepared to leave Spring Hill, he had warned that too many claims were being filed, considering the "probable aggregate of just claims," and urged an investigation into board activities in Bexar County, where 475 certificates had already been issued.[12]

Bexar County records show that Maverick made forty-one actual land purchases in the county in 1838 and 1839, either simply as buyer or as "assignee," an agent to whom a claim was transferred. He also received 640 acres as a donation grant for his participation in the siege of Béxar.[13]

Back in Pendleton, the elder Maverick was channeling funds to Texas in the form of bank drafts and writing encouraging letters. In June, 1838, Samuel wrote that "the vast emigration & natural increase of the people will insure great profits in lands, no matter where situated," and in October he wrote, "Now is your time, in my opinion, If you should entirely fail you will recollect that I have Hog & dumplin & plenty of poor land for you all and to spare."[14] The next year, while acknowledging the dangers of land speculation, he was nonetheless moved to write with longing, "Was I 30 years younger I would be alongside of you" surveying and investing in Texas "irrigating lands."[15]

The Mavericks, father and son, acted on the assumption that settlers would soon pour across Texas. The elder Samuel was so certain of it that when he learned in 1840 of his son selling a parcel, he wondered "whether you are not doing yourself a great injury in selling your land at such an under price" when it might be hard to replace and when, if Maverick could just hold out, "Mount Etna will pour out his lava of emigrants."[16]

However, emigration slowed after 1838, and through long years ahead, the Mavericks would hold acreage without seeing their hopes realized. As Mary later wrote in her memoirs, her husband envisioned a southwestern empire flourishing through the efforts of industrious emigrants, but "they came not to Texas; they settled in the great North West, and there they built up the empires of which he had prophesied."[17] This meant much early discouragement for pioneers such as the Mavericks, who had chosen to cast both their financial and personal fortunes with the new Republic.

The discouragement is reflected in a letter heavily tinged with homesickness that Mary wrote to her mother on September 8, 1839. "We have not realized our expectations of Texas and San Antonio," she wrote, recalling how they had anticipated a more stable government and greater settlement. But hard economic times and "a combination of accidents" fused so that "every body does not come to Texas: the fact is very few come of late—So few that they make no show in this wide uncultivated waste."

As a consequence, land was cheap, "getting down to nothing," Mary reported. Her husband was still "dabbling" in headrights and land, but could not sell for much more than half the cost. And San Antonio itself, though still "the same healthy & beautiful place as far as the gifts of nature go," was "condemned" by the "thieves and mean wretches who inhabit it." In short, she explained, "the frontier situation of the place, and the fact of so general a want of population in Texas, have kept families from moving out here."

Despite the bleak outlook, the Mavericks were already financially and personally committed to staying. They held on to the dream of a settled, prosperous land and philosophized about the disappointments and privation they endured. Both distrusted the enticements offered by the crowded cities to the east, as evidenced by Mary's earlier surprise at finding young women of heart and sensibility in a city such as New Orleans. In the same September, 1839, letter to her mother, written after the birth of a second son, she consoled herself with the thought that she had "what thousands in the busy crowds of the world, surrounded by every luxury which art or fortune can command with countless friends and flatterers, sigh for in vain"—a loving husband and two boys. Her husband reasoned that if he had remained in Alabama, he might have gone into business in Mobile and lost all in the Panic of 1837, causing, Mary wrote "a disappointment to his wife as well as himself, for living in a fashionable place we would have been fashionable. Whereas here we have not so many artificial wants, and are no doubt learning useful lessons for life, and it may all turn out very well."

They put down roots in a number of ways. Maverick obtained his Texas law license in November, 1838, and soon began arguing cases in district court.[18] In Texas at the time, there were more lawyers than legal work, but the successful ones shared with doctors the important political and cultural positions.[19] Indeed, in January, 1839, Maverick was elected Bexar's mayor, or "president" of a city council composed of six councilmen of Spanish and Mexican ancestry and two Anglo-American councilmen, as well as an Anglo-American treasurer and collector.

Legend has it that Maverick never sought office during his years of public service in Texas, instead being elected on the basis of popular appeal. In truth, he would actively seek public office in later years, though usually at the urging of others. In this case it is fair to assume some truth to the legend, as he was out of town for at least two weeks before the January 7 election. At the installation ceremony the next day, former mayor John W. Smith was named mayor pro tem until Maverick's return from a business trip to Mobile and Tuscaloosa. On March 1, city hall records show, "the President elected presented himself took the requisite oath and proceeded acting as such."[20]

Maverick was to continue to enjoy popular support in the next few years, as he was to be voted onto the city council and into the Seventh and Eighth Republic congresses. Election returns and newspaper accounts from this early period do not survive to provide clues as to who voted for him and why, but obviously his previous residence in the city, his past role as a delegate to the independence convention, and his educational and legal qualifications were assets. Bexar County archivist John O. Leal has suggested that impoverished Mexican citizens of the community may have voted for him in these early years in gratitude for his help in arranging sales of land rights or in buying those rights.[21] To the few American emigrants who had been in Béxar before the revolution, Maverick was one of them, a real "Texian," whereas to newcomers he would be an old-timer with impressive credentials.

By the time he began serving as mayor, the Mavericks had moved into their own home, after renting a second house for a few months. Their purchase was "the Barrera place," a three-room stone dwelling on the northeast corner of the Main Plaza. The house stood less than a block from the spot on which Maverick had caught the fatally wounded Milam during the Béxar siege. Now the new occupants converted a shed on the property into a kitchen and servant's room, built a second adobe servant's room, constructed a stable, and put a picket fence around the garden filled with fig and pomegranate trees. The San Antonio River arched through the northeast corner of their property line, and they erected a bathhouse and wash place under the branches of a massive cypress tree.

In March, 1839, shortly after moving into this new home, Mary gave birth to second son Lewis Antonio with a "Mrs. Black from the Alamo" serving as midwife.[22] Named for the city of his birth, Lewis would become known as the first Anglo-American child to be born and grow up in San Antonio.[23]

Fragmentary records of his first term as mayor reveal that Sam Maverick grappled with the usual problems of an ethnically mixed frontier community, helping to settle disputes and trying to meet the threat posed to all by Comanches and Mexican desperadoes. He attempted to defend the city by instituting a guard plan and by soliciting the Texas government for help against depredations. The government itself faced the same problem, however, as Houston's successor, Mirabeau B. Lamar, was removing the capital from relatively safe Houston to an even more exposed site than San Antonio, tiny Austin on the banks of the Colorado.

Another continuing cause of concern was the lack of finances to provide needed city services. Not only was money scarce, but Maverick's council inherited a confused set of accounts for a paltry sum from the previous city treasurer. Maverick's mayoral predecessor had ordered a tax of one dollar on every cart entering the city with merchandise and two dollars on every wagon carrying freight in an attempt to raise money for much-needed bridge and road repair. But bridges and roads remained a headache, as did such other municipal matters as garbage disposal and maintenance of a clean water supply.

By the end of his one-year term, Maverick found himself acting as treasurer as well as mayor. He also was serving as a precinct justice of the peace.[24] He apparently refused to be considered for re-election to the mayor's spot, as in the next vote John W. Smith won another term overwhelmingly against former independence convention delegate José Antonio Navarro and councilman Antonio Ruiz.

During Maverick's mayoral service, a few Anglo-American emigrant families had trickled into town, providing the beginnings of an Anglo-American society. The Mavericks gravitated toward these people of similar background and culture while gaining at least a limited knowledge of Spanish and maintaining good social and business relations with the established Mexican families of the town.[25]

The record of relations between the Mavericks and their aristocratic Mexican neighbors is one of mutual respect, but the cultural gulf was great. For example, Anglo-American and Mexican men generally had vastly different attitudes toward time and work. When William Fairfax Gray shared lodging with Béxar residents Navarro, Lorenzo de Zavala, and José Francisco Ruiz at the independence convention, he found them enjoyable and courteous companions, but "indolent" and surprised by his own "industry in writing and studying."[26] In a similar vein, Sam Maverick wrote to his wife on December 29, 1838, from Houston that he had delayed en route to have the company of Mexican friends, but having before him "a full view of the dilatory, procrastinating, unresolved character of the Mexicans," he finally pushed onward alone.

The men were at least bound by common business and political in-terests, but the women moved in separate domestic spheres. In her published memoirs, Mary wrote that as the small Anglo-American fe-male society formed, "we exchanged calls with the Navarros, Sotos, Garzas, Garcias, Zambranos, Seguins, Veramendis and Yturris." In her unpublished draft, this is followed by the comment, "but never felt like being at all intimate & could never think of letting our children go anywhere to stay awhile—because they let theirs go almost naked &cc with few exceptions."[27]

The Mavericks' first neighbors from the United States had arrived in the summer of 1839. William Jacques brought his wife and two small daughters to a home on Commerce Street, and William and Eleanor Elliott settled with their son and daughter in a house near the Mavericks.

Meanwhile, Mary's brothers came and went, trying their fortunes in various ways. William's business quickly failed, a result, Mary wrote, of the extension of credit to Mexicans in Coahuila by his clerk Lance-lott Smithers, from whom Maverick had bought land in 1836. William returned to Alabama and took Robert, for, Mary informed her mother, "Robert says he wants to be at school and I know he ought to be for he is learning nothing here & growing fast to the age of a man."[28] William refused to give up on his own Texas dream and in October, 1839, brought brother Andrew with him to begin farming.

Farming was a particularly dangerous occupation in the San An-tonio area, for Comanches could swoop down on a solitary farmer or his crops at any time. The Mavericks had put slaves Griffin and Wiley to work cultivating a labor above the Alamo, but they had had to give it up after the Indians chased the two workers into the river and stole their animals. William and Andrew found their plow animals "con-stantly stolen" when they put in a crop on leased land at the mission of San Francisco de la Espada.

Even more dangerous than farming was the surveying work neces-sary to convert land into someone's duly measured property. Yet Sam Maverick "took the greatest delight in the surveying camp," as his wife later wrote, and spent much of his time living out of the saddle locating lands. He would through the rest of his life continue to buy certificates—headright certificates, bounty and donation certificates, railroad reserve certificates—with which to locate lands, often band-ing together with other locators on extended surveys.

Maverick had called himself a wanderer, and in this work he could remain a wanderer, pushing farther and farther westward through the brush-dotted hills, the watered valleys, and sprawling arid plains of Central and West Texas. The grand vistas corresponded with his grand vision of settlement, and he exulted in the challenge of living apart from civilization. He would give his support to organized religion, but it was the trips into the wilderness, with their ascetic demands, that repeatedly meant for him both physical and spiritual renewal.

He was fortunate that they did not mean death. The Comanches called the compass "the Thing that Steals the Land," and a surveying party usually included guards to watch for Indians while the surveyors worked, as they had to leave their rifles too far away to do them any good in a surprise raid. Often in his haste to get out of Comanche country, a surveyor would locate only two or three corners and figure the other side or sides.[29]

Just how dangerous the work was became all too clear early in Maverick's locating career, when in the fall of 1839 he departed a surveying camp on Leon Creek early because of a promise to his wife. Either the afternoon he left or that evening, Comanches raided the camp, killing all but one chain bearer. Searchers found thirty-year-old surveyor Moses Lapham some distance from the camp, scalped and with an arrow in his body.[30]

The strain of waiting and wondering in the face of such dangers would eventually surface in Mary Maverick's diary. Like most pioneer women, she often had to face alone the difficulties of life in a frontier environment, not knowing where her wide-ranging husband was or if he was safe. In addition to his frontier activities, Maverick periodically returned to the States on business, leaving his small brood for months at a time.

His first such trip was taken during the winter of 1838–39, when in his absence, he was elected mayor of San Antonio. He traveled to New Orleans to collect money being sent him by his father. Discovering that it had not arrived and that the Maverick business agent in New Orleans, John Aiken, had gone to Tuscaloosa to attend the legislature, he determined to go to Tuscaloosa himself and collect some business debts. "When I think of leaving you at all in San Anton[io] I am horrified," he wrote to Mary. "But Will[iam]s men are there: and the French upon Mexico. God be with you my dearly beloved wife, and make me

88

return to thee again, a better man who is ever thine own in life and in death, now and forever."³¹ Maverick's emotional words called forth an equally strong response in his wife, who endorsed the letter by writing, "Tis my own Gus – O may God bless him prosper him & return him soon, soon, soon beseech thee."³²

The most anxious times occurred when Maverick and other settlers rode out of San Antonio on the heels of raiding Comanches. Led by Jack Hays, an unprepossessing but intrepid Tennessee native barely out of his teens, the "Minute Men" kept horses and provisions ready and were prepared to respond to the call of the San Fernando Cathedral bell within fifteen minutes. Maverick's "War Horse" was kept padlocked to a mesquite picket, with saddle, bridle, arms, and such supplies as coffee and salt handy nearby.

The bell rang out its warning repeatedly during the Mavericks' early years in San Antonio, for Comanches often hid in the trees, grass, and gullies surrounding the town, waiting for a chance to attack. Sometimes they would fall upon a solitary cart driver, sometimes upon a well-armed party that had ventured too far from the settlement. With no efficient system of frontier protection provided by the struggling government of the Republic, the Minute Men could only drop their affairs and respond to the latest discovery of a scalped and mutilated body, pursuing the Indians in hopes of recovering stolen horses and captives, of confronting the marauders in battle, and of destroying their villages.

A typical series of events occurred in June of 1839, when Maverick accompanied Hays and the other Minute Men, plus a Mexican company under Alamo veteran and city military commander Juan Seguín, on a retaliatory pursuit. They followed the Comanches to the Cañón de Uvalde and destroyed the Indians' newly deserted villages, then continued, spurred onward by sightings of Indians throughout the hills and rocks.

After ten days Seguín returned, announcing, Mary later wrote, that those who continued the pursuit were sure to find death at Indian hands. Mary waited through five more "terribly anxious days," having found a note to "Beloved Wife" apprising her of a few small debts to be settled, should the writer not return. But he did, along with Hays and the rest, "dreadfully ragged, dirty, and hungry," having killed a few Indians and captured a few ponies.³³ This incident followed the standard pattern of Indian-settler warfare through all of frontier Texas for years to come, in that the settlers invested a large amount of time and energy in a dangerous pursuit that netted little result.

The most dangerous and unsettling Indian encounter for Bexar residents, however, occurred in the heart of the city in the Council House Fight of March 19, 1840. In her memoirs, Mary was to devote much space to her eyewitness account of this debacle, and subsequent accounts have relied heavily on her narrative, which re-creates the confusion and recklessness of that "day of horrors" in which thirty-five Comanches and seven Texans were killed.[34]

On the nineteenth, sixty-five Comanches entered the town ostensibly ready to bargain for the ransom of white captives. The visit was part of a pattern established in colonial America long before the line of settlement reached Comanche country—white authorities, sure of their own cultural and ethical superiority, confronting Indians who possessed their own "daunting self-confidence" and an ability to manipulate the encounter to their advantage, if only temporarily, by piling on demands.[35] For the white men, the meeting represented part of a continuing frustrating process whereby they attempted to redeem settlers' friends and relatives en masse, only to get an occasional solitary captive, evasion, and lists of demands. Texas Ranger commander Henry Karnes had met with three of the chiefs in Bexar in January and had recommended to Texas secretary of war Albert Sidney Johnston that if the next bargaining party did not bring promised white prisoners, the bargainers should be held as hostages until the captives were returned. In preparation for such action, Johnston had dispatched three companies of regulars to Mission San José south of the Alamo.

Now the Comanches arrived bringing only two captives, fifteen-year-old Matilda Lockhart and a Mexican boy. The teen-aged girl had spent two years with her kidnappers, and her body was a map of bruises and sores, with her nose, as Mary remembered, "actually burned off to the bone—and the fleshy end gone, and a great scab formed on the end of the bone."[36] Recent scholarship shows that American Indian brutality toward captives was often inflated in the minds of ethnocentric whites, but the Comanches indeed practiced exceptional cruelty toward many of their captives. A lucky few would be adopted into the tribe, but only after proving their bravery through harsh trials.[37]

Grimly, Gen. Hugh McLeod and William J. Cooke, quartermaster general of the Texas Army, met with Chief Muguara and his warriors in the courthouse, or "council house," on the Main Plaza and listened to Muguara's new demands. Then they stated that he and part of his band would be detained until their tribesmen brought in the remaining captives, at which point the ransom would be paid.

Mary and a neighbor, Mrs. Thomas Higginbotham, were peering through a picket fence outside the courthouse, watching Indian boys shooting arrows at coins, when a great war whoop erupted from the building. Upon hearing the edict, the warriors had begun firing arrows, and the soldiers present responded with a gun volley that killed several Indians and two whites. The mêlée then spilled out onto the square and through the city, as civilians and soldiers chased down fleeing Indians.

Mary ran for her home and there found her husband and brother Andrew "sitting calmly at a table inspecting some plats of survey." Raising the alarm, she hurried through the house looking for the children while Maverick and Andrew grabbed their guns. Maverick ran into the street while his brother-in-law raced into the backyard with Mary.[38]

Here they found that three Indians had entered the gate, heading for the river, and encountered Jinny the cook surrounded by her own children and the two Maverick boys. The undaunted slave woman stood clutching a huge rock and informed the nearest Indian that she was willing to smash his head with it. As the three Comanches resumed their flight toward the river, Andrew shot two of them and hurried up Soledad Street while Mary hurried the children indoors.

She continued to watch the drama unfolding. To a white man leveling his pistol at an Indian lying on Soledad Street, she called, "Oh, don't, he is dying," and the man responded, "To please you, I won't, but it would put him out of his misery."[39] A street struggle between an Indian and the finely dressed Col. Lysander Wells, veteran of the Battle of San Jacinto, proved so engrossing that Mary, possessed of a youthful sense of invincibility, wandered into the street "almost breathless" and had to be ordered back by another lieutenant.[40] Later, she recalled that she went in without feeling any fear, concluding, "I was just twenty-two then, and was endowed with a fair share of curiosity."[41]

The skirmishing and bloodletting continued until all but two of the visiting Indians were dead or captured. The two took refuge in the Higginbothams' kitchen and remained understandably recalcitrant in the face of appeals to give themselves up. Finally, a number of young men congregated and dropped a flaming candlewick ball into their refuge, then killed them as they emerged.

Writing of the incident in more peaceful times, when a younger generation could wax elegiac about the Indian, Mary Maverick felt the need to justify subtly all actions of her countrymen in the conflict. "All [Indians] had a chance to surrender," she wrote, "and every one who offered or agreed to give up was taken prisoner and protected."[42] Indeed, the participants saw no dishonor in chasing through the streets and slaying the Comanches who had made their lives so precarious. They had only to look at Matilda Lockhart's scarred body, a sight that caused Mary herself to comment, "Ah, it was sickening to behold, and made one's blood boil for vengeance."[43]

In the aftermath of the conflict, the citizens of San Antonio began counting their own dead and injured. Among the fatally wounded was G. W. Cayce, a young man who had only that morning arrived on the Maverick doorstep with a letter of introduction from his father. Infantry captain Mathew "Old Paint" Caldwell, who had signed the Declaration of Independence with Maverick, had also been visiting the family and returned from the fray with a bullet through the leg. The Mavericks' neighbor Thomas Higginbotham, "as peaceful as a Quaker to all appearances," had participated and received a slight wound. A lieutenant had fared worse, with a bullet through the lungs. He was tended in a home across the street, where his cries and groans echoed through the night.

All of these medical emergencies were treated by a Russian surgeon named Weidman whose colorful and grisly exploits led Mary Maverick to devote a whole chapter of her memoirs to him. Weidman, who had successfully prescribed for baby Sammy's teething discomfort, was not only a doctor but a naturalist sent by the Russian czar to make scientific observations in relation to the land and its inhabitants. This he did with an enthusiasm that could only border on the macabre to the less scientifically inclined. After the hostilities Mary saw the exultant doctor deposit first one, then a second severed Indian head on the Higginbothams' windowsill. He announced that he had chosen the heads and two complete bodies as specimens for study. Two days later, horrified San Antonio residents realized that Weidman had not only boiled the heads and bodies to obtain skeletons but had emptied the liquid into their drinking water supply.

There were other worries besides the quality of the drinking water, of course. The day after the massacre, a Comanche woman was released to return to her camp and report what had happened. She was instructed to offer an exchange of prisoners—the Indians in San Antonio for the fifteen Americans and "several Mexicans" known to be Comanche captives. Military officials set a twelve-day truce to give sufficient time for the exchange to be carried out. Then, with the captive Indians biding time in the jail adjoining the courthouse, everyone waited and hoped for peace. Indian troubles were not yet over, but Sam Maverick was again heading east on business.

Only two days after the Council House Fight, he departed San Antonio on a fund-raising trip to New Orleans that would extend until late June and lead him all the way back to South Carolina.[44] Aware that he was leaving his wife and their two small children in a frontier community just recovering from the bloody Council House Fight and under threat of Indian reprisals, Maverick was lulled by the presence of his brothers-in-law and of the family's adult male slaves, as well as by the strengthening of the military garrison near San Antonio. The events of March 19 had actually benefited the city's residents by ensuring continuing troop protection.[45]

On March 23, 1840, Maverick wrote Mary from Gonzales that a company there was being formed "to render you any assistance San Antonio may need on the return of the Squaw Courier." In regard to his family's safety, he wrote simply, "Take care of my wife & boys: and I will do the same by your husband; so my love I am in a hurry to get back, so fare thee well." A week later, he wrote from Houston, "Beloved kiss our boys for me, and take especial care (without dull care) of thy precious self—until we meet again, which (with all my speed) will be an age."[46]

Mary managed to fare well enough, but reminders of Indian dangers continued to appear. On March 26, a browned and buckskin-clad woman plodded into the city carrying her three-year-old child. Mrs. John Webster, an escaped Comanche captive, had spent nineteen months among the Indians after seeing her husband and youngest child killed near Austin. Mary joined Catherine Jacques, Eleanor Elliott, Maria Smith, and Mrs. Higginbotham in tending the former prisoner. Years later, Mary recalled how the woman's clothes smelled so bad that Catherine Jacques affected a ladylike swoon. Mary was sent for a bottle of cologne but picked up pepper vinegar, "which caused her to revive instantly."[47]

Mrs. Jacques' apparent "possuming" caused the women to have a "great laugh," but again they heard tales of extreme suffering with the knowledge that a similar fate could await them and their children outside the relatively secure confines of San Antonio. Mrs. Webster stayed in the Maverick home two weeks. Her eleven- or twelve-year old son Booker still remained among the Comanches.

Two days after Mrs. Webster's arrival, a large body of Indians arrived on the edge of town led by Isimanica, a fiery young chief who rode into the main square, hurling insults at the inhabitants. He was directed to the garrison at San José, where the acting commander maintained the truce by barely holding off a confrontation.

The truce period had already passed on April 3, when another band of Comanches appeared, this time to bargain for a captive exchange. But all the Indians could provide for trade were a Mexican boy, a five-year-old Anglo-American girl, and Mrs. Webster's son Booker, who reported upon his release that the other captives had all been tortured and killed when the "Squaw Courier" reached camp. The remaining captive Indians in San Antonio were "strictly guarded for a time" but eventually "stole away to their ancient freedom," as Mary poetically phrased it in her memoirs.

Meanwhile, Sam Maverick was finding his journey dismayingly long. Once again, he had ranged farther than intended when hoped-for funds did not materialize. His letters and business records hint that he collected monies from a number of sources on these trips east—from his father's enterprises, from the sporadic merchandising efforts in New Orleans, from rents on a few Alabama properties he held, and from the sale of his own South Carolina and Alabama landholdings, never extensive and now dwindling as he focused his energies and purchasing power on Texas acreage.

Now he found the Panic of 1837 still affecting financial transactions, as the economic depression it created spread from east to west. He wrote a breathless, guilt-tinged letter to Mary on May 15, from New Orleans, explaining that not a single dollar had been waiting for him there. Consequently, "I was forced to go on to South Carolina with the deeds we executed." On a whirlwind visit to Charleston, he had read in a newspaper that the Mexican Central Army was near San Antonio, a piece of intelligence that "threw me into the horrors." He soon found it contradicted, "but the possibility that my sweet Mary might be alarmed made me redouble my exertions to get here."

Maverick had bypassed Tuscaloosa, unable to face his mother-in-law's plaintive queries, but with "the times being worse than you could conceive," he had returned to New Orleans only to be delayed again, and could not promise his wife a return date before the middle of June. Meanwhile, he had heard nothing of Comanche matters except "that 2 captives are brot. in & the exchange going on."

Throughout his trips eastward to finance his land empire, as well as his trips westward to locate land, Maverick remained uneasily aware of the tension between his family role and his personal ambition. On a journey eastward in 1844, he would write, "A plague on this business, — how much better if I were nursing my little daughters & teaching my sons to read & write. But I am started & never could see backwards in my life. Go ahead! Slave on! I fear me it is an evil genius of paltry gain that carries me off so. If so, dearest, maybe you can see it and you must tell me so. Are we not one & thou the medicine chief of my whole tribe?"[48]

However, the self-effacing Mary was not one to criticize her husband, choosing instead to blame herself for weakness when his frequent absences became too much. Only once among their extant correspondence would she sound a questioning note, writing in 1845, "Ah! my dear husband, I feel that we too often risk your life."[49] Her letters and diaries show a consistently loving, even adoring, attitude toward the man whom she called in 1839 "the gentlest of instructors, the most sympathizing of friends." Her veneration of her husband perhaps in part reflects their fifteen-year age difference and her early loss of a father. She endured "black and desolate solitude" in Maverick's absence, but always she awaited the next joyful reunion.

Such a reunion took place as promised in June, while Indian troubles continued to intensify. The Comanches were "constantly stealing and murdering" and making travel especially unsafe.[50] For once San Antonio did not bear the brunt of Indian attack, as the Comanches banded together with marauding Kiowas and moved southward through the American settlements. Reaching the coast, a large band under Penateka Comanche Buffalo Hump terrorized and pillaged Linnville, a settlement on Lavaca Bay and a seaport for San Antonio.

Sam Maverick had shipped supplies to Linnville on his trip to the United States, and he had planned to go down and accompany them to San Antonio. But two years' supply of provisions was destroyed in the raid, including clothing materials, a set of silver spoons for Mary, and whiskey and brandy bought, as was the custom, for surveying expeditions. In addition, a set of law books carefully shipped by the elder Samuel from Pendleton was lost. The Mavericks heard that "they were strung to the Indians' saddles by strings run through the volumes, and used for making cigarettes." The wife of the Linnville customs collector, who was briefly captured, reported that she had been strapped to the back of a mule and forced to read from a law book as the Indians laughed and hooted.[51]

On their return trip from the coast, the Comanches and Kiowas were defeated by militiamen assembled near Lockhart in August, 1840, at what became known as the Battle of Plum Creek. This subdued Comanche raiders, but did not remove the Indian threat from the far western frontier of which San Antonio was a part.

Meanwhile, both Samuel Maverick in Pendleton and Agatha Adams in Alabama were disturbed by news of Texas Indian troubles and begging for more correspondence. On November 23, 1840, Mary's brother Robert wrote from Tuscaloosa that their mother had grown "easily alarmed" and urged pointedly that Mary write twice a month "for the gratification of your aged mother." Just a few days later, Samuel wrote from Pendleton, "I wish you would write me oftener than you do, and let me know and see matters as they are with you." Ever ready to provide a maxim, he closed with one: "Suspense is a canker to the soul, but knowledge is the bright path through life, and that reaches to God." Earlier, he had written, "You will better excuse the anxiety I feel, when our Teeny Sam shall have settled on the Pacific Ocean."[52]

Actually, members of both the Adams and Maverick families were feeling the lure of Texas, despite reports of Indian depredations. That fall of 1840, both Lydia and William Van Wyck and Mary Elizabeth and Joseph Thompson visited Pendleton and contemplated moving to the Republic. The elder Samuel had already given his son money to begin buying Texas lands in trust for the grandchildren. In a November 1 letter to his father, Maverick encouraged a scouting visit by his brothers-in-law but qualified his enthusiasm: "I fear that I have heretofore given my opinions too freely & foolishly in favour of this country—but I am content to feel that whatever I said of the health & richness of the country was said in candor & I say it again. Only God knows I could not foresee our eternal warfare & insecurity."

Mary's brothers William and Andrew had chosen to stay in Texas and had moved their farming operations north to the San Marcos area, while Robert was talking about returning. Other relatives were also looking westward. Mary's Uncle John and Aunt Ann Bradley in Alabama had talked of coming to Texas for two years, and in December, 1840, they arrived in San Antonio with their brood of young children, greatly augmenting the small Anglo-American society and leading Mary to write, "I promise myself much pleasure in having them for neighbours."[53]

For Mary, this increased family companionship and the birth of her first daughter, Agatha, in April of 1841, ushered in a golden period. Years later, she recalled the summer of 1841 as one in which she and the other transplanted American women "led a lazy life of ease," adopting the Mexican practice of afternoon siestas and daily river bathing. Mary and Eleanor Elliott and their children had one reminder of the uncertainty of their frontier lives in a near-brush with Indians on a berry-picking expedition. But the year moved placidly along, the women reading novels, picnicking, and gossiping about news from home and San Antonio events. "We joked and laughed away the time," she later wrote wistfully, "for we were free from care and happy. In those days there were no envyings, no backbiting."[54]

While Mary enjoyed the laste carefree period of her life, Sam Maverick continued his land quest. Records of 1840 showed him owning 4,605 acres under complete title from the General Land Office and 12,942 acres under survey. He was by no means the largest landowner in San Antonio, however, for John W. Smith possessed 9,406 acres clear and 31,284 under survey, and father and son Erasmo and Juan Seguín owned 20,000 acres under complete title.[55] The men with land, Anglo-American and Mexican, continued to run city affairs, and Maverick returned to public office in 1841 as treasurer of the City Council.

President Lamar visited the city in June of that year, raising support for the Santa Fe Expedition, which sought to claim for Texas jurisdiction over the Santa Fe area and a part of the lucrative Santa Fe trade. By an act of December, 1836, Texians had claimed eastern New Mexico as part of their newly independent territory, despite the fact that New Mexico was still claimed and controlled by Mexico. Now Lamar raised a civilian and military force to march westward with trading goods and invitations to the people of New Mexico to unite with the young Republic.

The undertaking proved a disaster, with expedition members suffering through a difficult journey across the plains and finding New Mexican officials hostile to their cause. When the weary travelers were captured by Mexican forces and imprisoned in Mexico City, suspicion fell on one of the most prominent men of the San Antonio community, Juan Seguín. It was rumored that Seguín, jealous of Anglo-Americans assuming power, had alerted Mexican officials to the expedition. Most modern historians consider the suspicions unjust, and Mary Maverick retained a careful neutrality toward Seguín years later, stating that many "suspended judgment," in part because of the high esteem in which his father, Erasmo, was held.[56]

As 1841 drew to a close, Maverick continued to pour most of his energies into locating and acquiring promising land. An October 27 letter from Maverick to ranger captain John Hays requested that Hays make a number of surveys for him to the northwest, along the branches of the San Saba River and at Enchanted Rock, a massive dome of solid granite in present Gillespie County.[57]

Meanwhile, the Mavericks awaited a visit from Mary's mother. Agatha Adams had not seen her daughter for four years, nor had she seen Lewis and her namesake Agatha. At one point, she made plans to come to the Texas Coast and meet the family there, but, Mary wrote, "I had too many babies to make such a journey, and the risk from Indians was too great, and we did not encourage the plan."[58] In August of the year, Agatha wrote how anxious she was to visit, but "I am dependent on George, you may judge of the probability of my coming."[59] A spendthrift who kept bad company, George moved in and out of his family's lives, causing them all grave concern. William had tried to get him to come to Texas but to no avail.

Finally, Agatha corralled George and made plans to leave for Texas on October 1, not only to see her loved ones but to consider settling. The news of her coming did not reach the Mavericks until late October, and soon thereafter came word that Agatha had taken ill in late September and died of congestive chills the day after the planned start of her long-awaited trip.

The death was especially bitter for Mary, both because it was the first great sorrow that she had to face as an adult and because she felt guilt over the unaccomplished reunion. She blamed herself for not agreeing to a coastal meeting and wrote, "Her heart had been so set upon seeing me that I felt almost as if she did not even go gladly to Heaven," denied a reunion.[60] In the margin of her memoir draft, she wrote, "*Poor* mother! *Dear* mother!" Mary had been twenty when she last saw Agatha, and now she felt the pain of a daughter aware that she would never have the opportunity to develop a mutually loving adult relationship with her mother. Yet Agatha had never questioned Mary's place with her husband, writing frankly in 1838, "I will not attempt Mary to tell you how much I feel your absence so far away tho I know it was your duty and that you have too much good sense to repine or not be cheerful and conduce all you can to your husband's interest or happiness."[61]

Agatha's death was for her daughter "a sudden awakening from a fancied security against all possible evil."[62] As 1841 gave way to 1842 and Texan-Mexican enmity flared once again, Mary Maverick moved toward trials that would shatter what was left of that fancied security.

7

"The Time to Prove the Heart"

*I will live & luxuriate in the hope of returning to the dear home
where thou art. You have much to do dearest, to take care
of our jewels [children] & thy precious self. Now is the time
to prove the heart.*

—Mexican prisoner Sam Maverick to his wife, October 16, 1842

REPEATEDLY during the winter of 1841–42 the Anglo-American residents
of Bexar were warned by friendly Mexicans that Mexican troops would
soon be coming. Finally, in February, 1842, word came that a force was
moving toward the town. Reinstated autocrat Antonio López de Santa
Anna was sending his troops into Texas in part to keep his country's
claim on the Republic from languishing and in part as a reaction to
the Texans' Santa Fe Expedition.

Reluctantly, the Americans in San Antonio made hurried preparations to leave, hiding many nonportable items. The climate of fear is
reflected in a Mexican neighbor's willingness to take into safekeeping
only under cover of darkness Mary's bureau filled with valued keep-
sakes such as her wedding dress. On March 1, a large caravan of families including the "tribe of Maverick" and brothers William and Andrew Adams started eastward in what became known as "the Runaway of '42." With the carriage and Kentucky wagon that had brought
them to San Antonio in need of repairs, the Maverick entourage made
do with horses for Sam, Mary, Griffin, and Wiley, and Granville drove
a wood cart carrying Jinny, Rachel, and the children.

Mary later remembered the journey eastward as particularly pleasant. "The weather was charming, the grass green and the whole earth
in bloom," she wrote, "and I cannot forget the gay gallops we had going
ahead and resting 'til the others came up."[1] After almost four years
in San Antonio, this was her first opportunity to leave her domestic

confines for any length of time, and she enjoyed being able to ride freely over the landscape and to listen to the campfire jokes and stories provided on their second night of camping out by members of scout Ben McCulloch's armed band heading for San Antonio to "meet the enemy."

On March 3, the San Antonio families reached Seguin and accepted the invitation of farmer-rancher Michael Erskine to stay on his ranch by the Guadalupe River about twelve miles southeast of the town. The next day, many of the men of the party, including Maverick and the Adams brothers, headed back toward San Antonio while the rest pushed onward to Erskine's ranch. Here Mary, Eleanor Elliott, and Catherine Jacques set up housekeeping in a blacksmith shop on the Erskine property while the slaves pitched tents nearby. On March 4, in the midst of the settling-in activity, Mary paused to write her husband, "Beloved above all earthly things I beg you to consider your own safety and for the sake of your wife and children be cautious."

Early on the morning of March 6, the sixth anniversary of the fall of the Alamo, the women in the blacksmith shop were awakened by a knock on the door and Capt. Samuel Highsmith's solemn pronouncement, "Ladies, San Antonio has fallen." Mary Maverick later recalled that "we were seized with a vague sense of terror," Eleanor Elliott falling to her knees, Catherine Jacques "weeping hysterically," and Mary herself taking "a shaking ague" while the children "waked and cried" and the slaves came in "with sad and anxious looks."[2]

Word soon came that no battle had been fought, that the Americans had decided to fall back to Seguin until the strength of the Mexican army's numbers could be ascertained. But all day rumors flew, including speculation that a Mexican force was marching toward the Erskine farm, planning to cross the Guadalupe there. After dinner, Mary later recorded, "we all went out to the public road and sat down on a log, all in a row" to see the enemy army approach. Instead, they saw brother Andrew, sent ahead by their husbands to reassure the refugees.

Soon Maverick and the other men joined the party and, following Capt. Jack Hays' directions, took their families to Gonzales. That community's residents had fled eastward, too, and Mary was soon established in a vacant house with another San Antonio wife, Mrs. Wilson Riddle, who had been delayed in Bexar by the birth of her baby.

Maverick and the other men headed once more for Bexar, following

Hays and a band of three hundred sent to retake the city. The Mexicans fell back across the Rio Grande without a fight, leaving great destruction in the American residences. Maverick found the walnut mantelpiece in his home ripped from the wall, and a neighbor's piano had been axed.

Meanwhile, Gonzales was still in a state of nervous tension. A false Indian scare brought a flood of people into Mary's temporary home, eating all the carefully stored provisions and keeping the residents awake all night. Gonzales was too close to the insecure western frontier, and Sam Maverick needed to return to the States on business again. He determined to take his family northeastward, to the vicinity of La-Grange, the seat of Fayette County on the Colorado River.

They began traveling once more on April 17—the Mavericks, their three small children and slaves, and brother Andrew. They crossed a "bald prairie" known for its Indian trails and planned to bed down for the night in a deserted log house on the west side of the Navidad River, a home often used by wayfarers since the Indian massacre of its occupants. But Mary took one look into the doorless cabin and asserted that something would happen to the party if they stopped there. Maverick and Adams laughed at her premonition, but she remained adamant, and the group pushed onward along the west bank of the Navidad through a violent rainstorm. They reached a settler's house after midnight and had to ford a flooding ravine to do so. But Mary's premonition proved true when a later traveler informed them that the cabin Mary had rejected had collapsed during the storm, the roof and logs a mass of debris.

With the Navidad impassable for three days, the Mavericks moved into their host's corncrib, then bade goodbye to Andrew, who was turning back, and traveled onward to the Colorado. On April 21, they reached the homes of Texas senator Jon Winfield Scott Dancy and of the Enoch Jones family on the west bank of the Colorado. Both were away—the Jones family fled eastward and Dancy reconnoitering against the Mexican army.[3] However, a brother, Griffith Jones, and the Colorado ferryman living there welcomed them, and the family spent a week at the spot before arranging for board at Francis E. Brookfield's on nearby Buckner's Creek.

On April 30, Maverick left for Alabama on business and to get Mary's eighteen-year-old sister Elizabeth, who had been boarding with Dr. R. N. Weir in Tuscaloosa. "She is in a good family and also one of the most respectable families in Tuscaloosa," brother Robert had written Mary after their mother's death. "But I should like for her to be in Texas with her relations."⁴

Again, Mary waited, but this time in anticipation of having her sister for company during Maverick's long absences. Lizzie had been only thirteen when Mary left home, and Mary's attitude toward her had been both maternalistic and moralistic. "I expect our Lizzy is growing fast & I hope improving rapidly," Mary had written to her mother in 1838. "I wrote to her by the last mail, I want her to keep alive the correspondence so that I may judge how she Cultivates her mind: it is my fondest wish to find her a sensible and intelligent woman."⁵ However, Lizzie had proven an infrequent correspondent.

She arrived with Maverick on June 11, and the family moved to widower Jon Dancy's on the twenty-first. Taking note of their arrival in his diary, Dancy commented that Elizabeth was "a pleasant young lady."⁶ The bland adjective little reflects the personality of Lizzie Adams, who had a tart tongue, an independent outlook, and frankly negative views on love, marriage, and children. Mary was the moralist and traditionalist, Lizzie the sharp-tongued cynic. Despite their different approaches to life, Lizzie's subsequent letters to Mary, written after they had established separate homes in Texas, show that the sisters sought each other's company and maintained a supportive relationship over the years.

In that summer of 1842, however, it was hard to look beyond a month-to-month existence. Relations between Mexico and Texas were as precarious as ever. The Texas Congress in late June had voted for war with Mexico, to be financed by the sale of up to ten million acres of land. Sam Houston, who had succeeded Lamar to again serve as president, vetoed the resolution, and matters were once more at a confused impasse. Maverick wanted to be in San Antonio—indeed, needed to be to oversee his land purchases and serve out another term on the City Council, but he could not in good conscience move his family back to the city, where he had already had three close calls with a Mexican military presence.⁷

His son's continual tempting of the fates caused the elder Samuel to write in exasperation on July 15, "You will please to recollect that should you lose your life in this scuffle in Texas that it will be fatal, not only to your family but to our whole family. I am (near) 70 years old & there is no male among us, except the children, to take charge of our affairs. My Estate is crumbling to pieces by the loss of thousand & tens of thousands of dollars, for want of out doors attention which I am unable to give it." Indeed, he reported, "our whole affairs are in a critical situation," yet "we have enough now left except we both should leave soon, in that event the probability is that all our Exertions will be principally lost."

However, Sam Maverick had invested too much energy and money and hope in the future of Texas to turn back now. On August 21, he purchased from Dancy twenty-six acres along the Colorado River as a possible temporary homesite. The next day, he departed once more for San Antonio to attend the fall term of district court. Along with sister Lizzie and Jon Dancy, Mary accompanied her husband and Gonzales lawyer and Texas congressman William E. Jones for the first few miles. She was so depressed by the parting that Maverick exclaimed, "Almost you persuade me not to go." "Alas!" Mary wrote later, "too surely and swiftly came a terrible sorrow."[8]

On September 5, 1842, the Fourth District Court of Texas, also known as the Western District Court, commenced its fall term in San Antonio. "No invasion expected," wrote presiding judge Anderson Hutchinson in his journal.[9] However, a few days later a Mexican citizen warned John W. Smith of the approach of a Mexican force numbering fifteen hundred.

The Anglo-Americans in Bexar remained dubious, surmising that the threat, if one existed, probably came from a smaller force of Mexican marauders, as both Mexican and Anglo-American brigands had been harassing the trade routes between the city and the Rio Grande. John Hays and five other scouts did go out to check the report, but before they could return, Gen. Adrian Woll marched to the outskirts of the city with an army estimated at one thousand to eighteen hundred Mexican soldiers.

Maverick was defending Shields Booker against the city of San Antonio in a dispute over an allegedly unpaid fifty-peso fee.[10] Apprised simply of the presence of an unknown force, the Anglo-Americans at court sent three "old and respectable Mexicans" to meet it with a white flag, but Woll detained the delegation overnight, surrounded the city, and staged a predawn occupation in a dense fog. The Anglo-Americans, numbering less than sixty, attempted a defense at the Maverick home on the northeast corner of the Main Plaza in a confused skirmish that proved fatal to a few soldiers and left San Antonio merchant John Twohig injured.

Sam Maverick and his compatriots steadily maintained to Woll that the Americans thought they were defending themselves against a large band of frontier desperadoes rather than a regular army, citing the presence of such bands in the area, Woll's detention of the Mexican emissaries, and his arrival at the city by a "new and untravelled route." To Mary, Maverick wrote on September 11, "I avoid explaining the disagreeable affair of this morning—only, that at dawn and in a fog we mistook an invading army for 2 or 3 hundred robbers. We found it *necessary* at last, to surrender as prisoners of war (53 of us)."[11]

As one of four negotiators with Woll, Maverick had argued against the surrender.[12] The French commander in Mexican service, seeing that he had netted only a small party of civilians, promised kind treatment and a recommendation for the men's release at San Fernando. "I wanted to stand out in spite of those deceptive terms, refusing to surrender at all," Maverick later wrote from the Mexican prison of Perote. Instead he wanted to demand that the Americans be allowed to retire together and armed. However, "the majority prevailing, we were, in the end, through the specious promises of that general, coaxed into the horrid condition in which we now find ourselves."[13]

The men captured by Woll were some of the most reputable citizens of the Republic. Judge Hutchinson was a respected jurist and author of a digest of Mississippi state laws. Robert Simpson Neighbors, attending court as a member of John Hays' volunteers, was former quartermaster of the Texas Army and was to serve as a state legislator and dedicated Indian agent. Maverick, Jones, D. C. Ogden, Ludovic Colquhoun—all had served or would serve in the Republic and state legislatures.

In September of 1842, however, they were captives facing an indefinite detention, and Maverick's letter to his wife on the day of surrender reflects the uncertainty the men felt. Afraid that Galveston might be attacked, he advised her to risk being overtaken in the interior by the Mexican army, which he felt would not harm families, rather than to flee to a low and sickly place. "A tear almost comes into my eye—a soldier's tear—when I think of my precious family," he wrote, "but yet I have not shed a tear: when I do it will be to thee, my beloved." Despite his predicament, he showed no regrets over his choice to return to San Antonio, concluding fatalistically that "I will not now mourn over what could not be avoided." He urged her to be cheerful and smile, adding, "I need it; it is the sunshine of my soul."[14]

The Americans were held in the Maverick home until September 15, when they began a long forced march toward Mexico under a guard of about 150 infantry and cavalry. "Mr. Maverick with about twenty others have been permitted to ride horses," William Elliott reported to Mary.[15] The Elliotts as British subjects had felt confident enough to return to the city, and Maverick was able to place a handful of gold doubloons for Mary in Eleanor Elliott's keeping.

As the prisoners journeyed southward, the news of the latest Mexican incursion led volunteers to congregate on Cibolo Creek above Seguin. Under the leadership of Mathew Caldwell, they soon moved to a new camp on the Salado about six miles east of San Antonio. Here a company led by John Hays drew San Antonio's invaders into ambush on September 18. The Battle of the Salado, with Mary's brothers Andrew and William participating, resulted in the loss of about sixty Mexican soldiers and the death of one American.

A more costly skirmish for the Texans flared about a mile and a half from the battle. Capt. Nicholas Mosby Dawson had raised a company of thirteen to sixteen men in LaGrange. Crossing the Colorado at Dancy's place on their way to join Caldwell, they began picking up additions. One was John Bradley, "at the spot looking after the welfare of his niece, Mrs. Samuel Augustus Maverick."[16] Another was the Maverick slave Griffin, who had protected Mary against the Tonkawas four years before and now was trying to perform an even greater service. At the news of her husband's capture and removal, Mary had called Griffin to her and asked him to pose as a runaway bound for Mexico in hopes of freeing or aiding his master. He gladly assented, she later reported, adding that he had responded to the offer of freedom by saying, "I do not want any more than I have, master has always treated me more like a brother than a slave."[17] Thus, Griffin joined the party, "armed to the teeth and riding a good mule." He was carrying ransom funds, "the only man of the command who had any money."[18]

As the Dawson group, now fifty-three strong, neared the Salado battle, they were surprised by a Mexican cavalry detachment that immediately brought up artillery. As the artillery inflicted casualties on the American force, Dawson and some of his men tried to surrender, only to be cut down. Three of the Dawson party escaped, but fifteen were taken captive, among them Mary's uncle. Griffin fought valiantly but was one of the thirty-five slain.

In the aftermath of the Salado battle, the victorious Texas troops pressed their advantage as Woll withdrew from San Antonio and began falling back toward Mexico. On September 22, John W. Smith reported, "Yesterday the Texian Army was within four miles of the ____ rascals" and predicted that in a few days the invaders would be "in the hands of the Texians."[19] But squabbles over leadership in the American camp caused a loss of confidence, and Woll was able to retreat safely while disgruntled American volunteers returned to San Antonio.

Meanwhile, Sam Maverick and his fellows were herded across the Rio Grande, their journey barely begun. Over the next three months, they would be marched deeper and deeper into Mexico, reaching the grim, seventy-year-old prison castle of Perote east of Mexico City in late December after a journey of at least two thousand miles.[20] They would sleep in manure-filled sheep pens and on bloody rocks where cattle had been slaughtered, drink water only after it had been muddied by the horses of their guards, and endure the taunts of soldiers and citizens. Yet pages from Maverick's journal of the ordeal could be interspersed with pages from his 1835 land-surveying journal without the reader's noticing a significant difference in tone. Indeed, after his return, Maverick would write of a certain relish for the journey in which he "saw and experienced a thousand new thrills."[21]

For a man of Maverick's adventurous bent, ascetic temperament, and speculative land interests, the trip did hold an element of wonder and delight. After crossing the Rio Grande, he noted with approval the rich, irrigable plains and prairies near Nava, the well-wooded and watered San Juan River valley, the refreshing water of the Sabinas, "finest water I ever drank."[22] They stopped at haciendas that he termed "splendid," with good water and flourishing sheep- and corn-raising operations. One such fifty-league estate, he wrote wistfully, was mortgaged by a widow for forty-one thousand dollars.

As they continued southward along the western edge of the Sierra Madre Oriental toward the garden spot of Saltillo, Maverick was most taken with the mountain views. "The profile of the Candela mountains is so striking, for beauty, variety and high sublimity I cannot forget it," he wrote, and later, after passing through Monclova, he noted a "remarkable mountain top above clouds." But from Saltillo to San

Luis Potosí, the peaks were bare, people few, and water "scarce and brackish."[23] Here the ranches were poor, and often deserted.

After San Luis Potosí, the scenery gradually improved once more as they neared Mexico City, with wooded mountains and fertile valleys again catching the traveler's interest. They came within sight of the great volcano Popocatépetl and of Mexico City itself without entering it, instead veering eastward across a "splendid plain or valley" to Puebla, where water oozed "in a thousand little springs out of the sides of the many ditches in all the fields" and the road was "a shaded avenue with running water in the ditch on either hand."[24]

Maverick showed an appreciation not only for the physical environment but for the recent history of the troubled nation through which he was journeying. Along the way, he noted the spot where liberal federalist Antonio Zapata had been executed after an 1840 attempt to defeat the centralists and the place where "poor Gen'l Mexia was shot by order of Santa Anna" in 1839 for the same offense. The precariousness of the San Antonio prisoners' own situation was brought home by the fact that Mexía's executioner, a "brute lieutenant with red, bulldog eyes," now goaded them onward. "God! What a perfect villain!!" Maverick wrote.[25] The prisoner could lose himself in the landscape only so long before the uncomfortable reality of his situation intruded.

Maverick's journal hints at what the captives had to endure along the way. On spotting a place to drink, they were often denied water, and the journal matter-of-factly reports nights camping in "cow dung a foot thick" and in damp quarters "which appeared to be used as a privy." Sometimes the people they encountered were "villainous" or at least abusive; at San Fernando de Agua Verde, Maverick recorded, one woman called in Spanish, "How many buck goats are there, damn you?"

However, in the same city another woman, Marina Rodrigues y Taylor, sent three daily meals for Maverick and four other prisoners during their eight days there, and in many places they received small kindnesses. One little boy at a spot where the prisoners camped brought fruit hidden inside his shirt every day.[26] At Puebla, when Maverick tried to pay a peasant boy for helping him buy food for the prisoners, the child pressed the money back into Maverick's hand, and a "brave old Englishman" on their departure from the city "went out a mile or two cursing our guard and walking in our ranks, giving cigars, etc."[27]

Friendly couriers, too, carried missives from the captives; Maverick entrusted letters to whomever he could—to Mrs. Taylor, to Mexican military officials, to other travelers—and made and sent duplicates when possible. From Saltillo he wrote of his plight to Waddy Thompson, the U.S. minister to Mexico in Mexico City, hoping for assistance from the South Carolina native related to him by marriage. Along the route, he also wrote encouraging letters to his wife, two of which survive. The first was penned October 6, after John Bradley and the other survivors of the Dawson Massacre had joined the San Antonio prisoners across the Rio Grande. Maverick rejoiced in the news that William and Andrew Adams, Jon Dancy, and Griffith Jones had escaped unharmed, but mourned the death of "my poor Griffin." "God knows I feel his death as the hardest piece of fortune we have suffered in Texas," Maverick wrote. "Poor faithful, brave boy! I owe thee a monument and a bitter tear of regret for thy fall, I mourn thee as a true and faithful friend and a brother, a worthy dear brother in arms!"

With his fate, and even his destination, still unclear, Maverick could only encourage his wife from afar. "I have confidence in you to do with yourself & our precious ones what shall seem best in this great emergency," he wrote. With what he knew about Mexican troop movements, he was not eager to have her leave Dancy's, but he admitted that she would perhaps be better off in Tuscaloosa. Leaving the decision to her, he asked that she let his agent in New Orleans, Leonard Dobbin, know of any move.

Meanwhile, he urged her to be as merry as possible and to ride with Lizzie for exercise. "Be lively and laugh, dearest, and let me meet you as I found you & more so," he wrote. "But take care of my little blue eyed one my Agatha, and my Sam and my Lew, and God be with you and help the brave, and love to all, and write father, and I kiss thy hands &c." Ten days later he wrote from Monclova, now aware of the long journey ahead but underestimating the distance they were being forced to traverse. "We have now gone 1/3d of the distance, say 400 miles & have now before us 800 miles," he explained. "I doubt not we will go safely through & be liberated in Mexico in a few months or weeks perhaps." Until then, he wrote, he placed his hopes on "returning to the dear home where thou art." Acknowledging that "you have much to do dearest, to take care of our jewels & thy precious self," he counseled, "Now is the time to prove the heart."

Mary later wrote that she tried to follow her husband's advice and remain cheerful, "but I was then only twenty-four years of age, and almost a child in experience and I had the care of three helpless little children and the birth of a fourth to look to in the future."[28] She had received word of her husband's capture while nursing Lewis through a severe bout of typhoid fever, she remained a refugee at Dancy's, and she was indeed expecting a fourth child. The eight months of waiting for her husband's release she recorded in a sporadically kept diary as a time of "loneliness – sickness – anxiety & sorrow too deep for expression," later adding, "all this time I was extremely spiteful my organ of combativeness raged."[29]

The situation improved only slightly when the family was able to move in mid-November to a log cabin slaves Granville and Wiley built with the help of Griffith Jones on the Colorado River property Maverick had purchased near Dancy's. The new home was a cramped structure – a sixteen-by-eighteen-foot room with a kitchen and shed room attached, the latter for Jinny and her children. Brother William Adams soon arrived and helped Granville and Wiley build a second cabin adjacent to the first before he departed for Alabama. Then Aunt Ann Bradley and her brood arrived on the Colorado and settled at Dancy's, providing an opportunity for Mary and her aunt to console each other and for Lizzie to enjoy the company of the older Bradley girls.

While Mary was moving into the first cabin, Maverick's Pendleton relatives finally heard of his capture. It was the second blow of the year for the family, as they had lost Sam's sister Mary Elizabeth in Alabama to illness in June. Her five children – three from the Weyman marriage and two from the Thompson union – remained in Alabama with widower Joseph Thompson, but the financially distressed Lydia and William Van Wyck had returned to the Pendleton area, where Lydia ran a school and William was "attending the grinding" at the elder Samuel's Rock Mill.

On November 6, a letter from Mary arrived with the news that Maverick had been taken, and Samuel quickly wrote Waddy Thompson "to ask your immediate assistance in discovering where he may be, and in procuring his *release*, and in furnishing him with two or three hundred Dollars if his necessities should require it, or some more if he wishes it." He enclosed a letter from friend and neighbor Barnard Bee, former Texas secretary of state and minister to the United States from Texas, affirming that he was personally acquainted with the younger Maverick, and "a more honorable and respectable man does not exist."[30]

On November 18, Thompson received the letter Sam Maverick himself had written from Saltillo, and the next day sent a response to San Luis Potosí, reporting that he had left a message for the minister of foreign relations "asking your release & that of Mr. Wm. E. Jones as a *personal* favor to myself" and promising to ask "at a fitting time" for the release of the other prisoners. "I have no doubt you will all be soon released so bear up," he concluded.[31]

However, by the time Maverick and his fellows reached the walls of Perote on December 22, it was apparent that the Mexican government was not to be hurried. "I have not yet received an answer to my application in your behalf," Thompson wrote on December 20, adding, "I cannot calculate on this government about anything." He was hopeful that with Santa Anna's impending arrival in Mexico City, a release could be arranged. Otherwise, when he returned home in March, he expected Maverick to be released to him as a favor.[32]

Meanwhile, the Seventh Congress of the Republic of Texas was meeting without two of its members. Both Maverick and William E. Jones had been elected representatives after their capture. The voters of Bexar County had elected Maverick despite the fact that he had moved his family to Fayette County. Again, a lack of electoral records and contemporary newspaper accounts makes analysis of Maverick's support difficult, but Bexar residents obviously perceived that, despite his 1842 removal from the City Council, he had retained his allegiance to the county, as evidenced by his return for district court. Now the other Texas House members, despairing of the two absent members' quick release, voted the men's seats vacant.[33]

The Republic's government had not been inactive in attempting to retaliate against the Mexican army as Maverick and his companions marched southward. In early October, President Houston had delegated to Alexander Somervell the job of invading Mexico, if practicable, with the Texas militia and volunteers. Somervell, leading an expedition of about seven hundred men, had captured Laredo on December 8, but he soon saw the folly, with only limited troops and equipment, of attempting to inflict any serious damage on the sprawling nation. On December 19, he called off the campaign.

More than three hundred men refused to disband, and on the day Maverick and his companions reached Perote, the remainder of the Somervell Expedition under William S. Fisher stationed themselves on the Rio Grande opposite the Mexican town of Mier. Known as the

Mier Expedition, they engaged in battle with Mexican troops in the town on Christmas Day and surrendered to the Mexicans' superior numbers on the following afternoon. The luckiest of the expedition survivors would arrive at Perote some nine months later.

Like the San Antonio prisoners, they would be entering a limited, harsh world. The fort and prison of Perote sat forbiddingly among barren foothills on the road between Mexico City and Vera Cruz. Surrounded by a dry moat, the outer stone walls measured thirty feet high and fourteen feet thick at the base. The twenty-six-acre compound housed cavalry, infantry, and artillery troops, and prisoners were housed in bare stone cells in the interior of the main wall.[34]

Maverick, unaware of the Mier disaster, wrote a brief, optimistic letter to his wife on December 30, reporting that he was in good health and hoping to be liberated in a few weeks. But his situation quickly worsened. William Jones later recalled, "The first four days after our arrival we were allowed to go about the castle. On the fifth we were chained in pairs—and on the eighth or tenth day we were put to work, packing sand stone, lime, etc. into the castle" from a nearby mountain.[35] On January 5, 1843, Maverick was placed in solitary confinement for complaints made on behalf of "the majority of my fellow-sufferers for whom I was deputed to act." He had protested that "the slavish labor exacted from us at the point of the bayonet" was contrary to the conditions of their surrender and to the laws of civilized nations, particularly considering the almost nonexistent food rations.[36]

Despite his confinement, Maverick refused to be silenced, writing an indignant letter about two and a half weeks later to Mexican secretary of state and foreign affairs José María Bocanegra. In it, he protested their detention, yet he wrote not asking for liberation but only for humane treatment. "We are chained by the legs, with heavy ox chains, coupled like beasts, two and two together," he reported, "and forced at the point of the bayonet side by side with your shameless convicted felons,—robbers and murderers."[37]

It was not the work he complained of, he explained, "but the kind of work, and the work without adequate food." Minuscule portions of bad bread, unwholesome beans and rice, and Irish potato broth sometimes containing "bones, grissel, and the voluminous entrails of a beef" constituted their daily diet; occasionally they received a "beef ration" made up primarily of bone and gristle. The "crafty and covetous" captain in charge of provisions turned a deaf ear to prisoners' complaints. In fact, three of their number had been placed in solitary confinement, "in chains, almost starved and nearly naked," for daring to ask for money promised them for carpentry labor in order to buy bread.

Maverick called on Bocanegra to remove the captain and to order that the prisoners be treated better and fed, asserting that the treatment they were receiving "would shame the Devil himself." He stressed that he was writing solely on his own responsibility, "because if evil instead of good come of it, the evil shall fall on me alone," and because "I am wholly insensible of any kind of fear in doing what I conceive to be right. I cannot conceive the idea [of] bad consequences in such a case; and if such follow, it is no business of mine."

Maverick forwarded this fiery missive through Waddy Thompson, who apparently chose to withhold it rather than risk an angry reaction as he pressed for the prisoners' release.[38] On January 26, he was able to report that Santa Anna had promised to liberate Maverick and Jones "very *shortly.*"

According to his memoirs, Thompson was able to hold out another avenue of escape, one that Maverick refused to take. The Mexican government wanted recognition of its sovereignty, and if Maverick would say he was in favor of the reannexation of Texas to Mexico, he could have his freedom. Thompson explained to the captive that the Mexicans simply wanted to save face with an agreement nominally recognizing Mexican sovereignty while giving Texans broad independent powers. Maverick wrote in reply, "I cannot persuade myself that such an annexation, on any terms, would be advantageous to Texas, and I therefore cannot say so, for I regard a lie as a crime, and one which I cannot commit even to secure my release; I must, therefore, continue to wear my chains, galling as they are."[39]

Maverick was uncomfortable as well with the possibility of Thompson's procuring his release before most of the other San Antonio and Dawson prisoners received theirs. "I somehow cannot feel that I can or ought to go before my companions in arms, Mr. Bradley Messrs Hatch Hutchinson & Johnson &c &c," he wrote Mary on January 27. He told her of his letter to Bocanegra, confiding that "the fact of some of us having money and procuring the necessary food, I of course kept out of sight." He had carried "a little" money with him from San Antonio, and Waddy Thompson had from the beginning urged, "If you want *money* draw on me for it."[40]

Trying to encourage his wife, on January 27 Maverick also expressed appreciation for "the force & energy of your style, my love" and suggested that she try producing some articles for publication, should she feel up to it. Yet his spirits drooped under the specter of a continued indefinite imprisonment and the lack of any news from home. Maverick begged his wife to write and "say with all your candor how near you have come and will keep to that serene state of mind which I have constantly prayed may be enjoyed by us both." He reasoned that "there was never anything in the whole history of our love, to make memory sad, and why should we suffer our past felicity to become a source of unhappiness now." Stoically, he prayed for resignation, patience, and cheerfulness, "for God himself has filled human life with accident, trials and death." Yet never had he been more aware of the "daily hazards to which we have been subjected" as "poor luckless Texians," and he expressed anxiety over the impending birth of their fourth child.

A week later, Maverick reported to his wife Santa Anna's promise to release him, as well as the intelligence that all the prisoners were to be liberated in a month. "How much better it is that I am not to go alone but with unlucky but brave compan[ions]," he wrote. "If I really reach your dear presence, my own precious love, I shall not regret what I have seen and suffered."[41]

Yet the month came and went without any signs of liberation. During that time, the Mier Expedition prisoners marching south staged a mass escape at Salado, only to be recaptured. Santa Anna ordered the 176 prisoners executed, but the Mexican government altered the order to specify that every tenth man would forfeit his life. In the infamous black bean episode, the captives drew from an earthenware jar containing white and black beans; the seventeen drawing black were summarily executed.[42]

American captives were not the only ones determined to resist Santa Anna's regime. The dictator paid a brief visit to Perote on March 1 before proceeding to Mexico City, where he immediately had to quell a native revolt against his dictatorship. "I conclude that the greater and to him more interesting events of his first days in the Capitol has prevented his attending to what he promised the Amcn. Minister in my behalf," Maverick wrote glumly to Mary on March 16, adding, "I have to tell the whole truth. I lived and breathed on this promise ever since it was communicated to me. I do not stop to consider the hu-

mility of our situation, my anxiety to be in your presence without dishonor is now paramount."

The prisoners had finally gleaned a little news from home. From
a letter written in December by Dr. John Chalmers of LaGrange, Maverick had learned that his family had been ill but was improving. Yet
too many questions remained unanswered. "O dearest how have you
past the fourth trial attendant on our love?" Maverick asked. "Have
my prayers and pure love helped thee in that hour? Are you again in
good health; are my precious children alive and well. Great God how
I have longed to know these particulars."

Maverick swore to his wife that he was in excellent health physically, but his cool, logical, reasoned approach to life was giving way
to mystic, poetic musings in his bleak situation. "Our five senses are
confined to a very limited field (say the castle and once in a while,
the city of Perote)," he wrote, and now "instead of facts, (such is our
situation) reflections, memories, inferences, and dreams have occupied
my soul. In spite of my former indifference to dreams they now occupy
me much; and are in fact the most interesting events of my life." He
dreamed frequently, pleasant scenes from his youth and childhood, and
always Mary was there—"How just and true it is that thou my good
angel, shouldst be the principal personage in every agreeable scene of
my life, *though many years before we met.*"

Scarcely had Maverick sent this letter of March 16 when he finally
received the first and only direct word from his wife during his captivity. Mary's missive of January 7 reported all well in the Colorado River
cabin but mentioned nothing of her pregnancy, causing Maverick to
wonder if he had been mistaken concerning a fourth "trial and hardship incident to our love." But soon, he felt sure, he would be home
to learn the situation for himself. On March 22 he wrote that he, Jones,
and Judge Hutchinson had had their chains removed a few days before and horses now stood ready to take them to Mexico City to receive their official release.

The relief he felt at the impending liberation and at receipt of his
wife's letter sent him into an eloquent reflection on his actions and
affirmation of his love. If she should ever again follow him, as she did
on their last leave-taking, with "that sweet thoughtful face, that reluctance, that almost tearful smile of Love," he vowed, "I shall not go.
Even the rough duties I owe to our affairs, and the higher duties I owe

to poor Texas, these are such that I cannot turn a deaf ear to them, but oh how much stronger—pshaw! I cannot compare anything to that compass in my bosom" drawing him ever homeward to Mary.

In Mexico City, the three prisoners were "first paraded for a quarter of an hour ragged and dirty in front of the Palace—then escorted into it and finally sent to prison" temporarily.[43] Santa Anna officially liberated them on March 30, the same day Mary gave birth in her cabin near LaGrange to a sickly daughter, "child of a captive father, and for him named Augusta."[44] The former captives remained briefly in Mexico City, boarding at the same establishment as Waddy Thompson and moving about freely. Then they removed to the port of Vera Cruz, and on April 5 boarded the American naval ship *Vincennes*. Maverick and his companions traveled through Pensacola, Mobile, and New Orleans before sailing for Galveston on April 22.[45]

He reached the home he had never seen on May 4. The Mavericks' eldest son, Sam, later remembered that his father rode up crying "Ave Maria," and Mary wrote in her diary, "Joy! Joy! Joy! *Blessed be God our Father.*"[46] From Pendleton, the elder Samuel wrote, "I hope you have brot. away at least a link of the chain, as I have often wished that my father had the handcuffs from the old Jersey prison ship (1778) that on the goodness of *God*, your grandchildren may hold the iron in their hands, & see the inscrutable working of his almighty power."[47]

Sam Maverick *had* carried home the chain that bound him in Perote. It symbolized an ordeal, but also an adventure. The incarceration had been galling, of course, but the journey, despite its hardships, had for him resembled a long surveying trip, demonstrating the extent to which he thrived on land exploration and in the midst of harsh living conditions. He now would complain of physical ailments only when forced into the hot rooms and unwholesome diet of civilization, where he would find himself while attending the state legislature in the 1850s.

Maverick was to refer to his Mexican march as a pilgrimage, indicating that he invested the time spent traversing broad plains and ragged mountains with a degree of mystical religious meaning. Along with physical invigoration came spiritual renewal, a fact that would become most apparent with his participation in the Chihuahuan Expedition a few years later.

His other source of spiritual sustenance through the Perote ordeal was his wife, his "good angel," who inhabited every pleasant dream dur-

"I hope you have brot. away at least a link of the chain [which bound you]," Samuel Maverick wrote to his son upon learning of the latter's release from the Mexican prison of Perote in 1843. *Courtesy Texas Memorial Museum, Acc#1721-273, Austin.*

ing his incarceration. "I am conscious of . . . *having been, or tho't, his ideal*," Mary would write some years later.[48] Indeed, there are many indications among the couple's letters and journals that each idealized the other. The depth and constancy of their love is apparent in Maverick's letters from Perote, in Mary's great joy at his every homecoming. However, they did not live in an ideal world; they were human beings, not romantic icons; and they were to face trials even harder than Perote.

8

The Quest for Stability

I am ashamed of the miserable position in which I think Texas now stands. . . . But there is no manner of danger of ultimate defeat; suspense [and] delay is all I deplore."
—Sam Maverick to R. N. Weir, August 15, 1843

WHEN MAVERICK ARRIVED at the log cabin on the Colorado, relations between Mexico and Texas remained as unsteady as ever, continuing to cloud the personal futures of those who had cast their lot in the Lone Star Republic "We are desirous to return to S A [San Antonio] & hope to be justified in returning before another summer," Maverick wrote a few months after his homecoming to R. N. Weir, the Alabama doctor who had given a temporary home to Lizzie Adams and who now served as Maverick's Tuscaloosa business agent. Otherwise, they would have to go to Tuscaloosa "for a while."[1] Actually, Mary, sister Lizzie, and the children would remain on the Colorado for a year and a half after Maverick's return before sickness and the continuing instability of political affairs drove them in a new direction—to the Texas Gulf Coast.

Maverick himself had barely settled in before he resumed his pattern of ranging westward and eastward, in June returning to San Antonio on court and land business. He reported to his father that no important land papers had been lost in the events of the preceding autumn, and he waxed as enthusiastic as ever over the acreage and future of Texas.

To continue financing Texas lands, Maverick instructed Weir to sell his plantation near Tuscaloosa, as well as two town lots. "My dear friend now is the time for investing something in the soil of Texas," he wrote. "It is bound to result in great profit." The political situation with Mexico, he admitted, had Texans "all in the dark without much to hope for" and almost "palzied in the cringing attitude of beggars." But he confidently looked to a time when the Republic's "abundant native strength and resources and valor to boot" would triumph.[2]

Many Texans had long favored annexation to the United States as a resolution of the Republic's predicament. But the U.S. government had backed away from such a move for diplomatic reasons, an obvious one being the possibility of war with Mexico over the issue. Now, in 1843, Pres. John Tyler became alarmed at the intrusion of England into the affairs of Mexico and Texas. The English, eager to stop the United States' westward expansion and to engage in advantageous trade with Texas, were acting to prevent any possibility of annexation. Tyler responded by opening new negotiations with Texas through his secretary of state, A. P. Upshur.

The negotiations between Upshur and Texas president Houston sputtered and died over Houston's insistence that U.S. troops be on hand to protect the Republic from invasion and that the negotiation be carried out in secret. Meanwhile, many Americans eager to migrate to Texas and many Texans eager to renew their ties with the United States and enjoy increased security waited and wondered in mounting frustration. Among them were the Mavericks.

Sam Maverick hoped to do something to further annexation efforts, as Bexar residents had re-elected him to the Republic's House of Representatives and this time he was free to serve. Maverick's own record of the election results shows that in the three-man race he received the highest number of votes with 202; runner-up F. L. Paschal received 135 and was also elected.[3] On December 6, 1843, Maverick and Paschal were seated in the Eighth Congress of the Republic of Texas. Three days later, fellow Perote prisoner William E. Jones joined them.

The congress of the struggling nation met at Washington-on-the-Brazos rather than in Austin, the capital selected in 1839, in part because of the continuing exposure to Indian and Mexican raids that Austin and other frontier settlements faced. The main issues facing the delegates when they met December, 1843, through February, 1844, were empresario contracts, Houston's discharge of Texas navy commander Edwin W. Moore, and annexation. In all of these matters, Maverick stood with those openly critical of the president.

At Houston's urging, in February, 1841, the Sixth Congress had empowered the president to grant empresario contracts in hopes of filling the Republic's empty coffers and providing a buffer of emigrants between settled areas and Indian country. The next year, a general colonization law had added impetus to the empresario colonization system, with colonizers receiving ten premium sections, each to be settled by one hundred families. The government retained alternate sections in hopes of selling them after the colonizers had done their work of settlement.

However, the men who seized this empire-building opportunity stumbled among the many hardships involved in extending civilization wholesale into areas barely charted. W. S. Peters and Associates, Charles F. Mercer, Henri Castro, and Henry F. Fisher and Burchard Miller all mounted large settlement efforts but were hampered by a host of problems, from dissatisfied colonists to difficult contract terms to general ill-feeling directed against them by individual settlers.[4]

Sam Maverick was not opposed to large-scale emigration efforts, which, after all, could enhance the value of his own lands, and he voted with a House minority in favor of incorporating the Texas Land & Emigrating Company. But he was opposed to confused, ill-thought-out colonizing attempts being made as a result of the reopening of empresario contracts. He was also distrustful of Sam Houston and his attitudes toward land distribution. Indeed, Houston's reasoning on land matters was often difficult to fathom and appeared tinged with hypocrisy in regard to the rights of the small landholder. For example, in a campaign speech the hero of San Jacinto, who had eleven-league claims pending around the Red and Trinity rivers, had pledged that, if his hand should ever sign a patent (an official land grant), "I hope God will strike it free from my body."[5]

Disillusionment with Houston's empresario system was so great that a bill was proposed repealing the president's authorization to make colonization contracts and calling for forfeiture where colonizers had failed to meet contract conditions. On January 3, 1844, Maverick successfully added a phrase specifying that future failures to meet contract terms would result in forfeiture as well.[6] The bill was eventually passed over Houston's veto by both House and Senate.

Another point of contention between the Congress and the president was the case of Com. Edwin W. Moore. The previous Congress had voted secretly to sell the ships of the small Texas Navy, a move prevented by popular sentiment. But Houston had charged the naval commander with insubordination when Moore, with no money forthcoming from Texas, directed his ships in a Yucatán-financed campaign to smash a Mexican blockade of Yucatán. Moore was tried and acquitted of all but four minor charges and brought his case for reinstatement into the navy before Congress. On January 24, Maverick wrote to Mary that Moore was a "capital fellow" and that Congress would soon "do him justice" despite Houston and his backers. Indeed, Moore was soon reinstated.

Besting Houston became more difficult when the subject was annexation. Houston's secure negotiating position as president and his insistence on secret dealings drove Maverick and others anxious for annexation almost to distraction, as they were unable to determine whether he wanted annexation and if so, how he was attempting to get it.

Maverick was already glum on his arrival at the congressional session, referring to Houston as "the Arch plotter" and commenting to Mary on December 11, "I really fear he is quizzing or humbugging the public & if so I trust it will be exposed." In mid-January he reported to his wife the news of Tyler's reopening of negotiations in October, only to be stalled by Houston.

A week and a half later, Maverick wrote to Mary that he seldom spoke in the House but that he had scored against Houston what William Jones called "the best hit, and the best and truest & strongest thing that has been said here this session." Pressed into describing the president's position on annexation, the representative from Bexar had stated, "Whether it was our destiny to go as a province & dependency of England, or to become annexed to the N [*sic*] States of Am[eric]a, or to become Independent, or to revolve back to Mexico, the President has the papers and the witnesses to show that he had produced the result." Maverick observed that the government in Washington, D.C., seemed to think that Texans were reluctant to be annexed. "We are obliged to leave much to him [Houston]," he observed, "and I am sorry to leave in such suspicious keeping a thing so valuable to us all."[7]

Even if the two men had not differed on the issues, Maverick's straightforward style clashed with Houston's penchant for intrigue. "Excellent, High Secretary, do I write too plainly?" the former had written to Bocanegra while confined in Perote, and throughout his public career he would favor the direct, open approach, chafing under the florid speech making and machinations that were part of legislative decision making.

Now, instead of plain information, the legislators got only tantaliz-

ing rumors of critical movements in the United States toward annexation. Houston's secretive handling of the issue led on February 5 to
a split between his supporters and opponents, as the House voted 20
to 19 against a resolution expressing confidence in Houston, despite
"unfounded aspersions" on his character.

Maverick voted in the majority. He also signed, along with five
other members of the Committee on Foreign Relations, a majority report
excoriating Houston for refusing to supply them with information on
annexation negotiations. The report compared Houston's attitude to
that of a carriage driver taking his passengers in a "precisely opposite
direction" from their desired destination and informing them that "they
have no right to enquire where they are going, or to interfere in any
way with his driving until they are set down at the end of the route
he has chosen for them."[8]

Maverick served not only on the Foreign Affairs Committee but
chaired the Enrolled Bills Committee, certifying that bills had been
correctly enrolled and submitted to the president for approval. He was
a member of the Finance, Public Lands, and Indian Affairs committees, the last of which also took Houston to task for giving Indians
money meant for frontier protection and appearing to favor them over
settlers.[9]

Personally, Maverick introduced and saw passed a bill to amend
the criminal laws of the Republic, a set of judicial adjustments including the stipulation that should a district judge find it impossible to
raise a jury of twelve because of "the sparseness of the population" in
one county, he could adjourn to another county in his district.[10] He
also presented bills for the relief of San Antonio and some of its Mexican and Anglo-American citizens.[11] Nor did he and Jones want to
forget friends from their recent captivity. Jones had written Maverick
in August that Waddy Thompson was financially distressed, having
advanced thirty-six hundred dollars to the Santa Fe Expedition prisoners released in Mexico in 1842. The two men worked to get Thompson reimbursed and officially thanked for his efforts on behalf of all
the Texan prisoners.

Many Texans remained in Perote—most of the San Antonio captives, the Dawson Massacre prisoners, and the Mier survivors of the
black bean episode. Maverick and Jones found it hard to incite anyone
to action on their behalf. In January, Maverick shared with his wife
part of a letter from Perote prisoner George Van Ness, who reported

widespread sickness and death among those still held captive. The sad situation, Maverick wrote, "bespeaks the deep abasement of the Texian Character. We might at least have tried to do something for our poor friends," but he observed that only invasion seemed to arouse public sentiment.[12] Meanwhile, he lived with the knowledge that he had been freed "from the mere accident of being cousin to the Minister Thompson." He had written Weir, "Only think how much better off (tho' undeservedly) than my poor fellows I have been."[13]

Feeling that Texans needed the full power of the United States behind them to avert such situations, he went home from the Eighth Congress still disturbed over the lack of progress toward annexation. Pendleton acquaintance Richard Franklin Simpson had been elected to the U.S. Congress, and at the end of February Maverick penned a letter to the Democratic congressman outlining his views on the subject. He reported that Houston was opposed to annexation and playing a delaying game. Maverick also saw in the Texas president a "hatred of the western section" that could lead, with Houston's control of the Republic's Senate, to a stipulation for peace "with 1/2 only of our proper soil." In a very threatening development for those such as Maverick who looked westward for the Republic's future, Houston and the Senate could agree to a Nueces River boundary "or even less," giving away the Rio Grande, which was "as important to our prosperity and extension, as the Mississippi is to the U.S."[14]

Finally, Maverick worried over the duplicitous actions of the U.S. chargé in Texas in the matter. "I do not know but he is honestly intent on carrying out the wishes of your government," Maverick admitted, but "I would not have chosen him in a matter where plain sailing is better than circumnavigation."

In February, Maverick's old neighbor John C. Calhoun took over the negotiations for the United States and made better progress, signing an annexation treaty with Texas commissioners Issac Van Zandt and James P. Henderson in April. However, it was rejected by the U.S. Congress that June.

Meanwhile, the Maverick family continued its impermanent existence on the Colorado, experiencing periodic bouts of sickness that confirmed Maverick's low opinion of the lands to the east of San Antonio. When he had come home the preceding May, he had found the family ill with bilious fever. Baby Augusta was, in Mary's words, "sick and almost dead for weeks," and both young Sam and Agatha came close to death of the fever themselves during that spring and early summer. Another sickly summer lay ahead.

The couple continued to consider departing temporarily for Tuscaloosa. From the Congress in January, Maverick wrote his wife that he had not made up his mind about such a visit but would leave it up to her, adding, "If you conclude write me: but we can't go till the roads are passable, even to Houston, say April or thereabout." A brief, hopeful letter about annexation followed, however, with Maverick writing, "if annexation is about to take place, we must stay to attend to the formation of the State Govt. and forego for this year the pleasure of visiting our friends."[15]

The Mavericks often were to make plans for a family trip to Alabama, but it never materialized. For one thing, Mary was usually pregnant or caring for a new, and often sickly, baby, as well as a number of other small children. She would experience ten pregnancies and births over a period of almost twenty-one years, with six children growing to maturity, and she would feel perpetually tied to child tending and supervision of the Maverick slaves, the number of which varied from a few adults and children to twenty during the Civil War.

Thus, in traditional fashion, Mary Maverick maintained the homefront. She had become wife and mother in a time when women's role was strictly defined as "angel of the house," a moral presence presiding over the domestic sphere. Mary struggled faithfully to fulfill the responsibilities inherent in the role, accepting home as her sphere, home management and moral nurturing of the family as her sacred duty.[16]

Her husband continued to travel, returning through cold rains to San Antonio for district court in March of 1844. Again, the specter of Mexican invasion hung over the city, for he wrote his wife on March 6, "There is every precaution taken by Capt Hays and we are all on the look-out. But I am well convinced there is no truth in the report about the Mexicans coming. . . . And they cannot come without our finding it out."

He returned safely from Bexar only to leave in late April on a business trip to New Orleans.[17] Apprised of Maverick's movements by a letter from the Louisiana city that reached him on May 24, the elder Samuel in Pendleton revealed exasperation over his son's continuing risk taking. Samuel had repeatedly warned his eldest child of the dangers of becoming a martyr to Texas or to his business interests and urged him to remember in the event of another military action that Waddy Thompson had won his release only on the promise that Maverick not take up arms against Mexico.

Now he wrote, "If it had been to save the life of yr wife or children or yourself, I should have approved of your going to N.O. at this time, it is certainly very imprudent, (& you must use all possible precaution) you have escaped so many accidents & hazards, that I am somewhat surprised at your venturing this time at this season of the year, But may God be with you."[18]

Maverick's own guilt at this latest tempting of the fates led him to write to Mary on May 11 from Galveston a letter in which he expressed the fear that "an evil genius of paltry gain" was motivating his movements and concluded that it would be better for him to be tending his children. Yet, as he said, "I am started & never could see backward in my life." He was always pulled eastward by the need for more money to finance his Texas lands, lands he was reluctant to sell, given the economic times and his own acquisitive desire. He was pulled westward by the lure of the lands themselves.

These movements continued to create an uneasy tension between his passion for empire building and his responsibility to his "precious jewels." Time after time, despite his avowals that wife and family came first, empire building took precedence, and he expressed his guilt and anxiety in breathless reiterations of love and concern. "All my solicitude & anxiety goes to the poor little cabin where my treasure is laid up," he wrote on May 11, calling on God to "in thy mercy save that dear home from sickness and sorrow."

Before arriving in Galveston, Maverick had stopped at the fledgling community of Port (or Passo) Cavallo, located at the entrance to Matagorda Bay. "I am much pleased with this place," he wrote to Mary on April 30, "and am about to take an interest in it. It is cooler than San Antonio and the orange trees are 7 ft. high." He suggested that the family come to the Pass during the summer, after his return. "But I shall yield to your pleasure with the greatest satisfaction," Maverick wrote. "In case of annexation the temptation to go to San Antonio, will be great I am sure."

From Galveston he wrote that late news made San Antonio seem out of the question, but he now contemplated a permanent move to the coast. "If we were at Port Cavallo (The Pass) I would really be glad," he said. "We could then get off to the states or where we pleasure, and would not be half so exposed to the Mexicans as even at La Grange."[19]

When Maverick returned home that summer, the balance of the San Antonio prisoners were also making their way home, finally released by Santa Anna after repeated requests from U.S. diplomats.[20] John Bradley had been released a few months earlier through the intervention of Andrew Jackson and was campaigning for a seat in the Republic Congress while his family remained on the Colorado near Maverick's. But in September, he died, a victim of "inflamatory rheumatism, contracted in the dungeons of Perote."[21] The self-reliant and resourceful Ann Bradley took her seven children and moved back to San Antonio, where she opened a thriving boardinghouse.

Meanwhile, the Mavericks almost lost one of their own in August, 1844, when eldest daughter Agatha went into convulsions after being kicked by a horse belonging to Andrew Adams, visiting on his way to Alabama. Both parents sat by the child's bed "almost hopeless" at her condition. But she slipped into a quiet sleep about midnight, waking before dawn to ask her father for a drink of water and eliciting from him an emotional "Blessed be God."[22]

The family continued to be plagued with illness, and twenty-six-year-old Mary herself weakened so during the summer that she was an "invalid" during the fall.[23] On November 9, Maverick sold the twenty-six acres on the Colorado to Dancy, and within a week the family had set off to establish a home on the coast.[24]

Mary was so reduced by illness that she rode lying among pillows and quilts in a carriage, accompanied by her two little girls, while the boys rode in one of the two accompanying wagons, and Maverick and his sister-in-law traveled on horseback. They had a hard journey, pushing southward in cold, wet northers, crossing swamplands that mired wagons and oxen, and boiling water to drink from cattle tracks on the prairies. On December 3, they reached the Gulf of Mexico, and Mary rhapsodized over the "magnificent, calm, gently heaving water" and the "beautiful, smooth, hard beach." But three days later, camped on the cold beach and breathing the smoke of a camp fire, she "lost all admiration for the 'deep and dark blue ocean,' and was most miserable and sick."[25]

They journeyed down the long, flat, sandy peninsula, which jutted southwestward to enclose Matagorda Bay, arriving on December 7 at the tip, called Decrow's Point and situated across the entry to the bay from Port Cavallo. The family would spend almost three years at these two fledgling settlements in a further attempt to establish a permanent Texas home.

At the Point lived former Republic congressman Gen. Alexander Somervell, who had led the punitive and ill-fated expedition against Mexico while Maverick was in Perote. Somervell was now collector of customs for the port, and the Mavericks moved into the house occupied by the general and his brother, agreeing to maintain the home and furnish board for the two men.

Hardly had the family reached its new home than overnight guests arrived—Prince Carl of Solms-Braunfels and his entourage. The German land-buying association of which the prince was a part had bought the Fisher-Miller Land Grant, one of those awarded by Houston and threatened with forfeiture by the Eighth Congress. The prince was pressing onward with colonization plans for western and coastal Texas acreage, arriving with his first settlers at the pass as the Mavericks settled in. On December 12, the royal party stayed with the Mavericks and Somervells, and Mary later remembered that the sight of two attendants lifting the royal personage into his pants led General Somervell into "one of his famous fits of laughter," which echoed over the Point. She described the party as "very courteous and polite," but concluded in a nice bit of understatement, "They wore cock feathers in their hats, and did not appear quite fitted to frontier life."[26]

As the winter waned, the Mavericks planted a garden and delighted in the climate that produced flourishing vegetables and watermelons, flowers, grapevines, and orange trees. Both husband and wife took a keen interest in growing things, and Maverick's father often sent them advice and tried with infrequent success to arrange the safe delivery to them of seeds and cuttings from his own plants.

The climate was salubrious for the family's health as well, and Maverick helped his wife recover by remaining at home more and by taking her every evening to bathe in the salt water. But they had another scare with daughter Agatha, badly burned after her clothes caught fire in March, 1845. She gradually recovered, and in June Maverick once more set off for San Antonio on land business. In Bexar County and Bexar Territory to the west, tax rolls show that in 1844 he held 35,229 acres by title and 20,077 by survey, as well as twenty-one San Antonio town lots. In addition, in 1845 he accumulated over 11,000 acres for his father to be deeded to the Weyman, Thompson, Van Wyck, and Maverick grandchildren.[27]

He was outdistancing many of his fellow speculators in San Antonio; even without the lands held in trust, he had tripled his 1840
total. John W. Smith had moved in the same time from 41,000 acres
to about 47,000; however, William Elliott had quickly acquired over
88,000 acres under title. The chief Mexican landowners in Bexar still
held around 20,000 acres; in 1844, José Antonio Navarro held 20,003,
and Ignacio Cassiano, "in connection with" José Cassiano, held 22,412.[28]

Maverick was bringing important land papers home with him in
late June when the boat in which he was sailing from Port Lavaca to
Port Cavallo overturned in a sudden squall, nearly drowning the passengers and plunging the papers into the bay.

Hearing of the near-fatal accident and the loss of the land records,
the elder Maverick wrote to his son a thoughtful assessment of the
affair. At seventy-three years of age, Samuel had just weathered a painful illness. He had been trying to put his own extensive affairs in order
and questioned what his own prudence and initiative had accomplished.

He had gloried in the accumulation of land and still felt the urge
to continue buying. But without trustworthy agents spread across the
South, he could not maintain good control over his possessions, and
he was alarmed by legal measures in South Carolina to void or transfer
land purchases. Favoring fair representation for all, he nonetheless felt
the mass of nonlandholding residents had power through the ballot
box to negate the hard work and ingenuity of those who had built
up estates. "A free Negro & a free holder stand very much on the same
footing with us, pretty much outlawed," he had reported the year before. "Any scamp may with impunity insult & rob him & be sustained
in court or out of court by an overwhelming majority."[29] Indeed, in
many of his letters to his son, Samuel likened the United States to
a pirate ship in which confusion and avarice reigned, with supposedly
Christian men dispossessing the Indians and being dispossessed by other
emigrants in turn.

Now he counseled his son to learn from the near-fatal accident something of the uncertainties of life and the need for a simple dependence
on God and nature. "If all the Land you have purchased are lost forever, although they cost you years of Privation, distress of mind & body,
& although the winds & the waves threw you to the sharks yet God
shut the mouths of the sharks, to open your eyes," Samuel wrote on
August 6, then shared some of his doubts over the course he had pursued and now saw his son pursuing:

> You and I Sam are like the boy who was to have all the apples he could carry in his arms, he took too many, & like our lands, all dropped out. It puzzles me to pay Taxes & keep up the marks. If I had my life to live over again I would instead of purchasing the most . . . purchase the best & in no place where it was unhealthy, there I would set down & like a Hindoo Yoga look at the point of my own nose. We have been both working for our grand-children, and whether what we have heaped up is for their good or for their bad, we know not, it is even more difficult to know whether they will ever get it or not.

Nonetheless, in the same letter, Samuel thanked his son for the purchases of Texas land made for the grandchildren in his behalf and asked, "Had I not better order from N. York 1 doz. spades & 1 or 2 doz. stone hatchets & chisels, & a man to go round & put up a Mound 6 foot high at every corner of the tract of land & mark large substantial rocks at every corner 'Maverick' & set up at where the lines crosses Road & at other conspicuous places?"

As if to reinforce Samuel's counsel on the power of God and nature, the Mavericks had a second, if less harrowing, boating accident soon after Maverick's return from San Antonio. Out sailing for pleasure one afternoon, Sam and Mary and their two sons, Lizzie Adams, General Somervell, and some visitors to the Point got caught in a sudden fog and wound up running aground near a small cabin where they were forced to spend the night. Early the next morning, they returned to anxious family and friends who had spent the night blowing foghorns and tending large fires on the beach.

Mary was greeted by her two daughters, who, she learned, had cried themselves to sleep. She was able to dismiss the experience as one that "gave us many hearty laughs thereafter," but Mary alone of the lost party had lain awake all night and "hailed with delight the dawn of day." The hazards and uncertainties that the young mother had faced over the last eight and a half years were beginning to crowd in on her.[30]

One great uncertainty was resolved that summer of 1845. In February, the U.S. Congress had finally adopted a joint resolution conditionally offering Texas statehood. The next month, English and French diplomats had convinced Houston's successor, Anson Jones, to wait ninety days to decide on the annexation question, and in May the English had secured for Texas a preliminary treaty with Mexico recognizing Texas independence on the condition that the nine-year-old

Republic not be annexed to another power. However, on June 16, the Texas Congress met and chose annexation. In July, a constitutional convention also gathered, voted for the annexation, and prepared a state constitution. Mary wrote, "Thank God, we are now annexed to the United States, and can hope for home and quiet."[31] It was a hope to cling to, but one that would be only imperfectly realized for years to come.

9

"Let Us Hope That We Are Beloved"

Ah! my dear husband, I feel that we too often risk your life. . . .
Are we better than others, that we deserve so much of the care of
Providence over our little affairs?—alas no. Are we peculiarly
beloved of our Father?—let us hope that we are beloved.

—Mary Maverick to her husband, November 16, 1845

THAT SUMMER when annexation to the United States finally became
a reality for Texans, William Van Wyck, recovered from his financial
failure and again practicing law in New York City, wrote to his brother-
in-law Sam Maverick, "I congratulate you on the annexation and hope
that you will now reap a reward sufficient to compensate you for all
your trials and sufferings."[1]

Indeed, the Mavericks were enjoying a relatively worry-free interlude on the coast, spending about two and a half months at Tres Pa-
lacios, a summer retreat on Cox's Point near the community of Matagorda. Incorporated in 1830, after Stephen F. Austin's selection of the
town site, Matagorda with its schools and churches possessed a reputation as a cultural center with "probably the most cultivated society in
the state," as Mary wrote in her memoirs.

Even people who found little to like in Texas commented favorably
on this community at the mouth of the Colorado River. One such
critic in 1835 reported that it was "the best port on the coast & is rapidly improving & [I] am told contains the best society of any town
in the Colony."[2] Englishman William Bollaert in his travels through
Texas in the early 1840s wrote of visiting in a Matagorda home where
his host was an accomplished violinist and harpist and added, "The
Society I met at his house both of Ladies and Gentlemen left nothing
to be desired—beauty, talent and friendship."[3]

Mary was equally pleased to find that Matagorda had an Episcopal minister who could baptize her children, and his wife she discovered to be a former teacher of hers in Tuscaloosa. Her own involvement in the pleasant society of the place was limited, however, by her advanced pregnancy and delivery of the fifth Maverick child, George Madison, on September 7, 1845, at the home of Maggie Shortridge Pearson, a sister of Mary's old school friend E. A. Shortridge Lewis. Meanwhile, Maverick and his sister-in-law Lizzie attended such Matagorda social events as the marriage of Annie Fisher, whose father, S. Rhoads, had signed the Texas Declaration of Independence.

In late October, they sailed back across the bay, and Maverick made hurried preparations for another business trip east. The family was now renting a private house across the point at Port Cavallo, but they wanted to build their own home, and Maverick, who had bought one-third interest in Decrow's Point, wanted to start developing the place. He needed to obtain funds and he had business debts to collect in Tuscaloosa and a tract of land to sell near Florence, as well as other business to conduct for himself and his father in New Orleans and Mobile. He also had a house sale to complete that would take him, reluctantly, all the way to Charleston.

He planned to take twenty-two-year-old Lizzie back to Tuscaloosa for the winter. She had lived with the Mavericks for more than three years, but extant family papers tell little about her niche in family life during this time. As the Maverick children neared school age, the eldest later related, Lizzie was pressed into service as their teacher, but finding her charges reluctant, she drew pictures to entertain them.[4]

On October 28, 1848, Lizzie sailed with her brother-in-law on the schooner *Mary* for New Orleans. Again, the trip was filled with anxiety for both of the Mavericks, as Mary waited with five children under eight years of age at the sparsely settled port through a cold, stormy winter and her husband found himself straying farther from home, with repeated delays. His initial passage through a choppy Gulf led Mary in a letter of November 16 to question the repeated risk of his life, "that life which is all of light and love this world contains for your wife and children—5 helpless ones remember."

How, she wondered, could they hope for the continued care of Providence, for the special protection of a loving God? Yet she did, for "in that divine love of a merciful Father for his helpless children rests my immoveable faith & hope." Sounding a theme that would be repeated in her diary through subsequent trials, she wrote, "Unworthy that I feel myself to be beloved of him, yet this sweet trust alone could sustain me under heavy afflictions."[5]

Maverick himself was particularly apprehensive about being gone from home this time. Political stability was finally being achieved; John C. Calhoun, whom he called on in New Orleans, told him that the newly annexed Texas would be admitted as a state before long.[6] Yet about the personal welfare of his own family, Maverick admitted to his wife in a letter from Tuscaloosa on November 19, "I feel more uneasy than I ever did in my life. I feel guilty of leaving you almost out of doors." His guilt was probably compounded by his being at Mary's old home among her friends and relations as he wrote. Mary's brother Andrew was studying medicine in Tuscaloosa, and youngest brother Robert had married and settled on the family plantation, putting it once more into cultivation. With Robert, Maverick visited the graves of Agatha and William Adams on the property "and paid our tribute to sad memories," he informed his wife, knowing how much she would have valued performing this duty herself.

His guilt, however, sprang in large part from the fact that once more he was extending his trip. "I have not been able to raise any money at all," he reported in the November 19 letter, "and I had to come to the determination (whilst at Mobile) to go to South Carolina." It would be a "fatiguing journey & in a hurry all the time," but, he wrote, "I shall mind nothing so bad as absence."

Maverick was conscious of the fact that his wife no longer had relations nearby from whom to draw support. Lizzie, Andrew, and Robert had all returned to Alabama, brother William had moved to Freestone County, and Aunt Ann was in San Antonio. Other Maverick relations were talking about packing up for Texas, however, and while in Tuscaloosa, Maverick took time to write to them.

G. Jones Houston, a member of the family to whom Maverick had sold his Lauderdale County plantation, had married Maverick's niece Elizabeth Weyman, also known as Routez, at Pendleton the preceding year.[7] "The match was made up in Alabama," the elder Samuel wrote apprising his son of the news. "He appears to be a decent smart man, & I hope all will be for the best."[8] The Houstons returned to Lauderdale County, but showed interest in moving to Texas. Thus, Maverick in Tuscaloosa invited them to Port Cavallo, offering to help Houston locate a place to settle in January or February. "I told him that you had always desired me to get Routez if possible to come to us in Texas," he wrote Mary, "but that I had never made up my mind to advise friends to quit civilization &c for Texian misery—until now, and that you and I felt much interest in those relations."[9]

Meanwhile, Maverick pushed eastward to Pendleton, where his father remained in poor health after suffering a "suppression of urine" and agonizing catheter treatments the previous summer. Maverick suggested that his father come live with them, but Samuel declined. "Nothing would please me better than to live in the neighbourhood of my Son & his family and dear children the remainder of my time if we could find a healthy comfortable neighbourhood of honorable men," he wrote, but, given human nature, he considered this as much of an impossibility in Texas as in South Carolina.[10]

Father and son spent twelve and a half days together in what both sensed would be their last meeting. Maverick found his father "improved greatly in faith & philosophy, more humble & relying, and less worldly in practice." The elder Maverick had indeed developed a stoic reliance on the Almighty that he counseled his son to adopt, stating, "It is God who made us; & let him dispose of us as suits his sovereign pleasure."[11]

The visit left the son feeling melancholy and reluctant to break the ties of remembrance by continuing on his journey. It was Samuel who urged him onward. "Strange to say, he did not expect or desire me to stay longer; but thought I ought to go & take care of our little ones," Maverick wrote to Mary on December 10.

There was nothing very strange about a grandfather urging his son to see to his family responsibilities, particularly when by the son's own admission he had left his wife and children "almost out of doors." Maverick's mild surprise at his father's injunction says something about Maverick himself—that, despite his loving, guilt-infused letters to Mary, he was still greatly absorbed in the roaming business life he had established before his marriage.

Now he found that "the State of exchange, risque &c of my business" required a trip to Charleston. "As soon as I can raise some funds I must send you a remittance," he wrote Mary, "for I am afraid you are almost starved & shivering in the Northers."[12]

Christmas came—a Christmas Maverick had hoped to spend at least in Tuscaloosa, if not home—and then New Year's, and he remained in Charleston. On January 4, 1846, he wrote Mary, "I had no heart to write you a Merry Christmas or New Year's letter. I feel much worse I assure you, than when I was in the Prison of Perote." His quest for funds in the city had been a successful but protracted one. "I am sad and impatient," he confessed, "worn out with delays, and as home-sick & sinking at the heart as ever was poor forlorn unfriended, whipt schoolboy after the holidays."

His guilt had grown, for he wrote, "When I broke my parole & ran off from Tuskaloosa away to Carolina without your express knowledge, dearest, I brought upon myself trouble enough, and a heavy punishment" in the form of bad weather and "long-winded & slow motioned people." Yet in this abject stance, he could not resist a flash of humor, concluding that "whilst I did tremble in a sort of *petit judgment* I did not quite give up—I did not give up atall, but purchased 3 blankets which I put on my bed in addition to the ordinary complement."[13]

Now he prepared to return to Tuscaloosa and Mobile, having purchased four slaves—Frances and her son Simon, seamstress Naoma, and twenty-four-year-old carpenter William—in Charleston to add to the family retainers.[14] This subject, too, he had to broach diffidently to his wife, who already had charge of more slaves than she cared to have and found supervision as irksome as did her husband. Rachel and Wiley had been traded to Thomas Decrow as partial payment for the third interest in Decrow's Point, where William was to help erect buildings. The Mavericks had retained nine slaves, including Granville, Jinny, Jinny's children, and a girl named Emeline deeded to Mary as part of her mother's estate.[15]

Maverick justified his purchase of more workers by surmising that, "if they do not turn out as well as I have reason to hope, then all I shall have to do will be to transfer them into hands as good or better than those out of which I took them." He judged Charleston "little better than a slave market," concluding that a curse evidently hung over a slave country, "but as long as we continue in it the way is to submit to the necessity, and to use without abusing the institution."[16]

Maverick's attitude reflected that of many members of his antebellum social class—ethically uneasy over slavery but economically inclined to take advantage of the system. Like many owners, however, Maverick would discover that slaves were often a poor investment.[17] Mary Boykin Chestnut, complaining that her father-in-law's money went to support a "horde" of Africans, would comment that few slaveholders had found either their hatred or love of slavery "remunerative as an investment."[18] Maverick's addition of new mouths to feed and bodies to clothe usually meant increased economic expenditure with little economic return, particularly since the Mavericks' primary need was household help. This need and Maverick's dislike of brandishing authority meant that adult male slaves would gradually be sold off from the Maverick home; by 1850, the couple would own only two adult males, twenty-year-old Jack and thirty-year-old Granville, and eight females. Ten years later, they would own a twenty-two-year-old male, a thirteen-year-old male, and sixteen females, eleven under the age of twelve.[19]

To Mary, more slaves meant more expenditure of her own energies in directing them and more frustration as many of them naturally tried to subvert such control. In the only tart comment in her memoirs, she writes, "This purchase of negroes in Charleston soon proved to be a perfectly worthless investment," and in her diary the next year she rejoiced when Frances, "the most devilish and insolent negro I ever knew in my life," was sent away to be sold.[20]

Maverick did dispatch from New Orleans a more welcome boarder in the form of schoolteacher Lucius Peck, who accepted the tutoring of the oldest Maverick children in order to reside on the coast and improve his health. Peck arrived in late January, in advance of his employer.

Maverick finally reached New Orleans once more on February 1, after stopping in Tuscaloosa to pick up Lizzie. "I am truly sorry to tell you that Elizabeth refused to return," he wrote Mary on February 4.[21] Nor was he yet ready. He was buying building supplies and reluctantly turning toward Mobile to get lumber for the house. "I see every thing holding me back," he wrote. "It won't do for me to go home without material complete for building." He had found only two old letters from Mary waiting in New Orleans, and he feared the family sick. "God save you my love," he prayed, "and keep my poor household from starvation & misery; for their father is a poor, miserable, insufficient man — But he truly loves you all."

At last, on March 9, Maverick departed Mobile by sea, bound for home. Now all too aware of the hazards of Gulf travel, he stopped to pen a letter of farewell to his wife. "Dearest, I leave freely to your good judgt all of my business, which you must administer as you think best," he wrote. "My confidence in you is perfect & unlimited." He gave her leave to marry again, concluding, "But I shall claim in Heaven (I hope) your loving companionship. You gave me your first love, & I have given you my whole heart forever."[22]

As Maverick traveled westward, G. Jones Houston and his brother Ross had arrived at Port Cavallo in response to Maverick's invitation of a few months earlier. Turbulent weather, however, convinced them that they were not interested in settling near the Mavericks. Mary reported that during their visit "the north wind blew almost a gale and the bay rose very high, and the water of the bay seemed higher than the land, as it was driven southward through the Pass."[23] Maverick himself traveled through another threatening gale before arriving with the slaves on March 17, after a five-month absence.

Meanwhile, political events once more required watchfulness on the part of Texans. As Calhoun had predicted, President Polk had signed the act making the annexed Republic a state on December 29, while Maverick was in Charleston. Now, due in part to this action and to another centralist victory in Mexico, a confrontation was looming between the United States and Mexico.

Aware of the tension annexation would cause and eager to reinforce American claims to the Nueces strip, Polk had in June, 1845, dispatched Gen. Zachary Taylor with fifteen hundred men to Corpus Christi, in disputed territory beyond the Nueces. As Maverick returned to Texas, Taylor was marching an expanded force to the Rio Grande on Polk's orders.

In late March, 1846, the general reached the river and established bases at Port Isabel and at a bend of the river opposite Matamoros, a site that came to be known as Fort Brown. On April 12, Mexican commander at Matamoros Gen. Pedro de Ampudia warned Taylor to retreat across the Nueces. Taylor did not. On April 25, Mexican troops sent across the Rio Grande surprised a small American force from Fort Brown, killing eleven and capturing the rest. This gave Polk the impetus he needed for waging war. A few weeks later, after Taylor had proceeded to victories over the Mexican army at Palo Alto and Resaca de la Palma, Polk announced to Congress that a state of war existed because of the April incident in which, he declared, Mexican troops had intruded upon American soil and spilled American blood. The Democrats in Congress responded by quickly producing a war bill, and on May 13, Polk signed the declaration.

Again, Samuel Maverick wished his son and family were safe in Pendleton, as he worried about the likelihood of Mexican schooners making raids along the Texas Coast.[24] To Texans such as the Mavericks, however, this conflict called forth less worry over personal safety and possessions than had previous troubles, for now they had the full power of the United States behind them. Most Texans could simply follow with satisfaction the movements of U.S. Army troops on their southern border and be "gladdened," as Mary wrote, by American victories.

A disquieting note was sounded in August, 1846, however, for those who, like Sam Maverick, maintained an interest in western Texas. Texans still claimed most of the territory of present-day New Mexico, using the Rio Grande as the southern and western boundary. But the Mexican government and residents of New Mexico still disputed the claim, and as part of the annexation treaty Texas had agreed to let the United States settle border questions with Mexico. In August, 1846, Gen. Stephen Kearny occupied Santa Fe with his Army of the West and set up a mixed military-civil government for New Mexico, ignoring Texas claims despite President Polk's assurances that those claims would be considered.

The Texas boundary disputes would drag on, with Maverick eventually becoming involved in the controversy. Meanwhile, the Mavericks continued to call Port Cavallo home and to hope that it and Decrow's Point would become busy communities. In August, sister Lizzie Adams wrote to Mary, "I am very glad to hear you say that Passo Cavallo is improving; I hope it will yet be a flourishing place" attracting "people of worth and intellect; so that in after times you may enjoy yourself sufficiently to compensate for all past privations."[25]

Despite her refusal to return with her brother-in-law some months before, Lizzie was planning to return to the Mavericks as soon as Andrew finished his medical studies and could accompany her. While in Alabama, Lizzie supplied her sister with family news and caustic comments on love and marriage. Conveying the information that brother William had recently married Letitia Ann Goodman in Freestone County, Texas, she added her own thoughts on the institution in response to a missive from Mary. "What did you mean by that long lecture on love and marriage?" Lizzie asked. "Don't catch me in that scrape yet awhile; if ever. Liberty is sweeter to me than matrimony."[26]

In June, 1846, Lizzie reported to Mary the death of brother George in Aberdeen, Mississippi. The cause was identified as both congestive chills and an apoplectic fit. But even this intelligence did not tame her pen for long, for in the same letter she commented that she had not heard again from William and concluded, "Maybe he has not recovered from the fright into which marrying threw him." She also wrote, "You ask me how the young men of Alabama compare with those of Texas; I answer they are a set of sopheads."[27]

Mary sadly recorded her brother's death in her diary. Attributing his waywardness to the early loss of their father, she wrote, "Alas! that a loving sister's hand should have it to record—he grew dissipated—and as a common consequence—fills an early grave."[28] Ten years later, she would write to her second son, Lewis, that if she reprimanded him overmuch for temper, it was only because he reminded her of George, a "generous, brave & gifted" young man who had come to a bad end through the untimely death of his father and through yielding to "an impatient and imperious temper." "Poor fellow his fate was hard," she would write, "and no one but me, I think, understood him if I did."[29]

Mary was gladdened, however, by the arrival at the Pass of her Matagorda friend Maggie Shortridge Pearson, now living in Victoria but visiting the Pass for her daughter's health. Together the women could talk over old times in Tuscaloosa, as well as share their experiences as mothers nursing sick children. Despite the relative healthiness of the Pass, the Maverick offspring were experiencing a medley of childhood ills, with Lewis, Agatha, and Augusta taking whooping cough during the summer and all five children catching the measles in September.

Meanwhile, Maverick was once more anxious to get back to Bexar to better attend to his landholdings, including fighting in court for his claim to some of the acreage he had located. The land picture was still cloudy in Texas, and not only because of the war with Mexico. Conflicting claims had multiplied during the Republic, when thirty million acres had been granted in various attempts to fill the nation's coffers, settle its wild areas, and reward those in its service.[30] During these hectic years the handful of people composing the General Land Office had tried vainly to keep track of it all and prevent duplication of claims. But disputes over landownership could reach back into the eighteenth century to determine who had the right to sell and under what circumstances, and in Maverick's business, he could hardly avoid litigation, either as a plaintiff or as a defendant.[31] Now he was in danger of losing a particularly choice tract.

The elder Samuel, from the perspective of one casting off worldly pursuits, advised his son to concentrate on taking care of himself rather than on traveling around worrying over the lands. "We have plenty

A sketch of San Antonio's Main Plaza showing property in litigation provides an example of Samuel Augustus Maverick's land notations. *Courtesy Barker Texas History Center Map Collection, Austin.*

of this world's goods," Samuel wrote, assuring his offspring that "if we lose the Barrera tract, it is of no earthly consequence whatever, I desire that you employ a lawyer if you think proper at my expense to attend to the suit."[32]

Sam Maverick was fully aware of the problems of holding on to a land empire in light of his father's experiences, and he tried to fight the urge to buy more, reporting to Mary on a November trip to San Antonio that "land I believe is a poor drug yet in this country: Tho' it has risen enough to shut me out from the class of purchasers – or else I am not so *mad* as I used to be." He had even managed to turn a deaf ear to the news of two available leagues fronting on the Rio Grande and regarded the Mexican bearer of the information, who had previously kept him informed of western lands for sale, as a sort of tempter to be resisted.[33] Nonetheless, on this trip Maverick did continue to accrue San Antonio houses and lots. He already owned twenty-two city lots; now he bought three more, in addition to renting out two houses and purchasing a third.[34]

Boarding with Mary's Aunt Ann Bradley, Maverick found much sickness in the city; in fact, one of the Bradley children had died two weeks before his arrival, and Maverick reported the situation so severe that "some hundreds have died." As his wife had done a year before, he marveled at their own good fortune, urging that the two of them "offer up our praise to Almighty God for having suffered us his unworthy poor servants to escape so many and such dread perils, and to enjoy the ineffable bliss of constant love with *all* the pledges of that love under our wings."[35]

Both Mavericks had a sense of being undeservedly blessed, but the tension of feeling about to fall from this state at any moment was beginning to tell on Mary, left so often to wait and wonder. As Maverick went on to Austin in December and failed to return by Christmas, Mary spilled some of the strain into her diary. On December 30, she wrote, "No husband and rumours of Indians at Austin My God oh how many times in this miserable existence have I been reduced to the brink of despair – but yet and at length he always did return let me hope, Oh let me pray a merciful God, a loving Father to allow again that beloved companion to cheer this black and desolate solitude."

Mary's was the cry of many a pioneer wife; indeed, her next plea strikingly paralleled that of Margaret Lea Houston, another young Alabama bride brought to Texas and experiencing her own desolation. Mary mourned, "Oh my husband if you knew the full bitterness of this misery you would not leave us again," and Sam Houston's wife wrote to him, "Oh my love if you could look into my heart at this moment, I know you would never leave me again."[36]

When Maverick did return on January 3, 1847, Mary turned again

New Years-day 1847 sadly passes this day with, ah how miserable I am, how my heart aches. And yet two acquaintances arriving to-day from Port-La Baca assure me that the rumor of indian depredations was altogether false, and they even tell me they had heard of My husbands being safe & in good health. This greatly relieves one for a time - but oh I want confirmation I am afraid they only tell me so to quiet my apparent trouble; his last letter told me he hoped to be with us in 2 weeks - tis nearly four. But blessed be God I can yet hope. I have no certainty of evil. Oh may I not God has again blessed me supremely and now in gratitude I must try to be good. Saturday 7 oclock P.M. my dear husband came back 3rd of Jan 1847 he has been in neither danger or sickness — What happiness inexpressible Bear testimony this heart and hand Our God is all mercy, all love, and my Farther above, the incense of pure love, and adoration ascends from two human hearts to thy footstool this lovely Sabbath. My the poor offering be accepted here in thy sight. Farther son

An 1847 entry from Mary Maverick's 1842–50 diary. *From Maverick Family Papers, Barker Texas History Center, Austin.*

to the diary to record "happiness inexpressible" and praise to a God "all mercy, all love." Again, for a time, she could breathe more easily. But her health reflected an underlying tension, with references to nervous headaches and a sick stomach beginning to make frequent appearances in her diary.

Ironically, after all his narrow escapes on his journeys, Maverick injured himself in March while working on the couple's new house, falling twelve feet down a flight of stairs and absorbing the force of the fall on a shoulder. The accident left him unable to feed himself or to sit up for more than a week. Meanwhile, Andrew and Lizzie had arrived from Alabama to find the family living in the kitchen and outhouses of the new home. Lizzie once more moved in with her sister, and Andrew returned to his farm on the San Marcos River.

In April, Mary planted garden seeds and the Mavericks moved into their long-awaited house, a spacious three-story frame building constructed to withstand Gulf tempests. Barely had they settled in before Maverick was once more on the road to San Antonio, his shoulder aching on the long horseback ride. In the city he found a large number of soldiers forming a cavalry regiment to join U.S. troops fighting the Mexican war. Two months before, General Taylor had won the Battle of Buena Vista. Now San Antonio brimmed again with adventurers looking for action. Their commander, old Maverick friend Col. John Coffee "Jack" Hays, was at Seguin marrying Susan Calvert, with Aunt Ann's daughter Mary Bradley in attendance. When Mary, a favorite of the Mavericks, returned, Sam Maverick tried to entice her to join his wife on the coast for awhile, but without success.[37]

Actually, despite the new house and garden, the Mavericks were seriously considering returning to Bexar. "It is understood here that you are coming: and that I will not be far behind," wrote Maverick to his wife on May 3, "'tho without your determination, they think I would never return."

Maverick's statement has an ironic undertone. Although in her memoirs Mary talks as if she were eager to return to the "dear old place" of her early married years, it is apparent that Maverick himself motivated the move. He had tried to stay busy on the coast, improving Decrow's Point and buying a half interest in the steamboat *Delta*.[38] However, as Mary reported, through his trips to the city he was "making new investments and knitting his interest and his sentiments more and more with the life and growth of San Antonio and the surrounding country."[39]

In Bexar, Maverick could return to his first love, for despite his rejection of the leagues on the Rio Grande a few months before, he was still buying certificates. In 1849, S. W. Fisher of Matagorda would report that he had obtained for Maverick several 640-acre certificates at prices "much inside your limits."[40] Furthermore, when Maverick obtained certificates, he looked to the lands west of San Antonio. He could never turn his eyes from Bexar for long.

Not only did he want to return, but he was hoping to establish a permanent home on land he had purchased on Alamo Plaza, near that "old Golgotha" that held so many memories of revolutionary days.[41] But the ownership of the Alamo mission and its grounds was under dispute. After the 1836 battle, the Alamo had been left neglected, a near-ruin that drew curious observers. Mary Maverick herself prepared a sketch of the structure for her father-in-law sometime between 1838 and 1848.[42]

In 1841, the Republic had granted the mission to the Roman Catholic Church, but with the annexation of Texas, the U.S. government claimed the complex as an old fort. In July, 1847, Maverick wrote from Port Cavallo to Cap. S. M. Howe of the United States Army contingent in San Antonio concerning the Alamo's ownership. If it was indeed an old fort, the military could lay claim to it, but if it was a mission, the military could not rightfully appropriate it. Maverick erroneously insisted that the Alamo had not been used as a fort by the Mexican military until 1835, when General Cós converted the structure by casting down the church arches in order to make a cannon ramp and erecting various cannon mounds.[43] He urged the military commanders in Bexar to talk with the old Mexican residents of the town to confirm this, concluding that his own "foolish prejudice" to reside on the spot from which he had made "almost a solitary escape" led him not to ask a favor but to "confidently look for justice."[44]

Meanwhile, the Mavericks still owned their home on the northeast corner of San Antonio's Main Plaza, and in October they packed up their belongings and headed once more for this residence. Mary, Lizzie, and the younger children, with servant Betsy, who was Jinny's daughter and George's nurse, traveled by stage from Lavaca to San Antonio while Maverick, the two older boys, and the other servants moved the family's belongings northward in wagons.

The move, of course, meant that the family would be less isolated, with relatives and old friends to welcome them in San Antonio. Yet Mary expressed some ambivalence, writing in her diary, "I felt really sad to leave; any place which is not disagreeable and has been a home 3 years, is loved. We leave here a delightful summer house, fine gardening soil, the fish and the sea breeze, etc." However, there was no use looking backward, and with a touch of out-of-character sarcasm, she concluded, "We will surely find something in exchange in that earthly Eden Bejar."

They left a few of the slaves, including Jinny and her son Jack, on the peninsula—not at Decrow's Point but farther up the sandy strip at Tiltonia, a farm that Maverick had bought in February from Charles Tilton. By their agreement, Maverick was to pay Tilton three dollars a head for an undetermined number of cattle calculated at about 450, with any over that number gratis. In addition, Tilton was to sell Maverick his land and houses for five hundred dollars "and to throw in without charge whatever hogs there may be, also an ox cart and ox yoke, and all lumber, logs &c lying about the premises."[45]

The purchase was significant because it began Maverick's less-than-successful venture into cattle raising, an enterprise that would eventually give rise to the term "maverick" to denote an unbranded calf or independent thinker.[46] Informed of the investment by letter, the elder Samuel's mind strayed back sixty years to a time when his Uncle William Turpin's firm took five or six hundred head of cattle in payment for a debt and drove them to Pendleton, "then a good wild pasture." He reported that the experiment proved a bother and financial failure. "Cattle like an army of men don't thrive," he concluded. "They can't be kept & fattened that way, the very smell of one another gives them disease."[47]

There was no such problem with land, of course, and despite Samuel's admonitions to his son to disentangle himself from worldly business cares, he could not resist further advice in this department. "I would sell no lands at present," he wrote two months before the Mavericks returned to San Antonio. Instead, he urged his son to "be patient; you will have flood time before long" with water falls "like gold mines to your Boys to establish Cotton Mills."[48]

Indeed, Sam Maverick's return to San Antonio signaled the beginning of a renewed emphasis on land buying and land locating that would make him one of the two biggest investors in West Texas acreage during the 1850s and 1860s.[49] Again, the potential for frontier settlement looked promising; "flood time" seemed to be around the corner. A few months after the Mavericks' return, the Treaty of Guadalupe Hidalgo brought peace between Mexico and the United States, with the former acknowledging the Rio Grande as the boundary between the two nations and ceding to the United States most of New Mexico and Arizona, as well as the portions of Colorado and Wyoming it held, and all of Nevada, Utah, and Alta California.

San Antonio itself was beginning to attract a larger number of emigrants from the United States and Europe. In 1846, German scientist Ferdinand Roemer estimated the city's population at 800; by 1850 it was to soar to 3,448.[50]

Bexar was far indeed from an earthly Eden for the returnees. They had to adjust to the dust, extreme heat, and bustling growth; their old home had deteriorated, with floors worn away to dirt and an unkempt garden; colds and diarrhea abounded in the city, with many deaths reported. Still, it was pleasant to visit with the Bradleys and with other old friends, such as the Elliotts, and to hope that health and fortunes would improve.

Maverick was soon on the move west again, during the Christmas season surveying property and potential silver mines around Enchanted Rock. While he was gone, on the afternoon of December 24, 1847, Mary gave birth to the couple's sixth child and fourth boy, Willie, after two nights and days of labor. Despite the long labor and severe afterpains, she reported that she "recovered sooner than common." But the baby "dwindled to a skeleton," with dysentery "in spite of all attention," and it was not till mid-April that she could report him improving.[51]

By this time, her husband was off on another surveying trip to one of his favorite locations, near the headwaters of Las Moras Creek, where he planned to locate his headright.[52] The Comanches were still strong in this area beyond the settlements, and Mary wrote in her diary, "It is dangerous, but I have been tried so often this way I have almost grown callous to fear and thus I confidently expect him back again."

On his surveying expeditions, Sam Maverick was penetrating to the edge of territory explored by Anglo Texans, and May, 1848, found him on the Rio Grande at the mouth of Las Moras Creek in present-day Maverick County. Here in the juncture between the two streams, he wrote to his wife on May 9, was "one of the prettiest spots on earth on a splendid mesquite plain." When Maverick wrote, the surveying

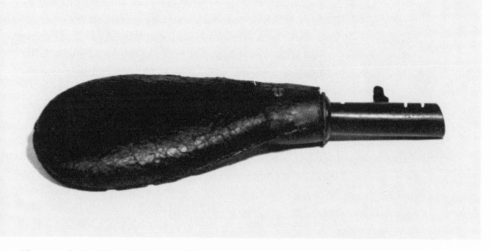

Shot pouch that Samuel Augustus Maverick carried with him on his surveying trips. *Courtesy Texas Memorial Museum, Acc#263, Austin.*

party of fourteen men had already located surveys along the Rio Grande, explored northwestward until they reached a stretch of the "Puerco," or Devil's River in present Val Verde County, and were now preparing to locate acreage along the creek. "My avaricious (or land loving fury) is fully satisfied," Maverick assured Mary, "and we have the best land in the country & a plenty of it."

The outdoor living and work, as always, agreed with him. "I am in the best of health & a most voracious appetite," he wrote. However, as always, despite his obvious pleasure in the work and the strenuous life, he expressed worry about how Mary and the children were faring, and vowed that "all this is nothing—not worth a moment's considera-tion compared with the health of my family." Letters from San An-tonio had reached the camp without any word from Mary, who had been nursing sickly four-month-old Willie when her husband left. Uneasily, Maverick anticipated that it would take another month to finish his survey and return home. "This is all I ask," he wrote. "God protect my own beloved wife my daughters & my brave boys."[53]

Across the letter Mary Maverick wrote, "What sorrow unutterable in reserve for my poor husband!" Just a few hours before Maverick penned his missive at Las Moras, seven-year-old Agatha, whom the couple had lovingly nursed through more than her share of childhood mishaps, died after a sudden, painful illness of over a week. She was a victim of bilious fever and, her mother suspected, of stomach problems brought on by eating too many whole green mustang grapes. "My God oh my God grant me submission," Mary wrote in her diary, "'twas thy will, to it, thou knowest, I endeavor to yield. Oh comfort her poor fond father, who on his return will find this, his favourite earthly treasure, gone, gone—all dead and buried."[54]

Indeed, this eldest daughter had been Maverick's favorite, and his letters home since her birth repeatedly asked after "my blue-eyed one, my Agatha," first among the children. From Perote, Maverick had written longingly, "Are Agatha's eyes the same shade of blue?"[55] Mary later wrote in her memoirs that the child "was the idol of her father, and in return for his devoted affection for her, she idolized him."[56] Mary evidenced a deep devotion toward all her children and a strong sense of responsibility for their welfare.

Agatha's death was to alter permanently the way her mother and father looked at the world. No longer could they feel a Divine Providence ordering and protecting their affairs, nor would they be able to draw much comfort from each other. Theirs was a mutually loving and supportive relationship, but Maverick had chosen to be absent so often and he and Mary had each idealized the other too much. She was his "good angel," his "blessed Mary"; he was a man "by nature eminently just and gentle."[57] Now two real, aching human beings were to experience a sense of disorientation that would affect their relationship by plummeting Mary into spiritual turmoil and her husband into grieving withdrawal.

Maverick came home earlier than expected, two weeks after the death, but without any suspicion of what awaited him. Eleven miles outside San Antonio, he met an acquaintance and learned of his daughter's passing. Mary later related that her husband went immediately to the grave and "threw himself down upon it," then came home and announced that he was trying not to murmur at God's will. "He said we should humble ourselves in sack cloth and ashes," she wrote, "and he never removed that sack cloth in spirit whilst he lived—was ever after a sad changed man."[58]

10

"Oh World of Trial! Oh World of Grief!"

THROUGH THE MONTHS after Agatha's death, her parents could find no relief for their sorrow. "Cursed land, cursed money," Maverick said, "I would give all, all to see her *once* more. She has wandered off in the dark and we will never more on Earth be able to find her." To his father he wrote, "Oh, Almighty and all just God, teach us how it is that the poor little boon of the breath of life, could not be spared from thy great storehouse to animate a little dear thing which thou hast made so perfect."[1]

The elder Maverick in Pendleton could only commiserate from his own sad experience, communicating that, "I have before went through the same horrors, that you and Mary now feel" with the death of Sam's four-year-old sister Caroline in 1809. The loss "put a damper on me, and partly weaned me from the world, made it insipid, and almost worthless," he wrote. "My path has been checkered & rugged ever since, nor can I see through the mysterious ways of providence."[2]

Mary Maverick was struggling with these mysterious ways in her diary, wrestling with two basic questions. *Could* it be the will of God that had caused this thing "which wrings our hearts with almost incurable agony"? Or could it be "some neglected or violated law of nature" in which she and her husband had to assume culpability? She sought peace through prayer and confession of human unworthiness in her diary, like her mate figuratively humbling herself in sackcloth and ashes.[3]

Meanwhile, there were earthly cares to attend to, including the wants and needs of five other children. Augusta had taken the same fever a few days after her sister's death, but quickly recovered, and baby Willie continued to fare poorly, almost dying of dysentery during the summer before Mary found pomegranate root tea to be a strengthening elixir.

Mary's correspondence and diaries attest to the fact that she, like most women, shouldered a heavy load of responsibility in regard to curing illness in the family. Medical doctors might or might not be available; if they were, their knowledge might be scant, as an individual could set himself up as a physician with little or no medical training. Even if a doctor were relatively well trained, he might be schooled in a method of treatment actually injurious to the patient, as was the case with the physician who nearly killed the young Sam Maverick by giving him a cathartic when he had chills.

Thus, the family nurturer felt compelled to be a doctor as well, with the lives of her family depending on her knowledge and skill. Mary sadly recorded a promising treatment for bilious fever in her diary the summer after her daughter's death, lamenting the fact that "for all we may read and think knowledge only comes after sad experience."[4]

While the Mavericks nursed their grief, more auspicious events were occurring in their extended family, with Aunt Ann Bradley and sister Lizzie both marrying and departing San Antonio. Most of Aunt Ann's children were grown when she entered into a second union, this time with John Allen Veatch, a forty-year-old captain of the Texas Mounted Volunteers guarding the frontier. She went to live with him in his camp on the Rio Grande, leaving her youngest daughters Pauline and Ada boarding with a woman on the Salado.[5]

Twenty-five-year-old Lizzie moved back to the coast, the bride of Bob Clow, a genial thirty-seven-year-old merchant from Pennsylvania who had courted her before the family departed Port Cavallo. Clow lived at Saluria, another tiny Matagorda Bay community. On April 29, he had arrived in San Antonio and the couple had begun making wedding preparations. No sooner had they started than Agatha was struck with her fatal illness. Two weeks after the girl's death, Lizzie and Clow were married in a quiet early morning ceremony and left immediately on the stage for Saluria.

Lizzie's first letter from her new community in June encouraged the Mavericks to return to the coast, promising that "you would now like this side [of the bay] better than the other; and if you would come back, you would remain." Indeed, she vowed to Mary, "if you were only living here, then I would be perfectly contented." Mary's response indicated that the Mavericks instead were planning to build a new home in San Antonio, for Lizzie in July wrote, "From the tenor of your letter I imagine you will not return here, which is not surprising; for with an elevated, airy house you would be much better situated where you are."[6]

The Mavericks talked of moving away from their old house, which now contained such painful memories, but they stayed on the corner of the Main Plaza, and Maverick began to show physically the strain of his daughter's loss. Jack Hays, appointed commander of an exploring expedition to El Paso, wanted the forty-five-year-old Maverick to accompany him and brushed aside Mary's protest that her husband was not well by arguing, "Don't you see Mr. Maverick is dying by inches? Everyone remarks how gray he has grown, how bent and feeble he looks, and this will be the very thing for him—he always thrives on hardships, and his mind must be distracted now from his grief." Mary wrote, "I recognized the truth and force of this reasoning and that Hays loved him dearly and I set to work to persuade him to go."[7]

San Antonio merchants had raised eight hundred dollars for Hays' expedition, an attempt to find an all-season trade route between the Texas settlements and Mexican Chihuahua. Commerce existed between Chihuahua and El Paso, a ranching headquarters on the Rio Grande that was just becoming a way station for California-bound gold seekers and cattle drovers. Therefore, if the expedition could find a good route to El Paso, the undertaking would prove a success.

For the most part, they would be traveling over lands inhabited only by roaming bands of Indians. Castroville, founded in 1844 by European emigrants and situated twenty-five miles to the west of San Antonio, was the only community in the almost six hundred–mile stretch between Bexar and El Paso, aside from a few small Mexican enclaves along the Rio Grande. Men such as Hays and Maverick had ranged up to two hundred miles west and southwest of San Antonio, but beyond that, little was known of the territory.

Promoters hoped that the fixing of a route to El Paso would not only draw some of the Santa Fe–Mexico trade into Texas but provide the first link of a highway to San Diego and San Francisco. The U.S. military, too, planned to send a contingent of soldiers along to study how to deploy troops along this arid, intimidating frontier.[8]

On August 27, 1848, a party of thirty-five citizens with Maverick among them departed San Antonio under Hays' command, accompanied by a band of Delaware Indian guides and a Mexican named

Lorenzo who claimed to know the territory beyond Devil's River. Hays calculated the distance to El Paso to be about seven hundred miles and planned to make the round trip within three months. He knew it would be a difficult passage, but not how difficult. Before their outward journey was over, they would be chewing shoe leather, looking forward to the taste of stringy pack mule, scrambling along seemingly endless rock ledges, and suffering a thousand torments of heat and thirst.

At Hays' request, and out of personal habit, Maverick kept an abbreviated journal of the expedition, meticulously recording miles traveled. Seldom on this journey did he record more than locations and distances. At Fredericksburg, the civilian contingent met Capt. Samuel Highsmith's company of thirty-five soldiers, an aide, a surgeon, and Delaware Indian chief John Connor. Together they proceeded southwestward to the headwaters of Las Moras Creek, crossed a stream already known as Maverick's Creek, and camped on San Pedro Creek, where Maverick recorded in his journal for September 19 that he had dreamed of "my poor dear Tita [Agatha] and of Augusta and Mary."9

Now the toughest part of the expedition began as they worked their way "roughly along the great northward curve of the Rio Grande."10 First the explorers faced the Puerco, or Devil's River, so named by them because of the difficulty they met in crossing the twisting stream. To advance one mile could mean eight treacherous fordings, and the high banks and chasms bordering the water forced the men to walk and lead their horses between crossings.11 Finally leaving the river, they pushed northward to the Pecos, fighting intense thirst and chewing their boot tops along the way. "To the Pecos — *in great thirst*," Maverick recorded on September 26.

The muddy, swift stream proved to be even more difficult than Devil's River. The men crossed and recrossed, at one point "crawling like flies" on the side of a mountain and gaining only three miles for the day.12 On October 2, they reached the Rio Grande, where Maverick recorded, "We killed and ate a panther."13 Now they stayed close to the stream, conscious that they could not stray far from this water source. Maverick's entry of October 7 shows their predicament: "7TH. Going W.N.W. Camp on edge of impassable ravine. Go back 1/2 m. to water horses. No food on hand; had scant breakfast. Here we begin to eat bear grass. 16 [miles]."

They met a band of Apaches who directed them to an Indian trail, but Indians also stole some of their horses and mules, the latter now prized as a food source. By October 12, one member of the party had gone out of his head with hunger and "rode off in a fury," as Maverick noted in his journal. Attempts to capture and hold him were unsuccessful. The explorers pushed onward, crossing to the Mexican side of the river to avoid the intimidating canyons of the Big Bend. They went without food for twelve days before reaching the Mexican settlement of San Carlos, where they rested and bought provisions. From San Carlos, it was a relatively easy journey along the Mexican side of the river to another settlement, Presidio del Norte, where they again crossed the river and entered the private American trading post of Fort Leaton.

At the fort, the expedition stopped. The men were worn out, and Highsmith's orders included a fast-approaching time limit. Besides, they were within 150 miles of El Paso, with a known and level route existing between the trading post and the town. Thus, Hays and Highsmith determined to turn around. First, however, the men rested for more than a week, having traveled almost 750 miles.[14]

Hays and Highsmith determined to try an alternate route on their return trip, and on the last day of the month the expedition set out over relatively level land to the northeast. Again, they had to go long periods without water, but cool weather arrived to reduce their thirst. The men recrossed the Pecos and, realizing that they were too far north, began moving downstream. "The Pecos water is quite salt but I like to drink it," Maverick confided in one journal entry.

They spent eleven days traversing the Pecos before striking off northeast again, then southeast to the headwaters of Devil's River. Here the expedition, facing a continuing scarcity of water, divided into three groups. The soldiers took a direct route toward their headquarters, twenty-eight of the civilians moved on a direct route to San Antonio, and Hays and thirteen others, including Maverick, slowed to explore the Moras area.

Further investigating the area he had delighted in on surveying expeditions, Maverick soon let his land-appraisal instincts surface. "League of fine mesquite and live oak land here," he wrote on December 1, camping north of Las Moras Spring. "Prime land, timber and water and very suitable for a ranch, & fat deer."

A reminder that this land was not very safe came in the form of two Comanches herding fourteen stolen horses and transporting a Mexican boy. Hays' group recovered the Mexican captive and horses and captured one of the Comanches, but when he escaped, they had to begin camping without a fire to avoid meeting a hostile Indian band. Despite such dangers, the small group arrived in San Antonio on December 10, having shortened their route to 556 miles on the trip home. Hays recommended Highsmith's return route to the federal government, but actually the whole expedition, going and coming, had blazed too tortured and circuitous a trail to be successful. The significance of the Hays-Highsmith Expedition lay in the fact that it spurred Gen. William Jenkins Worth to send a Topographical Engineers expedition to study the route. This study, conducted in 1849, resulted in a "lower route" across West Texas, which became "an important link in the western military road system."[15] At the same time, Robert Simpson Neighbors and John S. Ford were surveying an equally useful northern trail.

Despite the Hays-Highsmith Expedition's lack of success, the rigors of wilderness survival had renewed Maverick's health and spirits. Lewis reported to his grandfather Samuel in a letter that "Papa" had come back from the expedition "fat," and Mary reported that Hays had called him the "most enduring and least complaining man of the party." She judged her husband returning in improved health and in a "more cheerful and hopeful" frame of mind.[16] Mary, too, was feeling much better able to cope with the uncertainties of life, for in her husband's absence she had experienced a spiritual renewal, joining the fledgling Methodist church in the city with Hays' wife, Susan, with whom she had developed a deep friendship.

Mary had always possessed strong religious and moralistic leanings, but seldom since coming to the frontier had she had a chance to participate in a church. Now, though she still preferred to worship in the Episcopal faith, she entered wholeheartedly into the Protestant community that was available just when she most needed spiritual direction to help her deal with Agatha's death. She also read religious works, mentioning in her diary Martin Luther's writings and Swiss historian Jean-Henri Merle d'Aubigné's popular *History of the Reformation*. On October 22, 1848, the day that her husband reached Presidio del Norte at the meeting of the Río Conchos and Rio Grande, Mary wrote in her journal, "Calm & sacred & holy is the joy of my soul O God most high. For thou hast visited and redeemed through the sacrifice of the *lamb* which taketh away the sins of the world."

With the passing of the difficult year 1848, reunited with her husband and with her five surviving children in good health, Mary optimistically confided to her diary, "New Years day 1849 bright and beautiful, delightful temperature and cheerful hopes!!" But that very month, cholera appeared on the coast and began working its deadly way into the inland settlements.

Sam Maverick was ready to rid himself of his coastal investments, which were not proving at all profitable. Lizzie had written the summer before that the cattle at Tiltonia were "starving for grass and water," and Jinny was fretting in her caretaker position, anxious to see her children with the Mavericks in San Antonio.[17] In addition, the coastal communities were not developing as Maverick had hoped. In early 1849, Decrow's Point, where he had planned to erect and rent buildings, had only Thomas Decrow as a resident, and of Port Cavallo Lizzie wrote, "an uglier more deserted looking place you cannot imagine."[18]

Finally, the steamboat *Delta* had turned out to be, in Maverick's words, "dead capital." In late January, he wrote Decrow that they had better sell it and promised to visit in the spring "for the purpose of either selling or moving my cattle" to the Cibolo, "as they will not prosper on their present grass."[19]

Another tempting opportunity was unfolding for enterprising men in early 1849—reports of riches were filtering in from the California goldfields. "I hope you will not think about the gold of Calif[ornia]," Samuel wrote to his son on February 12. Two weeks later, Lizzie wrote to Mary, "Have you the California fever? The ladies seem not to have escaped its infection." However, she added, she had heard from an acquaintance that "Mr. Maverick has sworn off from wild trips: so I suppose you will now make a settlement for life."[20]

Nothing in the record indicates that Maverick felt the lure of California, but a number of the men of his extended family did. Captain Veatch became a goldseeker, leaving Ann after less than a year of marriage and going on to an illustrious career as a scientific curator, geologist, and professor in California and Oregon.[21] Mary's brother Andrew, who had been serving as a surgeon in Veatch's frontier company, also started for California. And Robert Clow, always struggling to keep his latest mercantile venture solvent, talked more than once of becoming a forty-niner in the long, affectionate, and chatty letters that he wrote to his sister-in-law.

Clow and Lizzie had moved to Lavaca shortly after their marriage, with Clow dissolving a faltering Saluria business partnership. The couple traveled in the fall to the old Alabama home place, where Robert Adams, now a Baptist minister, lived. When they returned, Clow stocked a Lavaca store with goods bought in New Orleans.

His letters to Mary show a genuine openness and affection that endeared him to her and provided a contrast to her own husband's increasingly withdrawn nature. In 1852, she would record a visit from the Lavaca merchant in her diary with the words, "He is so full of life & hope & good fellowship to all—great company—a general favourite."[22]

Mary and her brother-in-law early formed an alliance based on what to do about the independent Lizzie. Three months into his marriage, Clow wrote in frustration to Mary of his wife's "horror at some future day of being cursed (!) with a *squalling* family." He reported that some of the ladies of Lavaca had teased her on the subject, eliciting the comment that "she prefers death."[23]

Lizzie was already more than a month pregnant when her husband wrote, and as her pregnancy progressed she refused to discuss the subject with him. In February, 1849, two months away from delivery, Lizzie abruptly left Lavaca to stay "until after a *certain event,*" Clow wrote, at Mrs. Nash's boardinghouse near Seguin, where she had once stopped with Mary. She would not even agree to take their one slave, Mary, brought from Alabama.[24]

Mary wanted to take her sister to Sutherland Springs, mineral springs a short journey southeast of San Antonio, and stay with her there. Clow heartily approved the plan. "I cannot feel satisfied unless I *know* you are with her," the expectant father wrote, answering Mary's "several inquiries" by informing her that "I think the '*certain event*' will take place between now and the last of Ap'l, I do not believe that she has prepared herself with any information on the subject, unless she done so previous to marriage, but up to the point she left she stood that *peculiar situation* better than anyone I ever knew."[25]

Even as Clow wrote, his wife was returning to Lavaca, having judged Mrs. Nash's too public and having spent almost a week with Mary in San Antonio, where she apparently had become reconciled to her fate. Her niece's death so close to Lizzie's marriage may have put a dread of childbearing into her, but Lizzie had always acted cynical about love, marriage, and babies and continued to do so, with her devoted husband staunchly insisting that she had a tender, maternal side. On April 18, Lizzie gave birth to a daughter, Kate, at Lavaca. In reporting the event to Mary, Clow commented, "Our Bl[ac]k Mary will follow *suit* in two weeks—& then I will have to be *nurse* cook & washer. This is rather too much—of a good thing."[26]

As Clow wrote happily about his new daughter, the Mavericks were about to lose their second one, just when Mary began to become somewhat reconciled to the loss of the first. On March 7 she had recorded in her diary that with Agatha's death she "lost all concentrativeness except on religious subjects," but that God had granted her a spirit of resignation and calm. Maverick himself was working to establish an Episcopal church in San Antonio, banding together with a number of other prominent Anglo citizens to make an unsuccessful offer of "at least 450 dollars" for one year of service by an Episcopal clergyman.[27]

Maverick gave generously of his time and money to the church that was eventually established, but he did not enter as wholeheartedly as did his wife into religious inquiry and church work. A highly rational man facing a seemingly irrational world where children could die suddenly, he, like his father, subscribed primarily to a fatalistic faith in an almighty power.

He would need whatever faith he could muster as sickness drew closer and closer to the Maverick door. Influenza, smallpox, and cholera were all spreading through the Texas settlements in those early months of 1849. The latter struck Bexar's Mexican population at the beginning of April, then thrust its way into the Anglo-American community. Mary wrote vividly of the "fear and dread" the scourge brought: "Into every house came the pestilence, in most houses was death, and in some families one-half died! All had symptoms and the weather continued close and damp and dismal. Men of strong nerve and undoubted courage shrank in fear—many drank hard and died drunk—one poor fellow cut his throat when attacked."[28] She reported twenty-one cholera deaths in San Antonio on one day, April 22. The night before, the Mavericks' only remaining daughter, six-year-old Augusta, had had a dream that made her mother tremble to hear. The girl talked of wearing a flowing white dress and riding in a carriage to a church in which people dressed in white were gathered. "It was prophesy of her shroud and burial and resurrection," wrote Mary, for on the evening of April 23, Augusta became ill and by nine the next morning, she was dead. "Oh world of trial! Oh world of grief," Mary wrote in her diary. Shortly before Augusta died, Mary had gathered her onto her lap and asked her if she wanted to see God and her sister. "Yes, mama," she replied.

"They buried her the next day by the side of Tita," Mary wrote in her memoirs. "I could not go."[29]

The grieving mother could not attend in part because she herself had been stricken with cholera, as had sons Lewis and George. In fact, everyone in the house except eldest son Sam and slave Betsy experienced the illness to some extent. All rallied except for Augusta. "Both my beautiful ones gone and no girl to grace & gladden our fireside," Mary recorded sadly in her diary.

As the Mavericks groped for some way to deal with their latest loss, father Samuel in Pendleton reported his own deterioration in health from a possible mild stroke. He explained that his tongue was "thickened in articulating words," his walk "weak & stumbling."[30] Only a few months earlier, Samuel had contemplated his march toward death in a letter, promising his son and daughter-in-law to "not forget or neglect if it is in my power, to convey your love to dear Agatha," as well as to share with them "all the information concerning the Great first cause, & the destiny of man" if possible. Yet the latter he considered unlikely, having deceased friends who had futilely promised to do the same.[31]

As Samuel struggled with his new infirmities, his daughter-in-law remained prostrate with illness and grief. Finally, in July, Sam Maverick took his family to Sulphur Springs on the Cibolo to recuperate, and Mary recorded in her diary that the exercise did her good, as she "had never sat up one entire day before since the death of my gentle Augusta" two and a half months earlier. Still, they could not escape illness by removing to the small community on the Cibolo, and the death of a girl in a house in which the Mavericks were staying overcame Mary once more. "We felt no improvement by our visit to the springs," she notes later in her memoirs. One good change came out of the visit, however, for while Mary and the boys remained briefly on the Cibolo, Sam Maverick moved their household goods to an old Mexican home he had bought on Alamo Plaza as a prelude to building their own two-story house nearby.

After their return to San Antonio, the Maverick boys continued to experience a medley of ills, from bilious fever to chickenpox. But as another hard summer waned, their mother, pregnant yet again, began to gain a sense of control by changing doctors and beginning a study of alternative medical treatments, which she would pursue avidly through her remaining child-bearing and child-rearing years.

The early nineteenth century had seen the rise of botanical medical systems that challenged standard medical doctrines. Practitioners rejected mercurial medicines and such harsh treatments as bloodletting, instead favoring agreeably administered botanical remedies. Mothers in particular were attracted to the mild, natural treatments, which promised less suffering for their children. Many embraced the Thomsonian system, a highly popular approach to health.

Samuel Thomson, a New Hampshire farmer, had turned to steam baths and herbal remedies to improve the health of his often-ill wife and children. By 1839, he claimed three million followers, almost one-sixth of the population of the United States.[32] Mary found the Thomsonian approach much to her liking, calling it "a harmless & safe system" and resolving, "Now I will not dread every sickness as death but with God's blessing will hope for health again."[33]

Still, she mourned the deaths of her daughters. "O God teach me resignation," she prayed in her journal, "and the blessed truth *always* that *thou* hast taken them. How else can human nature ever be reconciled." Her solace lay in thinking of Agatha and Augusta as angel spirits, occasionally touching her own all-too-human one with their presence.

They appeared to her in a dream that summer. She had had other dreams of them, but in this one, Mary dared to ask Agatha if she was happy in heaven. Agatha did not reply, looking uncomfortable with the question, and Mary could only berate herself as an infidel for even asking. Yet she praised God for these dream moments, "the meeting of angel spirits with mine, yet vile and unclean."[34]

She drew little solace from anyone during this difficult time. Susan Hays had become a treasured friend, but she was yet childless. Sister Lizzie wrote fond condolences, admitting that as a new mother, "I can to some extent understand what your feelings must be, when compelled to resign to the cold earth the child that has drawn nourishment from your breast." However, at the same time, Lizzie continued to exhibit a tactlessly callous attitude toward motherhood, writing flippantly to her bereaved sister that during the first few days of daughter Kate's life "I was on thorns for fear she would live: but as I saw she did not gratify my selfishness, I began to think better of the matter, and now I like the little brat very well."[35]

Mary could not look to her husband for loving companionship in grief at this point either, for in September she complained for the first and only time in her journal of his lack of sympathy, his silence and aloofness. The fault, she wrote, must be her own, as "I thought him by nature eminently just and gentle." Yet part of her rebelled at the idea when considering the devotion she had felt toward her mate. "If I had lov'd & served the Lord my God with half the devotion—he would not turn away or leave me desolate in the days of my affliction," she asserted. In the next entry, however, she repented such harsh thoughts, concluding, "My poor husband is very unhappy. He has lost all his precious daughters and like Rachel 'will not be comforted,'" as he could not after all believe the deaths a part of God's will. "His grief is ever fresh," she wrote, "& at times appears moroseness or utter indifference to all things—approaching despair."[36]

No cheering news was coming from Pendleton, where on September 15 Samuel wrote in a failing hand of the death of Sam Maverick's nephew Augustus Weyman in his last year at West Point. "Augustus wrote me that he hoped to finish his studies & graduate in June next, & I wrote & advised him to go to you in San Antonio," Samuel explained. But "God only knows what is Best to be done in this Life. We must all trust in the living God to guide us through this life. I feel very badly over this . . . bereavement."

These lines ended the last legible letter the elder Maverick would write, for in early November he suffered a stroke that would render him almost helpless. In addition to carrying the news of his grandson's death, Samuel's final missive amply illustrates many of the themes of his long correspondence with his far-away son. "Land is the only article now in the U.S. that is selling for less than its intrinsic Value," he wrote, inquiring not for the first time whether Sam had obtained clear title to Rio Grande lands. The admonitions were there, too: "For Heave[n's] sake take care of my dear *Son*. If you & I both die shortly it would ruin the whole family. Lydia Ann writes me that she is afraid that WVWyck looks badly."[37]

It was the Van Wycks, however, who returned to Pendleton from New York after the stroke to begin a long stewardship of the elder Samuel and his affairs. Both William and Lydia wrote Maverick as the year neared its end, urging him to come and see his father.

Maverick instead wrote his father in December listing some treatments for paralysis and signing the missive "Yr undutiful & repentant son."[38] He was hemmed in by more immediate cares—the impending birth of an eighth child, his wife's and his own weakened emotional states, plans for a new house on Alamo Plaza at last, and administra-

tion of his business affairs. Tax records show that in 1848 he was paying taxes in Bexar County on thirty San Antonio town lots and on
over eighty thousand acres of land, including the eleven thousand held
in trust for the elder Samuel's grandchildren.[39] In addition to these
holdings and his coastal properties, he held large tracts in Guadalupe,
Gillespie, and San Patricio counties.

On the coast, the cattle remained a problem he was not quite willing to relinquish. General Somervell had offered him half a league on
the Lavaca River in exchange for the beeves, and in November John
Graham wrote from Matagorda that the Maverick slave Jack "finds it
quite impossible to pen and brand your cattle on the Peninsula and
the stock is consequently becoming more wild and unmanageable
daily."[40] Maverick had devised a brand by adding to the previous owner's brand, changing it from

Yet many of the cattle were indeed going unbranded, and this was to
give rise to references to any unbranded cattle as "mavericks."[41]

Another letter from the coast in November came from Lizzie, who
now in her worry over her sister's mental state began to write Mary
in a more sensitive vein, as well as a sensible one. A mutual acquaintance had visited Lavaca and "spoke in the most feeling manner of
your sad misfortune and the lonely life which you now lead," Lizzie
reported. "She says you have but one fault, that is you are entirely
too good." Lizzie warned her sister against letting "unavailing sorrow"
overcome her and "throw a shadow over your home," affecting the
dispositions of her children as the sadness in their own childhood
home had affected the Adams siblings. "Other and brighter feelings
will come," Lizzie predicted.[42]

Indeed, in December Mary's diary entries show that she had achieved
a greater degree of tranquillity. She always seemed to become imbued
with spiritual strength during the Christian holy days, a condition
reflected by the fact that prayers of praise replaced pained pleas for faith
and victory over the flesh in the private journal. With the new year,
she received spiritual succor from the civilian Episcopalian church effort newly established by John F. Fish, the U.S. military post chaplain
assigned to the San Antonio garrison.

The Mavericks' sixth boy, John Hays, was born in February and given his name in honor of Maverick ancestors named John and the Mavericks' friend John Hays. He was a small and sickly infant from the start, leading visitors to speculate that he could not live long. Mary rejected their prognosis, determined to nurse this one to health. "Yet am I thankful 'tis not a girl," she admitted to her diary, and she again fell into long periods of bleak despair. "Mrs. Elliott tells me that you have lost all life and spirits," Lizzie wrote in late May, adding, "I think you should rouse yourself up, take a trip someplace" so that Mary could lose herself in "action and variety."[43]

But once more, Mary was putting most of her energies into the tending of a sick baby. Second son Lewis wrote to his grandfather and the Van Wycks in Pendleton that the baby was beginning to grow healthy on goat's milk and that his mother "thinks he gets better every day."[44] The child had been baptized along with Willie on April 4, the same day their father was elected a vestryman by the members of Fish's small Episcopal congregation. Mary hopefully recorded the infant's slight weight gains through June and early July, only to note finally, "July 19th he died of a sudden & violent attack of cholera infantum. . . . In Jesus' name give me faith."

Shortly after the baby's death, Mary's brother Andrew wrote her from Chihuahua, Mexico, where he had been living five months, struggling with bronchitis and continuing to contemplate a trip to California. Unaware of the latest trial his sister had passed through, Andrew nonetheless wrote in the same oppression of spirit she felt, concluding that "[I] long to see the day arrive that I may be enabled to leave this world in peace for Life for grown wearisome."[45]

Lizzie at least refused to adopt such an attitude. On hearing of John Hays' death, she wrote to her sister, "I must renew to you my old advice, traveling. You now have no excuse for not doing so." Mary had apparently protested that she could not afford such activity, for Lizzie wrote in exasperation, "You say that you have not the means to travel. . . . Where are the acres on acres of wild land that your husband possesses?" She argued that Maverick could sell half his holdings and "still have enough left to satisfy even an inordinate craving for land." Thus, she urged Mary to "take my advice, get Mr. Maverick to sell some of that trashy land—and then seek a change."[46]

Lizzie's tart comments in her letters to her sister reflect the fact that Sam Maverick was getting a reputation as a wealthy and eccentrically frugal man. "I understand that you are having a new house built," Liz-

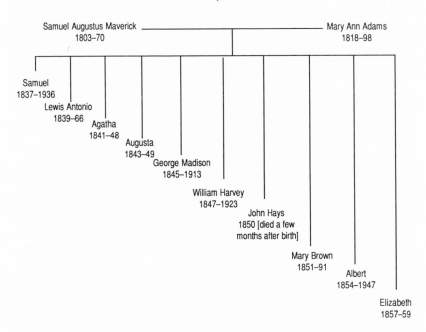

Samuel Augustus Maverick–Mary Ann Adams family tree.

zie had written to Mary the preceding November. "I am very glad to hear it for I am tired of being so often told of the old ruins in which you live. People will say 'I wonder why Mr. Maverick doesn't live in a better house.'"[47] In early 1851, she would write that people considered Maverick "quite a lump of riches," and "I always say yes."[48]

Maverick was indeed wealthy by contemporary standards, but most of that wealth was tied up in land speculation, and this circumstance enhanced his natural frugality and preference for plain living. Both Maverick and his father expressed admiration for the simple Quakers and distrusted worldly fortune.[49] Thus, the two men's philosophies stood in counterpoint to their shrewd acquisitiveness. "The loss of a fortune frees us from a frivolous world," Sam Maverick had written in a cryptic entry in his journal during his first few months in Texas, and repeatedly the elder Maverick reminded his son that "a little is enough in this checkered uncertain world of ours."[50]

Mary, too, with her strong spiritual yearnings, shared her husband's disdain for worldly living, and the record reveals no incompatibility on the subject of finances. The couple did show a liberal spirit toward their children, their relatives, and projects such as the Episcopal church. When the children began leaving home, their parents repeatedly encouraged them to draw on the family's financial resources. They provided frequent gifts to the Clows and contributed to various San Antonio charitable and civic efforts. Sam Maverick's eulogist would relate how during a time of great sickness and privation in San Antonio, Maverick had appeared at the mayor's door with a thousand dollars to be distributed to the poor, with the stipulation that the donor's name not be mentioned.[51]

The Mavericks, then, were not miserly, but Sam Maverick occasionally appeared so to some of his contemporaries because of his caution in personal expenditures and disregard for some of the comforts money could procure. Mary's assertion to her sister that lack of funds precluded a trip thus can be seen as a reflection of the couple's cautious attitude—or as a convenient excuse for continuing an introspective existence at home. Besides, family demands for nursing seemed unending. Son Lewis broke his right arm in a fall from a tree in early October and became ill from an abscess below the elbow. He did not regain use of the arm until the end of November, and Mary perceived correctly that the limb had healed crooked.

One positive change the family could look toward was the two-story house going up under the giant pecan tree in the northwest corner of the Alamo grounds. Maverick had engaged another South Carolinian, Francis Giraud, to survey the mission site, and Giraud had drawn a boundary around the inner line of the buildings, emphasizing their use as a mission and lopping off the northwest angle and the corral on the northeast. The U.S. Army, defeated in its bid to claim the mission as government property, rented the dilapidated complex during the year the Maverick home was built, making the Alamo a quartermaster's depot for grain and hay storage.[52]

On December 1, 1850, the Mavericks moved into their spacious new house on higher ground and hoped for better health and fortunes. Mary was pregnant again. Maverick had continued to accumulate town property, and deed records and plats show that he planned an "Alamo City" residential area around his new Alamo Plaza home, perhaps hoping to attract more Anglo-Americans to the east side of the river.[53]

He was beginning to assume an important role in the business life of San Antonio as the city experienced greater growth and change. Together with other influential citizens such as Frank Paschal, with

Samuel Augustus Maverick

A middle-aged Samuel Augustus Maverick. *From Rena Maverick Green, ed.,* Memoirs of Mary A. Maverick.

whom he had served in the Congress of the Republic, Maverick had in April become a member of the "body corporate" of the Bexar Manufacturing Company, formed to produce cotton and woolen items.[54] Many of the organizers of this enterprise were also involved in the September, 1850, creation of the San Antonio Railroad Company to obtain a railway between the Gulf and their city.[55] Both manufacturing and railroad building were in their infancy in Texas, and Maverick, elected treasurer of the railroad with the incorporation, was to be taxed with many headaches in trying to create in frontier Texas a transportation system even remotely resembling the ones that developed with such rapidity in the industrial states of the North.

Maverick was also moving once more toward political involvement in the affairs of Texas. Shortly before the death of John Hays, he had chaired a San Antonio public meeting on the dispute over the state's western boundary. After Kearny had angered Texans by setting up a New Mexico civil government deaf to Texas claims in 1846, the Texas legislature had countered by designating a large chunk of present-day New Mexico east of the Rio Grande as Santa Fe County. Now New Mexicans were making it clear that they intended to work toward statehood despite the Texas land claim, and it looked as if the federal government was throwing its weight behind the New Mexicans as the debate over the extension of slavery further complicated the issue.

Mass protest meetings were held across Texas. In San Antonio, the assembly chaired by Maverick produced a resolution asserting that the Rio Grande boundary fixed by the first Congress of the Republic should stand and that the federal government could only insult Texas by offering payment or a "pretended concession" to part of the disputed land while refusing to recognize the state's claims.[56]

Various compromises were proposed nationally, with the final agreement passing the U.S. legislature on September 6, 1850, as part of the Compromise of 1850. For renouncing its claims to two-thirds of present-day New Mexico, Texas would be awarded $10 million, with half of that being retained by the U.S. government to settle the Lone Star State's revenue debt. Eventually, the United States would pay $7.75 million to holders of Texas securities to eliminate this debt. Meanwhile, the state paid its nonrevenue debt holders $1.25 million from the $5 million it received.[57]

The relinquishing of the New Mexico land claim proved a setback to the hopes of Texas land speculators such as Maverick. However, the state now had $3.75 million in its coffers, and much acreage remained to be explored and claimed within the new Texas western border. Now that the line was firmly established and the U.S. Army was extending its Texas frontier posts into lands far beyond the settlements, Maverick could better extend his own empire westward. And having reentered the political fray, he was about to be called on to help direct the fortunes of Texas once more.

11

"Take New Courage from the Race"

*I feel like shirking off a sort of heaviness that threatened to come
over me from years that have passed and take new courage
from the race (short or long) that lies before.*

—Fifty-year-old Sam Maverick from the state legislature
to his wife, January 9, 1854

WITH THEIR MOVE to Alamo Plaza, the Mavericks were at long last to
find some stability. Turbulence in Texas affairs had been followed by
turbulence in their personal lives, but now came years of relative calm,
with Maverick's energies going into business and political enterprises
and his wife's into family and spiritual matters. Both pursued their
courses out of a strong sense of duty only heightened by their recent
suffering. Maverick mused in a letter to his wife during this period,
"Time and experience ought to make us better able to act reasonably,
and consistently with what we have found to be our duty to God, to
ourselves, and to other people."[1]

If that task proved difficult and tiresome, as it often did, the couple
now could at least rejoice in their settled life, in the continuing survival of their four sons, ages three to thirteen at the time of the move,
and in the birth of another, longed-for, daughter. Mary Brown Maverick, named for her father's Quaker great-grandmother, was born in
June, 1851, seven months after the family settled into its home under
the giant pecan tree. "I trust my heavenly Father will allow me to keep
this one and teach me how to bring her up," Mary wrote in her diary.
"She is inexpressably dear to my heart."[2] Informing G. Jones and Elizabeth Weyman Houston in Alabama of the news, Sam Maverick commented, "I do not despair of raising myself to a just appreciation of
this blessing."[3] Indeed, Mary Brown's presence was to draw some of

the old warmth and affection from his nature, easing his distant relationship with his wife.

Thirty-three-year-old Mary herself came close to death with this eighth birth, losing much blood and the power of speech. She fainted twice after the birth and felt "no pain but some indescribable peace, as if it might be the presence of guardian angels." As she liked to think of her two departed daughters as angels, it was tempting to cross over into the spirit world. But she prayed for life yet to care for her five living offspring.[4] Mary had been confirmed a member of the Episcopal church two months before, giving her renewed hope in dealing with the uncertainties and tribulations of her existence.

Her husband, too, was trying to put the family tragedies of the last few years behind and heighten his involvement in the affairs of San Antonio and Texas. Elections were scheduled for two Bexar and Medina County seats in the fourth Texas state legislature, and in July, he entered the race, the sixth and last candidate to announce. Acknowledging in a newspaper statement of July 21 that he ought to state his politics and position, Maverick declared, "To claim to be a *democrat* would seem to be too easy to be of any reliable use: besides I must say that I have for years felt great relief from being out of the strife of party."[5] He addressed the continuing states' rights issue, as he had years before in South Carolina, by warning against either the federal or state government's usurping the other's power.

He also set two priorities for which he would labor in the legislature: creating a state primary school system, and improving transportation. "We have for years been wasted by war; and had neither the time nor means for anything but self-preservation," he wrote. Now, "relieved in great measure from these sore afflictions," he wanted the state to pay off its debts with the money provided by the U.S. government and use the interest from the remainder to finance common schools.[6] Maverick's own growing boys continued to receive schooling from tutors and attend small private schools, but his city would lead the way educationally in 1854 with Texas' first "genuinely free school system."[7]

For the legislative candidate, a victory would mean winter months spent away from his family in Austin. During the summer and early fall, he showered solicitude on his wife and new daughter, buying a carriage to take them for evening drives. On September 28, Mary happily confided to her diary that Mary Brown, or "Maly," as they called her, was getting "rosy & playful & good," and "my husband is so kind and God my Father blesses me so in the health of my dear children."

Elected that fall, Maverick embarked on five terms of continuous service in the Texas legislature. Election records do not survive, but newspaper accounts from the decade of the fifties indicate that Maverick had the support of old Texians and at least a portion of Bexar's Mexicans and other ethnic minorities.

Now that annexation was complete, the Mexican war over, and boundaries firmly established, the state was facing a period of unprecedented growth, with a population that would almost triple between 1850 and 1860.[8] Legislators struggled with a variety of complex administrative tasks as determined emigrants pushed northward through the prairies to the Cross Timbers and southward along the coast to the Nueces. Despite this upsurge in settlement, however, San Antonio and Castroville remained westernmost communities, with the exception of those Spanish-established settlements on the Rio Grande, and Maverick's remained a frontier constituency.

During his legislative career, Maverick would repeatedly travel by horseback and later by stage northward over the rolling prairies to Austin to work on the priorities he had laid out for himself: transportation, common schools, and resistance to secession. He would also work to foster fair and liberal laws for land acquisition and ownership, to provide frontier protection, and to ensure a fair and efficient judicial system.

Austin in 1851 was just beginning to take on the air of a promising and substantial settlement. It had flourished briefly from 1839 to 1841 as the capital of the Republic, only to lose this status with Sam Houston's re-election to the presidency. Houston considered Austin too exposed to Indian raids and too primitive for a state capital and temporarily moved the seat of government to Washington-on-the-Brazos, where Maverick joined the Eighth Congress. In 1845, Austin was again designated the capital—until 1850. Yet in 1849, Rutherford B. Hayes, later president of the United States, still judged it an "inconsiderable village" with "not more than one or two passable buildings."[9]

Austin's greatest impetus for growth came in 1850, when voters statewide made it the permanent capital. When Maverick arrived at the end of 1851, the legislature was still meeting in the old one-story frame capitol building at the corner of what is now Colorado and Eighth streets, but a variety of public and private buildings were under construction. In the first four months of the year, at least one hundred homes and businesses had been erected.[10]

On November 3, 1851, Maverick was introduced to the House by fellow Bexar and Medina representative Robert Simpson Neighbors, a former Perote prisoner who like Maverick had explored West Texas and helped organize the San Antonio and Mexican Gulf Rail Road venture.

The newcomer was soon busy on the Judiciary, Contingent Expenses, and Internal Improvements committees.[11] He liked second-term governor Peter H. Bell, "an honorable highminded man" and a sensible one, as he concluded in an early letter home.[12] Under Bell's administration, the legislature would focus much of its time and energy on reducing the state's public debt, defending the frontier, and untangling the land claims of colonizers of the Republic period.

Maverick found many acquaintances in the legislative halls, including Jon Dancy, William Menefee, and Barnard Bee's son Hamilton. The latter would become, along with Maverick, one of the few members to serve consecutive terms through the 1850s. Most of Maverick's colleagues were southerners like himself, products of antebellum plantation culture. The majority were farmers or planters themselves, and a substantial number were lawyers. Most were "of the successful middle class in wealth."[13]

Maverick's letters home from the legislature during the 1850s reflect a keen impatience with the speechmaking, showmanship, and machinations that accompanied the legislative process and a desire to be with his family or out surveying instead. At the legislature in 1856, he would liken all of society to a "company of actors performing a continuous role" and would muse to his wife, "I feel that I was intended to act in that part of the drama which passed by before Annexation."[14]

In November, 1851, he wrote, "It's the most abominable thing my coming here. George & Willy I miss very much." In an allusion to the topography of Rome, he concluded, "If I had them here we would have fine times on these 7 hills."[15] A month later he complained that he was devoting himself "entirely to business" in order to finish and get home, but the "showy young men" in the legislature were busy building their own careers through "striking speeches."[16] His obvious homesickness and solicitous inquiries caused Mary to write in her diary on November 16, "He is so thoughtful and affectionate about us—how it falls like a blessing from *heaven on my heart!*" Indeed, on December 12, he wrote, "You must, dear Mary, relax your mind more by diverting or cheerful scenes,—otherwise we shall indeed grow old too soon, my love."

As Christmas approached, Maverick introduced a bill to incorporate a line of Gulf steamers and offered a resolution that Governor Bell's antisecession message of November 10 be sent to the governor and legislature of South Carolina. Bell had argued that Texas could help to avert "a coming storm" by pressing for constitutional amendments and reminding South Carolina that secession was "a remedy of dernier resort."[17] Yet, as historian Billy D. Ledbetter has noted, throughout the 1850s, the ultra–states' rights wing of the Democratic party was to command party machinery in Texas and dominate the state legislature.[18]

Serious national concerns were pushed aside at Christmastime, when Maverick returned home to greet the G. Jones and Ross Houston families. G. Jones and Elizabeth Weyman Houston, now with two daughters and a son named after Elizabeth's deceased brother Augustus, were finally making the long-talked-of move to Texas, arriving in San Antonio at the end of November and staying with the Mavericks through the holidays. In January, both Houston families located on land Maverick had offered them on the Cibolo southeast of San Antonio, and the Mavericks and Houstons began a long and pleasant intercourse, with much visiting back and forth.

Returning to the legislature, Maverick continued to infuse his letters to his wife with warmth and concern. "I am afraid you are harassed by untoward cares & bad servants," he wrote on January 9, 1852. "Don't take too much to heart. I hope I shall be with you in a month: and am ready to do anything you like." He also wrote to their eldest, fourteen-year-old Sam, urging him to "give mama a kiss, without telling her anything about it" and setting before his son the example of Thomas William Ward, who had lost a leg in the siege of Béxar. "Sam never give way to despair my son," Maverick wrote. "Do your duty and never fear the consequences."[19]

Maverick did his duty in the House by introducing a bill to regulate courts in the Fourth Judicial District, of which Bexar was a part, and acting to clarify and regulate a number of land matters. Representative of his efforts was a report and bill he prepared as a member of the judiciary committee to assist "a large number of the most respectable native and adopted citizens of Bexar county," who were petitioning the legislature for relief against people trying to locate on their already titled lands.[20]

Another land matter that Maverick entered into was the issue of a statewide geological survey. He and C. B. Stewart were appointed a select committee to consider the need for such a survey, and on February 2, 1852, they submitted a report recommending that as a start "three or four thousand dollars, or some moderate amount be put into the general appropriation bill, for Geological and Mineralogical explorations" to be made in the next two years.[21]

Maverick had shown keen interest in acquiring mineral deposits himself, but now he joined with Stewart in pointing out that private entrepreneurs might locate and profit from such mineral riches to the loss of "the body of the people" of the state, and that a geological survey could enhance the development of "practically useful science" in Texas. For example, they argued, "no doubt we needlessly go to expense in the transportation of lumber for building, when there is every reason to believe, that for much less money, houses might be built out of the dirt under foot." They reported themselves "almost tempted to recommend the appointment of a State Geologist and Mineralogist, for the sole purpose of experimenting for the next year or two, on the admixture of earth, sand, and what not, for making a good durable wall."[22]

It was exhilarating to think about the potential of Texas lands, but thorny problems concerning their apportionment remained, and Maverick became involved in debate over the settlement claims of colonizers Henry Francis Fisher and Burchard Miller.

The two men, failing to meet the terms of their contract, had assigned the principal interest in the contract to the German Emigration Company represented by Prince Carl of Solms-Braunfels without giving the society a full understanding of the isolated nature of the western lands granted or of the contract's stiff terms. Now that the German group had settled a few thousand emigrants, most outside the isolated Fisher-Miller lands, Fisher and Miller were attempting to perfect titles to the lands for which they had received certificates. The men asserted that they had a judgment for this action, but the General Land Office commissioner rejected their claim, and it was brought to the legislature.

John O. Meusebach, Prince Carl's successor as commissioner for the German emigrants, was naturally resentful of the two colonizers. So was Sam Maverick. As pointed out earlier, Maverick was not averse to properly administered colonization efforts, as they could enhance his own western holdings and help build the grand democratic empire he envisioned. However, he knew that most of the German colonization had been carried out more in spite of than because of Fisher and Miller's grand designs. Meusebach later reported that when the two colonizers' claim came up in the House, "the Hon. Sam Maverick, of Bexar, got up with a fulminant speech, which—thundering that you could hear it in both houses—he concluded with the following words: 'They say that they got a judgment; it is a snap judgment; gotten up in a dark corner; it is a fraud, a fraud, a fraud!'" Most of the Congress agreed, because the claim was rejected, though it would reappear.[23]

Shortly before the House adjourned in February, a resolution was presented to submit to the voters a plan for dividing Texas into two states, with the Brazos the dividing line. Sam Maverick, who had fought a year and a half before to retain all the territory claimed by Texas in 1836, voted with a minority to keep the resolution alive.[24] His vote reflects how clearly his allegiance and fortunes lay with West Texas. After all, he had identified the country east of the Guadalupe River to Mary in 1838 as an unhealthy one men would simply scheme to get away from to "the blessed climate of the West."[25]

As his legislative term ended, Maverick collected on an old service claim, receiving $503 compensation "for services and losses while a San Antonio prisoner" during the Republic period.[26] He then turned homeward to San Antonio, uneasily aware that more than six years had passed since his last visit to his father at Montpelier, and that more than two had passed since a stroke rendered the elder Maverick nearly helpless.

Periodic reports came from his sister and brother-in-law. William Van Wyck had written soon after Samuel was stricken, reporting that friends such as Barnard Bee were visiting but that only "Washington" could decipher the old man's whispers.[27] Samuel was confined to a wheelchair, still alert and able to see and hear but unable to communicate except by signs, as he could not write legibly. On the death of the Mavericks' baby John Hays, sister Lydia reported that their father spent hours trying to write a condolence note, only to give up in exasperation.[28]

Shortly before the birth of Mary Brown, Lydia had sent a gloomy report on life at the family home. "Father is anxious to hear from you which he constantly makes known to me by signs & gestures," she wrote. "A few days ago whilst I was sitting near him, I heard him whisper distinctly that he wished you would come to see him." She judged his health and spirits good, but he still could not stand alone nor feed himself. Thus, it fell to her to take care of his needs as well as the demands of her growing brood. Like Mary, Lydia faced one pregnancy after another, eventually bearing nine children.

But it was not childcare or care for her aged father that made her extended stay at Montpelier "far from being agreeable." She, like her brother, drooped under slave management. Lydia characterized her father's slaves as "from long indulgence" given to stealing and drunkenness and referred to the family home in a telling phrase as "this place of misrule *still*," indicating that Samuel had never exercised much control.[29]

A year later, two months after Maverick returned to San Antonio from the legislature, Lydia anxiously reported her father failing with dropsy. On April 28, 1852, seventy-nine-year-old Samuel breathed his last. "His son never ceased to regret that he did not go out to see him, ere he died," Mary wrote in her memoirs, "but he seemed to be tied here all the while, still hoping to start soon, and yet finding something to detain him."[30]

In truth, father and son had said what there was to be said six years before. Samuel had consistently stressed independent industry and increasingly urged simple reliance on a mysterious Providence, and his son had absorbed and lived these precepts. Now Samuel was buried on his property at Montpelier. He was survived by two children, sixteen grandchildren, and three great-grandchildren, the latter belonging to Elizabeth and G. Jones Houston. The extended family was spread from Texas to Virginia, where Elizabeth Houston's brother Joe Weyman attended college. The only two family members on Maverick's side remaining in Alabama were Elizabeth and Joe's younger half-sister and half-brother, Josephine and Samuel Maverick Thompson.

On Mary's side of the family, brother Robert remained in Alabama with his wife and children, and Andrew was adopting Mexico as home. William had started a family and continued to reside in Freestone County, Texas, and Lizzie and Robert Clow were still at Port Lavaca, where Lizzie had given birth to a second daughter only a few days before Mary Brown's birth.

As her own family grew, Lizzie renewed her entreaties to her sister to return to the coast. "I wish I could be persuasive enough to induce you to come here to live: we can have more comforts, and at much less expense than you ever could in San Antonio," she wrote in June of 1852, and Clow added an invitation to divide a choice twenty-six acres he owned on the bay with "brother Maverick." Yet staying in Lavaca had not improved the Clows' financial fortunes; they were living in a public inn and struggling to keep the store solvent. The ever-affable Clow could not resist a barb at his sister-in-law in February of that year, writing, "I note your remarks in regard to estimating riches too high, I think they are proper.—But I tell you, that you and Mr M have *the name* of thinking a great deal of 'the root of all evil.'"[31]

Failing to lure Mary to the coast, Lizzie and her girls arrived in July for a visit of three months. Lizzie frankly found her sister's life too isolated, "she being used to much company at a public house," Mary confided to her diary. Lizzie's observations caused Mary to give way to bitterness at her lot in the privacy of her diary, where she characterized herself as "almost a hermit kept at home with sick babies, or miserable servants, for years past, and almost [having] broken off all intercourse—but that I find at home, God help me! *The slave of slaves.*"[32]

Mary had borne eight children in fourteen years, while managing and providing for the needs of nine to thirteen slaves, over half of them children. Often, her husband had left her in cramped quarters for extended periods with sick babies and servants who seemed to delight in sabotaging her attempts at supervision and harmony. Mary could not look at slavery from an enlightened, humanitarian viewpoint, but could only approach it from the position of one struggling within the authoritarian system.

She had already confided to her diary, "My poor Father used to say that the institution of negro slavery was the greatest curse under which man laboured—and I in sorrow and with brimming tears agree with him as far as my personal evidence can go." Now she wrote, "My lot is to struggle with them alone, unaided, without sympathy, or sympathy only for them! I who would be so happy to be at peace with all who pray to God for *them* all daily."[33]

Mary was not alone in such feelings. Sister-in-law Lydia had written in April, "Oh how unpleasant, I often think I would rather be on a scanty island in the sea than to live with them, but so it is."[34] They both might well have agreed with Mary Boykin Chestnut's comment on the peculiar institution in *A Diary from Dixie:* "Mrs. Gibson said her mind was fixed on one point; she never would own slaves. 'Who would that was not born to it?' I cried." In fact, Chestnut's famous Civil War diary reflects many of the attitudes contained in Mary Maverick's journals. Both women felt imprisoned within a system that forced southern mistresses to live with and see to the daily welfare of a group of people whom they considered part of a lower and degraded class. Chestnut considered her female relatives martyrs to "a horde of idle dirty Africans," and Mary Maverick complained of slave character in similar terms.[35]

Yet both were uneasily conscious that these slaves were human beings, and if their lives were not lived according to the values their mistresses held dear, it was at least in part because of the difference in circumstances. Chestnut railed against the miscegenation forced on slave women by their masters, and Mary's deep sense of her own unworthiness before God made her feel that she had "no right to condemn" her charges. She repeatedly humbled herself in sackcloth and ashes as "the worst of Christians, wives, mothers, mistresses," imploring, "O *Father pity me & teach me how to do better*."[36]

While Mary continued her spiritual struggle at home, her husband was finding more public demands on his time. Stockholders of the San Antonio and Mexican Gulf Rail Road elected him a director in October, 1852, two days before Robert Clow arrived to pick up his family.[37] The Clows, too, were excited about the railroad, as it would originate on the coast, and competition was keen among the coastal communities to become the point of origin. Yet the directors were already facing severe problems. For example, in July, the committee to examine titles on land being offered in exchange for railroad stock had reported no progress, "as they had neither abstracts nor claims of titles on which to base an opinion" and found most of the offered land being overrated.[38]

Still the promoters remained optimistic. The San Antonio and Mexican Gulf was the first Texas railroad authorized to use city and county bonds for construction capital, and the city of San Antonio had been authorized to issue bonds totaling up to fifty thousand dollars for the effort. In addition, the state had recently agreed to encourage railroad construction by granting eight sections of land for each mile of railroad built.

Despite these incentives, all the Texas railroad builders of the period would find their task almost impossible, as ability to dream outstripped ability to deliver. The elder Samuel had written his son almost five years earlier, "I prophesy that you will have Rail Road & Telegraph Bubbles to form in Texas to empty the pockets . . . as they have here."[39] In December, 1852, the directors felt they were making progress by finally selecting Saluria as the point to be linked with San Antonio by railroad. Maverick and fellow surveyor and land speculator John James were appointed to obtain Sam Antonio city bonds with interest coupons attached.[40]

As the new year 1853 began, Mary and the children visited the Houstons on the Cibolo while Maverick attended an extra session of the Fourth Legislature, serving on a select committee to resolve the affairs of the German Emigration Company and its creditors. On February 2, 1853, he and fellow member H. B. Andrews reported that a tentative agreement had been reached between the two parties and referred the matter to the Judiciary Committee.[41]

While dealing with legislative matters, Maverick came down with "bilious cholic" after drinking "some villainous rotten limestone water."[42] On his arrival home at the session's conclusion, Mary doctored him with her new botanical knowledge and managed to keep him in bed for a number of days.

However, as always, Maverick's cure for ill health was a sojourn in the surveying camp, and he departed in early March for the newly established Fort Chadbourne on land he was leasing to the U.S. government in present-day Coke County above San Angelo. During the 1850s, Maverick was to locate numerous claims in this area.[43]

Chadbourne was not the only fort on Maverick land. Maverick and other speculators such as John James had located the sites with the best water and best timber in advance of the army's movement of forts into West Texas.[44] In 1852, Maverick had leased to the federal government the land for Fort Clark, perched on a limestone ridge bordering Las Moras Creek 125 miles from San Antonio, and he would continue to do so until the outbreak of the Civil War. He also owned the land on which Fort Terrett was situated, west of Junction in present Kimble County.[45]

Thriving with cold air and exercise, he wrote Mary on March 14 from Fort Mason, in present Mason County northwest of Austin, with a familiar report: "I find that I much underrated the distance the difficulty the Time. If we get back in a month it will be as much as I now expect. And if I should find you my dear & our little Mary & our

FRONTIER FEDERAL FORTS*

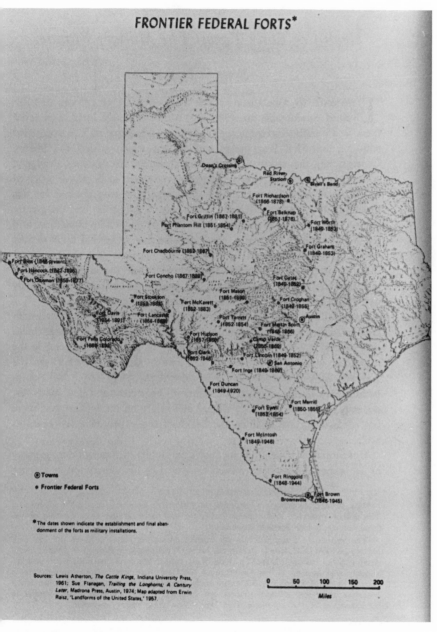

Federal frontier forts, including those on land owned by Samuel Augustus Maverick.
From James O. Breeden, "Health of Early Texas: The Military Frontier," Southwestern Historical Quarterly *80, no. 4 (April, 1977): 358.*

boys all well and be able to present myself in improved health we will not complain of the loss of time."

He pressed onward to Fort Chadbourne, enjoyed the officers' hospitality there, and returned in good health the end of April, finding his family well and busy. The older boys were attending school and dancing lessons, and Mary was involved in Methodist and Episcopal church fund-raising activities. The women of the tiny Episcopal congregation had actually bought a lot and started a church building, only to have the effort falter and die. Now a new pastor, the Rev. Charles Rottenstein, arrived to take charge of the thirteen-member parish.[46]

Mary Maverick's spiritual quest was to veer into new channels of inquiry shortly after her husband's return. When old friend, now gubernatorial candidate, Jon Dancy visited in mid-May, he suggested that they try calling up the spirits, or "table-rapping," then pronounced Mary a spiritual medium.

Spiritualism, the belief in souls living on after death and in human mediums' being able to communicate with them, was spreading across the United States with a vigor and a broad appeal not felt before or since in American history.[47] "What progress do the 'spirit rappings' make in your town? I would like to see something of it," Lizzie had written to her sister only the month before Dancy's visit.[48] The Fox sisters of northern New York had touched off a flurry of excitement with their fraudulent reports of spirit rappings in 1848, and a young man dubbed the "Poughkeepsie Seer," Andrew Jackson Davis, was attracting attention among a wide cross-section of Americans in the 1850s, with his ability to diagnose and prescribe for illnesses while under hypnosis. Many were also taken with his Swedenborgian belief in a tangible spirit world where souls grew toward perfection.[49]

Dancy, who had suffered the loss of a young wife before migrating to Texas, showed great enthusiasm for the topic, frequently recording in his diary attempts to call up the spirits. Former minister to Mexico Waddy Thompson was "nearly distracted on the subject," Maverick would report to his wife when he visited with Thompson in New York in 1856.[50] Mary Maverick, too, found the spiritualists' ideas most enticing, and it is not hard to see why. If there was the possibility of actually communicating with the spirit world and receiving guidance concerning the treatment of illness, then she could commune once again with her lost loved ones—daughters, parents—and perhaps prevent the loss of others so dear to her heart.

Mary had quested after spiritual righteousness in hopes of drawing nearer to her daughters; now she found herself drawn to the possibilities of communion and purification that spiritualism offered. Of Dancy's visit she wrote, "I took pencil & paper & very soon my hand wrote legible wonderful things purporting to be from departed spirits brothers, mother, friends, many!!!!! O God I pray thy guidance that my immortal soul be not led astray."[51]

As Mary began studying and experimenting with the tenets of spiritualism, her husband was running for another term in the House. On June 1, 1853, the Texas *State Gazette* reported seven candidates for representative from Bexar County, concluding, "We would not interfere in the election at all but will just express the hope that our Bexar friends will not leave at home their former able and faithful member, the Hon. S. A. Maverick, for a more worthy and capable member was not in the last legislature."

Re-elected, Maverick again joined with men with whom his history and the history of Texas were intertwined, including Ranger captain Henry McCulloch and Charles Edward Travis, son of Alamo martyr William Barret Travis. Dancy's gubernatorial campaign had been unsuccessful, but the new governor was another acquaintance from Maverick's early days in Texas, and one much to his liking. Elisha M. Pease had attended the independence convention and had served the Republic and state in a number of key positions since arriving in Texas in 1835. Like Maverick, he was a judicious and moderate man opposed to southern secession sentiment. His administration would focus on creation of a public school system, Indian removal, and internal improvements, primarily in the form of transportation charters.[52]

Maverick was appointed to the Judiciary and Public Debt committees, then secured an appointment on the Internal Improvements Committee.[53] Here he could work on behalf of the San Antonio and Mexican Gulf Rail Road, as well as on other attempts to link West Texas with the world. His efforts were rewarded when the legislature in January doubled section grants for railroads to sixteen per mile. It was a boost for the troubled railroad venture, which had fallen prey to "malicious rumors" in San Antonio after company president Enoch Jones and board member Thomas Jefferson Devine had received the contract for the railroad's construction.[54]

During this session, Maverick also could write to his wife that, as he had hoped, "we appropriated the proceeds or interest of 2 millions, today, to common schools." The legislature had done nothing less than to create a permanent endowment for public schools in the most important act of Pease's administration.[55]

While at the legislature, Maverick was reminded of more stirring times by a visit from Ben Milam's brother James, who had traveled from Kentucky to take the fallen hero's bones home. Maverick dissuaded him, and James Milam departed satisfied that "the good people of San Antonio were not willing that they should be taken" and would provide a more fitting internment.[56]

As Maverick worked in the seat of Texas government, he and Mary discussed the possibility of her visiting Austin with the children. "I cannot conscientiously say that Austin is much of a place at present, but you ought to see it and the Capitol," Maverick wrote on November 28, 1853, "and I think you might spend a short time here pleasantly enough." The town now stretched fourteen blocks northward from the banks of the Colorado River, with construction of permanent government buildings proceeding in its "Capitol Square." Austin's prosperity would soon far surpass that of San Antonio, but its greater distance from the coast meant that residents had to wait longer for many of the commercial comforts then filtering into Maverick's home city to the south.

In early December, son Lewis became ill with chills and fever, and Mary decided against the Austin visit. Instead, Maverick returned home briefly for Christmas. Back once more at the legislature on January 9, 1854, he wrote his wife a thoughtful letter, gently remonstrating with and encouraging both himself and her. He talked about duty to themselves and to others and to God, including the duty to avoid becoming morose with the passing years and sad experience. "It is ungrateful to cultivate a brooding sadness: 'To enjoy is to obey,'" he counseled. "I trust, my dear M that you may continue to cultivate in your own generous heart and in the bosom of your next friend, a desire to perform our social duties [to] our own happiness and that of those who are connected with us in any way whatever."

Age, Maverick had heard, increased the selfish passions such as avarice, and he asked his wife's assistance in "coax[ing] me away from that fault or fatality. So that I may not quite disgrace the intention of my limited existence." He was ready, he wrote, to "shirk off a sort of heaviness" and to "take new courage from the race."

Mary was taking new courage from her studies in botanical medicine and spiritualism, but she was uneasy and diffident about dabbling in these alternative methods of dealing with illness and death. She wanted to take classes from a Professor Ryan, who was lecturing on biology and psychology to "scant audiences" in San Antonio and promising knowledge especially valuable to mothers in handling illness, from headaches (curable through mesmerism) to epidemics. He had a men's class and would take a women's group of ten, but, Mary reported to her husband in a letter of December 11, 1853, "I only hear of 6 *ladies* willing to learn—I am afraid I will lose some knowledge that *might* prove of great importance to our children."[57] Cholera was again breaking out on the coast, and fourteen-year-old Lewis was given to bouts of illness and eight-year-old George suffered from harsh headaches.

George's headaches, Mary reported, had been the subject of a "spirit communication" she received through her father in her capacity as a writing spirit medium before Ryan's arrival. The "distinctly written" message promised her an "enlightening of the wisdom principle to manipulate, for the purpose of curing George's head, and other diseases." So, she concluded, "besides my long undefined respect for this science—I am now influenced by a mysterious belief (which is nevertheless a belief till it be proved to me delusion) that a dear son may be cured of a great affliction thru its teachings."

She had been subjected to some ridicule from acquaintances on the subject but swore to her husband, "it shall not give me one passing embarrassment if I have your approval." Chafing at the lack of women to complete Ryan's class, she complained, "I don't understand why knowledge & science is forbidden to woman, I know 'tis not Our Father's will which denies us. Man, vain man—only, I know you are an exception. So I hope you can still trust me since I have yet no desire to put on the Bloomer costume or set aside the natural or legitimate rights of man—but am glad to live on in the time honored custom to 'love honour and obey.'"[58]

The practical, logical Maverick was skeptical of spiritualist thought. Reporting Waddy Thompson's interest in the subject in 1856, he would write to Mary, "Admitting it were spirits, I should like to see some good resulting to somebody."[59] But he lovingly and consistently supported his wife, now pregnant with their ninth child, in her efforts at greater understanding, commending her on her study of botanical medicine and encouraging her to seek out what truth there might be in spiritualism. Of her medical regimen he wrote on December 5, 1853, "The

Mary Maverick and her children, early 1850s. *Clockwise, from upper left:* Samuel, Lewis Antonio, William Harvey, Mary Brown, George Madison. *From Rena Maverick Green, ed., Samuel Maverick, Texan.*

truth is that if you had not fallen on the Botanic practice, half or more of us would (I think) be dead," and when she and their two eldest sons began taking Ryan's classes in January, Maverick wrote warm, encouraging letters from the legislature. He suspected that Ryan "has not yet put his own temper into a philosophical trot," but he concluded on January 13, "these erratic geniuses are apt to do more for mankind than for themselves."

As for his wife's philosophical questing, Maverick reassured her that he was "much pleased" with "the liberal spirit with which you are disposed to look into new and important [propositions]—with a desire to believe the truth," adding, "Most people, I fear, look more for the gratification of pride or prejudice, than for the truth." A week later, he responded to a self-deprecating letter from Mary by writing that he was eager to learn from her and their eldest Sam and reminding her, "Perhaps it is a good thing to feel humble and unworthy. There is then, at all events, some hope of improvement, and who does not deserve & need improvement."

As the legislature moved toward adjournment, Maverick began turning his mind more to his own business. He and fellow long-time San Antonio speculator John James exhibited a friendly rivalry, and on February 17 Maverick revealed an oft-hidden relish for gamesmanship when it came to land matters, writing Mary that James and a partner planned to sue him on his return concerning whether he or they had the right to field notes of locations made the preceding summer. She could help him "get ahead of Herndon & James" by sending the notes to Austin. "The main point is for me to be summoned & brought to trial without having in hand the thing sued for," he explained, adding, "It would be fun to beat them . . . in that way. We'll see!" Eventually, Maverick and James would agree to half-ownership of disputed lands, including the site of Fort Hudson, established in 1857.[60]

Besides land matters, Maverick's mind was turning toward his farm and straggling cattle herd on Matagorda Peninsula. Over the four years since John Graham had written that Jack found it impossible to pen and brand the cattle, Maverick had received further troublesome reports and repeated offers from coastal residents to buy or trade for the cattle. James Stanley in 1850 had offered to buy the herd, reasoning that "they have been awfully neglected, not Branded ever since you left, and will do you very little good situated as they are." That same year, James Lytle had offered to exchange half a league of land near

Brenham for the beeves. The following year, Charles Power had written wanting to make a deal, and S. G. Cunningham suggested buying the cattle for the New Orleans market and shipping them from Decrow's Point. In spring of 1853, while Maverick was on his Fort Chadbourne surveying expedition, Mary received an anonymous letter from "A friend to justice" on the coast.

> Send some one to look after your stock of cattle immediately or you will not have in eighteen months from this time one yearling nor calf to ten cows. It is said and that by some of our most respectable citizens that yearlings and calves may be seen by dozens following and sucking your cows and branded in other peoples brand. While I am writing this I am informed that Morrison, Gove, and Worcester have each written to Mr Mavrick [sic] on this same subject But for fear that you are not apprised of it and hearing that Mr Mavrick is not in Texas I give you this information In haste.[61]

When Maverick returned from the legislature, this letter was already nine months old, and he could not put off action any longer. He was not interested enough in cattle ranching to have done anything before this, but he was loath to give up the enterprise.

In late March he finally acted on his plans to move the cattle, departing with young Sam and Lewis for the peninsula with the intention of driving the herd to a location on the San Geronimo. He wrote Mary from the peninsula on April 25 that they had had "a rough and hard time" collecting about 250 of the beeves and could not be home before May 20. A few weeks later, he wrote from Goliad that the delicate Lewis had been experiencing chills. "I have Jinny & Jack & Harriet and an ox waggon and 400 cattle, 150 of which I bought on the route," Maverick reported, explaining that he was now heading for the Conquista to establish the ranch near present Floresville rather than the San Geronimo, as Indian troubles were severe in the San Geronimo area. "Dear Mary if it would be better for me to go home, write me so," he concluded.[62]

Mary did just that on May 26. She had borne a sixth son three weeks before and was listening with alarm to reports of Indian raids along the frontier more severe than for some years. Many families had arrived in San Antonio seeking safety. Her weakened condition and distress over the Indian raids caused Mary to throw aside all attempts at stoicism and plead with her husband to return.

"I write to beg of you for pity's sake to come home and bring our dear boys," she implored. "You cannot know how many and atrocious the murders and depredations of the Indians have been." She insisted that she would "joyfully give all ranches & all stock in creation to *see* you three alive and well at home once more," concluding, "Oh come, do not say there is no risk, or refuse me this boon—I am alone & sick and God only knows how weary with expecting and miserable with disappointment."

After more than sixteen years in Texas, Mary Maverick was still facing the same uncertainties she had had to face when her husband rode out of San Antonio in the late 1830s following marauding Indians. But now it was worse because experience had taught her that sorrow could strike to the heart of their home and because she now had to worry not only about her husband but about her growing sons.

In a fortuitous turn, Maverick and his elder boys arrived home on the same day that Mary wrote. That summer, they established their Conquista Ranch and left Jack in charge once more. Meanwhile, Mary had another delicate baby to nurse. She recorded his care in detail in her diary, but it is apparent that she felt reluctant to name the child, to give him a concrete identity when she feared she might lose him yet. Finally, diffidently she did. "I begin to fear he is not fattening much or is at a kind of stand still but all tell me 'tis fancy & I hope so," she wrote, "He weighs 10 lbs, not any more than a week ago but bless God I have much very much to be thankful for & hope & pray to keep this dear little boy we sometimes call Albert."[63]

Mary continued her keen interest in spiritualism, admitting in her diary that whereas some thought her a spirit medium others considered her "a self deluded enthusiast." "I don't know truly if I am, or am not, either," she wrote, but she found it a "great joy & very natural" to believe that "our friends in the spirit land" could look down upon, love, and assist the living. Like her husband, she saw "little of physical manifestations, nothing to make me fixedly a convert." Yet still, she concluded, it was "a most sweet trust & I will repose faith in it."[64] Her belief in spirit friends would carry her through the family separations that lay immediately ahead. Her boys were growing up, and her husband soon would be off again, running the race he had set for himself along the paths of public duty and personal gain.

A "Respectable and Rather Venerable Senator"

I enjoy myself much less here now as a respectable and rather
venerable senator . . . than I did with chains 1200 miles on foot
and a prisoner between Texas & the City of Mexico.
—Sam Maverick to his wife, July 16, 1856

HAVING RE-ENTERED the political world, Maverick was to remain active
in Texas affairs of state until the aftermath of the Civil War brought
sweeping changes in government from the local to state levels. The years
1854 through 1856 would find him taking a stand for the principles of
democratic equality and continuing his involvement in state issues ranging from frontier protection to landownership for settlers on the vacant public domain. Much of his energy during this time, however,
centered on railroads.

Since the 1840s, national interest in a transcontinental railway had
escalated, with northerners naturally favoring a northern route and
southerners envisioning a railroad from the trade centers of Memphis
or New Orleans to Texas and California. In December of 1853, the Fifth
Texas Legislature, of which Maverick was a part, had passed a bill to
provide for the construction of a railroad across Texas as a link in a
railway system to the Pacific. The following summer, Maverick and sixteen other prominent men together submitted a bid for construction
of such a road. They proposed to lay out a route from the eastern
boundary of Texas to "a suitable point on the Rio Grande, at or near
the town of El Paso," to "finish and place in running order" fifty miles
within eighteen months, and to complete one hundred miles "each and
every year thereafter."[1]

The ambitious proposal was made by such established and reputable
Texans as Maverick, Hamilton Bee, Matt Ward, J. Pinckney Hender-

son, and John Hancock in alliance with eastern railroad promoters R. J. Walker and T. Butler King, directors and agents of the Atlantic and Pacific Company. Walker had impressive credentials as former secretary of the U.S. Treasury and author of the successful Walker Tariff, but he was also involved in a number of dubious grand financial schemes. He had plunged into railroad speculation with the Atlantic and Pacific Railroad construction charter, obtained from the New York legislature with authorization to issue one hundred million dollars in capital stock. As this effort faltered, he and Georgia Whig King latched onto the Mississippi and Pacific charter.[2]

On August 5, Maverick wrote to his wife from Austin that he thought the governor would accept the group's proposal, adding, "I shall endeavor to keep clear of the possibility of ruining myself, by entering into any contract. I neither wish to make nor to lose: but only to see the great work go on—to the benefit of all."

Maverick's statement is borne out by Julian P. Greer's analysis of the records of the San Antonio and Mexican Gulf Rail Road effort, in which he found not only self-interest but "much laudable, selfless striving" among the directors, despite conflicts of interest that would create a furor today. For example, in the San Antonio and Mexican Gulf Rail Road venture, not only had company president Jones and director Devine received the construction contract, but Maverick and his fellow directors sold tracts to the company. They did so at reasonable prices for the time, however, usually under a dollar an acre, depending on the location, and with the purpose of getting the venture off the ground.[3]

Pease approved the new trans-Texas railroad alliance's proposal, but he soon declared the contract forfeited, judging inadequate the stock deposit made by Walker and King on behalf of the contractors. In this judgment he was backed by a public already weary of shaky railroad ventures, so that "it was useless to dwell upon the high standing, integrity, and unimpeachable honesty of the company."[4]

As 1854 neared an end, Sam Maverick joined the other contractors in a Montgomery, Alabama, meeting, with Walker and King, who argued that they had complied with the law, that the contract was in force, and that the company should proceed with organization. Maverick and the other Texas promoters refused to go along. "I broke ground in one of our conferences with those humbugs Walker & King, and told them flatly that the Governor of Texas had only done his duty," Maverick wrote on December 20. "We Texians refused to contest the point of sufficiency of the Deposit and would not organize a company."

Not only did this end the trans-Texas railroad venture before it had fairly begun, but the San Antonio and Mexican Gulf Rail Road was in dire straits. Over four years after its incorporation, not a foot of track had been laid, and as Maverick reached Montgomery, Jones and Devine forfeited their contract.

The problems plaguing Maverick and his companions were common to Texas railroad entrepreneurs of the period trying to raise capital with vast amounts of land nearly worthless to eastern capitalists. Eleven railroads were to be constructed in the state by the time of the Civil War, most of them in the 1850s, but they were precarious and exorbitant undertakings—the eighty-mile stretch of road between Harrisburg and the Colorado River carried a price tag of over a million dollars, three times what it should have cost.[5]

Leaving Montgomery, Maverick turned away from railroad business to take up a long-neglected personal duty. Since his father's death almost three years before, he had received periodic letters from brother-in-law William Van Wyck regarding the disposition of the elder Samuel's estate. Now the prodigal son journeyed to the Anderson District courthouse and Pendleton to check the records for himself.

Despite Samuel's repeated assurances to his son that his affairs were in order, two wills had been found—the second protecting his daughters' portions from being lost by their husbands—but neither had been admitted to probate.[6] A judge in February, 1853, had ordered the elder Maverick's personal property sold. Accordingly, in April, 1853, the slaves were sold for $24,471, other personal property for $1,540. Van Wyck purchased for Maverick the family clock, a large silver cup, and portraits of the elder Samuel and of his son as a child. Van Wyck also saved Samuel's clothes and the family Bible for his brother-in-law.[7]

The land would be next, and neither Van Wyck nor Maverick evinced much interest in trying to hold onto a portion of the South Carolina–to–Alabama land empire Samuel had built up. Van Wyck had been drawn to Pendleton and to participation in his father-in-law's land business once because of his own financial need, and a second time because of Samuel's stroke. Duty rather than affinity for land administration had led him to become involved in his father-in-law's business affairs, and Maverick had chosen to build his own land empire outside the perimeters of his father's.

When Maverick finally traveled to Pendleton after his meeting in Montgomery in December, 1854, Samuel's lands were in the process of being sold by order of the Court of Equity, with proceeds to be divided among the surviving children and grandchildren.[8] Van Wyck was struggling mightily to handle the situation for the benefit of the family. He had reported on October 23 that the Anderson District lands had been sold that month for disappointing prices. "I stood alone and bid them up as high as I dared to do, and not have too many fall in my hands," Van Wyck explained. On October 14, he had halted the sale of Samuel's Pendleton lots, "for which I have been greatly censured by the community," he wrote wearily. They were going too cheaply, and he hoped to realize more by waiting for construction of a railroad. Meanwhile, lands in other districts were being appraised in preparation for sale.[9]

Maverick did not notify the Van Wycks of his coming; consequently, his arrival in Anderson District found them in Charleston. They hurried home to greet him while he surveyed his father's estate business in the Anderson District courthouse probate office, visited family friends at Pendleton, and sold a tract he still owned in the area. He seemed unconcerned with seeing his sister and family and impatient of the delay, sending word that they need not come, then starting for Charleston to see them, then finding himself "provokingly detained" by meeting William and Lydia and their four youngest children en route and having to return to Pendleton.

Maverick's letters written from Pendleton to his wife have a curiously detached tone, as if all his ties to home had eroded. This stemmed in part from the fact that Montpelier had burned in early 1850, and Samuel and the Van Wycks had rebuilt on a nearby knoll. "Mr Van Wyck's SM place," Maverick wrote at the top of a letter of January 2, 1855, in which he reported noncommittally, "I find our friends generally well, and nothing new to mention." Of his business, he wrote indifferently, "I thought it important to see Mr. Van Wyck and have an insight to the business of the Estate—especially as I feel like not often repeating so long a journey as I have made to this place."

In truth, Maverick was beginning to earn his reputation as a reclusive eccentric. On his trip to move his cattle operations the preceding year, he had bypassed the Clow home, leading Robert Clow to write to Mary, "Why did not Mr. M. come through this place on his way to the Peninsula? I think he might have given us a call." Writing to announce the birth of a third daughter while Maverick was on his Pendleton trip, Clow returned to the subject by conjecturing, "I presume he was in a hurry, or it was in the night or something of that sort, I will only say we would have been glad to have seen him. What would you say if I was to go through San Antonio, and not even call to ask how you were? But you will say Mr. M. is eccentric and you [Clow] are not."[10]

Maverick *did* stop to see Mary's brother Robert in Tuscaloosa and to sell a Tuscaloosa tract on his way home in January, then scribbled a brief will in a letter to his wife as he once again boarded a vessel at New Orleans for the chancy Gulf crossing. Like his father, Maverick had taken care to remain virtually debt-free, and now he bequeathed to "my immaculate Mary A. Maverick" all of his property "both personal & real . . . also all that shall come from my father's estate. Like the Roman Catholics in regard to another Mary I have full faith in this one. She knows better than I, how to deal with the children, and whether property ought to be given them,—when, & how much." He also expressed the wry hope that "she may find some better use for [the property] than I have had time to discover." Mary endorsed this missive by writing, "A precious letter. . . . What unvarying confidence in a poor ignorant wife—yet one earnestly aiming to do right & hope."[11]

The traveler returned safely to a San Antonio buzzing with political excitement as the American, or Know-Nothing, party, came to prominence. A secretive nativist group originating on the Eastern Seaboard, the party was anti-Catholic, pro-Union, and opposed to foreigners holding office. It had managed to get its slate of candidates elected to San Antonio city office the year before, and now city residents were becoming more aware of the threat it posed to harmony among the diverse ethnic and religious groups of the city. Not only did San Antonio retain a heavily Mexican population, but it had become the home for a substantial number of European, primarily German, emigrants, as well. The Know-Nothings posed a clear threat to the democratic rights of both of these groups.

Until the arrival of the Know-Nothings, political party affiliations had remained tenuous in Texas, with political adherents usually dividing into pro-Houston and anti-Houston factions. Now the new party forced Democrats, Sam Maverick among them, to organize and speak out for Democratic party principles.[12]

Who was a Know-Nothing and who was not? Maverick, again a candidate for the Senate in the summer of 1855, found himself quizzed along with other candidates by the Democratic Committee of Correspondence of Bexar County through the pages of San Antonio's English- and Spanish-language newspapers.[13] Maverick's reply left no doubt as to where he stood. "I am not, and have not been, associated with the 'Know-Nothing' society, nor do I approve of their principles," he asserted, characterizing the principles as "Chinese or Turkish, or anything but American." In fact, he considered "the getting up, and the carrying on of such a society as this . . . a dangerous conspiracy against the peace and dignity of the country." He warned that "if good men will not suppress and utterly denounce secret political clubs like these, we shall straightway see even more treasonable counterplots."[14]

Maverick provided a ringing defense of San Antonio's Mexican Catholics against Know-Nothing attempts to exclude them from government. He had remained on warm terms with such San Antonio natives as statesman José Antonio Navarro, and he had not forgotten their contribution to Texas independence. "These Catholics threw in their share with the others," he wrote, "and they bought this country, and I find that they like it, and I am happy to see it." Indeed, he argued, they had paid "with a parcel of their blood" for the freedom Texans enjoyed.

Maverick completely repudiated the whole idea of excluding portions of the electorate from having a say in government. America's gates "are open to all the world," he wrote, "and who would shut them." No group could claim to be "exclusive proprietors"; instead, the continent was to become, "under God, the field for the regeneration of all mankind," a place where emigrants could "come and learn that men are still friends, though they do not think alike."[15] In addition to lashing out against Know-Nothingism in print, Maverick chaired a mass protest meeting "OF THE DEMOCRATIC PARTY, And all others opposed to SECRET POLICE ORGANIZATIONS," as the San Antonio *Ledger* trumpeted.[16]

During this summer, 1855, campaign, Maverick forged a strong alliance with Governor Pease, also running for re-election. At a Bexar County public meeting to endorse candidates for governor and lieutenant governor, Maverick said of Pease that "a better and safer man, or one upon the whole, of sounder and more practical views, could nowhere be found."[17] A Democratic party slate soon emerged in the county, with Pease for governor, Maverick for senator, and a German director of the San Antonio and Mexican Gulf Rail Road, Jacob Waelder, for representative. Among those endorsing the slate were an alliance of German American Bexar citizens and Henri Castro's colonists, who passed strong resolutions against the Know-Nothings.[18]

The Democrats were victorious in Bexar County, but the Know-Nothings were able to place about twenty representatives and five senators in the Texas legislature.[19] When Maverick returned to that body in early November, he wrote his wife of his hope that "party differences will not prevent harmonious action." Immediately, a conflict erupted between established Democrats such as Maverick and a loose coalition including the Know-Nothings over a relatively minor matter, the awarding of the state printing contract, with the Democratic *State Gazette* getting the nod by a narrow margin in both houses. Maverick wrote to Mary of the incident on November 9, 1855:

> If we had been beaten I should have been mortified, and perhaps not so patient and philosophic as to say that this sort of array is better in many respects than unanimity. If it serves as a moral check to keep us on the watch to be right and consistent, it will doubtless do more for the country than all these Know Nothing gentlemen could ever perform (if they should recant and do their best to repair their errors).

In this sixth session of the state legislature, Maverick was serving on the Finance and Internal Improvements committees, and in the latter capacity he fought against breaking up the railroad reserve land set aside by the previous legislature for a trans-Texas railroad. As the Mississippi and Pacific venture had come to naught and settlers and speculators were locating on the reserve lands, a majority of the Internal Improvements Committee favored repealing the action reserving the lands.

Maverick and two other members did not. It had been argued that keeping the lands closed would be unjust to locators, but in a minority report on November 26, Maverick argued that Texas still offered "a boundless domain of hill and dale, outside of the Rail Road reserve" and that speculators were behind the claims of injustice. The lands set aside along the thirty-second latitude, he wrote, remained "the shortest, the least expensive, and most practicable" of continental routes, and Texans should take a long-term view by keeping them open for the eventual coming of a railroad, which could prove "our chief means for all sorts of Internal Improvements." He remarked, "We are, so to say, founders of the State, and should legislate for posterity," doing "what we conceive to be our duty, let come what will."[20]

Maverick also quickly became involved in another dispute in this session. He opposed a bill offered by Henry McCulloch for protection of the frontier against Indian incursions. No one could dispute the need for such protection, for Indian raids along the western frontier seemed endless and had again grown in intensity. In October, Maverick joined five other prominent Bexar citizens in calling in the pages of the San Antonio *Sentinel* for a citizens' expedition into Mexico to combat Mexican aid to the raiders.[21] Now McCulloch reported some western areas "almost entirely depopulated" and approximately forty people killed within sixty miles of San Antonio in the preceding eight months.[22] The Mavericks themselves, while visiting the Houstons on the Cibolo in August, had spent a night "forting up" with a crowd in the Houston home as seventeen-year-old Sam and fifteen-year-old Lewis joined in pursuit of Comanches who had killed two people and stolen horses.[23]

McCulloch's bill bothered Maverick, however, because it called for raising a militia of a thousand men to serve six-month terms, acting as a vigilante force along the frontier with unlimited freedom to pursue and punish whomever they chose. Maverick was afraid that a regiment raised under this broad mandate would be made up of opportunists who would become a law unto themselves and would also engage in filibusterism against Mexico. Thus, he spoke against the bill on the floor of the Senate when it was brought up for discussion on November 16.[24] The next day, he succeeded in referring McCulloch's proposal to a joint committee from the two houses and, as chairman of that committee, he was able to substitute his own alternate bill calling for the mustering of minutemen from among frontier families.[25]

He continued to be concerned as well with increasing the number of frontier families, arguing for a preemption bill giving 320 acres to settlers on the public domain. Some senators felt that the time for providing such inducement for settlement was past and that the state should hold onto its land in hopes of eventually profiting financially. But Maverick, calling the grants "the true policy of our State," asked, "Do we not need population to settle up our frontier—to locate upon the millions and millions, that are now, and probably will be for a long time to come, in a wilderness condition?" Only with settlement, he argued, could the resources of the state be developed, railroads built, and an extensive system of internal improvements put into effect. "It is idle to talk about holding back our lands to make money out of them," he asserted.[26]

He was doing just that privately, of course, but for those lands to be worth anything, the tide of settlement would have to be helped along. Maverick acted out of self-interest as well as commitment to the public good, but the two motives dovetailed nicely in his vision for the future of Texas.

That vision, as noted earlier, included a network of common schools, and in December Maverick spoke out strongly against a state university funding bill as premature. "What, half a million dollars for one or two universities, before we have built two school houses, or put in operation one school for the space of a year!" he declared. Instead, he observed that "my best hopes would be fulfilled if I could be permitted to see, spread abroad, common schools and common sense," and he felt the electorate would support him in this matter.[27]

As the time drew near for Governor Pease's inauguration in the new three-story limestone capitol building, Maverick encouraged his wife to come to Austin for the festivities, and this time Mary agreed. The children were in good health, although Maverick's letters home indicate that the slaves continued to frustrate her. Maverick wrote on November 16, "I am truly sorry, my love, that you have so much real hardship with the plaguing negroes." Calling himself a "recreant governor of negrodom," he shouldered the blame, "which I know that I deserve, in not arranging and adjusting things better at home." Still, he urged his "Dear Mary" to "wear your wonted placidity, and bid defiance to the cares of life—if you can!"

On December 20, Mary arrived in Austin with the four youngest children and the couple's seventeen-year-old niece Joey Thompson of Alabama for a two-week stay at the boardinghouse where Maverick roomed. With Joey leaving a wake of Austin admirers, the family returned to San Antonio shortly after the new year. "I presume you reached home safely but that you did so with any degree of satisfaction I have my doubts," Maverick wrote on January 4, 1856. "The sleepy children, jolting stage, and rum drinking judges, gave you trouble enough."

Mary and the children did not stay in San Antonio long before they were back visiting on the Cibolo while Maverick wrapped up business at the legislature, introducing a bill to aid the troubled San Antonio and Mexican Gulf Rail Road and seeing a county created that bore his name. The act to create Maverick County, formed out of Kinney County and bordering on the Rio Grande, became law on February 2, 1856.[28]

Maverick returned from the legislature bringing his slave Jack's wife Rosetta and their three children, whom he had purchased in Austin at Jack's request.[29] He had written Mary that they could sell the whole family, Jack included, back to Rosetta's previous owner if things did not work out, concluding that "we will be more like[ly] to lose temper than money by the trade."[30]

This purchase proved no more fortuitous than Maverick's Charleston one, and Mary in an undated early 1856 diary entry entreated the spirit of her father to "encourage a poor unhappy child tonight," wondering, "Did you feel the miseries of an inharmonious life? . . . Did you deprecate the curse of slavery.—I too am *ground up* in this relentless *most* unholy system."

Her husband remained away from home as frequently as ever, in late April joining a party to survey along the Red Fork of the Colorado up to the Arkansas-to–New Mexico emigrant trail established by Randolph Marcy in 1849. At Fort Chadbourne to get packs for mules on May 6, he wrote that he was "sound and hearty" and that Chadbourne was "beautiful," with cold, almost frosty nights. But the expedition was marred by tragedy when member William McDonald accidentally shot himself with a double-barreled shotgun and died instantly. Writing Mary of the incident on May 15, Maverick reported that it would still be at least a month before he could return home, as they were going ahead with "a couple of hundred surveys or more" on the Concho.

He returned home in time to see seventeen-year-old Lewis off to college. The Mavericks had puzzled about where to send their eldest sons for further schooling, particularly Sam, who showed little inclination for higher education. When Maverick had visited Pendleton the previous year, he had written to Mary, "I find the same difficulty here as with us about schools" and reported that one friend was afraid to send his sons north to college, "lest they lose a relish for S.C."[31]

Now, in June, 1856, Lewis chose to leave for the University of Vermont at Burlington, the alma mater of his San Antonio schoolmaster George Dennison.[32] His father did see at least one advantage in a northern school in that Lewis might be more easily led astray by *"good fellows* and *friendly fellows* and trifling fellows" in a southern college.[33] To Mary, the choice was simply very far away. "I felt as if some dear one had died," she remembers in her memoirs, "and I missed my dear Lewis dreadfully."[34]

With Lewis' departure, the entries in Mary's diary, never plentiful, dwindled and died as she turned her energies toward writing letters to her son, many of which survive. She worried about Lewis, more than she would about Sam when he followed his brother to distant places. Sam with his broad face and open features looked like his mother, but he was hearty, frank, cheerful, and fond of good times; Lewis, with the slender, intense look of his father, had inherited an introspective, brooding, sensitive temperament that Mary felt was too like her own. Soon after his departure, she warned him against accepting professions of friendship too readily, concluding that "in this selfish world we all must learn cold reason and your Yankee classmates will be a profitable chapter to study." Of her own emotions at his absence, she told him, "I think my blessed spirit-friends help me to hope & trust & I am telling my heart when it aches—That it must be strong [as] this is only the beginning—for one after another must go to school, must leave Mother for their own good."[35] Indeed, the Mavericks were planning to place Sam in a school in the fall, but the question remained where.

Meanwhile, Maverick attended a summer session of the Sixth Legislature, suffering through a sweltering Austin July and August and reporting the temperature to be one hundred or over for days at a time and his bed "hot to the hand like clothes held to the fire or just taken out [of] the sunshine."[36] Boarding at the establishment of merchant and Swedish emigrant leader Swen Swensen, he noted on July 28 that his host had a number of Swedish families there, "industrious, good people," who washed and cleaned shoes "in old-country Style" and made the establishment "get along very well without blacks."

Still, he wished for a room situated on a breezy hill. "I am going through a fiery trial," he wrote on July 16, "and I would be glad to resign if it was not for putting a large constituency to so much inconvenience about a small matter connected with my personal convenience." Maverick had over the years devised a personal health regimen built on plenty of fresh, cool air, cold water bathing, and vigorous scrubbing of the skin with a brush. Now he suffered from the heat and poor ventilation. Comparing his ordeal unfavorably to the one he suffered while a prisoner in Mexico, he wrote, "The very houses they now build are so constructed they are a greater torment to me, to Sweat in, than the Prisons of Mexico."

Then there was the interminable business of the legislature. "I am in despair about adjournment," he wrote, mentioning that the loquacious Dancy, William Ochiltree, "and some 20 of that sort in the House are in full blast and talking like men who seem to have no other occupation nor hope of Heaven but the privilege of talking."[37]

Maverick himself took the floor at least once in the session, arguing in favor of a bill to allow the use of Spanish before Justice's Courts "in certain cases" and in courts west of the Guadalupe River. He reminded reluctant colleagues that the state's Spanish-speaking inhabitants were the original possessors of the territory and loyal subjects of Texas who would benefit greatly from the law. As for arguments for the superiority of the English language, he contended that "one of the elements of its superiority consists in its facility to receive additions" from other languages.[38]

Again, much of his time at the legislature was spent on railroad matters. Walker and King had reorganized the trans-Texas railroad effort under the auspices of the Texas Western Railroad Company, using a charter transferred to their Atlantic and Pacific Company before the Mississippi and Pacific Railway effort. Now the Internal Improvements Committee of which Maverick was a part was caught in a dispute between the railroad promoters and Governor Pease, who remained wary of the promoters and disapproving of the fact that the group's charter made no provisions for keeping control of the venture in Texas. At the same time, a select committee dealing with the Missouri and Pacific Railroad reserves east of the Brazos was appointed with Maverick as a member, and the committee reluctantly concluded that these reserves should be open for settlement, as "the object for which the reserve was made has entirely failed to be accomplished."[39]

The San Antonio and Mexican Gulf Rail Road, too, was occupying Maverick's time. With ten miles graded and a quantity of crossties on hand, the board of directors in April had entered into a contract with Col. Benjamin Osgood to build the first stretch of road from Powder Horn and Lavaca to Victoria, about thirty miles inland. That same month, Maverick and Francis Giraud had been appointed to open books of subscription for one million in capital stock.[40] Now he was being summoned by another director to go to New York with company president William Clarke to obtain bonds. "It's a pressing case I believe, but I shall refuse to go there—and afterwards," he wrote to Mary on July 28, "I think I am quite sick of the Rail R business and want to stay a little at home."

In addition to being sick of the railroad business, he was ready to get out of the cattle business. "I did not promise Cornelio Delgado or anybody whatever to let them have cattle or oxen," he wrote in the same letter. "I am on a trade, I expect, with Mr. Toutant for all the cattle." Rancher A. Toutant had convinced Maverick "that it is your interest to sell and mine to purchase." On arriving at Maverick's Conquista Ranch, Toutant found slave Jack and a white man on the premises reluctant to round up the cattle, which Jack now estimated at about two hundred head. On July 18, Toutant wrote, "Now I must conclude that the negro boy is not over anxious that you should sell your stock, either because he has there, indeed, an enviable birth [sic], or because he does not wish you to be convinced, by counting, of the gross negligence of which he has been guilty." Nonetheless, Toutant offered two thousand dollars cash for "the whole stock as it now stands."[41]

From the legislature, Maverick countered with an offer of $2,250, to include "the wagon, yokes, hogs and horses, that are mine." But he soon accepted Toutant's offer, glad to get out of a deteriorating situation, as Jack and his white companion, now identified as a member of a cattle-stealing gang, had been run off the property, taking Maverick's pistol with them.[42] Thus ended Maverick's only documented experience with cattle ranching, despite the cattle baron myths that were to cluster around him.

When he returned home from the summer session, he reluctantly reconsidered his refusal to go to New York and agreed to make the trip on behalf of the railroad. He would take with him nineteen-year-old Sam and see if they could find a college for the youth, as well as visit with Lewis in Vermont. Accordingly, father and son departed San Antonio in late September, traveling to the coast and this time visiting the Clows before sailing to New Orleans. Clow reported to Mary, "Lizzie and myself both remarked that Mr. M. looked better than we had ever seen him. He was in fine spirits, too, and he and Sam anticipated a pleasant journey."[43] It would be a journey of discovery for both. The younger man was to learn something of the world beyond the Brazos; the elder was to learn something of his son.

Maverick had spent very little time with his children, and now he observed his eldest with a bemused incredulity. This unstudious and rough-and-ready product of the frontier got into two scrapes on the voyage to New Orleans, coming to blows with another fellow in the baggage section and enraging a sailor by accidently spitting into the man's soup. Maverick wrote his wife from New Orleans, "The more I see of Sam the more I think it would be folly to put him 4 years more at *Latin & Greek.*" Instead, he felt it would be best to "get him into some practical scientific & modern language school." He found his son "very abstracted," as likely to have his collar in as out, yet "of most noble nature." Summing up, Maverick wrote, "He is both as mild as a lamb and as brave as a lion. I never saw anything like him in my whole life."[44]

Arriving in New York and embarking on railroad business, Maverick met the son of one of his old Yale classmates and a recent graduate of the University of Edinburgh. This gave the Texas father and son a new direction to mull, and on November 8, young Sam sailed on the *Atlantic* steamer for Liverpool, en route to the Scottish university. Waiting to hear of the steamer's safe arrival, Maverick wrote his wife on November 27, "I am under a heavy responsibility about Sam: More than I first thought, when he and I together got up this business of his going to Europe." A week later, with news that his son had reached England, Maverick wrote, "I pray that my telling Sam go to Europe may turn out well. I think he needed to be sent somewhere to experience & learn something that I did not find here."

With his son gone, Maverick turned more intently to railroad business. He and Clarke had come to have bonds engraved and printed, to "dispose of 200 of the bonds on the best terms obtainable" for railroad capital, and to obtain iron and other materials so that construction could begin in earnest at Lavaca. If contractor Osgood had managed to obtain the iron and other materials, they were to pay him with bonds. If not, they were to pay other subcontractors who looked as if they could deliver.[45]

Excitement ran high back in Texas, with Clow in October reporting the citizens of Lavaca "quite in good spirits" since the departure of Maverick and Clarke. He reported to Mary, "The citizens say 'We know that Mr. Maverick would not have anything to do with the matter, if there was any duplicity or humbug about it.'" Indeed, he continued, "Mr. M. I need not inform you, has an enviable character throughout the state, for probity, sincerity and honesty of purpose."[46]

Maverick was hopeful, too, about effecting a real start, signing a contract with Osgood and partners on November 15. "I am quite in hopes
they will go vigorously forward to finish 25 miles by July next," he wrote
Mary.[47] On November 27, he reported having signed contracts for an
additional twenty-five miles. But the business proceeded slowly, with
Maverick spending "short, cold, dark and rainy" days conferring with
railroad men and lawyers. "I feel quite a martyr to the Rail Road," he
wrote on December 4, feeling his optimism slipping, "and all I can write
you is that I hope it will go on as contracted for."

Much as they tried, however, Clarke and Maverick could not raise
enough capital in the eastern financial center, where potential investors
not only questioned the Texas law granting sixteen sections per acre
but generally disdained the land that could be the Texans' only col-
lateral security of any substance.[48]

As he continued what he called his "nondescript service" for the
railroad through the month of December, Maverick also took in some
New York events, including the Women's Rights Convention being held
in the city. Only eight years since the groundbreaking Seneca Falls convention, America'a and England's leading women's rights activists were
using a New York gathering as a means of furthering their cause, sub-
jecting themselves, as Maverick reported, to "a storm of hisses" from
a gallery packed with jesting critics. He attended the convention on
the evening of November 26 and wrote his wife the next day of his
impressions on listening to Lucy Stone Blackwell, Ernestine Rose of
England, and that "fine old Quaker" Lucretia Mott.

Maverick evidenced great sympathy for the speakers and their cause,
particularly in regard to the importance of education for women. He
reported that Mrs. Rose "spoke very well indeed, on the Educational,
the Industrial and the Political wrongs suffered by woman, in all ages,
even yet. I must say that I agree with her."

However, the tone of the convention carried too much bitterness
toward "man as an oppressor" and too much urgency in regard to suffrage to suit him. "It is idle to say that man is woman's enemy," he wrote
Mary. "The habits and customs of both man & woman are woman's
enemy. We love & cherish our daughters as much or more than our
sons; and yet *you* as well as I bring them up in a manner less defended
against the wrongs of society." He foresaw a day when women would
and should have the political power they sought through the vote, but
was put off by the advocacy of the "zealots" for immediate political ac-

tivity in the Irish wards of the city, concluding that they needed to practice prudence and moderation in righting the "abundant & real" wrongs.[49]

The suffragists were not the only ones who might practice more prudence and moderation. Lewis came from Burlington to visit his father in December and like his brother showed a propensity for falling into scrapes, refusing to take off his hat in the second gallery of the theater at the preemptory request of another theatergoer and attacking a storekeeper whom he suspected of trying to cheat his father. In the first incident, Maverick reported to his wife, "I then asked him myself [to remove the hat] and afterward joked him about the bad policy of a fight in that seat, when it was 30 feet or more to the pit." In the second, father and son were hauled off to the city judge, who "discharged Lewis as an indiscreet young hothead." Treading gingerly with the wife to whom he had left most of the child raising, Maverick asserted that he had no fear the youth would eventually learn prudence, concluding, "I am not uneasy about Lewis: but like him very much."[50]

As the dimly lit winter days passed in New York and Maverick's railroad work drew toward an unsatisfactory close, he took time to ruminate on philosophical matters. Old benefactor Waddy Thompson was in town, too, eager to share with Maverick his fascination with spiritualism. But Maverick was growing impatient with spiritualism's emphasis on a distant heaven or improbable heaven-on-earth. He wrote to his wife on December 4, "It all appears to be speculation & enquiry about the mysteries of a hereafter life—without regard to what we instinctively know to be our moral obligations to our Creator and our duties to our neighbor."

Maverick promised to remain open to his wife's search for truth among spiritualist doctrines, but he found them in conflict with "my most solemn convictions and my constitution & nature." The emphasis, he insisted, should be on man as an accountable free agent with "moral, social and eternal obligations." What these obligations were, and how they could best be carried out, would become the subject of intense debate in Texas as Maverick returned to a state edging steadily toward secession from the Union.

13

Love, Honor, and Duty

We see how everything was made to love,
And how they err who in a world like this
Find anything to hate but human pride.
— Lines from a poem sent by Mary Maverick
to son Lewis, February 1, 1857

Our highest honor is our strictest duty.
— Sam Maverick arguing in the Texas Senate
against giving recognition to filibuster William Walker
as Nicaragua's president, February 3, 1858

AS HER HUSBAND'S STAY in New York lengthened and Lewis and Sam took up new lives in new places, Mary Maverick struggled with familiar feelings of loss and change. These feelings were intensified by the news of her youngest brother Robert's death in Alabama in September, 1856. She took the loss hard; Maverick wrote from New York, "I pray you may continue well—with your mind softened to a just sense of pious resignation."[1]

Brother William Adams had passed away in 1853, so Andrew Adams, practicing medicine in Sonora, Mexico, was now the only surviving male sibling in Mary's family. She received one of his infrequent communications at about the same time the news came of Robert's demise. Andrew's gloomy missive could certainly do nothing to cheer his sister's thoughts, for he described his seven years in Mexico as full of "trials afflictions Povertys and distresses Spiritual and temporal," capped by the recent death of a wife whom he alluded to obliquely as having left him with three small children.[2]

Andrew reflected Mary's own propensity to brooding, but the third surviving sibling, Lizzie, maintained an acerbic and practical approach to life. "You must feel very lonely with the boys and Mr M away, but

I think you are too despondant," she wrote to her sister in December, pointing out that "Sam and Lewis will get along bravely without your wasting so many sad repinings about them." Instead, Lizzie advised to "let trouble in only when it *does* come—let fancy work on the bright materials, throw the dingy ones aside."[3]

Mary, weighed down by grief, fears, and a sense of her own inadequacy, could not follow such counsel. In the last entry of any substance in her diary, on New Year's Day, 1857, as she waited for her husband's return from New York, she lamented her lost and absent family members. "The buried ones are associated in my heart—with the absent living ones," she wrote, calling it a "deep abiding sorrow" to be parted from one's own.

Just as heavy as this separation, however, was the continuing sense of her own weakness. Her diary entries for the year just ended show that she judged herself a failure as slaveowner, wife, and mother, with "glaring defects and vile tempers" overriding her "high aspirings" and "noble impulses." Her husband she continued to view as "so much better than me"—gentle with the children and noble-hearted, while she was uneasily conscious of *"having been, or tho't his ideal."* Now, she mourned, "I strive, I pray to do good, to feel an unwavering and abiding trust in God's love & mercy & power, but I never entirely succeed in any of these." Perhaps, she reasoned, even her introspective search for righteousness was that of "a great egotist." Critical self-examination led her into a maze of miseries. "Is it so with others?" she wondered, "this struggle, this inconsistancy, this repining weakness which yet *conquers* all your good."[4]

She still clung to the idea of "a spirit land where youth & hope & trust & innocence & purity *may* be regained," but continued to approach the subject warily. "There is danger in spiritualism, as in everything else, in believing too much, in fanaticism," she would soon write to Lewis on hearing that he had attended a lecture by Poughkeepsie seer A. J. Davis and wife. Yet, she concluded, "we may *hope* that our departed friends *enjoy the privilege* of watching over & impressing us for good."[5]

Mary would come to a firmer peace, but not without further emotional suffering. "Mothers as a class have much to bear which only God knows or can lighten," she had written to her second son shortly after his departure.[6] With Maverick's return she was soon to become pregnant a final time and plunge anew into the fight to save a baby with a tenuous hold on life.

Meanwhile, her husband was growing even more deeply involved in political matters. The year 1857 saw Texas political allegiances shifting, as Democratic candidate H. R. Runnels and independent Democrat Sam Houston battled for the governorship. Houston had associated himself with the Know-Nothings the previous year, but now the Know-Nothing star was fading and state Democrats were breaking into two camps—the Jacksonian Unionists, who favored Houston, and the mainline Democratic party, Calhoun states' rights advocates who backed Runnels. Former congressman H. W. Sublett suggested that Maverick run for lieutenant governor and draw the western vote.[7] The San Antonio *Ledger* reported that a candidate from West Texas appeared to be a "settled thing" and mentioned Maverick and Francis R. Lubbock, both "capable and popular, and tried and true democrats," as the most prominent names being considered.[8]

Maverick was caught in a quandary, for he discovered himself aligned with his old nemesis Houston on the secession issue, which was becoming uppermost in everyone's minds. However, the Bexar senator had established himself firmly as a mainline Democrat from whom the states' rights advocates expected support. John Marshall, chairman of the Central Democratic Committee, wrote to him in May asking him to see that literature supporting the Runnels slate was distributed among the Mexican and Anglo citizens of the Rio Grande counties. Marshall announced, "Every Democrat must now do his duty. I intend to review Sam Houston's votes to satisfy the people of Texas that he is a dangerous representative of the South in Congress."[9]

Houston was defeated for the only time in his political career. It would take two more years of southern secessionist agitation for old Democrats with Union sympathies such as Maverick to come out in his favor.

Maverick himself had chosen to run again for the Senate and had won re-election. As he prepared to return to the legislature, he and his wife mourned the suicide of old friend Thomas Jefferson Rusk, who had been serving in the U.S. Senate and promoting Texas boundary and railroad interests. Rusk had visited San Antonio a few years earlier, taking Mary to the theater, and he had exchanged infrequent letters with Maverick. Now Mary wrote, "This is a great loss for Texas to deplore, and an unhappy private mystery."[10]

She was expecting again, and her tenth and last child, a girl, was born on October 17, 1857. The baby was "a wee teeny creature," and as with the previous child, Mary showed reluctance to name her when her survival seemed uncertain. She made a game of the matter, however, writing to sons Sam and Lewis soliciting names.[11] In his first letter from the legislature on November 6, her husband wrote, "I haven't yet found a name that I would like to give our little dear tho I have thought of it constantly—and of you my love—whose health I pray may be soon restored and preserved." He was also thinking of their eldest in Scotland and still feeling that a practical business course would be best for the youth, perhaps one provided by Dolbear's Mercantile College in New Orleans and favored by San Antonio judge George Paschal. "P. thinks he could have done something worthwhile if he had learned or been early drilled into methodical practice," Maverick explained to Mary on November 13, adding, "I suspect he is right—in my own case I feel that this want of method is the great deficiency of the American Men of the age."

Maverick playfully reported that he and Clow, who was joining his brother-in-law in the legislature, were boarding with "a pretty widow named Robertson." The comment got a response, for a few days later he vowed, "The good looks and good conduct of our landlady can have no other effect upon the married gentlemen than to increase their admiration if possible of their beloved wives, and their respect for everyone of the sisterhood who is struggling for a living."[12]

Maverick was serving in this session on four standing committees: Counties and County Boundaries, Private Land Claims, Claims and Accounts, and Indian Affairs. As a member of the last, Maverick signed a report of January 25, 1858, recommending that an agent be appointed for the Alabama and Coushatta Indians who had been placed on a reservation in 1854, as "they have been, and unless some method be provided to remedy the evil, must continue to be in every instance the losing party" in disputes with whites.[13]

Maverick also shepherded another extension of the San Antonio and Mexican Gulf Rail Road charter through the Senate, but railroads and Indian administration took a back seat in the Seventh Legislature to two pressing issues, the possibilities of calling a southern states convention and of framing a response to recent events in Nicaragua, where American filibuster William Walker had failed to maintain his hold on the presidency.

The debate over slavery and secession had risen to new, more inflamed levels with the controversy centering on Kansas Territory, where voters were given authorization to decide whether their future state would be slave or free. The resulting violence and intimidation had turned the territory into "bleeding Kansas" and led to further estrangement between pro- and antislavery forces nationwide. In February, 1858, the Texas legislature passed a resolution charging that proslavery southerners were being excluded from Kansas affairs and authorizing the governor to send delegates to a convention of southern states, if one should be called, or to call a special session as prelude to a state convention on the issue. Maverick, despite his unionist sympathies, voted with the majority.[14]

He refused, however, to countenance a set of resolutions supporting William Walker in his Nicaragua filibustering attempt and condemning Commodore Hiram Paulding, who had arrested Walker and forcibly removed him from the Central American country. What galled Maverick most was that Walker supporters were attempting to compare the filibuster's fight with the Texas fight for independence. "As an old Texan," Maverick declared on the floor of the Senate, "I [am] unwilling to let it pass, and go forth, that a Texas Legislature should at this early day, so far forget, and thus grossly detract from, the truths of our early history, as to compare them with Nicaragua or General Walker."[15]

Walker was, Maverick argued, a "presumptuous intermeddler in the affairs of other people," whereas the Texas colonists had acted on their own behalf, taking up a just cause only after handling their situation with prudence and forbearance. As for the language of the resolutions calling Walker Nicaragua's rightful president, Maverick reminded his colleagues that "the people are the only rightful source of power," and the Nicaraguan people had not been able to support the man whose purpose was "self-aggrandizement, spoilation and plunder." Nor did he believe Texans would support such a usurper's actions. Texans, he averred, "entertain no self-conceited, Know Nothing notions of forcing their own ideas right or wrong, on ignorant outside barbarians."

Some of the legislators were drawn to Walker's support by his promise to make Nicaragua a haven for southern slaveholders, a possibility Maverick deplored as drawing some of the strength from the South. "Sir, the safety of the South lies in quite the opposite of this," he commented; "it consists in a habitual constant and immovable resolve to avoid all filibusterism, and to maintain, unimpaired, all the guarantees of law and constitution."[16]

Maverick worked steadily in the Senate, serving briefly as president pro tem.[17] He was aware that once more he had left Mary struggling with slaves and sick children. Jack and his family had proven troublesome, and Maverick had already tried to sell them back to the family's previous owner, planning to keep only the child Julius, "for the reason that he has been constantly misused by his mother & ought to be separated."[18] However, the previous owner no longer wanted them, and in November, 1857, Maverick directed his wife to arrange for their sale through a San Antonio businessman, commenting, "They can't sell *below* their *value to us.*" At the same time, he sold Granville, one of the slaves who had been with the Mavericks since their emigration to Texas and who had recently run afoul of gambling laws.[19]

The Mavericks soon took Granville back and kept Jack and Rosetta and their children as well, actions which indicate that the couple felt some moral responsibility toward all but the most recalcitrant of their human charges. Maverick could not bring himself to whip a slave; when the law required it in Granville's gambling case in 1857, the duty fell to the sheriff, with Maverick paying the fine and costs.[20]

The slaves remained an aggravation, but Mary's real worry was over the precarious health of her children. The baby was still so tiny. G. Jones Houston visited and pronounced her healthy, leading Maverick to reassure his wife, "I wonder why not, to be sure?! Don't you remember how very little you were at first?—That's the way I suppose to make a beginning to become large. In all probability she is to follow your example & to become the largest of our children (sex considered)."[21]

While Maverick was at the legislature, however, three-year-old Albert developed typhoid, and Mary received distressing reports of ill health from Lewis in Vermont. A few months earlier, fearing he was sick, she had written, "I suffered such a scorching away of all self happiness & almost cheerfulness from losing three dear children that I fear to think what I might be, if life survived another such loss—which God be merciful to spare me." Now she wrote emotionally to Lewis to "remember always what blank and broken hearts would miss you from the home circle and then do your best to keep that circle entire."[22]

Maverick was not as worried about this son's health as he was about his decision-making abilities. Lewis had informed his parents that he wanted to become a medical doctor, and his father reacted with angry incredulity, calling the practice of traditional allopathic medicine "a swindle" and complaining to Mary, "He must have known my often declared opinion about the M.D. & yours too, or has a bad memory."

He also admonished his wife not to share any of her spiritual books with this impressionable student. "I should think these better be let alone by such as Lewis while at his studies," he wrote. "Children ought not to be put to such studies. But they ought to be taught plain facts and be trained by exact sciences. Forgive me this is my serious conviction."[23]

Mary attempted to ameliorate the situation by supporting Lewis in his resolve but directing him toward the botanical medical practice she and his father had embraced. Diffidently, she wrote to him on February 14, 1858, "I can myself—in default of a better teacher learn you the botanic practice, since I have in my family & among some friends tried its virtue for *nine* years—always finding it better." She continued to be doctor and nurse to her four-month-old unnamed daughter, reporting to Lewis that the family's planned trip to visit him that spring would have to be canceled on account of the baby's health. Finally, in May, she wrote him that "my little Lizzie baby" was getting well. "I called her Elizabeth one night when I thot her dying," she confided, "but as Pa says it is a name 'will do to live by too.'"[24]

Lizzie still did not grow at any appreciable pace, but the other Maverick children at home were growing rapidly, and that summer of 1858 Mary sent Lewis descriptions of each. Twelve-year-old George was "serious studious truthful & good"; ten-year-old Willie "boisterous, mischevious" and fond of a fight; seven-year-old Mary "very smart & very affectionate & unselfish," as well as "earnest & matter of fact"; four-year-old Albert, recovered from typhoid, she characterized as grave, affectionate, and strong-willed.[25]

A new worry intruded, however, with the intelligence that Lewis had been expelled from the University of Vermont for joining classmates in tampering with a bell in a bell tower. On hearing the news, Maverick dashed off a supportive letter recommending that Lewis do what he could to re-establish himself and counseling, "I really think it would be time well spent if by a tribulation in sackcloth for 2 years you could get reinstated . . . it would make a man of you indeed: you would bless the day my son. Cheer up my son."[26]

Having returned from the legislature in February, Maverick was again busy with land and railroad matters. He had located and bought up tracts throughout West Central Texas—in Bexar County, in surrounding counties, and in unincorporated land to the west. Tax records for 1857 show that he held 103,115 acres in Bexar County and in the territory outside established counties, including 16,043 acres as trustee for his father and 4,937 as agent for John MacKay. In addition, he had 36,384 acres in other counties, for total Texas landholdings of 139,499 acres.[27]

Now his desire for western lands had him looking all the way to distant El Paso. Early that fall, he traveled by stage to the border community, where he soon engaged the surveyor of the El Paso town site, Anson Mills, to do survey work for him. Maverick became the future brigadier general's "principal employer," and Mills later recalled both how Maverick expressed "bitter" opposition to secession and how he accompanied Mills on the surveying expeditions, "following my tracings and examining my notes."[28]

At the same time as Maverick's El Paso journey, the San Antonio and Mexican Gulf Rail Road was actually becoming a shaky reality, but too late for the financially embattled directors to sustain it. The state engineer confirmed that five miles of track were completed and operating from the coast, but the line ended in open prairie. Furthermore, in the face of numerous lawsuits for recovery of land, the directors had been forced to mortgage the road to acquire the iron for Osgood. After Maverick's return, the directors made plans for sale of the road to pay their debt to Reid and Tracy, the company from which they had contracted for iron. In December, 1858, terms were reached with the company, with reduced notes accepted. Maverick had committed himself to the largest amount by signing a note for twelve thousand dollars and was now responsible to Reid and Tracy for a reduced note of sixty-five hundred dollars.[29]

Not only was Maverick confronted with railroad problems on his return from El Paso in October, but he found a wife distracted with Lizzie's drooping health and news that Lewis was ill with liver trouble and inflammatory rheumatism. Lewis had won full reinstatement to the university, but he asked his father's permission to come home for a year. Maverick, with his characteristic disdain for assuming authority in interpersonal relationships, wrote with curt exasperation to his son that he "need not have talked about *permission*" but could return if he wished. Mary, temporarily removed to the Houstons' on the Cibolo to nurse Lizzie, wrote that she wanted him to come but feared his health would worsen during the long trip.[30]

Even more, however, she feared his being at the mercy of allopathic doctors. Informed by Lewis that his physician had said he could not

travel until January, Mary wrote on November 30, "How can you believe that any M.D. can *know* that you will not be able to travel before January? Why Catholics have no more faith in the Pope!" Should
he die away from home, she wrote two weeks later, "I fear indeed I might
fail in fortitude to bear it." By Christmas, however, about the time
Maverick had determined to travel to Vermont to get him, Lewis reported himself improving and out of a doctor's care.

Lewis soon began his homeward journey, while his father continued to be taxed with railroad headaches. In January a man who had
traded Saluria town lots for stock without receiving the stock sued
Maverick and the other directors, and the defendants advertised the
railroad for sale on the first Monday in April.

Maverick's fellow legislator and railroad director Isaiah Paschal refused to give up, writing to him in early March that he thought ar-
rangements could be made with a London firm without selling the road
and asking Maverick to lend him twenty-five hundred dollars to go
to London to effect this.[31] Maverick's reply is lost, but it is unlikely
the request was honored, as he was not involved in Paschal's subsequent efforts. Instead, Maverick chaired a general stockholders' meeting on March 8, attempting to bring everything to as satisfactory a
conclusion as possible. He had purchased over twice as many shares
as any other individual.[32]

As Maverick's railroad venture wound to an unsatisfactory close,
he and Mary were visited with another personal tragedy, the death
of seventeen-month-old Lizzie on March 28. Mary had entertained high
hopes for the child as late as December, writing to Lewis that the baby
was "plump and getting rosey." "What say you I was her physician, after
two M.D.'s gave her up & all my old lady friends," she had boasted
joyfully.[33] The two final entries in her diary simply record the baby's
birth and death. She had no time or heart for anything more.

A week after the child's death, the San Antonio and Mexican Gulf
Rail Road, now slated to go as far as Victoria and connect with another railroad, was bought by a company that included Paschal and
fellow director Jesse Wheeler. "They will have to make a pretty strong
and palpable demonstration, before every confidence can again be re-
vived with the great unwashed down this way," Robert Clow wrote from
Lavaca.[34]

Maverick's own disenchantment with the way things had gone may
have been reflected in his response to a letter of January 17 in which

Hugh Hawes asked him to allow himself to be appointed president of a new steamship company. "My mind is early made up," Maverick wrote on the back of the letter, "that it would be wrong to lend my name to the management of any affair that I could not control & superintend. And there is hardly anything I know so little about as the . . . Steamer business."

The land certificates given to the railroad company by the state were scheduled to go on sale in June, and records show that Maverick was to buy some of the certificates through the years.[35] He was not alone among the directors in taking this opportunity to recoup something from the failure, one of many transportation defeats in those early days of statehood. The line would be completed to Victoria before the outbreak of the Civil War, but not without further problems for the string of investors who followed Maverick and his friends.

As he extricated himself from the railroad effort, Maverick again turned to the political arena as another statewide election loomed. For the governership, a second showdown between Democratic standardbearer Runnels and Houston was brewing. In May, former governor Pease wrote Maverick urging him to join Houston's independent ticket as a candidate for lieutenant governor. "I think it very probable that [Houston] will be elected to fill the vacancy in the Senate and in that event I should feel that the administration of the state government was in safe and reliable hands," Pease explained. He felt, furthermore, that a ticket with Houston and Maverick on it would prove a powerful vote-getter, rallying those who opposed secession. "The announcement of your names will at once unite all who are not desirous of seeing Texas placed in an attitude hostile to the union, when there is no occasion for such a course," Pease explained.[36]

Whether Pease had discussed the selection with Houston and whether Maverick considered such a move is not known. When the independent Houston faction of the Democratic party met to select a slate of candidates, Edward Clark was nominated for lieutenant governor, Gustav Schleicher for Maverick's Senate seat, and Maverick for a House seat.

Maverick did throw his influence solidly behind Houston. "Old Sam is the right man for *this* delicate occasion," he would soon write to his wife.[37] He worked that summer of 1859 to combat the secessionist drift he felt Runnels only exacerbated. In March he had shared a podium with fellow declaration of independence signer José Antonio Navarro as they observed the twenty-third anniversary of the signing, and that summer Maverick invited Navarro to join him in addressing a pro-Houston rally in San Antonio. Navarro responded with a stirring letter asserting his support of Maverick's and Houston's positions, reaffirming his faith in the American union, and inveighing against "políticos de media noche" and the "diablo revolucionario" (midnight politicians and the devil of revolution). Maverick endorsed the missive by writing, "Splendid letter."[38]

He remained busy campaigning with Pease on the antisecessionist platform. Mary reported to son Sam, returned from Scotland and spending the summer with the Van Wycks at Pendleton, that Maverick and others "addressed a great crowd" in July before the newly opened Menger Hotel beside the deteriorating walls of the Alamo chapel. "Old Sam Houston is to be our next governor it seems—the least of two evils," she wrote.[39]

Not everyone thought so. The San Antonio *Ledger*, previously friendly to Maverick, refused to endorse him for representative, commenting, "Everybody knows him and everybody respects him, but we certainly were surprised, and regret much, to find him flinching from the standard. He was about the last man we would have expected to have done so."[40]

On July 30, the Austin *Intelligencer* picked up a story in the Galveston German paper, the *Union*, reporting an assertion by Maverick that Runnels had in speaking to him come out in favor of "dissolution of the Union." It was not until after Houston's election, on August 1, that Maverick requested a denial, stating that he had only argued "the existence of a weak faith in the Union" on Runnels' part, as inferred from the tone of one of the governor's public messages during the previous legislature. Maverick swore that the item damaging to Runnels had not been brought to his attention until August 6, when he promptly wrote to set the record straight. But the Clarksville *Northern Standard* maintained a skepticism concerning the "fortunate" mistake on behalf of the Houston forces and casting aspersions on the "artless innocence" of the retraction's timing.[41]

It seems probable that the item, published in papers outside San Antonio, had not come to Maverick's attention until a week after publication. But whether the timing of his denial was calculated or innocent, his feelings about Runnels are clearly reflected in a letter he would write to his wife from the legislature: "What a blessing it is not to have Runnels here now, aggravating the mischief, as he did all the time he was governor."[42]

After two terms in the Senate, Maverick was returning to the House. He was not the only family member on the move. Lewis had come home for the summer, then, still sickly, traveled to Alabama with his cousin Samuel Maverick Thompson. From Alabama, Lewis proceeded to the University of North Carolina, which he was to attend with his Pendleton cousin William Van Wyck. At about the same time Lewis departed San Antonio, his brother Sam arrived home after three years' absence in Scotland and Pendleton.

Soon after his eldest son's homecoming, Maverick returned to the legislature, still dominated by states' rights representatives despite the election of Houston. Through the preceding decade, the wealth of the average legislative member had doubled, and the proportion of members holding slaves had risen to over half.[43] These men had a large stake in the antebellum Southern system and felt a widening gulf between their interests and those of the industrial North. Outgoing Governor Runnels' message read to the House on November 10 struck a warning note. Citing John Brown's recent raid on Harper's Ferry, Runnels remarked that "events are fast converging to a fearful catastrophe," and he called on the legislature to make "a clear and unequivocal expression of opinion" on the subject of southern states' rights.[44]

As national civil strife loomed, the legislators became quickly occupied with a more immediate threat in the form of the Cortina Wars along Texas' Rio Grande border. Mexican rancher Juan Nepomuceno Cortina, dissatisfied with Anglo treatment of Mexican Texans and responding to the arrest of an associate in Brownsville, had staged a raid on Brownsville, killing a jailer and four or five others. He then defeated Anglo and Mexican militia based in the city and assumed control over the Brownsville area. State and federal forces were sent to combat Cortina, and most Anglos, with ethnocentric attitudes toward "greasers," unreservedly backed the troops sent to quell the insurrection. But Maverick decried the Texas militia's and Rangers' handling of the situation, commenting in a November 23 letter to Mary that "the Cortina humbug is disgraceful to the intelligence of the age: how ridiculous it became. From what I hear it would have been a good thing if he had killed twice as many as he did."

Maverick was at work in this session on the Internal Improvement, Apportionment, and Federal Relations committees. As a member of the first, he continued to work on behalf of railroads, introducing a bill for the relief of the Buffalo Bayou, Brazos & Colorado Railroad Company and its assignees and nurturing yet another bill to revive, amend, and continue in force the San Antonio and Mexican Gulf Rail Road incorporation.[45]

A contemporary newspaper gazette containing debates of the Eighth Legislature shows that Maverick spoke in the session on a variety of issues, including legislation against concealed weapons. He favored such action, although he felt it would not affect "us upon the frontier," where "men will carry arms, whether they do it secretly or openly." He also took the floor in favor of a bill he had helped frame that would give city voting rights to anyone in San Antonio who had a business or residence in the place. The bill's opponents disliked the fact that someone who was not an American citizen could vote under the bill's provisions, but Maverick responded by noting, "It is well known San Antonio is made up of people from different quarters of the world. Some of the inhabitants now residing there have not yet become American citizens. But they have bought and improved property there, and I don't want to make any invidious Know-nothing distinction."[46]

Bills earning Maverick's opposition included a preemption bill giving added inducements to settlers exposing themselves "beyond the reach of assistance." Maverick argued that, although he favored preemption, "I do not think it policy for us to increase the number of settlers who expose themselves unnecessarily." The frontier population, he predicted, would increase naturally without such an action. He also argued against a bill allowing a slave owner one-half of the slave's value if the slave were executed. The man who had termed himself a "recreant governor of negrodom" nonetheless contended that the responsibility for a slave's conduct lay in great part with the master, with good government on his part preventing such an end.[47]

Ultimately, though, all such matters paled beside the central issue facing the legislature—what to do about the widening rift between North and South. Sam Houston sounded the conservative theme in his January 13, 1860, address to the legislature, vowing that "Texas will maintain the Constitution and stand for the Union. It is all that can save us as a nation."[48]

On January 21, Houston reluctantly forwarded to the House the latest communication of the governor of South Carolina calling for a southern convention. Maverick wrote to his wife on February 1, "SC would be fool enough to go out of the Union, if she only had 3 or 4 States to go with her: Tho' all the departments of the Genl Govt. are in favor of doing justice to the South."

He prepared his own resolutions to counter the "mad-dog" South Carolina ones and presented them to the Federal Relations Committee, of which he was a member. Maverick's resolutions flatly denied that individual states had the right under the constitution to secede or enter into alliances with other states or foreign nations, rejected South Carolina's invitation to a southern convention, and denied there was any "present, sufficient" cause to secede.[49] The majority resolution that came out of the committee, however, was quite different, pledging to cooperate with other states "should it become necessary, to resist Federal wrong" and asserting that Texas would find "neither honor nor interest in the Union" if federal authority violated the state's rights.[50]

In mid-February the legislature adjourned, and Maverick returned to a burgeoning San Antonio. The city had changed greatly since he first entered it on horseback almost twenty-five years before. Population had more than doubled in the last decade alone, and with over eight thousand inhabitants, Bexar was now the largest community in Texas.[51] Most Anglo-Americans had built their houses near the heart of town, the Main Plaza with its new hotels and glass-fronted stores. Across the river at Alamo Plaza the Maverick homestead shared the square with a number of modest mud-plastered or adobe Mexican dwellings – and the impressive Menger Hotel. Numerous German emigrants lived on the outskirts of town in neat limestone homes.[52]

Despite the glass storefronts and new hotels, San Antonio remained a frontier community. Indians still periodically plagued the area, living conditions remained less than ideal, with streets still turning to muddy quagmires after each rain, and Frederick Law Olmsted on a visit in 1857 characterized "street affrays" as "numerous," with murders "from avarice or revenge" common.

Olmsted reported that Anglo-American inhabitants, still a relatively small group, held the capital of the community, Germans worked as mechanics and small shopkeepers, and Mexicans hauled goods from the coast to help make San Antonio a West Texas freighting and supply center. "Cash is sometimes extremely scarce in the town," Olmstead wrote, adding that "investments at present are mostly in lands. There are no home-exports of the least account."[53] Indeed, in 1860 there were only two factories in the whole state. Yet San Antonio's position as a trading center and as the hub of a quickly developing farm and ranch country lent it an air of growing prosperity. Construction had even begun at long last on an Episcopal church building, with Robert E. Lee, residing in Bexar as military commander of the Department of Texas, contributing generously to the effort.

The Mavericks were firmly in the midst of the life of the city—Mary through family and church activities, her husband through business, church, and civic enterprises. He owned 115 town lots, as well as tracts throughout the surrounding countryside.[54] He had donated 4 lots for the church's use and was active in its development.[55] When a public meeting was held on matters of importance to Bexar citizens, he often was called to the chair.[56] He had aligned his business interests with the interests of other members of a loosely organized Anglo-American and German American power network in the town while maintaining good relations with Mexican inhabitants. A Union prisoner living in San Antonio after the war's advent the next year and mixing with the population would report that Maverick was "considered by all a very honest man."[57]

Exaggerated stories were already growing about the reticent pioneer's wealth and landholdings, as the comments of the Clows attest. A description provided by an anonymous source in the Seventh Legislature gives a glimpse of perceptions of Maverick during this time period, as well as showing how his legend was already growing.

> [Maverick] is considered a sound and valuable member, generally silent in the House, but active on committees, and sometimes taking part in debates, though I never heard him. . . . He is somewhat given to a soliloquizing absent mindedness, and therefore the object of occasional pleasantries from his friends. . . . Mr Maverick is said to be the largest landholder in the United States, and of course very wealthy; but his republican simplicity of dress and manner give no indication of that fact.[58]

In truth, other speculators controlled more land than did Maverick —it has been estimated that Jacob de Cordova, a Galveston land agent with financial backing in New Orleans, had by 1855 gained control of over a million acres of Texas land.[59] Maverick's accomplishment lay in the fact that he acted alone and gradually built up impressive holdings with tracts often as small as 160 acres.

Neither was Maverick's wealth as great as many imagined, although it was substantial. In 1860 he had $177,000 in real property, $13,000 in personal property, and eighteen slaves. This made him one of the wealthiest, but by no means the wealthiest, in a group of 263 Texans, mostly planters, farmers, and merchants, who held over $100,000 each. Eight of these Texans had half a million dollars or more in individual property, and over half held twenty or more slaves.[60] Many of these men would lose all or almost all in the approaching clash between North and South.

In 1860, the national Democratic party split, with southerners refusing to accept party candidate Stephen A. Douglas and putting forward their own man, John C. Breckinridge. The first indication that Maverick was beginning to identify with the southern cause more strongly came in a letter that G. Jones Houston wrote to the younger Sam Maverick on October 12, 1860. "I am glad to see you are both good Breckinridge men," Houston wrote of father and son, confessing that "it gives me the greater confidence in my own position to have as good & prudent a politician as your Pa of the same opinion as myself."[61]

But the Democratic split only helped the Republicans to victory with their candidate, Illinois lawyer Abraham Lincoln, who was bitterly opposed in the South. On December 20, 1860, a South Carolina state convention voted unanimously to secede from the Union. On Christmas Day, 1860, an old school friend of Maverick's from Virginia, William M. Peyton, wrote him from New York, "All business is paralyzed, confidence totally destroyed. Exchanges deranged and the people standing with folded arms awaiting the shock of a convulsion which they feel they are impotent to arrest."[62]

Sam Maverick had for thirty years resisted a splitting of the American union, but with the impending secession of his native state, he reluctantly changed allegiance. Mary wrote in her memoirs, "At last he came to believe the quarrel was forced upon us, and that there was before us an 'irressible [sic] conflict' which we could not escape, no matter where we turned." Mary's own prewar views on secession are not reflected in the record, but as a native of the antebellum South, bound to the existing order through tradition and love of family, her sympathies went naturally to her fellow southerners, particularly when the husband whose opinion she regarded so highly came to embrace the southern cause. Thus, the Mavericks would cast their lot firmly with the Confederate States of America in a decision that would give their lives new focus and purpose but bring new heartaches as well.

14

Leaving the Consequences to God

We will do what the emergencies of the hour demand, doing what
we believe to be our duty and leaving the consequences to God.
—February 8, 1861, report of Texas secession commissioners Sam Maverick,
Thomas J. Devine, and P. N. Luckett

IN JANUARY, 1861, Sam Houston reluctantly called the state legislature
into extra session in response to frontier Indian depredations, a de-
pleted treasury, and the national states' rights controversy. Houston
still held out against any movement toward secession, as did a few legislators. However, Sam Maverick now joined the majority voting to
authorize a secession convention and to submit the question to the
people. The House also voted unanimously to repudiate any attempt
by the federal government to coerce a seceding state.[1] Reporting the
unanimous resolution to Mary, Maverick wrote on January 24 that he
was living comfortably at Austin's City Hotel and dining on corn bread,
bacon, cabbage, butter, chicken, mutton, venison, potatoes, and
honey—"in fact living like I had not yet seceded from the comforts
of life."

Indeed, for a few months it looked as if there would be no need
to forgo the comforts of life in a bloody war. As one southern state
after another joined the Confederacy, they did so in hopes that the
federal government would let them go unimpeded. The Texas Secession Convention met in Austin almost as quickly as the legislators could
approve it, running concurrently with the extra session from January 28
to February 4. House and Senate members moved between the legislative halls and the convention, where in a dramatic roll call on February 2, delegates voted overwhelmingly for secession.[2]

As the gathering ended on February 4, an interim Committee of
Public Safety was formed to handle state secession matters until the

delegates reconvened in March, after taking the issue to the people by ballot. The committee appointed three commissioners to meet with Maj. Gen. David Twiggs, commander of the U.S. Army, Department of Texas, headquartered in San Antonio, and demand that he turn over federal supplies to the state.

As one of the commissioners appointed, Maverick now began working industriously for the Confederate cause. At the outset, he and fellow appointees Thomas Jefferson Devine and P. N. Luckett had a delicate task: to convince Twiggs to give up the military posts, arms, stores, munitions, and other supplies under his control, valued at three million dollars, and to evacuate the federal troops in Texas, which composed more than 10 percent of the U.S. Army.[3]

Twiggs expressed sympathy for the southern cause but delayed while awaiting orders and thus made the commissioners uneasy. Perhaps, they reasoned, he was stalling in order to call his troops in from those remote frontier forts that Maverick had been renting to the U.S. government. After meeting with Twiggs on February 8, the commissioners reported to the Committee of Public Safety their unhappy conviction that "we must obtain possession of that which now belongs to Texas of right, by force, or such a display of force as will compel a compliance with our demands, and that without an hour's unnecessary delay."[4] Acting on this conviction, they followed the directions of the committee by sending word for former ranger and state legislator Ben McCulloch to bring his volunteer militia to San Antonio to force the issue.

Twiggs appointed his own commission, consisting of three army officers, and as McCulloch began marshaling his men to enter the city, the two commissions dickered over terms. Maverick, Devine, and Luckett knew what needed to be done to the advantage of their seceding state—all federal posts and supplies needed to come under state control, and the federal troops needed to be marched to the coast and put on ships. But in this new and unfamiliar situation they were unsure how much authority they had in working out the details. For example, Twiggs remained adamant that should he surrender, his troops would leave Texas retaining all their weapons. "What do you think of that?" Maverick and his fellows wrote to committee chairman John C. Robertson on February 10. "Please give the views of the committee on this and every other subject connnected with our mission as fully and speedily as possible."[5]

With the arrival of McCulloch's troops in San Antonio in the early morning hours of February 16, the time for arguing such questions was over. The volunteers came in two by two in the dim morning light, some mounted and some on foot, looking much like the ragtag army that had laid siege to Bexar twenty-five years before. "A motley though quite orderly crowd, carrying the Lone Star flag before them," wrote one observer.[6]

At six that morning, Maverick, Devine, and Luckett wrote a terse note to Twiggs requiring him to "deliver up all military posts and public property held by or under your control."[7] The general surrendered, only a few hours before his nonplussed replacement arrived. The Texas flag was raised over the Alamo once more, and the federal troops in San Antonio marched to the river to await their journey to the coast.

With McCulloch's help, the three commissioners had managed to accomplish peacefully a great stroke for their state. "We congratulate the able Commissioners on the successful accomplishment of their responsible mission," editorialized the Clarksville *Northern Standard* on March 9. Now Maverick, Devine, and Luckett turned to administrative matters, appointing southern loyalists to oversee the federal stores and publishing a general circular of their terms with Twiggs, who had been allowed to keep his men armed. The circular urged Texans to treat with consideration the men who had so recently been guarding their frontier.[8] The commissioners also ordered McCulloch to seize federal money being transported from the coast and called on federal officers for a property accounting.

While the commissioners were busy at their work, Texas voters cast their ballots overwhelmingly for secession and the convention began a second meeting, approving and ratifying the provisional Confederate government being formed in Mobile, Alabama. Yet many in Texas still decried or opposed secession. Maverick's friends and longtime business associates Isaiah and George Paschal remained outspoken unionists.[9] The German population of San Antonio, too, remained generally hostile to secession. Many German intellectuals, disheartened with their own country's failure to become a united nation, had fled to Texas in pursuit of a deeply felt principle of human liberty, and German farmers with small landholdings and limited funds "had little use for slaves."[10]

Col. Robert E. Lee arrived in San Antonio en route from a Texas fort with orders to Washington on the day of the surrender and asked,

San Antonio's Main Plaza in 1861, at the time of the surrender of federal troops and stores to Samuel Augustus Maverick and his fellow secession commissioners. *Courtesy Daughters of the Republic of Texas Museum, San Antonio.*

"Has it come so soon as this?" Refusing to join the secessionists, he hurriedly left the city, only to declare later his own southern allegiance.[11]

Governor Houston still refused to endorse secession. Consequently, the convention declared the governor's office vacant and installed Lt. Gov. Edward Clark in Houston's place. All state officials now had to take a Confederate loyalty oath, and when the legislature met in adjourned session in March, Maverick took the oath and voted with the majority that anyone who did not had deposed himself from office.[12] Added to the Committee on Retrenchment and Reform to try to pare state expenses, Maverick wrote his eldest son on April 8, "The state is wholly without means, and has everything on earth to do that any civilized state was ever called upon to do." The committee could make only a small start before the adjourned session ended on

April 9. Four days later, the federal-held Fort Sumter near the mouth of Charleston Harbor fell to Confederate troops, and the Civil War began.

For Sam and Mary Maverick the war brought new vitality and purpose by providing a chance to cast aside private miseries in service to the Confederacy. During the next few years they would work unceasingly in war support efforts and send four sons to fight.

At first, only Sam and Lewis were old enough to see action, and they welcomed the opportunity. Sam had been at loose ends since his return from Scotland almost two years earlier. An indifferent scholar despite his father's gentle urging toward independent legal study, he had tried establishing a small farm near San Antonio in the year before the war began, but had given it up. With the removal of federal troops from the Texas outposts, he volunteered for Henry McCulloch's First Texas Mounted Rifles guarding the frontier. Lewis, as melancholy at the University of North Carolina as he had been during his last months at the University of Vermont, quickly quit school and joined a North Carolina regiment.

Maverick was proud of his eldest son's decision, but impatient with the younger. Sam was performing a useful service for Texas under a man Maverick considered unsurpassed in the state in terms of firm yet fair command. But Lewis, whom his father considered ill-suited for the business of war anyway, had chosen to join his allegiance and fortunes with comrades from another section of the Confederacy.[13] In truth, neither of the boys had much in common with their father; third son George would inherit Maverick's prudence and solid, judicious character. But the matter-of-fact parent found it easier to relate to the actions of frank and open Sam than to those of moody and sensitive Lewis.

As a member of the First North Carolina Infantry Regiment, Lewis participated in one of the early skirmishes of the war, a Confederate victory at the Battle of Big Bethel in Virginia.[14] His fifty-seven-year-old father had come near a battle himself in an encounter with federal troops at Adams Hill south of San Antonio in May. Of course, San Antonio throughout the war had little to fear in regard to a Yankee invasion. But many of the federal troops called in from the frontier Texas posts were streaming toward the city en masse, and the citizens feared they were coming to fight rather than to surrender.

Actually, the troops were a bewildered lot needing direction. They

camped on the evening of May 8 on Adams Hill, a prominent land-
mark beside the source of the San Lucas Spring about fifteen miles
south of Bexar. The next morning, they were greeted by the sight of
a Confederate force led by Maj. Gen. Earl Van Dorn appearing over
the next ridge with a battery of six-pound guns. "Old Mr. Maverick"
led one company of about 100 "young men and boys."[15] The federal
troops deliberated and surrendered, 10 officers and 337 enlisted men
marching into San Antonio to the beat of a drum to become prisoners of war.

Lt. Zenas Bliss, one of the unfortunate troopers, later recalled that
"during the 1st part of our stay in San Antonio, we were treated very
well indeed, in fact it hardly seemed that we were prisoners." But after
the first Battle of Bull Run in the East, when both northerners and
southerners were awakened to the deadly seriousness and awful carnage of the conflict, Bliss reported that "the people became more bitter, and it was not so pleasant for us."[16]

As the war began to heighten in intensity, Maverick found how hard
it was to commit totally to the Confederate cause yet remain broad-
minded enough to remember that others held neutral views or the
unionist views he once had held. In December, 1861, he wrote Mary
from Austin of visiting with Swen Swensen and his family, "very kind
& pleasant people: and being a born foreigner—a swede, and a money
maker I have so far excused Mr. S. as not to insist on the extremist
points in our confederate politics."[17]

But as the South became more and more embattled, the lines were
more sharply drawn. In March, 1862, Austin printer and lawyer W. S.
Oldham, now a Confederate senator, wrote Maverick of arrests of "Lincoln sympathizers and traitors" in Richmond, declaring that such men
"will soon learn that our stock of forbearance and clemency has been
exhausted."[18] Across Texas, Union sympathizers were dispossessed and
even summarily hanged. In San Antonio, the Paschals were heavily
persecuted, and one resident later reported, "It was like living in an
asylum where every one was crazy on one especial subject; you never
knew what dangerous paroxysms were about to begin."[19]

Both Sam and Mary Maverick in their letters to each other and
to their fighting sons showed increasing bitterness toward the Yankees
and, by extension, to anyone sympathizing with them or failing to aid
the South in its fight. When Brownsville was taken by Union troops,
Mary would write, "It appears most of the citizens were willing—pity

[Confederate general Hamilton] Bee didn't burn every roof there." When Bee, the Mavericks' old friend from Pendleton and early Texas days, was facing censure as a poor commander, Mary wrote, "We have always thot him a high-minded gentleman and hope it may be disproved." But, she added, "nobody should be defended who can't prove a clear record now in our country's need."[20]

From the beginning, the Mavericks gave generously of their money and time to the war effort. Sam Maverick became an authorized agent in a statewide attempt to raise money to obtain loans for the Confederacy, and his own initial gift brought a grateful letter from Judge John Hemphill, former Texas chief justice and U.S. senator now serving in the Confederate Congress. "Your subscription of one thousand Dollars to the first Loan was not only a most patriotic act, but was to a delegate from Texas a source of great gratification," Hemphill wrote. "The subscription from Texas to that Loan was comparatively very small—and your advance was therefore more gratifying."[21]

Maverick also quickly became involved in efforts to outfit the Texas military companies being formed. In June, 1861, before the first Battle of Bull Run, he was already serving as treasurer of the Southern Defence Aid Society, whose primary aim was "to provide means for fitting out and support of those who have been or may be called into the service of our country."[22] He worked on the executive committee of the San Antonio Supply Association to provide goods at set rates to needy citizens, and in 1863, he introduced and pushed through the legislature a bill incorporating the San Antonio Mutual Aid Association, which was to provide a general mercantile establishment for city residents who were feeling the effects of the war in the form of scarcity of goods.[23]

Mary served as her husband's counterpart by acting as treasurer in the women's wing of the Southern Defence Aid Society and as president of the Ladies Aid Society. In these capacities, she helped raise money for war hospitals and soldiers' families and coordinated efforts to make and deliver such supplies as haversacks to companies raised locally. She also tried to keep her own sons well supplied, sending them everything from clothes she had stitched herself to coffee.

Henry McCulloch took note of the Mavericks' war efforts after visiting with them in early 1862. Unsuccessfully urging them to take money for his room and board, he wrote, "Your expenses are heavy at home, you have sons in the service that have had to draw heavily upon you and your daily outlays on objects of charity are considerable and you subscribe largely to the sum gotten up for the support of the families of those who have gone to the war."[24]

Sam Maverick recognized from the war's beginning that the North had the larger task in that it had to invade and coerce to win its point, whereas the South could simply defend its right to secede. Serving in the Ninth Legislature in November, 1861, he wrote to Mary that "having shown our ability, it is now not thought incumbent on us at all to attack the enemy." Instead, he predicted, the South could let the Yankees get dissatisfied with Lincoln and their generals as *they* delayed.[25]

Meanwhile, however, Texas was in straitened circumstances, and at the Ninth Legislature most of Maverick's work went toward trimming state expenses. He was serving on the Finance and the Private Land Claims committees and acting as chairman of a committee on the General Land Office. In the latter capacity, he wrote in the same November letter, "I will have to say how to put that affair on a cheap war footing."

Maverick took time from his legislative duties to write to fourteen-year-old Willie, whom he had left making cartridges for the Confederate Army. "How do you think old Abe Lincoln would treat you if he had you, after making all those thousands of cartridges?" Maverick asked playfully. But he was proud of his son's industry and anxious to emphasize its character-building value. "Steady, persistent application is beyond all question the first and greatest and most essential quality of the Southern man," he explained. "Nearly everybody is changing and experimenting and the result of it is failure & waste. It is so particularly here in the South. But give me the fellow whom you can't choke off from what he undertakes to do." That fellow was a "Napoleon Bonaparte," Maverick declared, showing that his early admiration for the powerful European conqueror and reformer had not waned. But as always, Maverick remained diffident about lecturing his sons. "I have said rather more than necessary," he concluded, "and I do not urge you on, beyond what is reasonable & agreeable to you, my son."[26]

With the war getting well under way, both of the elder Maverick boys were looking for new ways to participate. Lewis, his six-month enlistment up, returned to San Antonio while Maverick was at the legislature and soon formed his own company of Texas Mounted Volunteers, and Sam left the frontier militia to become a private in Terry's

Carl G. von Iwonski's painting of eldest Maverick son Sam (*center foreground*) in action with Terry's Texas Rangers. *Courtesy San Antonio Museum Association, No. 31-4801-157 L.*

Texas Rangers. Sixteen-year-old George joined Lewis' company as a private. Lewis and George would see little action, spending the rest of the war in Texas and Louisiana as members of Woods' Regiment, with Lewis eventually serving as a major on the staff of Maj. Gen. Xavier De Bray. Sam would see nothing but action east of the Mississippi, both as a hard-riding Ranger and as a member of an independent bushwhacking company.

As the Maverick sons joined their new regiments that spring of 1862, the war news was not encouraging. Federal troops were on the offensive in the West, laying claim to all of western Tennessee and positioning themselves to gain control of the whole Mississippi Valley. Staggering casualties continued—the Battle of Shiloh in early April claimed thirteen thousand Union lives and ten thousand Confederate ones.[27] Texas itself was threatened with attack from the coast, as the federals were extending their blockade of southern ports to include the state's coastline. The Sibley Expedition, a Texas attempt to push the federals out of New Mexico, was meeting a disastrous end, and Brig. Gen. Henry H. Sibley and his men were soon to straggle into San Antonio in defeat.

Nonetheless, by late summer, the Confederacy had improved its position considerably. Southern troops in the West were on the offensive to retake Tennessee and take Kentucky, and Robert E. Lee at the head of the Army of Northern Virginia was pushing into Maryland in the East. But the Battle of Antietam in September, pitting Lee against Maj. Gen. George B. McClellan, resulted in the failure of Lee's invasion, and the North was soon mounting new eastern and western offensives. In Texas that fall, the federal blockade forced state and Confederate troops to desert Sabine Pass and Galveston.

Lewis and George were stationed on the Texas Coast, quiet despite the federal incursions. They visited the Clows, now with four daughters, and spent Christmas, 1862, with the family of Mary's old friend Mag Pearson at their plantation on Caney Creek. Sam was with the Rangers in Tennessee, and his parents heard from him infrequently through the regiment's chaplain, former San Antonio Presbyterian minister Robert Franklin Bunting. Maverick reported to Lewis in early December that they had heard from Sam, guarding the rear forces of Gen. Braxton Bragg near Cumberland Gap. "He was well but ragged & out of means, & horse knocked up & then on a little Texas mustang," Maverick reported. "Your mother has now sent Sam 9 pounds of boots & clothes." As for the war effort, he could only repeat his conviction, now a strong hope, that the Yankees would "pull against one another" and bring about their own defeat.[28]

In addition to his war and legislative work, Maverick had spent the latter part of 1862 serving as San Antonio's mayor. More than twenty years had passed since he last held the office, but when chief municipal officer James Sweet resigned in mid-term, Maverick was appointed to finish the term. Again, Maverick dealt with the necessary details of community management, from appointing a city doctor to vaccinate "indigent persons" against smallpox to ordering bridge repairs and hiring additional police.[29]

In December, he was narrowly defeated for a second term by French-born P. L. Buquor, who had married into the Bexar Spanish-Mexican aristocracy. Maverick was upset enough to contest Buquor's qualifications "on the grounds that he holds a lucrative office under the Confederate States and has not paid his taxes."[30] The council voted five to three to uphold Buquor's election, but Maverick would soon have more public duties to fulfill.[31]

The year 1863 started on a positive note for Texas, with Confederate troops in January retaking Sabine Pass and Galveston. In addition, there was the news of Lee's sound rebuff of the Army of the Potomac near Fredericksburg, Virginia, in December. "With all our grand victories & all their losses, won't we have peace soon think you?" Mary wrote to Lewis on January 30.

Mary's letters to Lewis had undergone an obvious change in tone from his college days. When he was in Vermont, her emotional and sad missives had contained frequent sharing of fears and references to spiritualism. Now she no longer overtly indulged in melancholy speculation, instead adopting the matter-of-fact tone of sister Lizzie. Informed that Lewis was unhappy with his company's reaction on being switched from cavalry to infantry, Mary wrote, "It makes me grieve to know you are so unhappy but I think you magnify your unhappiness by brooding over it 'till it clouds all your sunshine & it is the wrong way." Instead, she urged, "learn just by a wrench of the will to make yourself cheerful & I know it is seemingly sometimes hard to do so but I've learned it & you can & you must, & when you do you can always *command* cheerfulness—when you will be independent of others opinions & self sustaining in content."[32]

Later that year, Mary summed up her new strength of spirit to her son by writing that "the secret of happiness or misery is all in the mind, or the capacity of the soul to attain equanimity." She mused, "As far as I know, a life of good intentions—if those intentions do not most of the time miscarry—is my solace—under oppressing care & trouble & I say 'begone dull care' and *hope* gilds the way ahead."[33]

Mary did not give up spiritualism completely, but she built on her traditional Christian faith for sustenance during the war years. Work on the church structure planned for the San Antonio Episcopal congregation's use had ground to a halt with the arrival of war, and the congregation remained tiny. But Mary continued a committed communicant.

She was also too busy to do much worrying. As the federal block-

Second Maverick son Lewis as a Confederate captain. *Courtesy Barker Texas History Center Photo Collection, Austin.*

ade affected the flow of goods into San Antonio, the family and slaves were making their own candles and soap, and Jinny was putting the spinning wheel to good use. Mary herself was learning how to spin. She took time, however, for her roses, particularly the ones named after her departed Augusta.[34]

During the war, Mary and her husband experienced their worse moments worrying over the brash, peripatetic Sam. In February they received news of the extended and ultimately meaningless battle fought between Bragg and federal general William Rosencrans in Central Tennessee as the new year opened. Casualties had been frightening, and Sam had been there. "My thoughts are often terrible to bear," Mary admitted to her second son, "yet amid every calm moment shines out gloriously my faith and hope in Almighty God—who rules all, that my spotless lambs will come back to home and us. . . . And I think I see glimpses of peace near ahead." Maverick, attending a February extra session of the Ninth Legislature could only write, "I don't know what to say. God grant we may have escaped in this last sad affair. Oh God have mercy."[35]

Quickly, however, they learned that Sam had performed heroically at Fort Donaldson, swimming out and setting fire to a Yankee boat, and that he had survived.[36] "God Almighty save the noble boy," Maverick wrote with pride and relief. However, he was afraid Sam's action had "the appearance of rashness." He concluded to his wife, "I shall write to him but I shall not oppress him with a heavy load of advice and council."

Maverick himself was unhappy over the gloomy tenor of the extra session, with reports of troops becoming demoralized. "We will break the state in a vain attempt to satisfy all sorts of clamors & complaints when the truth is we only need a good crop to be prosperous and recover from the effects of a seven years drouth," he wrote. "There is also a mean jealousy indulged by many against the rich negro holding, cotton planter—great complaint about the exemption from the army of 1 man for every 25 slaves &c—whereas, the rich men are doing their duty just as well as the poor."[37]

In response to the crop problem, while at the legislature Maverick offered a joint resolution to disband state troops called up by the governor the previous year, reasoning that they could go home and plant while remaining ready for service.[38] He remained disturbed by what he saw as "a most reckless waste of the credit of our state" by new members of the legislature anxious to prove themselves friends of the soldiers even if in the process they "break the constitution and the treasury & impoverish the country for fifty years, in a vain attempt to force the confederate currency, and throw away everything they can lay their hands [on] (honestly or dishonestly) in a gigantic scheme of funding the soldiers families."[39]

Maverick felt that Gov. Francis Lubbock, a South Carolina native elected over Clark in 1861, was joining in this bankrupting course. "I am truly sorry this Legislature met atall," he grumbled.[40] He initially backed M. M. Potter in the 1863 gubernatorial election, but saw elected Pendleton Murrah, another South Carolina native who had arrived in Texas by way of Alabama. Maverick himself won election that year as chief justice of Bexar County, a position he would hold until the removal of all Confederate chief justices after the war.[41] County Commissioners' Court records from the war years show that his time as chief justice was taken up in large part with petitions for assistance from soldiers' families and with the administrative duties of county tax collection.[42]

Meanwhile, the conflict dragged on, and the Confederacy was finding itself outmatched in terms of numbers of men it could put in the field. In Texas, and especially in San Antonio, some remained irritatingly cool to the war effort, and in 1863, Maverick chaired a public meeting at San Pedro Springs to get men to enlist.[43] "It would astonish you to see how many able looking men congregate on our streets & none of them going," Mary wrote to Lewis, "only talk-talk-& very few work on the fortifications. Your Pa does tho."[44]

Gen. Nathaniel Banks was in Louisiana mounting an offensive against Texas, and Mary feared Lewis and George would be sent to the unhealthy Louisiana swamps as part of an effort to stop him. Still she remained hopeful. On April 27, 1863, she wrote to Lewis, "When our gun boats get to work in earnest won't the Yankees see trouble! I hope so. Ah the turmoil & the grief they have crowded upon us can never be revenged. . . . Now can we ever be satisfied as a nation?"

The biggest events of that summer were the Battle of Gettysburg in Pennsylvania, with Lee and Gen. George Meade throwing their troops into the greatest single engagement of the war, and the surrender of Vicksburg to Maj. Gen. U. S. Grant. Despite a valiant performance at Gettysburg, Lee's troops simply could not get a steady toehold in northern territory. Even more ominous, the fall of Vicksburg meant that the federals would soon control the whole Mississippi River, cutting off Texas, Arkansas, most of Louisiana, and the secessionist portion of Missouri from the rest of the Confederacy.

Texas Confederates in September were encouraged by Lt. Dick Dowling's dazzling rout of federal troops from Sabine Pass, but in November Banks began taking points on the Rio Grande, and the Mavericks and other San Antonio residents had to consider the possibility of a repeat of the Runaway of '42, with the Union Army now taking the place of the Mexican troops. Mary seriously considered staying through an invasion, writing to Lewis on December 1, asking, "Cannot I too bear whatever of insult or robbery our many many . . .

noble southern women have borne—& What do I gain by running?"

Still, it was hard to believe that the Yankees could penetrate to San Antonio; more pressing was the lack of supplies the residents of the city were facing. In early February, 1864, Mary reported to her son that "the long talked of & looked for goods" had arrived at the Mutual Aid store, & "squeeze in was the only hope" as everyone in town hurried to the spot. Lizzie had sent eldest daughter Kate to stay with Mary for some months, and Kate was shoeless and the slaves were in rags. "I went & stood wedged up & swaying about till near 12," Mary wrote, getting for her pains a bolt of domestic cloth, a pair of shoes, and a dozen candles for a total price of $180.00. Maverick himself went the next day and got a coffee pot and twenty pounds of coffee for $85, "most reasonable thing they had."[45]

Again, the Mavericks were disturbed by lack of news from Sam. He had not been listed among the dead at the particularly bloody Battle of Chickamauga in which the Rangers participated in September, but, Mary reported to Lewis, "we never hear from him, we never hear of him," and she feared him dead. As they waited for word, the Mavericks were encouraged by the fact that Yankee newspapers were calling Banks' invasion a failure and that the peace party was swelling in the North. "Pa says he hopes they won't let us go till they pitch into each other up to the eyes," she explained.[46]

That February of 1864, Lewis tried to turn in his resignation after being embarrassed by the desertion of some members of his company. When the resignation was refused, Mary again reminded him to put duty over personal feeling. "I am glad your resignation was not accepted," she wrote on February 27, "altho I am unhappy that you are so uncongenially situated in that regiment—but the circumstances of our bleeding country require all imaginable sacrifices, and our educated and refined, tho as willing, if not more devoted, must suffer keenest of all." She was at least glad that he was in Brig. Gen. Tom Green's command, for Green, an old Texan, had been a friend of the Mavericks in their days on the Colorado.

However, within a month and a half, Green would die and Lewis would suffer a serious leg wound in the Battle of Blair's Landing on the Red River in Louisiana. Confederate general Richard Taylor wanted to cut off a federal flotilla on the river before the vessels could rejoin Banks' army, and on April 12, Green's cavalry regiments tried to do just that. They set up a punishing barrage from the riverbanks with musketry and a four-gun field battery, and the federals answered with their own heavy artillery fire. "No Confederate went aboard the fleet and no Federal came ashore; so there was a fine field of slaughter in which the imagination of both sides could disport itself," Taylor later wrote.[47] Casualties were few, but Green's death contributed to the Confederate withdrawal that ended the fray.

George Maverick, who received a graze on his ear, reported the battle to his family as "the most supremely ridiculous fight I ever heard of."[48] George moved Lewis to a nearby house and nursed him until he was able to rejoin the regiment. Their father wrote hoping that they would have no more battles. "It can't be long certainly before the Yankees fall out with one another," he wrote Lewis on May 25, adding sadly that "it seems the most convincing reasons can't stop the war."

Mary counseled Lewis that his wound might be God's providence "to shield your young life." She remained hopeful about the war's outcome, but wrote "'tis well to think upon Job."[49] She was hosting a stream of houseguests and visitors. Maverick's nephew Joe Weyman a few years before the war had established a ranch near San Antonio, and as he moved about Texas with his own Confederate company, his wife, Emma, and baby stayed long periods with Mary. Kate Clow also remained. She and the Mavericks' daughter Mary did not get along, but the elder Mary was conscious of being in the role of a mother to her for her extended stay, although Kate seemed indifferent to all attempts to make her feel at home. From time to time Aunt Ann Bradley or one of the Bradley girls, most of whom were now married, would drop in. Aunt Ann and the youngest, Ada, had moved to Austin with prominent Texan Thomas McKinney, a member of Austin's original Old Three Hundred colonists, and his wife, Anna. The childless McKinneys had taken a liking to Ada, and they would occasionally stop in as well.

The Mavericks also had visitors from the theater of war itself—the recruiting lieutenant from Lewis' company, a soldier from the eastern theater who had seen Sam. Always, members of the military were in and about San Antonio on business, and the Mavericks opened their home to them. Hearing that a Terry's Ranger who had served with Sam was in town, Mary vowed to invite him to tea and "ask 1000 questions if I can."[50]

The Mavericks were hoping that Lewis and George would soon be ordered back to Texas, as Banks had been driven back east of the Mississippi. "Won't the Yankees get whipped & killed enough to give up?" Mary wrote Lewis on June 12. San Antonio was bustling and she envisioned a stream of emigrants making it their home after the long and weary war. "And Pa's life time work of locating choice lands—will make you all rich right away," she wrote. "Ah! If the Good God spares all our lives 'till after the war—that will be the greatest of riches—Won't it Lewis?"

Mary was soon heartened by a long-hoped-for letter from Sam. They had learned that spring that he was in a bushwhacking company in Kentucky, but in June they received a missive from Sam himself, stating that he had rejoined the Rangers, turned down a commission, and, despite his desire to see the family, preferred to stay in the thick of the action east of the Mississippi. "We are all so happy at the letter from Sam," Mary wrote to Lewis, "and we hope to see you and George here before a great while—so that ours is just now a cheerful circle."[51]

Sixteen-year-old Willie remained at school in Bastrop, where the conscripting officers kept careful track of each schoolboy's seventeenth birthday, and was eager to join his older brothers. "He insists that George went at his age," Mary reported to Lewis on July 24. "I tell him 3 at a time is enough until he is old enough anyhow."

That summer saw the federal troops driven from the South Texas mainland by the frontier companies of longtime Maverick acquaintance John Salmon Ford, who had served as a Texas legislator, Ranger captain, explorer, and Secession Convention delegate.[52] But east of the Mississippi, the news was not so promising, as federal forces laid siege to Atlanta and to Mobile. "When will the war end Lewis?" Mary wrote that August. "Everybody is predicting that the hardest fighting is all over & the war to end right away—how is it? Do they only hope so?" San Antonio was now "flourishing," with crowded streets, flowing silver, and abundant goods, so that visitors from the East observed that the Bexar residents knew nothing of war. "But this is mockery," Mary protested. "Are not our dearest ones in that war, suffering and daring everything?"[53]

At the beginning of September, Sherman took Atlanta in a devastating blow to the Confederacy. Yet Mary wrote on September 8, "This war is the Almighty's, and we will succeed." She and her husband remained busy in support activities, with Mary vowing in October that "no soldier's family will suffer here" for want of necessities. "Patriotic old Bejar, if unionists do breathe our air," she wrote to Lewis, reporting a successful fund-raising supper given by thirteen-year-old Mary Brown's group, Daughters of the South. Even Maverick slaves Betsy and Rosetta had raised a hundred dollars for a Confederate hospital with a "patriotic supper" and dance at the Maverick home.[54]

Yet increasingly the Mavericks were aware that whatever the war's outcome, it had brought basic changes in the life of their city. No longer were the old Republic-era "Texians" the cream of the social structure, as new families and military men dominated the social scene. Neither Sam nor Mary Maverick had put much store in social affairs. Mary had enjoyed the early social circle that formed before the Runaway of 1842, when a small nucleus of Anglo women drew support from each other's company. As the Anglo social community grew and fell into bickering factions, she had become more observer than participant.[55] Now, in October, 1864, she noted greater change, with "a new aristocracy . . . springing up & the old lapsing out."[56]

By Christmas, Sherman had made his ravaging march to the sea, and federal troops had destroyed John Bell Hood's Army of Tennessee. Seventeen-year-old Willie put on the Confederate colors in January, but the war was rushing toward a close. A friend in Houston wrote to Lewis, "Our prospects for peace and recognition look gloomy enough. . . . They are expecting Galveston to be attacked and of course taken, and—then raids! A great many are leaving for Europe and Mexico."[57]

Early in the year, Sherman began a punishing march through the Carolinas, and in early April Grant penetrated the Confederate strongholds of Petersburg and Richmond. On April 9, 1865, Lee surrendered to Grant at Appomattox Court House.

Still, some Texans clung to their hopes. As late as May 8, Mary was writing to Lewis that despite "great disasters" God "has not decreed our conquest we will trust." Only in late May did the full hopelessness of the situation become apparent to all, and Trans-Mississippi Department commander Edmund Kirby Smith surrendered the last Confederate army.

In April, Mary had written that "to woman, to poor weak women, is perhaps the bitterest cup given to quaff" in terms of waiting, listening, hoping, and fearing. Now, in an especially bitter twist, some disgruntled Confederate soldiers who saw San Antonio as lukewarm or hostile to the lost cause looted stores and made blanket threats against the city's residents. In late May, Mary as president of the Ladies Aid Society prepared an address to "Soldiers of the Southern Confederacy" reminding them of the war work San Antonio women had contributed and concluding, "Is it not enough oh! brothers in a holy cause, is not the bitter agony of failure enough for us to bow under?"[58]

The Mavericks knew at the war's close that they were fortunate in having all four sons return to them—particularly when they looked at their extended family. Samuel Maverick Van Wyck, the firstborn of Lydia and William, had completed medical studies before the war only to be killed early in the conflict, leaving a young family in Pendleton. Samuel Maverick Thompson had lost a foot in battle, and Joe Weyman had served throughout the war only to die a few months before its end, leaving his own small family.

The Mavericks were fortunate in another way, as were most Texans, in not having to deal with invasion and the destruction that accompanied it. The most they could complain of in this respect was the heedlessness of Confederate troops who camped behind the Maverick fence and damaged it while pulling out brush to burn.[59]

Nor had the family suffered the tremendous financial losses felt by so many of the old aristocratic planter class, including many of the leading citizens of Texas. The couple suffered financially, of course, but Maverick had made his chief investment in land rather than in slaves and the plantation economy. Despite plummeting land prices throughout the state after the war, he would be one of the few Texans wealthy before the conflict to hold onto most of his real property as merchants and bankers replaced farmers and planters among the ranks of the wealthy.[60]

Yet the failure of the Confederacy was a searing loss for Sam and Mary Maverick because they, like so many southerners, had adopted it as a holy cause and worked wholeheartedly for its success. Maverick had tried for years to maintain a balance between his regional identity and his identity as a citizen of the United States, repeatedly asserting the importance of each. That fragile balance had been shattered when the split between North and South had widened to the point of war. In the years since, the Mavericks had found themselves emotionally absorbed in defending a way of life they had known since birth against an enemy that grew more vile and menacing in southern minds with every bloody conflict.

Now, having lived most of his life as a staunch unionist, Maverick was recognized as a prominent secessionist, and as such would become a target for bitter barbs from members of the new order determined to wipe out the old aristocracy. His last years would be weighted with political antagonisms and uncertainties.

15

"They That Wait upon the Lord"

*Pa I wish you would build us a new Home outside of town
a real Virginia Home where we might all feel at perfect liberty
to do & say just what we please & always to feel contented &
happy. I imagine then life would be something new & fresh
we would never feel dissatisfied but life would glide away
peacefully in a perfectly blissful channel.*

—Mary Brown Maverick, in school in Virginia, to her father in San Antonio,
January 13, 1870

ON JUNE 19, 1865, Maj. Gen. Gordon Granger arrived in Galveston and proclaimed a restoration of federal control over the state and freedom for Texas slaves. The twenty slaves belonging to the Mavericks could now savor freedom, but fifteen of these were children. Only one adult male had remained with the Mavericks at war's end, along with three young mothers and grandmother Jinny Anderson.[1] Some of the women and children may have stayed on temporarily in the relative economic security of the Maverick household, but by 1869 Maverick daughter Mary Brown would indicate that the family was employing only one household helper.[2]

Mary Maverick had felt "ground up" in the slave system, but she could only greet with mixed feelings the dissolution of a way of life she and her husband had known from childhood. The antebellum order was indeed passing away, and people who had faithfully represented it waited to see what would take its place.

Some prominent Texas Confederates fled to Mexico, but Sam Maverick was not about to make such a move. He had been a loyal unionist up until the point when he was "compelled to take his choice for or against his kith and kin," as Mary wrote in her memoirs, and he had hopes of a presidential pardon. Of course, there was the sticky

This photo carries the inscription "Aunt Jinny Fontleroy, who minded S. A. Maverick when he was a child" and is believed to be Jinny Anderson, who accompanied the Mavericks to Texas and stayed in San Antonio after emancipation. *Courtesy Maverick descendant A. L. Fenstermaker.*

matter of his actions as one of the secession commissioners seizing federal stores in February, 1861. Immediately following the commissioners' action, the federal government had brought a suit for trespass against them, and the suit was still pending.[3]

However, Maverick had the good wishes of some of the men who had remained loyal to the Union and were now returning to or resurfacing in Texas to guide a transition government. In Austin in September, he and friend Thomas McKinney visited former governor E. M. Pease, who had remained a unionist. Pease greeted Maverick "with *great cordiality*" and counseled him as to the best course to take with new provisional governor Andrew Jackson Hamilton.[4]

Hamilton duly forwarded Maverick's request for a pardon to Pres. Andrew Johnson, but the applicant remained on tenterhooks. In October, he bound himself as surety in a five thousand–dollar bond agreement for fellow commissioner Devine "to appear before any Civil Court to answer any charge that may be made against his conduct during the late Rebellion of the Southern States" in the coming year.[5] Devine was a particular target of the unionists because he had been involved in confiscating the property of Union sympathizers.

In November, Maverick wrote to Texan and new U.S. secretary of state James H. Bell asking him to check on the status of the pardon request. Maverick had heard that President Johnson, unhappy with Governor Hamilton's slow progress in reorganizing the state, had rebuffed the appeal of "some Texian who had an indorsement as 'long as his arm,'" and Maverick feared this was his own. He was also uneasily aware that Johnson's lenient policy toward the South was not finding favor in the North. "I don't know but the confiscation policy may yet be forced on the Govt.," he explained to Bell, "so I am anxious about my own case, and I long to get information of my pardon. I am wholly in your generous hands dear judge. . . . I want to know the worst and at the earliest moment."[6]

Bell responded with good news on January 4: "It gives me pleasure to be able to enclose to you your warrant of pardon," signed by Johnson on December 5.[7] The pardon would ultimately have little meaning in the punitive environment of Reconstruction Texas, but it had great symbolic value to the recipient, who had stood for union over disunion most of his adult life.

At home, the Mavericks had had one event to celebrate in the year of defeat, 1865; Lewis had become the first Maverick child to marry, wedding his cousin Ada Bradley on September 20. With his lean good looks and sensitive nature, Lewis had been a great favorite among the girls in San Antonio. Finally, as the war dragged to a close, the twenty-five-year-old Confederate officer settled on his twenty-one-year-old cousin. "Do you know I can't make up my mind whether you are in deep earnest there or not," Mary wrote to her son on the subject in April of the year. "(Forgive—only your happiness is my excuse) Because, if you are, pitch in strong is the style ain't it?"[8]

The Mavericks and Bradleys did not enjoy as warm and close a connection as they once had, but still the two families could be happy with their children's choice. Two negative considerations did surface: Lewis' failing health, and the feelings of Thomas and Anna McKinney, who had virtually adopted Ada and planned to leave their property to her. The McKinneys were friendly with the Mavericks, but apparently they were initially unhappy with the alliance, for Mary's letters to Lewis show that Ada was risking her McKinney inheritance by marrying him.

Mother counseled son to respect the dilemma Ada faced, but for Mary herself there was no question in the matter. "Is property of any importance?" she asked on May 8. "Is not the entire question of 'Love.' Then why make it secondary to anything—I think it wrong." Besides, Lewis was not exactly without fortune. Though land had dropped in price and Sam Maverick would be hard-pressed to keep up taxes on his empire during the postwar years, the Maverick family would remain in the stratum of wealthy Texans.[9]

The McKinneys accepted the marriage with good grace, but the second negative consideration could not be overcome. Lewis' health had been poor since his Vermont college days, and his war service and the wound he received at the Battle of Blair's Landing had only exacerbated matters. He and Ada made their home on the Colorado near Austin, but in June of 1866, nine months after the wedding, he died of "disease of the heart."[10]

It was a loss Mary Maverick had long feared, but she had learned that life goes on, however much the heart of the survivor may bleed. Much of her time now went to church activities, as the congregation of St. Mark's Episcopal Church attempted to renew the building of the sanctuary, which had been halted by the war. Mary became treasurer of the Dorcas Society, a women's group formed in 1866 to raise money for the project.[11]

Sam Maverick returned most of his attention to his land matters. Tax records for 1864 show that his holdings had almost doubled in seven years, jumping to over 278,000 acres. His Bexar County total had dropped because the western lands of the vast Bexar District that he had included on Bexar County tax rolls were becoming part of new counties and appearing on his tax list for other counties. But in 1864, he still owned over 62,000 acres in Bexar, plus 8,321 acres in temporary partnership with fellow San Antonio speculator Gustav Schleicher and 7,680 with G. Jones Houston. In other counties, the trustee lands for his father had grown to almost 20,000, and Maverick was paying taxes on almost 180,000 acres of his own in twenty-nine counties outside Bexar: Atacosa, Calhoun, Comal, Concho, Dawson, El Paso, Frio, Guadalupe, Haskell, Jones, Karnes, Kendall, Kerr, Kimble, Kinney, La Salle, Live Oak, Llano, Maverick, McCulloch, McMullen, Medina, Menard, Runnels, San Saba, Taylor, Uvalde, Wilson, and Zavala.[12]

Despite having to sell and forfeit a few tracts during the rough years of Reconstruction, he would continue to enlarge that amount. Late 1866 found him again in El Paso laying claim to one-third league "of what is known as the Guadalupe Salt Lake," a broad area of salt deposits mined by Mexicans and coveted by Anglo-Americans.[13]

That year had signaled some return to prewar order as Texans approved amendments to the state constitution and Pease lost the governor's race to James Throckmorton, who had served through the legislatures of the fifties with Maverick. Both Pease and Throckmorton were conservatives accepting of the old social order and not eager to take harsh measures against former secessionists.

However, on March 2, 1867, the first Reconstruction Act was passed in the U.S. Congress, ushering in an era hostile to the antebellum order. Southern state governments were deemed "inadequate and illegal," new southern constitutional conventions were called for to write black suffrage and other northern dictates into the documents, and military commanders were given full power over civil authorities and state laws.[14] Texas occupation generals Phil Sheridan and Charles Griffin used this act and the ones that swiftly followed to extend disenfranchisement and to pluck conservative Throckmorton from the governorship. The generals reflected the view of those who wished to strip of power anyone who had been part of the old regime.

In May, the ardently reconstructionist San Antonio *Express* reported gleefully that Maverick and Devine had "been summoned to appear before the Federal Court to answer for the three million dollars worth of U.S. property they receipted for as Rebel commissioners." U.S. Attorney General Henry Stanbery soon stepped in and ordered the case suspended indefinitely in a move that eased the immediate pressure on the defendants while keeping the specter of further litigation before them.[15]

As Texans struggled with the first punitive measures of Reconstruction and Sam Maverick struggled with his own legal involvements, the Mavericks received word that brother-in-law William Van Wyck had died at Pendleton. His twenty-seven-year-old son and namesake William, now a lawyer and the eldest Van Wyck sibling since his brother's death, wrote to Maverick about the possibility of coming to Texas. His uncle responded, "Come on here my dear nephew. I expect to break down at paying my own taxes on wild lands, but I will continue as heretofore to pay those of your mother & those of the Hrs of SM as long as I am able."[16] Two of Maverick's own four surviving sons remained in San Antonio: Sam, who was farming and studying law, and thirteen-year-old Allie. George and Willie had departed for the University of North Carolina after the war, then transferred to the University of Virginia, from which George would graduate the next year.

Slowly, as the Reconstruction military authorities tightened their hold on Texas, Maverick and his fellows began an organized resistance. With a vote on the new constitutional convention looming, Democrats and conservative Republicans held their own convention in Houston in January, 1868. Delegate Maverick was elected to the State Executive Committee, nominated a vice-president along with John H. Reagan, Hamilton Stewart, and J. W. Henderson, and appointed to the Committee on Resolutions, which urged voters to reject at the polls any convention created by the "Radical Party."[17]

However, the fact that most conservatives were not under law allowed to vote and confusion as to how best to achieve their aims contributed to a victory for proponents of the new convention at the polls in February, 1868. Maverick continued his work on behalf of the conservatives, traveling to Austin in May on convention business and meeting with Throckmorton and Richard Coke, former Texas supreme court judge.[18] Despite the grim times, he could report to Mary, "I have met a number of old friends & am having a very pleasant time of it.— talking 'Grape.'" His garden and his grapevines had become an even more diverting avocation for him since the war.

San Antonio post office, late 1860s. The man with the stovepipe hat in the foreground is said to be Samuel Augustus Maverick, but a notation apparently by Maury Maverick, Sr., on the back of the photo states that "Uncle Sam [eldest son of Samuel Augustus] says this is not true because Grandpa never wore such a hat and hated 'society.'" My research shows that Maverick indeed eschewed fashion and society. *From Maury Maverick, Sr., Papers, Barker Texas History Center, Austin.*

His principal vocation remained land buying. In September, 1868, the hostile *Express* reported Maverick's purchase of ten land certificates of 650 acres each, identifying them as "the last State certificates issued to the Mexican Gulf and San Antonio Railroad." The writer concluded, "Maverick lives in the most simple style—fences decaying and buildings crumbling to pieces; yet he is eternally buying lands. He is supposed to have more land than is embraced in Massachusetts. Where he locates, enterprise and improvements flees [*sic*] as victims are supposed to run from the plague."[19]

Such criticism had to be borne in the new reconstructionist climate. It held a grain of truth, for while Maverick had worked in the legisla-

246

ture for internal improvements, surveys, and other legislation that would open West Texas to settlement, as a private businessman he had primarily contented himself with locating lands in the hope that the natural tide of emigration would render returns without development on his part.

One silver lining for Maverick in the new harsh climate was the fact that old ally E. M. Pease had been named provisional governor after Throckmorton's removal. But in 1869, Pease resigned in protest of the reconstructionist policies being carried out by General Griffin's successor, J. J. Reynolds.

In March of that troubled year, Maverick had to deny once again a letter appearing over his signature in a state paper. The second convention had met, and under the leadership of former provisional governor Andrew Jackson Hamilton, now the moderate Republican gubernatorial candidate, they had hammered out a constitution that made concessions on such matters as black suffrage but remained too conservative in tone for the radical Republicans. The latter group was represented by Hamilton's brother Morgan and former Union cavalry commander Edmund J. Davis, also a gubernatorial candidate.

The radical Republicans initially opposed the constitution's adoption and, according to a letter published in the Houston *Times* on February 21, 1869, Maverick did, too, asserting that Texans "will work ourselves justice in repelling the offers of Governor Hamilton and his constitution."[20] The letter appears to be a radical Republican attempt to undermine the moderate document and candidate by making it appear that a conservative leader was rejecting them. Maverick quickly denied authorship in the pages of the San Antonio *Herald*; conservative Texas Democrats could easily see that Hamilton and this constitution were far less threatening for them than Davis and whatever wrenching changes he wished to impose.

Through the political turmoil, Maverick remained absorbed in land speculation, as an 1869 journal that he kept attests. If one places his 1835 journal on arriving in Texas and this journal side by side, the consistency is striking. Both booklets are filled with neat, cramped notations on lands to investigate and buy, as well as adages reflecting Maverick's disciplined personality. "Nothing so belittles as petty practices & pleasures," he recorded in this last notebook.

Despite his continuing interest in land, however, he was having difficulty holding onto what he had. In June, 1869, he wrote to George

and Willie at the University of Virginia that they should come home
or find schoolteaching positions that would pay their board, as his
money situation was serious.[21] The "dutch mayor" appointed by Reynolds was threatening to bring suit for three thousand dollars Maverick owed the city, the U.S. government was refusing to pay rent on
his Fort Clark and Alamo lands, and he reported "several conspiracies
got up here against me financially." He was having to sell town lots
and reluctantly considering parting with sixty acres above the Alamo
in order to be "relieved for a little while." Life had become a burden,
he reported, yet still he expressed the hope that "if we thank God for
past mercies with true piety, no doubt we shall turn every calamity
to our good."[22]

In September, he was once more called into federal court, this time
because of a land dispute. The *Express* reported dryly, "We learn that
S. A. Maverick, Sr. has been taken by the U.S. Marshall, to Austin
for refusal to obey a decree of the U.S. District Court, or rather, that
Mr. Maverick has business in Austin and could not well obey the decree without visiting the Land Office."[23]

Indeed, Maverick had formed a pattern in his years in the state
legislature of working steadily in the land office at every opportunity,
tracing landownership records. "I have not visitors any more," he wrote
to Mary on October 6, "but have attended to my business & made
vague promises & walked in the middle of the Avenue as a general
downneck habit." On October 26, he wrote, "I am still in fine health
& intent on getting through a thousand examinations & fixings up
with my miserable land business — making trouble for other people as
well as you & I." He had had to sell two tracts, explaining that "it went
very hard with me, but I was forced to sacrifice something to save the
rest if it can be saved atall." He asked her to send to Willie at school
"only what will barely do as I am two thousand dollars behind in this
year's tax or about that."[24]

Despite his avowal that he was in fine health, the sixty-six-year-old
Maverick's family saw his physical condition slipping, and they convinced him to take eighteen-year-old Mary Brown to school at the
Episcopal Virginia Female Institute in Staunton, Virginia, where some
of her mother's Lewis relations still lived. He wrote his will before departing, deeding half his lands and property to Mary, half to be divided equally among his five surviving children. To widowed daughter-
in-law Ada Bradley Maverick, he gave a San Antonio house "and such

other property as said Mary A. may think proper to convey to her."[25] Then he traveled eastward one last time. "Nov. 1, 1869," he recorded in his journal, "Set off for Staunton Virginia with daughter Mary B. via Columbus—Galveston &c."

Maverick may have wished for such simple problems as Lewis and Sam had provided on their initial trips and visits in the East with him, for fisticuffs with strangers were more easily dealt with than were the matters of the heart Mary Brown straightforwardly tackled. In September, she wrote him in Austin commenting on his "hard schooling," only mitigated by the softness in his eyes. "Thank God they often looked soft in spite of themselves when your tongue, 'That unruly member' said things that cut deep," she wrote on receiving a treasured loving letter from him. A few months later, she would write from school complaining about his lack of correspondence. "Think you that I have not feelings as well as yourself?" she demanded with Lizzie-like tartness, confessing that she had always longed for "a consciousness of your love & approbation."[26]

He had tried, at least with older children, to balance playfulness and affection with the sterner responsibilities of fatherhood. But demanding so much of himself in terms of public duty and private enterprise, he presented an imposing and often distant face to his family, a face made more distant by suffering over the loss of loved daughters this daughter had never known. He carefully endorsed the second letter with the date of his reply, but the reply itself is lost.

When Maverick had returned from Virginia, it was to a Texas coming even more firmly under radical Republican control. The conservative Republican constitution was approved by voters in late November and early December, 1869, but massive vote fraud at the same time propelled radical E. J. Davis into the governor's seat. Maverick traveled to Austin at the end of December on land business, and was there when General Reynolds hurried the Davis regime into power early. As Reynolds in February convened a new legislature composed primarily of radicals, the seven-term Texas legislator from San Antonio quietly returned home. Fourteen years earlier he had written to his wife that he felt his role in the Texas drama had ended with annexation. A sense of public duty had propelled him onward; now there was no place of public service for him.

He was still a business power, one of only eleven of the wealthy Texans from 1860 who still managed to hold over $100,000 in real and personal property in 1870. His real property in this, his final year, was valued at $160,000; his personal property at $5,000.[27] His land empire had continued to grow until it encompassed over three hundred thousand located acres in thirty-two counties spread through Central and West Texas.[28]

It is an impressive figure for an individual landholder, although put in perspective it loses some of its power. For example, this total represents less than half of the acreage of Big Bend National Park and comprises only a tiny fraction of the over 167 million acres of Texas soil. Rumors circulated during Maverick's lifetime, and persisted afterward, that he owned more land than anyone in the United States, and even in the world, with the exception of Russia's czar.[29] These rumors have less to do with Maverick's actual holdings than with his reputation as a reserved and somewhat mysterious purchaser of certificates and lands over a long period of time. At his death, he *was* the largest landowner residing in Bexar County, with fellow longtime San Antonio resident John Twohig running a distant second with over 126,000 Texas acres.[30] However, it is unlikely that Maverick was even the largest individual landowner in Texas at his death. The era of the cattle baron was beginning and vast ranches were spreading across the Texas landscape. In 1870, cattle rancher Richard King of Duval County was already the wealthiest person in the state, and his King Ranch would expand to one and a quarter million acres.[31]

Maverick still awaited the flood tide of western emigration that would add value to his lands as a new generation moved to center stage. George arrived home in late 1869 with a law degree from the University of Virginia; Sam had passed the bar in San Antonio in 1867. Allie was at school in Bastrop, and Willie and Mary Brown were in Virginia receiving their formal educations. Ada Bradley Maverick was marrying again, her groom the widowed Jacob Waelder with whom Maverick had served in the legislature and in San Antonio civic affairs. San Antonio itself was recovering from the war and beginning to boom as a mercantile center. The city's population had spiraled to over twelve thousand.[32] Bexar still lacked a much-needed railroad connection with the world, but it was beginning to enjoy such amenities as gas streetlights.

Thus, despite Governor Davis' imposition of a virtual police state across Texas, the future looked promising for those men of business able to weather this latest political transition. Soon mass resistance to

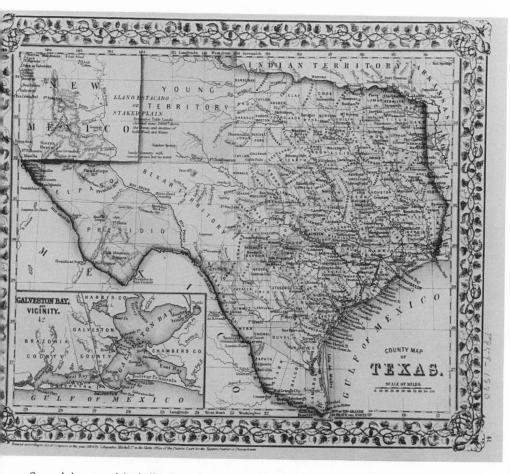

Samuel Augustus Mitchell's 1870 county map of Texas showing the state's growth in the three and a half decades after Samuel Augustus Maverick's arrival. *Courtesy Texas History Map Collection, Barker Texas History Center, Austin.*

Mill Bridge Crossing and the ford in the San Antonio River near Market and Navarro streets, 1870. *Courtesy San Antonio Museum Association, No. 248.*

the radical regime would solidify and the state's citizens would work their way back toward the Democratic conservatism of Sam Maverick. He would not be there to see the pendulum swing, however. "In the spring of 1870, Mr. Maverick became quite feeble," Mary later wrote in her memoirs. "At last in August, he became much worse and we no longer had any hopes of his recovery."

On September 2, 1870, at 5:30 P.M., Samuel Augustus Maverick died "after a wasting illness of more than two months" and was buried in San Antonio's first City Cemetery.[33] In going through his personal effects, his wife found a piece of the green muslin dress she had worn on the spring day over thirty-four years earlier when a chance meeting on horseback led to a life of Texas pioneering.[34]

Maverick home on Alamo Plaza, 1877. *Courtesy Barker Texas History Center Photo Collection, Austin.*

Mary Maverick would live twenty-eight years alone, devoting herself to family, church, and commemoration of Texas' pioneer past, and comforting herself with the thought that her husband was happy in the company of his blue-eyed firstborn daughter. She would see the frontier rapidly vanish and the settled West Texas of which her husband had dreamed take shape, as accelerated political, economic, and social changes continued.

Political turmoil continued until Maverick's old political ally Richard Coke wrested the governorship from Davis and took office in 1874. Meanwhile, San Antonio boomed. West Texas sheep and cattle ranching began to attract new emigrants to the city, to drive up land prices,

Mary Brown Maverick Terrell before 1875. *Courtesy Maverick descendant* A. L. *Fenster-maker.*

and to contribute to Bexar's growing prosperity, as wool reached forty cents a pound on the San Antonio market.[35] An 1874 traveler remarked that the city seemed far removed from the rest of the nation, with people even talking of "going to the States." But he found it a picturesque and prosperous community, with four banks, gaslights, two daily papers and a German weekly.[36]

The Maverick family was booming, too. The younger Sam Maverick married Sally Frost nine months after his father's death, and in 1872 Mary Maverick could hold her first grandchild, a boy inevitably named Samuel. That same year, George married Mary Elizabeth Vance of Castroville, and in 1873 Willie married Emily Virginia Chilton. Only surviving daughter Mary Brown would wed in August of 1874, selecting future ambassador to Belgium Edwin H. Terrell, and youngest Maverick sibling Albert would marry in 1877, taking as his bride Jane Lewis Maury, whom he had met while attending the University of Virginia.[37]

Mary was to enjoy having most of her extended family around her through her remaining years, as Sam, Willie, and Albert all settled into life as San Antonio businessmen. As one of the city's leading business promoters, Willie would welcome the first long-hoped-for train into San Antonio in 1877.[38] George chose to practice law in St. Louis, Missouri, for many years, but he, too, maintained business ties in San Antonio, and Mary often made extended visits to his home. George's wife, Mary Vance, later lovingly recalled how her mother-in-law would never make a distinction between her own daughter and her daughters by marriage and how she would choose nuts and raisins for dessert to spare her daughter-in-law extra work in the kitchen.[39]

The years were not without their troubles. Sam and Albert both suffered financial reverses—Sam through starting a bank that failed, Albert through land speculation as he and Willie continued their father's business by maintaining a Maverick Land Office. In 1881, the family was sued by a woman living in Mexico who asserted that she owned by right of an 1819 sale almost eleven acres in the center of San Antonio that Samuel Augustus Maverick had claimed. The land included almost two-thirds of Travis Park, which Maverick had deeded to the city as a gift, and lots that Mary and the children had already sold. Ada Bradley Maverick's second husband, Jacob Waelder, worked on the case on behalf of the Mavericks for years. With Waelder's death in 1887, former Texas governor John Ireland took up the family's defense and won a U.S. Supreme Court judgment in their favor.[40]

Mary was eager for the judgment, not so much for the land itself as for vindication of her husband's right to it. "Is property of any importance?" she had asked her son Lewis in 1865, instead asserting that love took priority. Indeed, upon her husband's death, Mary seems to have made a concerted effort to begin ridding herself of some of the troublesome lands. Bexar County court records show that, although Maverick himself had not sold more than twelve parcels in a single year, in 1871 Mary disposed of forty-three.[41] At the same time, she recognized the value of her town lots. At her death, her half of Maverick's landholdings had shrunk to less than twenty-nine thousand acres, but she held eighty-seven San Antonio lots or partial lots.[42]

Mary suffered one more difficult loss during her remaining years—the death of daughter Mary Brown in Brussels, Belgium, in 1891. As always, she turned to her Christian faith for sustenance. She had lived to see St. Mark's Episcopal Church thrive. Work on the church building had recommenced in earnest in 1873, and the next year Mary donated in her husband's name an old cannon found on the Maverick homestead property.[43] This relic of the Alamo siege was cast into a bell at Mary's expense, and in October of the year it returned from the foundry. On it was inscribed a star, with the word "Alamo" in the center, and the dates 1813, 1836, and 1874, each inscribed in a point. "Presented by Colonel Samuel A. Maverick," another inscription read, and "Gloria in excelsis Deo, et in Terra Pax." Finally, Mary and rector Walter R. Richardson had a longer inscription included:

Ye must be born again, the Master said,
And spoke of man's new birth
By water and the Spirit:
I too into the womb of mother earth
Have entered and been born again
From works of death to words of life
Through Christ's eternal merit.[44]

Mary donated church windows completed in 1875 as well—one in memory of son Lewis, one in gratitude to God for sparing the life of her grandson Sam when a violent storm sent a giant pecan tree crashing into the nursery of her home. She delighted in the place of worship she had so long dreamed of, writing in 1878 that "a feeling of local pride has been aroused, even among those who are not of us, that Old

St. Mark's Episcopal Church about 1879. *Courtesy Daughters of the Republic of Texas Library, San Antonio.*

San Antonio, in wilderness as she is and almost out of the world as she is thought to be, should possess such a fine church," though simple in relation to European churches.[45] Mary also remained active in the congregation, serving continuously as president of the Ladies' Parish Aid Society for over twenty years.[46]

She devoted much activity as well to keeping the pioneer history of Texas alive. In 1856, she had written to Lewis in Vermont of reading Henderson Yoakum's history of the state, concluding "'Tis an excellent work—tho more full & interesting details will be collected in time." Now she shared with her grandchildren the tales of early days in Texas, showing them how to hold a door shut with one foot while slipping the bolt against Indians.[47] Widowed sister-in-law Lydia Maverick Van Wyck visited the Mavericks in 1874 and reported to her own daughter-in-law that Mary "has been a heroine and it is interesting and thrilling to hear her relate some of her adventures and hairbreadth escapes from the scalping knife of the Indians &c."[48]

Mary became a prominent member of the San Antonio Historical Society and the Daughters of the Republic of Texas, helping promote the annual Battle of Flowers celebration in San Antonio to commemorate the Battle of San Jacinto. From 1879 onward, she served repeatedly as president of the Alamo Monument Association, keeping before the public the need for preservation of the historic site until restoration efforts were begun in the 1890s.[49]

In 1889, Mary prepared her own brief manuscript on the fall of the Alamo, sending it to grandson George Vance Maverick. The manuscript is disappointing to the modern researcher in that it appears not to have been drawn from any firsthand recollections supplied by her husband or others who departed before the fall. She did use information gleaned from survivor Juana Navarro Alsbury, but the account provides a standard recitation of the events surrounding the garrison's fall.[50]

Mary's memoirs are a different matter. Completed in 1881 and shaped for limited publication with the help of son George in 1896, while Mary was vacationing with his family in a cottage at East Hampton, Long Island, they brim with concrete detail concerning one woman's life in pioneer Texas and they carry some of the emotional power of Mary's diaries from 1842 through 1857. Mary used the diaries in preparing her manuscript, reliving, as she said, "the joys and sorrows of those dear old times."[51] Some things she found too painful or personal; for example, she eliminated all but a brief mention of her fascination with spiritualism. But she dedicated the volume to her husband and five children "in the Spirit-land," hinting that she retained some spiritualist philosophy, and she did not destroy the diaries. Carefully, she kept them and the family correspondence—a frank and affecting record of Texas pioneer life prepared at a time when San Antonio was boasting streetcars, a second railroad, a telephone exchange, indoor gaslights for the prosperous, and new electric lights.

Mary Adams Maverick died on February 24, 1898, less than a month before her eighty-first birthday, and was buried beside her husband. "She had hoped, and expressed the expectation only a few days before the change for the worse, that she should be able to attend the services on Ash Wednesday," wrote Richardson, "but alas! it was on that

Mary Adams Maverick as an elderly woman. *Courtesy Barker Texas History Center Photo Collection, Austin.*

day that she fell into the slumber which passed into the sleep of death early on the next morning."[52] The San Antonio *Daily Light* called her the city's "best beloved friend," and the women of St. Mark's placed a heavy brass cross in the center of the altar in her memory.[53]

Mary had written to son George nine years earlier during the Lenten season, citing the large number of people attending morning and after-

259

noon prayers at St. Mark's. "I am glad of it," she concluded, quoting Isaiah 40:31: "They that wait upon the Lord shall renew their strength." She had renewed her own strength again and again under adverse circumstances and had lived to see the flourishing of her family, her city, and her state.

Conclusion

MYTHS COLLECTED around Sam Maverick during his lifetime and continued to burgeon after his death. Rumors during his later years that he owned more land than anyone in the United States evolved into such speculations as Aurelia Mohl's that he was "the largest landowner in the world except the Czar of Russia."[1]

Such statements had at least a basis in Maverick's extensive land-buying activities, but his modest cattle-ranching experience was also vastly inflated beyond the one documented Matagorda herd. Anson Mills, who actually worked with Maverick in the late 1850s, later wrote that his former employer had "owned more cattle on the free public range than any other man in Texas," and by 1914 Texas Ranger Dan W. Roberts reported, "So large was the area of his cattle range, that he could hardly get over it in one season to mark and brand his calves."[2] The legend also gained an unsavory twist, apparent in a 1968 study of American language that carries the following surmise on the origin of the term "maverick":

> Old man Maverick, Texas cattleman of the 1840s, refused to brand his cattle because it was cruelty to animals. His neighbors said he was a hypocrite, liar, and thief, because Maverick's policy allowed him to claim all unbranded cattle on the range. Lawsuits were followed by bloody battles, and brought a new word to our language.[3]

Both the inflated land and cattle claims and the hint of outlawry were simply part of the grand Texas myths of bigness and lawlessness. They had little or nothing to do with the real man who settled on

Carl G. von Iwonski in 1873 painted this posthumous portrait of Samuel Augustus Maverick at the request of the Maverick family. *Courtesy San Antonio Museum Association, San Antonio, No. 79-72-138 G.*

the frontier and saw Texas grow from a sparsely populated Mexican territory of approximately thirty thousand people to a state of over eight hundred thousand.

In reviewing the man's life, it is even difficult to attach the term "maverick" to him. He was quite capable of taking a risky or independent stand, as he proved in running for the South Carolina legislature on an antinullification platform, in protesting the Texas prisoners' treatment in Perote and refusing to gain freedom through a lie, and in joining Sam Houston's independent ticket before the Civil War. He also held more enlightened views than did many of his fellows on the rights of Mexican Americans and women. Yet overall, his record is one of moderation, of working within the established southern Democratic order.

Stripping away the myths, the scope of Maverick's activities in Texas is still impressive. He fulfilled the legacy of his business-minded father by steadily and successfully building a frontier land empire through work that fed his ambition and his spirit, as he exulted in the sparse, liberating life of the surveying camp. At the same time, he fulfilled the public-service legacy of his grandfather by helping to chart West Texas lands and helping to develop his city and state. He worked on behalf of his adopted home of San Antonio de Béxar in the legislature of Texas, ensuring rights for its citizens of different ethnic backgrounds and giving of his time, money, and property to see it grow and prosper. Among his bequests were Travis Park and a station site for the long-awaited railroad, which only arrived seven years after his death.[4]

He had involved himself at each stage of the state's history between 1835 and 1870, helping establish the Republic, then pressing for annexation when it became apparent that Texans would find their conditions improved under the protective power of the United States. As a Texas legislator during the state's formative years, he fought to keep the Lone Star in the American Union and helped set policies on a wide range of issues, most notably frontier protection and expansion and internal improvements. As a secession commissioner and legislator during the Civil War, he worked to meet the needs of a state impoverished and fragmented by the conflict. After the war, he worked for a return to a conservative Democratic Texas.

Despite the political, social, and economic turmoil of his time and place, Maverick led a remarkably consistent life as a serious, rational man propelled onward by a sense of public duty and a passion for west-

Twentieth-century view of St. Mark's Episcopal Church. *Courtesy Maverick descendant Carey Rote.*

ern land exploration and empire building. His love for his wife penetrated his reserve, but only one event—the death of Agatha—seriously
threatened his sense of who he was and what he was about. He responded by retreating more fully into the patterns of public duty and
private gain that he had already established for himself.

Mary Maverick served in no state legislatures and made no trips
of exploration, but she, too, contributed to the development of Texas
through her perseverance in turning her eyes toward Bexar, through
her church and civic work, and through her raising of a family whose
descendants remain influential in San Antonio affairs up to the present day. She struggled with the demands of the traditional wifely role,
demands heightened by her uncertain and often isolated frontier life,

without seriously questioning that role. When she failed in it as measured against a nineteenth-century romantic and spiritual ideal, as she was bound to do, she judged herself wanting. Mary possessed a deep sense of her own inadequacy and shouldered too much blame for perceived failures of character that could be as easily traced to the unremitting cares she faced. However, her sense of inadequacy led to strength, for it spurred her on a spiritual journey that eventually made her a woman of faith and fortitude.

In their frontier fortitude, the Mavericks can be seen as the mythical "stalwart pioneers" previous generations have presented for our edification. However, it is my hope that in studies such as this one we can replace the cardboard figures of "stalwart pioneers" with real, aching, celebrating, willful, uncertain human beings who can be the more appreciated for their humanity.

Endnotes

1. William Menefee, who served as a delegate to the 1836 Texas independence convention with Maverick, characterized him as "one of the most polished members" of the convention, one whose "manner and general deportment indicated a refined nature." Menefee is quoted in Rena Maverick Green, *Samuel Maverick, Texan, 1803–1870: A Collection of Letters, Journals, and Memoirs*, p. 49.

2. See Gen. Robert Anderson File, Pendleton District Historical and Recreational Commission Archives, Pendleton, South Carolina.

3. Ibid.

4. Typescript of anonymous journal fragment, July [no year], found in Old Stone Church Book of Mrs. T. B. Anderson, Charleston, South Carolina, and included in Anderson File.

5. See *Pendleton District and Anderson County, South Carolina Wills, Estates, Inventories, Tax Returns and Census Records*, p. 44.

6. Quoted in Frederick C. Chabot, *With the Makers of San Antonio: Genealogies of the Early Latin, Anglo-American, and German Families*, p. 237. In 1660 this first Maverick wrote a "Brief Description of New England." As one of four royal commissioners appointed by Charles II to remove the Dutch New Netherland government from New York, he was awarded "a house on the Broad Way" in New York. He also received a grant of Noddles Island, East Boston.

7. Ibid.; James Slayden Maverick, *Maverick Ancestors of the Maverick Family of Texas*.

8. Samuel Maverick to Samuel Augustus Maverick, Dec. 12, 1841, Maverick Family Papers, Barker Texas History Center, University of Texas at Austin, hereafter referred to as MFP.

9. See A. S. Salley, Jr., ed., *Journal of the Commissioners of the Navy of South Carolina, Oct. 9, 1776–March 1, 1779,* p. 129, which identifies a [S]am Maverick as being paid "wages due him on board the Brigg Defence" by the South Carolina Navy in 1778. Also see Samuel Maverick to Samuel Augustus Maverick, Dec. 30, 1848, and to grandson Samuel Maverick of Texas, July 4, 1846, MFP.

10. Samuel Maverick to grandson Samuel Maverick of Texas, July 4, 1846, MFP.

11. Ibid.; Samuel Maverick to Samuel Augustus Maverick, Dec. 30, 1848, MFP.

12. See Samuel's letters to Samuel Augustus of Nov. 13, 1847, and June 23, 1848. Other sources report that he also traded with the Orient. He is quoted on the early difficulties of the cotton trade in Caroline Olivia Laurens, "Journal of a Visit to Greenville from Charleston in the Summer of 1825," *South Carolina Historical Magazine* 72, no. 4 (Oct., 1971): 222. Green, *Samuel Maverick, Texan,* reports that the elder Samuel was said to be the first American to ship cotton to England, but general studies show cotton was being shipped to the British Isles from Virginia before his birth. However, it appears that Samuel did participate in the beginnings of the antebellum cotton-trading boom.

13. Ronald Jackson, Gary Teeples, and David Schaefermeyer, eds., *Index to South Carolina Land Grants 1784–1800,* p. 92.

14. Beth Ann Klosky, *The Pendleton Legacy,* p. 39.

15. Rena Maverick Green, ed., *Memoirs of Mary A. Maverick,* p. 9.

16. Advertisements in 1803 Charleston *Courier* newspapers, Microfilm Collection, Clemson University Library, Clemson, South Carolina.

17. The 1810 U.S. Census lists Samuel Maverick and family both in Pendleton and in Charleston. Samuel himself fixed the date of their permanent move in a letter of June 23, 1848, to his son, in MFP.

18. Tilly Merrick to Samuel Maverick, Mar. 26, 1812, Maverick and Van Wyck Family Papers, South Caroliniana Library, University of South Carolina, Columbia.

19. See Klosky, *Pendleton Legacy,* p. 42; Ernest M. Lander, Jr., "Ante-Bellum Milling in South Carolina," *South Carolina Historical and Genealogical Magazine* 52, no. 3 (July, 1951): 126, fn; Pendleton *Messenger,* June 1, 1825, Microfilm Collection, Clemson University Library.

20. See lists of Pendleton Farmers Society members, 1815–61, Pendleton District Historical and Recreational Commission Archives.

21. Barbara Norton, "A Sketch of St. Paul's Church, Pendleton," *South Carolina Historical Magazine* 63, no. 1 (January, 1962): 44.

22. Elizabeth H. Jervey, "Marriage and Death Notices from the City Gazette of Charleston, S.C.," *South Carolina Historical and Genealogical Magazine*

45, no. 3 (July, 1944): 139. Elizabeth Anderson Maverick's prayer book does survive and is in the possession of Maverick descendant Jane Maverick Mc-Millan. It apparently was carried to Texas by Samuel Augustus Maverick or his wife.

23. *Miller's Weekly Messenger* of Pendleton, South Carolina, Sept. 24, 1807, Clemson University Library.

24. See characterization in Klosky, *Pendleton Legacy*, p. 39.

25. See Samuel's letters to Samuel Augustus, Oct. 13, 1845, and Feb. 27, 1846, in MFP.

26. New Haven *National Pilot*, Sept. 12, 1822.

27. Sam Maverick to Mary Adams Maverick, Dec. 4, 1856, MFP. He remembered the ship on which Fisher was sailing as having the same name as the ship on which his son sailed in 1856 but other accounts refer to the wrecked vessel as the "*Albion.*"

28. Reproduced in Green, *Samuel Maverick, Texan.*

29. Ralph Henry Gabriel, *Religion and Learning at Yale: The Church of Christ in the College and University, 1757–1957*, p. 84.

30. Ibid.

31. William R. Johnson, *Schooled Lawyers: A Study in the Clash of Professional Cultures*, p. 7.

32. Quoted in Gabriel, *Religion and Learning*, p. 111.

33. See Franklin Dexter, "Student Life at Yale College, 1795–1817," *Proceedings of the American Antiquarian Society* 27 (1917): 318–35.

34. Extract from "A Journey in New England," published in New Haven *National Pilot*, Sept. 19, 1822.

35. Gabriel, *Religion and Learning*, p. 84.

36. Memory Book, 1825, MFP.

37. The 1825 commencement program is on file at Yale; a letter dated June 30, 1986, from Judith Schiff, Yale chief research archivist, to me reports that Maverick was not among the commencement speakers in his class.

38. See letters of Samuel Maverick and Thomas Jefferson published in Green, *Samuel Maverick, Texan,* pp. 402–405. Also see Laurens, "Journal," p. 222.

39. Letter of Oct. 2, 1825, from Charles Livingston, in MFP.

40. Anderson County, South Carolina, and Tuscaloosa County, Alabama, Deed Records for 1825 and 1826, Anderson and Tuscaloosa County courthouses.

41. Klosky, *Pendleton Legacy*, p. 42.

42. All quotations from Sam Maverick's 1826 journal, MFP.

43. Sam Maverick's 1827 journal, MFP.

44. Sam Maverick's March, 1828 journal, MFP.

45. Louise Vandiver, *Traditions and History of Anderson County*, p. 15; Anderson County and Tuscaloosa County Deed Records for 1828.

46. In addition to Blackstone's *Commentaries* presented by Tucker, law students used James Wilson's lectures, published in 1804, and David Hoffman's lectures, published in 1817. James Kent was also producing a significant series of *Commentaries* as Maverick studied for the bar. See Johnson, *Schooled Lawyers*, pp. 8–9.

47. See Calhoun's transmittal of Feb. 5, 1828, to Adams in Clyde N. Wilson, ed., *The Papers of John C. Calhoun*, X, 344.

48. See Maverick's original law license in Box 2F6, MFP.

49. See Maverick's 1829 journal, MFP.

50. The draft of this address is included in the 1832 Nullification Papers File, MFP.

51. Maverick recorded the extent of his loss on a page included in early family correspondence, MFP.

52. See letter of March 28, 1831, in Wilson, *John C. Calhoun*, XI, 364; and Edwin Vedder, *Records of St. Paul's Episcopal Church of Pendleton, South Carolina*.

53. Undated letter to "Fellow Citizens," in 1832 Nullification Papers File, MFP.

54. Ibid.

55. Ibid. Maverick was appointed a delegate to a Union convention in Columbia in September, but was unable to attend.

56. For one account, see Green, *Samuel Maverick, Texan*, p. 18.

57. Most accounts, including Green's, state that Maverick moved to Lauderdale County, Alabama, with his widowed sister when he saw no opportunity for himself in South Carolina politics, but journals and letters in the Maverick Family Papers show that he began his southern sojourn in Georgia, then moved to Alabama, where his widowed sister later joined him.

58. Samuel Augustus Maverick's son Sam in "Reminiscences of Sam Maverick Related to his Daughter Mrs. Emily Maverick Miller, 1923," MFP, stated, "My father tried to run a gold mine in northern Georgia . . . [but he] quit the business, as it was not paying well." These reminiscences are shot through with factual flaws, but this statement is probably true, given the dates of Maverick's stay and his interest in minerals.

59. Maverick's 1834 journal, MFP.

60. Letter of Apr. 4, 1835, to Mary Elizabeth Maverick Weyman, MFP.

61. Letter of Mar. 14, [1833], MFP.

62. Letter from Dr. Darrell A. Russel, Natchez Trace Genealogical Society, to me, Aug. 1, 1986.

63. Letter of July 10, 1821, Anne Royall, *Letters from Alabama on Various Subjects*, p. 144.

64. See Sam Maverick's 1834 journal of trip, MFP.

65. Quote from letter from Sam Maverick to Mary Adams Maverick, Nov. 16, 1855, MFP.

66. Mary Adams Maverick to Lewis Maverick, Feb. 14, 1858, MFP. Calomel was a powder often used at the time as a cathartic.

67. See Samuel's letter of May 20, 1834, MFP.

68. Turpin also freed his slaves and gave many of them valuable New York property. His trusted servant Joseph got "several large buildings worth by estimation $75,000." (See letter of Apr. 4, 1835, from Samuel to son, MFP.)

69. This is drawn from the memoirs of the younger Sam Maverick of Texas, cited above. It has a ring of truth in light of the elder Sam Maverick's self-proclaimed aversion to slave management.

CHAPTER 2, THE ROAD TO INDEPENDENCE

1. See John Edward Weems, *Dream of Empire: A Human History of the Republic of Texas, 1836–1846*, p. 32.

2. For a fuller discussion of American settlers' attitudes toward landscape, see John Mack Faragher, *Sugar Creek: Life on the Illinois Prairie* (New Haven: Yale University Press, 1986).

3. William C. Pool, *A Historical Atlas of Texas* (Austin: Encino Press, 1975), pp. 42–44.

4. Weems, *Dream of Empire*, p. 39. Rupert N. Richardson, Ernest Wallace, and Adrian N. Anderson, *Texas: The Lone Star State*, p. 142, report a population estimate of 34,470 in 1836, in line with the under-thirty-thousand figure advanced for 1835 by T. S. Fehrenbach, *Lone Star: A History of Texas and the Texans*, p. 187.

5. See Maverick's 1835 journal, MFP. Maverick's son-in-law Edwin Terrell transcribed the journal, and Rena Maverick Green published the edited version in *Samuel Maverick, Texan*. Terrell omitted many of Maverick's entries on land matters, however.

6. For information on early land-selling policies, see Curtis Bishop, *Lots of Land*.

7. See "Maverick to Hightower," Lauderdale County Deed Record A-6, p. 340.

8. Undated letter in the elder Samuel's handwriting included in Box 2L105, Maury Maverick Papers, Barker Texas History Center.

9. Journal for 1835, MFP.

10. Quitclaim record, Box 2F8, Maverick Business Papers, MFP.

11. In 1838 Groce was paying taxes on sixty-seven thousand acres. See Groce entry in Walter P. Webb, ed., *Handbook of Texas*, I, 739.

12. The Rev. Walter R. Richardson, *In Memory of Mrs. Mary A. Maverick*, p. 14 (pamphlet in Box 2F6, MFP).

13. Charles Ramsdell, *San Antonio: A Historical and Pictorial Guide*, p. 13.

14. See San Antonio Bicentennial Heritage Committee, *San Antonio in the Eighteenth Century.*

15. It is difficult to obtain reliable population figures for the year Maverick arrived. Caroline Remy ("Hispanic-Mexican San Antonio: 1836–1861," *Southwestern Historical Quarterly* 71, no. 4 [Apr., 1968]: 564–70) reports that the population was about two thousand in 1834, before a cholera epidemic, and dropped to one thousand during the Republic.

16. Ibid.

17. Ibid., p. 568; Hermann Ehrenberg, *With Milam and Fannin: Adventures of a German Boy in Texas' Revolution,* pp. 102–17.

18. Undated entry in Maverick's 1835 journal, MFP. Mary Maverick in her memoirs refers to Smithers as "Launcelot," but his name is listed in deed records as "Lancelott Smither" and "Lancelott Smithers." Amelia Williams ("A Critical Study of the Siege of the Alamo and of the Personnel of Its Defenders," *Southwestern Historical Quarterly* 37, no. 3 [Jan., 1934]: 157–84) identifies Lancelot [sic] Smithers as one of the couriers from the Alamo during the 1836 siege.

19. I found no indication that Maverick had studied Spanish before arriving in Texas, but his choice of San Antonio as home and his land and legal work must have led to at least some familiarity with the language.

20. See Samuel Maverick's Land Book B, Box 4L115, and Business & Financial Papers, Box 2F8, all in MFP; also Maverick holdings in Bexar County Reverse Index to Deeds, Bexar County Courthouse.

21. Maverick's diary for October 8 reports that Ugartechea had set out "at the head of all his effectives" but returned.

22. Maverick reported the development of the fortifications in his journal, but it is unclear whether he was pressed into service at this point. His letter to S. M. Howe of July 3, 1847, simply states that he was a prisoner in San Antonio when "with great labor Cos for the first time turned the Alamo into a fort."

23. Maverick's journal reports, "on the 14th the comet was seen in the west 45 above the horizon, its train reaching 1/4 over the visable firmament." This is probably a reference to Halley's Comet, which made one of its periodic passages close to earth in 1835.

24. See Noah Smithwick, *The Evolution of a State: Recollections of Old Texas Days,* pp. 74–75.

CHAPTER 3, THE SIEGE OF BÉXAR

1. See Dr. Joseph E. Field, *Three Years in Texas.*

2. Nov. 28 entry, 1835 journal, MFP.

3. See undated entry in Maverick's 1835 journal, MFP.

4. The contents of the note are lost, but the tone of the diary indicates that in the beginning of the siege Maverick was able to write in a fairly free manner to his countrymen.

5. Field reported that, "during the siege, a correspondence was kept up with some Americans living in town, by means of Mexican friends, they not being permitted to leave." See Field, *Three Years*, p. 13. Other Americans were also present in the city. Maverick mentions Pleasant B. Cocke, partner in his first Texas land transaction, as being in Béxar during the siege, and Cocke rather than Holmes is identified as a captive with Smith and Maverick in the eulogy, "Life and Character of Samuel Augustus Maverick Delivered Oct. 1870 before the Alamo Literary Society by George Cupples, M.D." and included on pp. 128–33 in Green, *Memoirs*. But Maverick's diary makes clear that Holmes was the third man held in Smith's house.

6. See Klosky, *Pendleton Legacy*, pp. 45–46.

7. See Green, *Samuel Maverick, Texan*, pp. 35, 39.

8. Maverick's diary of the siege was published by Frederick C. Chabot as "Notes on the storming of Bexar in the close of 1835" (San Antonio: Artes Graficas, 1942) before being included in ibid.

9. Entry of Oct. 19 in 1835 journal.

10. See Ehrenberg, *With Milam*, pp. 41–45.

11. See *Dictionary of American History* (New York: Charles Scribner's Sons, 1976), IV, 239.

12. George Nielsen, ed., "Lydia Ann McHenry and Revolutionary Texas," *Southwestern Historical Quarterly* 74, no. 3 (Jan., 1971): 397.

13. Nov. 2 entry, 1835 journal. Maverick's diary makes Austin sound far less conciliatory than some historians have painted him.

14. Field, *Three Years*, p. 12.

15. It is unclear which women were present, although most accounts say one was Smith's wife. Over the years, a dramatic tale has sprung up in which Smith's wife makes an emotional and successful plea for the captives' lives, but Maverick's journal shows that it was Vidal who saved the three.

16. November 12 entry in 1835 journal.

17. Green, *Samuel Maverick, Texan*, p. 45.

18. Some accounts, such as the reminiscences of Maverick's eldest son in MFP, relate a dramatic escape, but as Green points out in *Samuel Maverick, Texan*, Maverick's journal makes it clear that Cós released the two men.

19. Dec. 2 entry, 1835 journal, MFP.

20. See Sidney Lanier's account of the storming in Green, *Samuel Maverick, Texan*, p. 46. Siege participant William G. Cooke, in a letter to his brother dated August 7, 1839, and included in the William G. Cooke Family Papers,

Barker Texas History Center, reported that a sentinel saw a man leave camp and enter the Alamo after a daybreak attack had been planned for December 4.

21. Ehrenberg, *With Milam*, p. 62.

22. Green reported that her grandfather made a stirring speech from atop a tree stump, and Milam followed with a call for volunteers. This scenario is not corroborated by contemporary accounts, but after the deserters arrived, Maverick and Smith probably renewed their urging for an attack. Cooke in the account cited in note 20 takes credit for rallying the men to fight, but other accounts, including Maverick's, do not bear this out.

23. Ehrenberg, *With Milam*, p. 73. Ehrenberg's account provides the basis for my summary of the five days of fighting.

24. For the quotation, see the portion of a letter from Maverick's son George, p. 23, Green, *Samuel Maverick, Texan.*

25. Samuel Augustus Maverick to his eldest son, Sam, Jan. 30, 1852, MFP.

26. Ehrenberg, *With Milam*, p. 87.

27. Ibid., p. 90.

CHAPTER 4, THE ALAMO, INDEPENDENCE, AND RETREAT

1. For a description of this interlude, see Ehrenberg, *With Milam*, pp. 102–17.

2. See Audited Military Claim Records, Texas State Library Archives Section, Austin.

3. Smith's bounty authorization can be found in the John W. Smith File, Daughters of the Republic of Texas Library on the Alamo grounds. Maverick's Bounty Warrant 165, on file at the General Land Office in Austin, raises questions, as bounty warrants were given for periods of three months' service, but his specifies the dates of the siege of Béxar, Dec. 5–10, 1835. Maverick did receive the standard donation certificate for the siege as well. His name does not appear on "Returns Made by Col. J. C. Neill of Men Remaining at Bexar When He Left," Muster Rolls, General Land Office, but the list is reconstituted and incomplete.

4. See Reverse Index to Deeds, Bexar County Courthouse.

5. See John H. Jenkins, ed., *The Papers of the Texas Revolution 1835–1836,* IV, 15. Neill reported Smith's sending his family to "the colonies," probably the Brazos settlements, where they would get transportation to New Orleans.

6. Of the three, only Martin, mentioned in Maverick's 1835 journal, died in the Alamo.

7. Jenkins, *Papers*, IV, 496.

8. See voting record of Feb. 1, 1836, in Libro Registro, Bexar Archives, Barker Texas History Center.

9. Jenkins, *Papers*, IV, 263–65.

10. The list includes such early Texas notables as Gail Borden, Jr., and Thomas Jefferson Rusk, whose address is listed simply as Nacogdoches.

11. See Richardson, Wallace, and Anderson, *Texas* (1970 edition), p. 92, which calculates "about 150 effective fighting men" by mid-February.

12. See Louis W. Kemp, *The Signers of the Texas Declaration of Independence*, p. 5. Badgett may have left earlier, as his discharge papers show he was given twenty days "to return home" (see footnote, p. 5). Badgett had ties in Arkansas and Louisiana and could have attempted a quick return to one of these states before the gathering.

13. Jenkins, *Papers*, IV, 237.

14. Ibid., IV, 423.

15. Amelia Williams, "A Critical Study," p. 156, states that there were never fewer than twenty men on sick call.

16. March, 1987, letter to me.

17. Green repeats this story in *Samuel Maverick, Texan.*

18. Letter of July 3, 1847, to S. M. Howe, MFP. Maverick says he was sent "only 4 days before the Mexican Advance appeared." His wording is curious, and could be interpreted to mean that he left four days before the troops even appeared in San Antonio. This would mean he departed on February 19. He is not mentioned or is barely mentioned in Alamo accounts; for example, Williams includes him only in a footnote to dispute a story placing him on a hill overlooking the Alamo on March 3. This has led some to speculate that he was not there as late as March 2. However, Kemp places his date of leaving as the second; Maverick's statement to Howe can be interpreted as indicating March 2, particularly since he refers to himself as "almost a solitary escape[e]"; and the time works well with the fact that Maverick reached Washington-on-the-Brazos late on the fifth and was seated on the sixth.

19. Brown said this was by Maverick's and Smith's "own honorable statements afterwards" to Sam Houston and Milledge L. Bonham, in Houston in 1836, but this assertion is highly suspect in light of other historians' accounts, particularly since no such statements have been uncovered and the record does not show Maverick in Houston at all after the Alamo's fall in 1836. Brown is quoted and disputed in Williams, "A Critical Study," p. 25, fn.

20. Quoted in Milledge L. Bonham, Jr., "James Butler Bonham: A Consistent Rebel," *Southwestern Historical Quarterly* 35, no. 2 (Oct., 1931): 132.

21. See Green, *Samuel Maverick, Texan*; and Kemp, *Signers*, who says Maverick arrived on March 5, and that "it appeared" Maverick and Smith arrived together. Maverick was seated at the same time the message Smith carried was read.

22. Weems, *Dream of Empire*, pp. 76, 82.

23. Jenkins, *Papers*, IV, 502–503.

24. See original "Journals of the Convention of 1836," Box 2-9/32, Texas State Library Archives Section. Two sets of minutes differ as to whether Maverick was seated before or after the letter was considered.

25. Williams, "A Critical Study," p. 157.

26. See Daniel Edmond Kilgore, *How Did Davy Die?*

27. See comments of Stephen W. Blount and William Menefee in Frederick Chabot, "The Mavericks: On the Occasion of Maury Maverick for Congress," p. 4.

28. Neither the original "Journals of the Convention of 1836," Texas State Library Archives Section, nor the convention minutes reproduced in Jenkins, *Papers*, Vol. IX, make clear which article was under discussion. There were three Section 15's at the time: the land claim rejection, a standard clause on compensation of Republic legislators, and a statement in the Declaration of Rights that "every citizen shall have the right to bear arms in defence of himself and the republic."

29. Maverick's letter of Oct. 15, 1836, to Thomas Jefferson Rusk, Rusk Papers, Barker Texas History Center.

30. Weems, *Dream of Empire*, p. 83.

31. See vote in original "Journals of the Convention of 1836," Texas State Library Archives Section.

32. Weems, *Dream of Empire*, p. 85.

33. Letter of Oct. 15, 1836, to Rusk, Rusk Papers. This letter fills a gap in previous accounts of Maverick's movements.

34. Ibid.

35. Samuel Maverick to Mary Elizabeth Maverick Weyman, Apr. 22, 1835, MFP.

36. Letter of Mar. 14, 1836, MFP.

37. Constitution of the Republic of Texas, General Provisions, Section 8.

38. Lydia Maverick Van Wyck visited the widowed Mary Maverick in San Antonio in 1874 and wrote to her daughter-in-law in conventional tourist fashion of her visit to the mission, where, "as lately as the year 1836, Texans who have driven out the Mexicans and were fighting for the liberty of Texas . . . defended this fort against a large army of Mexicans under Santa Anna." (See letter of Jan. 30, 1874, to Mrs. M. C. Van Wyck in Box 2R157, Charles William Ramsdell Papers, Barker Texas History Center.)

39. Y. P. Alsbury prepared his reminiscences of the battle at the request of Maverick and Duncan Weeks. The reminiscences are in the Barker Texas History Center Archives.

40. Maverick to his wife, Mary, Jan. 24, 1844, MFP. Maverick was commenting hopefully on the proposed annexation of Texas to the United States.

CHAPTER 5, "TURN THOSE SWEET EYES TOWARD BEJAR"

1. Maverick's 1835 journal, MFP.

2. Statement attributed to William Jacques in George Cupples' eulogy for Maverick appended to Green, *Memoirs*, pp. 128–33.

3. Will and statement included in a letter from Sam Maverick to Mary, Jan. 25, 1855, MFP.

4. The plaster cast was in the possession of the Mavericks' great-granddaughter, the late Mary Vance Green, who kindly showed it to me.

5. Mary Bradley to Mary Maverick, Aug. 17, 1848, MFP.

6. See "Mary A. Maverick's Account of Samuel Maverick of Pendleton and of Her Father William Lewis Adams," in the appendix of Green, *Samuel Maverick*; also 1884 letter from John Henry Brown to Mary, MFP.

7. Marion John Bennett Pierson, *Louisiana Soldiers in the War of 1812*, shows three William Adamses and a William E. Adams serving in Louisiana regiments.

8. William Adams is identified as "the first lawyer in the area" in Tuscaloosa Genealogical Society, *Pioneers of Tuscaloosa County, Alabama prior to 1830*, p. 2.

9. See Mary's account of her father's life in Green, *Samuel Maverick, Texan*, p. 410. William L. Adams is not mentioned in Edward E. Hill's full listing of Indian agents in *The Office of Indian Affairs, 1824–1880: Historical Sketches*.

10. Adams is quoted in Lucille Griffith, *History of Alabama, 1540–1900*, p. 48.

11. Tuscaloosa County Will Book, 1821–55, pp. 37–38.

12. George's birthdate is missing from family and official records, and he is sometimes listed after Mary. But he was not a minor in April, 1837, when he petitioned for division of the family slaves, along with Agatha, William, and Sam Maverick; this fact, and the amount of time between births, indicates that he was born between William and Mary, not between Mary and Andrew.

13. June, 1846, entry and undated 1856 entry, Mary Maverick's diaries, MFP.

14. Letter of Nov. 21, 1849, from Elizabeth to Mary in Jon Winfield Scott Dancy Papers, Barker Texas History Center.

15. Green, *Memoirs*, p. 58.

16. Details on Mary's schooling remain vague. Files of Tuscaloosa County at one time contained a "William L. Adams" file holding receipts from 1829 for the Adams children's tuition signed by an A. M. Robinson and showing that Mary's tuition had terminated in June. When she began attending school across the river is unclear. Elizabeth boarded at and attended "Mr. Williams's

academy," according to brother Robert's letter to Mary, Dec. 7, 1838, MFP. This was the Alabama Female Academy, which opened in 1830 and which Mary may also have attended. For information on early Tuscaloosa academies, see Matthew Clinton, *Tuscaloosa, Alabama: Its Early Days, 1816–1865,* p. 73.

17. See Mary's letter of Sept. 17, 1857, to her son Lewis, MFP.

18. See "Tuscaloosa: The Second State Capitol of Alabama," in Thomas McCorvey, *Alabama Historical Sketches.*

19. See Mary's letter of Sept. 8, 1864, to Lewis, MFP.

20. Mary's letter of Feb. 14, 1837, to her mother, MFP.

21. This and the following excerpts are from Maverick's Oct. 15, 1836, letter to Rusk, Rusk Papers, Barker Texas History Center.

22. Curtis Bishop, *Lots of Land,* reports on p. 21 that "letter after letter to [an early land commissioner] from surveyors tells of their being laid low by rheumatic affliction, cold on the lungs, bilious fever, or just 'the sickly season.'" In contrast, Sam Maverick's letters repeatedly reported that his health had improved when he got outside the settlements.

23. Agreement of Jan. 9, 1837, in Lauderdale County Deed Records, Lauderdale County Courthouse, Florence, Alabama.

24. Mary's letter to Agatha, Feb. 14, 1837, MFP.

25. Ibid.

26. Memo from Ellen Maverick Dickson to me, May 1, 1985.

27. See Green, *Memoirs,* p. 11.

28. See Pendleton *Messengers* of June 16 and July 7, 1837.

29. Green, *Memoirs,* p. 12.

30. Letter of Nov. 19, 1837, MFP.

31. Green, *Memoirs,* p. 12.

32. Ibid., p. 14.

33. Sam Maverick to Dr. R. N. Weir, Aug. 15, 1843, MFP.

34. Letter of Feb. 26, 1838, MFP.

35. Ibid. Maverick's records show that after long litigation, he was able to claim the Cibolo Creek tract, but of his seven Bexar County pre-Republic purchases, all filed on and listed in the Bexar County Reverse Index to Deeds, only one, purchased from Encarnación Delgado, is shown eventually going through. I could find no further mention of the Guild certificates for ten leagues (more than forty-four thousand acres), and Maverick's actual landholdings did not exceed this amount until after 1841.

36. John Bost Pitts III, "Speculation in Headright Land Grants in San Antonio from 1837 to 1842," M.A. thesis, Trinity University, 1966, p. 14.

37. Ibid., p. 17.

38. Ibid., p. 12.

39. Marsha M. Wells, unpublished paper titled "Samuel A. Maverick's Land Holdings in Texas," in possession of Emily Wells, shows how this worked. For

example, in 1847 José Gonzales hired Maverick as his legal counsel to prove that Gonzales was entitled to a headright. Gonzales accepted $500 payment from Maverick for the headright, which Maverick was able to claim after winning the court case on Gonzales' behalf in 1852.

40. See Headright Record 1, Bexar County Courthouse Deed Records. In accordance with the law's interpretation at the time, Maverick got a married man's portion, despite the fact that he had been single on March 2, 1836. The official document shows Smith and the others verifying that Maverick participated in the revolution as a single man and married afterward.

41. Letter of Feb. 26, 1838, MFP.

42. Ibid.

43. Letter of Mar. 13, 1838, MFP.

44. See Carl N. Degler, *At Odds: Women and the Family in America from the Revolution to the Present*, p. 38.

CHAPTER 6, "A FAMILY OF ADVENTURERS"

1. Green, *Memoirs*, pp. 18–19. It is quite unlikely that the Tonkawa would eat a baby, although they did practice the ritualistic eating of slain enemies' flesh.

2. Undated 1856 entry in Mary Maverick's 1850–1857 diary, MFP.

3. Green, *Memoirs*, p. 19.

4. Quotation in Donald E. Everett, *San Antonio: The Flavor of Its Past, 1845–1898*, p. 3.

5. Aug. 6, 1838, entry in Dancy's Diary, Dancy Papers, Barker Texas History Center.

6. Everett, *San Antonio*, pp. 23, 28.

7. Ramsdell, *San Antonio*, (1976 edition), p. 96.

8. Letter of Aug. 25, 1838, MFP.

9. Cassiano had witnessed one of Maverick's early 1836 land purchases and was to remain a helpful associate. In 1859, he wrote Maverick from El Paso to report that despite difficulties he had obtained a receipt Maverick needed and that he was ready to do anything else promptly and personally. (See letter of Mar. 8, 1859, MFP.)

10. One early observer noted that "gambling is a marked trait of the Mexican character and is carried to the greatest extent by all classes of people [in San Antonio]." See Pitts, "Speculation," to which I am indebted for the analysis of Mexican relinquishment of land rights.

11. Smithwick, *Evolution*, p. 151.

12. Pitts, "Speculation," p. 21.

13. See Index to Deeds, Bexar County Courthouse; and Thomas Lloyd Miller, *Bounty and Donation Land Grants of Texas, 1835–1888*, p. 442.

14. Letters of June 2 and Oct. 11, 1838, MFP.

15. Letter of Nov. 21, 1839, to Lewis Antonio Maverick, MFP.

16. Letter of Dec. 6, 1840, MFP.

17. Green, *Memoirs*, p. 52.

18. For example, the Audited Civil Service Claims for the Republic, Texas State Library Archives Section, show that Maverick in 1839 acted as special attorney for the Republic in a treason case against two Mexican citizens.

19. For information on lawyers in the Republic, see William Ransom Hogan, *The Texas Republic: A Social and Economic History*, ch. 10.

20. See "Journal of the City Council A, June 1837 to January 1849," San Antonio City Hall.

21. Conversation with me, Bexar County Courthouse, Mar. 9, 1987.

22. See Mary's draft of her memoirs, "Recollections assisted by notes taken at the time—Mary A. Maverick, early days in Texas," MFP.

23. See Green, *Memoirs*, p. 24, where Mary discusses the claim.

24. Election Register, 1836-42, Box 2-1/1, Texas State Library Archives Section, shows that Maverick became justice of the peace for the second precinct on Aug. 15, 1839, and was commissioned on Oct. 21, 1839.

25. Their subsequent letters and journals contain phrases in Spanish, and, according to family tradition, Mary's knowledge of the language was later good enough for her to be called on to interpret in court.

26. See Weems, *Dream of Empire*, p. 82.

27. See Mary's "Recollections assisted by notes taken at the time," MFP.

28. Letter of Aug. 25, 1838, MFP.

29. For a discussion of the early Texas surveyor's dangerous job, see Sue Watkins, ed., *One League to Each Wind: Accounts of Early Surveying in Texas*.

30. For two descriptions of this incident, see Green, *Memoirs*, p. 53; and Joe B. Frantz, ed., "Moses Lapham: His Life and Some Selected Correspondence," in Watkins, *One League*, pp. 252-59.

31. Letter of Jan. 5, 1839, MFP.

32. As noted earlier, Maverick was sometimes called Gus by his family.

33. Green, *Memoirs*, pp. 29-30.

34. These are the figures in Richardson, Wallace, and Anderson, *Texas*, (1981 edition), p. 138. Mary Maverick reported thirty-three Indians and six Texans killed.

35. See James Axtell, *The Invasion Within: The Contest of Cultures in Colonial North America*, p. 4.

36. Green, *Memoirs*, p. 44.

37. Axtell, *The Invasion Within*, argues that during the colonial period, Indians were usually kind to captives, adopting them into their tribes and proving more successful than the French or English in winning converts to their way of life.

38. Green, *Memoirs*, p. 33. The Mavericks' son Sam gave a different account in "Reminiscences of Sam Maverick Related to His Daughter Mrs. Emily Miller, 1923," MFP. He reported, "Uncle Andrew ran into the house and asked my father for his gun which he was cleaning. My father said, 'What do you want to kill the Indian for, what has he done to you?' Andrew ran and got his own gun and pouch, etc." This is an appealing and not completely improbable account. Sam Maverick showed some sympathies for the situation of Indians during his lifetime, as when he served on a legislative committee that tried to ensure the rights of the natives in disputes with their white neighbors. But the reminiscences, shared when the younger Maverick was eighty-six, contain numerous inaccuracies.

39. Green, *Memoirs*, p. 33.

40. In ibid. he is referred to as "Captain," but the entry on Wells in Webb, *Handbook*, vol. II, shows that he had reached the rank of colonel a few months earlier.

41. Green, *Memoirs*, p. 34.

42. Ibid., pp. 35–36.

43. Ibid., p. 44.

44. Mary later wrote that her husband commenced his trip in April, but letters in the Maverick Family Papers clearly show that he departed on March 21.

45. See Gerald S. Pierce, *Texas under Arms: The Camps, Posts, Forts, and Military Towns of the Republic of Texas, 1836–1846.*

46. Letters of Mar. 23 and Apr. 1, 1840, MFP.

47. Green, *Memoirs*, p. 45.

48. Letter of May 11, 1844, MFP.

49. Letter of Nov. 16, 1845, MFP.

50. Green, *Memoirs*, p. 48.

51. Ibid., p. 50; Weems, *Dream of Empire*, p. 186.

52. Letters of Nov. 28, 1840, and Oct. 11, 1838, MFP.

53. Letter to Agatha Adams, Feb. 21, 1841, MFP.

54. Green, *Memoirs*, pp. 56–57.

55. See Gifford White, ed., *The 1840 Census of the Republic of Texas.*

56. Seguín's own memoirs show rancor against John W. Smith, but mention "the Honorable Sam Maverick" only in passing as serving with Seguín in San Antonio government. See *Personal Memoirs of John N. Seguin from the Year 1834 to the Retreat of General Woll from the City of San Antonio in 1842.*

57. Letter of Oct. 27, Business Papers, MFP.

58. Green, *Memoirs*, p. 55.

59. Letter of Aug. 28, 1841, MFP.

60. See Mary's memoir draft, "Recollections assisted by notes taken at the time," MFP.

61. Letter of Apr. 22, 1838, MFP.
62. Green, *Memoirs*, p. 58.

CHAPTER 7, "THE TIME TO PROVE THE HEART"

1. Green, *Memoirs*, p. 61.
2. This passage was inadvertently misplaced in the 1921 printing of ibid., where it was inserted in the account of the second 1842 invasion. It was restored to its correct place in the narrative in Green, *Samuel Maverick, Texan.*
3. Dancy's diary contains a noncommittal note for Apr. 21, 1842: "Came home & found Mr Maverick and family at my house." See Jon Winfield Scott Dancy Papers, Barker Texas History Center.
4. Robert Adams to Mary Adams Maverick, Nov. 3, 1841, MFP.
5. Letter of Aug. 25, 1838, MFP.
6. Undated entry in Dancy diary, Barker Texas History Center.
7. Journal A, San Antonio City Hall, entry for July 16, 1842, shows that the council voted to consider Maverick's and John Bradley's seats vacated "as they were no longer within our limits or our county."
8. Green, *Memoirs*, p. 67.
9. See Anderson Hutchinson's journal published in E. W. Winkler, ed., "The Bexar and Dawson Prisoners," *Texas Historical Association Quarterly* 13, no. 4 (Apr., 1910): 294–95.
10. Weems, *Dream of Empire*, p. 234.
11. Letter of Sept. 11, 1842, MFP. Maverick's journal states that fifty-six were captured, with four of these released.
12. Maverick identifies only himself and Jones as "commissioners," but Hutchinson identifies George Van Ness and C. W. Peterson as well. Hutchinson reports that on the trip into Mexico Jones drafted a memorial complaining of the prisoners' treatment and that Jones and Maverick signed it as the group's representatives.
13. Letter of Jan. 21, 1843, to Mexican secretary of state and foreign affairs José María Bocanegra, in Green, *Samuel Maverick, Texan*, pp. 212–22. Sam Maverick's grandson Maury Maverick had the letter entered into the *Congressional Record* of Mar. 28, 1938.
14. Letter of Sept. 11, 1842, MFP.
15. Letter of Sept. 20, 1842, MFP.
16. Leonie Rummel Weyand and Houston Wade, *An Early History of Fayette County*, p. 155.
17. Green, *Memoirs*, p. 69.
18. Weyand and Wade, *Fayette County*, pp. 156–57.
19. Houston *Telegraph & Texas Register*, Sept. 28, 1842.

20. Joe Frantz estimates the distance in his introduction to William Preston Stapp, *The Prisoners of Perote*.

21. Letter of Aug. 15, 1843, to Dr. R. N. Weir, MFP.

22. See Maverick's journal as a prisoner, Sept. 1842–Apr. 1843, published in Green, *Samuel Maverick, Texan*.

23. Ibid., journal entries of Oct. 12, 21, 1842.

24. Ibid., journal entry of Dec. 17, 1842.

25. Ibid., journal entries of Oct. 7, Dec. 19, 1842.

26. In ibid., p. 177, Maverick's son-in-law Edwin Terrell notes that Maverick later sent "a fine set of China to Madame Taylor in remembrance of her kindness." The fruit-bearing boy is mentioned in a brief handwritten narrative in MFP by Maverick's daughter-in-law Mrs. Albert Maverick. She reports that "this same boy afterwards moved to S[an] A[ntonio] & told me that as long as Mr. Maverick lived he sent him a suit of clothes at Xmas."

27. Ibid., journal entries of Dec. 17, 19, 1842.

28. Green, *Memoirs*, p. 80.

29. Mary's 1842–50 diary, MFP. The arrangement of her memoirs indicates that she kept a diary even earlier, but only two volumes survive in the MFP—one covering the years 1842 to 1850, and a second covering the years 1850 to 1857, with a brief addition in 1859. There are often gaps of months between entries.

30. Copies in letter to Mary of Nov. 19, 1842, MFP.

31. Letter of Nov. 19, 1842, MFP.

32. Letter of Dec. 20, 1842, MFP.

33. See *Journals of the House of Representatives of the Seventh Congress of the Republic of Texas* (Washington, Texas, 1843), minutes for Nov. 30, Dec. 1, Dec. 2, 1842.

34. Weems, *Dream of Empire*, pp. 294–96.

35. See Jones' account of his captivity in Winkler, "Bexar and Dawson Prisoners," pp. 320–24.

36. Maverick related the reason for his solitary confinement in the letter to Bocanegra, Jan. 21, 1843. His son-in-law, in editing Maverick's prison journal, stated that Maverick refused to work and was placed in a dungeon, nearly starved, and threatened with death.

37. Ibid.

38. Thompson's grandnephew later sent the letter to Maverick's grandson Maury Maverick. See Green, *Samuel Maverick, Texan*, p. 212 fn.

39. Quoted in Waddy Thompson, *Recollections of Mexico*, pp. 95–97. Thompson characterized Maverick as "a man of fiery and impatient temper" who "chafed under his confinement, like a chained tiger." One captive, James W. Robinson, agreed to help Mexico negotiate with Texas and was released early.

In his letter of Mar. 16, 1843, to Mary, Maverick warned her to "tell Col. Dancy to watch J. W. Robinson, his business is secret & I know bad."

40. Letter of Nov. 19, 1842, MFP.

41. Letter of Feb. 2, 1843, MFP.

42. When Maverick heard of the expedition's capture in January, he wrote, "Poor fellows, it is a dreadful thing to be made prisoners to the coward Mexican:—and much worse for them, invaders of Mexico!" See his letter to Mary, Jan. 27, 1843, MFP.

43. See Jones' account in Winkler, "Bexar and Dawson Prisoners," pp. 320-24.

44. Green, *Memoirs*, p. 81.

45. Six San Antonio captives had been released at nearly the same time, for while Thompson had arranged the release of Maverick, Jones, and Hutchinson, the English minister had secured the freedom of W. H. O'Phelan, John Riddle, and W. J. Riddle. Two San Antonio prisoners had been released previously, and one had escaped en route to Perote and two from Perote itself.

46. See "Reminiscences of Sam Maverick Related to his Daughter Mrs. Emily Maverick Miller, 1923," and Mary's 1842-50 Diary, MFP.

47. Letter of May 17, 1843, MFP. The elder Maverick also wrote to Santa Anna on May 1, thanking him for Sam Maverick's release.

48. Mary's 1850-57 diary, 1856 entry, MFP.

CHAPTER 8, THE QUEST FOR STABILITY

1. Letter to R. N. Weir, Aug. 15, 1843, MFP.

2. Ibid.

3. Maverick's record of returns is in Maverick Family Correspondence, MFP.

4. See Richardson, Wallace, and Anderson, *Texas* (1970 edition).

5. Ibid., p. 130.

6. See *Journals of the House of Representatives of the Eighth Congress, Republic of Texas* (Houston: Cruger & Moore, 1844), minutes for Jan. 3, 1844.

7. Letters of Jan. 10, 24, 1844, MFP.

8. *Journals of the . . . Eighth Congress*, pp. 449, 463.

9. Ibid., pp. 451-52.

10. H. P. N. Gammel, *The Laws of Texas, 1822-1897*, vol. II, Eighth Legislature, pp. 18-19.

11. *Journals of the . . . Eighth Congress* show that Maverick introduced bills for the relief of, among others, José Cassiano and the family of Deaf Smith.

12. Letter of Jan. 24, 1844, MFP.

13. Letter of Aug. 15, 1843, MFP.

14. Substance copy of letter of Feb. 27, 1844, MFP.

15. Letters of Jan. 14 and late Jan. [undated], 1844, MFP.

16. For a discussion of perceptions of women's roles in early nineteenth-century America, see Degler, At Odds, chap. 2.

17. Mary states in Green, Memoirs, p. 81, that Maverick left in April for South Carolina, but the family letters that survive, including those from Maverick's father at Pendleton, show that on this trip he simply went to New Orleans and, possibly, Tuscaloosa. On Oct. 10, the elder Maverick wrote, "I have not heard from you since 14 May [a letter from New Orleans] & by N. paper 17 June to sail next day for Galveston."

18. Letter of May 24, 1844, MFP.

19. Letters of Apr. 30, May 11, 1844, MFP.

20. In Green, Memoirs, p. 84, Mary states that the prisoners came home in the summer of 1843, but this appears to be an error, as both contemporary and historical sources give the date as 1844.

21. See Chabot, Makers of San Antonio, p. 296, in which he publishes Santa Anna's letter releasing Bradley and quotes the newspaper account.

22. Green, Memoirs, p. 84.

23. Ibid.

24. For land transaction, see document in Dancy Papers, Box 3N186, Barker Texas History Center.

25. Green, Memoirs, p. 86, and Mary's eldest son's "Reminiscences of Sam Maverick Related to his Daughter Mrs. Emily Maverick Miller, 1923," MFP.

26. Mary, in Green, Memoirs, p. 87, refers to him as Prince Charles, but her further identification of him shows that she was referring to Prince Carl.

27. See 1844 Béxar County tax list, Microfilm Roll 59 (1837–55), Texas State Library Genealogical Section, and Maverick's 1845 tax records, Box 2F19, Business Papers, MFP. Maverick had purchased property for the grandchildren on the San Antonio, Leona, and Frío rivers.

28. Ibid.

29. Letter of Aug. 6, 1845, MFP. Mary, in Green, Memoirs, states that Maverick left for San Antonio on June 11, and remained gone six weeks. But her dating of subsequent events and the elder Samuel Maverick's letter of Aug. 6, 1845, show that he returned earlier. The elder Maverick referred to his son's letter of June 30 and to the boating accident of June 21, 1845, urging Sam Maverick to get official documents concerning the date and loss.

30. Pages apparently covering the years 1844, 1845, and 1846 were at some point removed from Mary's 1842–50 diary, leaving her mental state during this time open to conjecture. (From the diarylike style of the portion of her memoirs covering this period, it is apparent that she used the missing pages in preparing the memoirs.) But subsequent entries frankly show the increasing struggle she engaged in to deal with the pressures of her family's frontier existence.

31. Green, *Memoirs*, p. 89. The wording of this line, with a date preceding it, bears out the idea that Mary was referring to pages now missing from her diary in preparing the memoirs.

CHAPTER 9, "LET US HOPE THAT WE ARE BELOVED"

1. Letter of Aug. 21, 1845, MFP.
2. Nielsen, "Lydia Ann McHenry," p. 401.
3. Quoted in Joseph William Schmitz, *Texas Culture, 1836–1846: In the Days of the Republic*, p. 7.
4. See "Reminiscences of Sam Maverick Related to His Daughter Mrs. Emily Maverick Miller, 1923," MFP.
5. Letter of Nov. 16, 1845, MFP.
6. Maverick mentions calling on Calhoun in his letters of Nov. 8 and Dec. 10, 1845, MFP.
7. Routez and her brother Augustus M. Weyman had come to Pendleton after the death of their mother, Mary Elizabeth Maverick Weyman Thompson, and were attending school. Routez and Houston were married at the Maverick family church, St. Paul's Episcopal, on Apr. 5, 1844. See the Rev. Silas Emmett Lucas, Jr. *Marriage and Death Notices from Pendleton (S.C.) Messenger 1807–1851*.
8. Letter of May 8, 1844, MFP.
9. Letter of Nov. 19, 1845, MFP.
10. Letter of Sept. 1, 1845, MFP.
11. Letter of Dec. 10, 1845, to Mary, MFP.
12. Ibid.
13. Ibid.
14. Maverick's letter of Dec. 10 states only that he had bought a carpenter and a seamstress, but Green, *Memoirs*, p. 90, clearly states that he bought the four named slaves on this Charleston trip, and the number of slaves listed as Maverick's taxable property jumps from nine in 1845 to thirteen in 1846. (See Box 2F19, Business Papers, MFP.)
15. See copy of May 19, 1842, apportionment of slaves and property by executors of William L. Adams' estate to his children in family correspondence, MFP. Mary's share included "a Negro Girl named Emeline aged about 12 years," appraised at $600, "also one feather bed and furniture at $30, and one of the largest Silver goblets."
16. Letter of Dec. 10, 1845, MFP.
17. Catherine Clinton, *The Plantation Mistress: Woman's World in the Old South*, p. 185.
18. Mary Boykin Chestnut, *A Diary from Dixie*, pp. 163–64.

19. Texas Slave Censuses, 1850 and 1860, Microfilm Rolls 297 and 298, Barker Texas History Center.

20. Green, *Memoirs*, p. 91, and Apr. 27, 1847, entry in Mary's 1842–50 diary, MFP.

21. No reason was given for Lizzie's refusal, but it is not surprising that she found the social life and familiar associations around Tuscaloosa more appealing, at least temporarily, than the relatively isolated life with her sister's family on the Texas Coast.

22. Letter of Mar. 9, 1846, MFP.

23. Green, *Memoirs*, p. 91.

24. Letter of May 17, 1846, to his son, MFP.

25. Letter of Aug. 15, 1845, Clow Papers, Barker Texas History Center. These papers include correspondence from Lizzie and Andrew Adams to Mary, 1846, and correspondence from Lizzie and her husband, Robert Clow, to Mary, 1848–57.

26. Letter of Apr. 22, 1846, Clow Papers.

27. Letter of June 16, 1846, Clow Papers. Also see Lizzie's letter of Dec. 29, 1846.

28. June, 1846 entry, 1842–50 diary, MFP.

29. Letter of Aug. 23, 1857, MFP.

30. See Bishop, *Lots of Land*.

31. For example, a notice in the *Houston Telegraph & Texas Register* of Feb. 5, 1840, shows that Maverick brought suit against a number of other San Antonio businessmen to gain legal control of his 1835 Cibolo Creek purchase.

32. Letter of Oct. 24, 1846, MFP.

33. See Maverick's letter of Nov. 19, 1846, MFP, in which he states that he has resisted acting on Don Julio's news and adds, "It directly occurred to me, that many a time, this same Julio Iffla acted as if he were my genius or 'winged Mercury.'" The identity of this man remains unclear; he is not mentioned elsewhere in Maverick correspondence or in other sources I have checked.

34. See tax returns for 1845 and 1846–47, Box 2F19, Business Papers, MFP, and Maverick's letter to his wife of Dec. 7, 1846, MFP.

35. Letter of Nov. 19, 1846, MFP.

36. See Dec. 30, 1846, entry, Mary's 1842–50 diary, MFP, and Ellen N. Murry's "Promise in a Lonely Land," *Texas Libraries* 45, no. 4 (Winter, 1984): 140.

37. Maverick's letter of May 3, 1847, to Mary from San Antonio implies that Lizzie Adams had not yet arrived at Port Cavallo from Alabama, but according to Green, *Memoirs*, Mary's sister was already with her at the time Maverick attempted to get another female relative to join them.

38. Maverick and Thomas Decrow bought the boat and contracted with the state "to dredge out the logs obstructing the Colorado River at its mouth," according to son Sam in "Reminiscences of Sam Maverick Related to His Daughter Mrs. Emily Maverick Miller, 1923," MFP.

39. Green, *Memoirs*, p. 96.

40. Letter of Sept. 14, 1849, Business Papers, MFP.

41. Maverick refers to the Alamo as the "old Golgotha" in a fascinating but incomplete passage in his letter of Nov. 19, 1846, to Mary. He relates that upon his recent approach to the city with a company of fellow travelers, "we saw rockets shooting up from the old Golgotha and were electrified by the loud report of 3 heavy cannon." Immediately, the company suspected trouble from the Mexican army. The page ends with the words, "But on coming up (& finishing our 50 miles) lo and behold– " and subsequent pages among the papers do not provide a conclusion.

42. Mary's sketch, which was retained in family hands, is undated, but some Alamo experts place it before 1842. Historian Bill Green thinks that it was possibly done later than this from a published picture. On Feb. 24, 1848, the elder Samuel Maverick wrote from Pendleton, "I have [Mary's] beautiful drawings now laying before me of the Church of San Fernando de Bexar & the church of San Antonio Valero [the Alamo]."

43. Actually, the church had been used as a garrison sporadically since its secularization in 1793. Maverick may have been aware of this, but he wanted the land. The U.S. Army eventually, in 1850, leased the mission from the Catholic bishop.

44. Substance copy of letter of July 3, 1847, MFP.

45. See agreement of Feb. 9, 1847, in Box 2F9, Business Papers, MFP.

46. The *Oxford English Dictionary* identifies the term as "said to be named from Samuel *Maverick*, a Texan rancher about 1840 who habitually neglected to brand his cows."

47. Letter of Nov. 13, 1847, MFP.

48. Letter of Sept. 5, 1847, MFP.

49. See William Elton Green, "Land Settlement in West Texas: Tom Green County, a Case Study, 1874–1903," Ph.D. diss., Texas Tech University, 1981, pp. 188, 190.

50. Ramsdell, *San Antonio* (1976 edition), p. 44.

51. Apr. 23, 1847, entry, 1842–50 diary, MFP.

52. This was the grant of one league and one labor that Maverick received on Mar. 2, 1838, as a pre-Republic Texas emigrant.

53. Letter of May 9, 1848, MFP.

54. May, 1848, entry, 1842–50 diary, MFP.

55. Letter of Mar. 15, 1843, MFP.

56. Green, *Memoirs*, p. 78.

57. Entry of Sunday evening, Sept. 30, 1849, in Mary's 1842–50 journal, MFP.

58. Green, *Memoirs*, p. 100.

CHAPTER 10, "OH WORLD OF TRIAL! OH WORLD OF GRIEF!"

1. Mary quotes her husband in a May 26, 1848, entry, 1842–50 diary, MFP, and in Green, *Memoirs*, p. 101.

2. Letter of Aug. 12, 1848, MFP.

3. May 26, 1848, entry, Mary's 1842–50 diary.

4. June 2, 1848, entry, in ibid.

5. Accounts of Ann Bradley's life, such as the genealogical sketch in Chabot, *Makers of San Antonio*, omit mention of Veatch, as the marriage soon dissolved. Sketches of Veatch only refer to a wife Ann who divorced him in 1853. Correspondence between the Mavericks, Clows, and Bradleys makes Ann's identity clear.

6. Letters of June 2 and July 10, 1848, Clow Papers, Barker Texas History Center.

7. Green, *Memoirs*, pp. 101–102.

8. See James Kimmins Greer, *Colonel Jack Hays: Texas Frontier Leader and California Builder*, p. 217.

9. Maverick's journal is included in the MFP.

10. See William H. Goetzmann, *Army Exploration in the American West, 1803–1863*, pp. 227–30.

11. Greer, *Colonel Jack Hays*, p. 219.

12. See Maverick's entry of Sept. 29, 1848.

13. Maverick probably meant a mountain lion or puma.

14. Greer, *Colonel Jack Hays*, p. 224.

15. Goetzmann, *Army Exploration*, pp. 227–30.

16. See the elder Samuel's letter of Feb. 12, 1849, MFP; and Green, *Memoirs*, p. 102.

17. Letter to Mary of July 10, 1848, Clow Papers.

18. Letter of Feb. 28, 1849, Clow Papers. Lizzie talks of the two fledgling communities as if they were one.

19. See draft of letter of Jan. 23, 1849, MFP. In the elder Samuel's letters to his son, the steamboat caused the only mention of any father-son tension. Samuel thought that the boat had sunk and that his son had suffered other business reverses. Apparently informed by letter that these suppositions were untrue, Samuel wrote on Aug. 12, 1848, "I regret that I may have hurt your feelings, about your . . . losses. But you must attribute my feelings, by the feelings you will have after for your (our) dear Sam's welfare." Also see Samuel's letter to his son of Feb. 12, 1849, MFP.

20. Lizzie's letter of Feb. 28, 1849, Clow Papers.

21. For information on Veatch's career, see S. W. Geiser's biographical sketch, *Southwestern Historical Quarterly* 46, no. 2 (Oct., 1942): 169–73.

22. Undated 1852 entry, Mary's 1850–57 diary, MFP.

23. Letter of Sept. 6, 1848, Clow Papers.

24. Letter of Feb. 28, 1849, in ibid.

25. Letter of Mar. 14, 1849, in ibid.

26. Letter of Apr. 21, 1849, in ibid.

27. See Ella M. Darlington, "A Brief History of St. Mark's Protestant Episcopal Church of San Antonio, Texas," M.A. thesis, St. Mary's University, 1947; and Carey Rote, "Treasures of St. Mark's," unpublished manuscript, 1984.

28. Green, *Memoirs*, p. 105.

29. Ibid., pp. 103–105.

30. Letter to Maverick of June 17, 1849, MFP.

31. Letter of Dec. 30, 1848, MFP.

32. See Harris L. Coulter, *Science and Ethics in American Medicine: 1800–1914*, ch. 2. Thomsonians even established infirmaries, drugstores, and drug wholesale houses.

33. Late summer, 1849, entry (date unclear), Mary's 1842–50 diary, MFP.

34. Ibid.

35. Letter of June 7, 1849, Clow Papers.

36. Oct. 8, 1849, entry, Mary's 1842–50 diary, MFP.

37. Letter of Sept. 15, 1849, MFP.

38. Substance copy of letter of Dec. 5, 1849, MFP.

39. See 1848 Bexar County tax list, Microfilm Roll 59 (1837–55), Texas State Library Genealogy Section.

40. Letter of Nov. 25, 1849, MFP.

41. The term is generally traced to Maverick, but often with outlaw legends attached. Maverick's son George wrote a letter to the *St. Louis Republic*, which was printed on Nov. 16, 1889, and which explained how the term had originated with his father. A copy of the letter is in the Maverick Family Papers. Maverick's cattle brand was supplied by Maverick descendant Bebe Fenstermaker, who explains that a second brand appearing as Maverick's in the Scrapbook section of *Southwestern Historical Quarterly* 71, no. 1 (July, 1967) was devised by another Maverick descendant (letter to author, dated Nov. 4, 1987).

42. Letter of Nov. 21, 1849, Dancy Papers, Barker Texas History Center.

43. Letter of May 30, 1850, Clow Papers.

44. Lydia Maverick Van Wyck quotes Lewis in her Sept. 1, 1850, response, MFP.

45. Letter of July 28–Aug. 26, 1850, MFP.

46. Letter of Aug. 11, 1850, Clow Papers.

47. Letter of Nov. 21, 1849, Dancy Papers.

48. Letter of Feb. 24, 1851, MFP.

49. In a June 23, 1848, letter to his son, the elder Maverick lauded the sect for its "fear & trembling" before God, and Sam Maverick enjoyed listening to Lucretia Mott, "a fine old Quaker," on his trip to New York in 1856 (see letter to Mary, Nov. 27, 1856, MFP).

50. Sam Maverick's 1835 journal, letter of Feb. 24, 1849, from his father, MFP.

51. See George Cupples, "Life and Character of Samuel Augustus Maverick Delivered Oct. 1870 before the Alamo Literary Society," in Green, *Memoirs*, pp. 128–33.

52. See Ramsdell, *San Antonio* (1976 edition), p. 86.

53. In conversation with me, historian Bill Green has shared this deduction from a study of the property records.

54. See announcement of incorporation, *Texas State Gazette*, Apr. 6, 1850.

55. Ibid., Sept. 28, 1850.

56. Ibid., July 6, 1850.

57. Richardson, Wallace, and Anderson, *Texas* (1981 edition), pp. 172–74.

CHAPTER 11, "TAKE NEW COURAGE FROM THE RACE"

1. Maverick's letter of Jan. 9, 1854, MFP.

2. Summer, 1851, entry, Mary's 1850–57 diary, MFP.

3. Letter of June 20, 1851, MFP.

4. Summer, 1851, entry, Mary's 1850–57 diary, MFP.

5. San Antonio *Ledger*, July 21, 1851.

6. Ibid.

7. See Caroline Remy, "Hispanic-Mexican San Antonio: 1836–1861," *Southwestern Historical Quarterly* 71, no. 4 (Apr. 1968): 112.

8. Richardson, Wallace, and Anderson, *Texas* (1970 edition), pp. 148–49.

9. David C. Humphrey, *Austin: An Illustrated History*, p. 36.

10. Ibid.

11. *Journals of the House of Representatives of the State of Texas: Fourth Legislature*, pp. 9–23.

12. Letter of Nov. 14, 1851, MFP.

13. See Ralph Wooster, "Membership in Early Texas Legislatures, 1850–1860," *Southwestern Historical Quarterly* 69, no. 2 (Oct., 1965): 163–73.

14. Letter of July 16, 1856, MFP.

15. Letter of Nov. 14, 1851, MFP.

16. Letter of Dec. 12, 1851, MFP.

17. *Journals of the . . . Fourth Legislature*, pp. 62–64.

18. Billy D. Ledbetter, "The Election of Louis T. Wigfall to the United States Senate, 1859: A Reevaluation," *Southwestern Historical Quarterly* 77, no. 2 (Oct., 1973): 241.

19. Letter of Jan. 30, 1852, MFP.

20. *Journals of the . . . Fourth Legislature*, pp. 487-88, 572.

21. Ibid., pp. 680-85.

22. Ibid.

23. See John O. Meusebach, *Answer to Interrogatories in Case No. 396, Mary C. Pascal et al vs. Theodore Evans, District Court of McCulloch County, Texas, November Term, 1893*, Daughters of the Republic of Texas Library, San Antonio.

24. *Journal of the . . . Fourth Legislature*, pp. 867-68.

25. Letter of Mar. 13, 1838, MFP.

26. He had filed under an 1848 act "to provide for ascertaining the debt of the late Republic of Texas." See Public Debt Papers, Box 304-246, Texas State Archives.

27. See letter of Nov. 10, 1849, MFP. The reference seems to be to former slave John Issac Washington, whom Samuel had freed along with his mother, Margaret, many years earlier. See Samuel's letter to his son, Aug. 9, 1847.

28. Letter of Sept. 15, 1850, MFP.

29. Letter of Mar. 31, 1851, MFP.

30. Green, *Memoirs*, p. 112.

31. Letter of Feb. 5, 1852, Clow Papers.

32. Undated 1852 entry, Mary's 1850-57 diary, MFP.

33. June 14, 1849, entry, and undated late 1852 entry, in ibid.

34. See Lydia's letter of Apr. 12, 1852, MFP.

35. Chestnut, *Diary*, p. 229. Also see Mary's diary entry of Apr. 27, 1847, MFP.

36. Chestnut, *Diary*, pp. 163-64; undated late 1852 entry, Mary's diary, MFP.

37. For Maverick's election and other San Antonio and Mexican Gulf Rail Road information, see Julian P. Greer, "The Antebellum History of the San Antonio and Mexican Gulf Rail Road," M.A. thesis, Southwest Texas State University, 1968.

38. Ibid., p. 37.

39. Letter of Feb. 24, 1848, MFP.

40. Greer, "Antebellum History," p. 43.

41. *Journals of the House of Representatives of the Fourth Legislature, Extra Session*.

42. Letter of Jan. 31, 1853, from Maverick to his wife, MFP.

43. J. Evetts Haley, *Fort Concho and the Texas Frontier*, p. 134; Green, "Land Settlement," p. 188.

44. The fact that Maverick and James located their lands in some cases only a year or two in advance of the establishing of forts at the sites suggests

that the two may have selected acreage with the forts in mind or may have worked with the military in locating sites. However, Maverick's extant business correspondence contains no reference to these possibilities.

45. For Fort Clark information, see Harold B. Simpson, *Frontier Forts of Texas*, p. 64. On Apr. 6, 1861, Maverick wrote to his son Sam, "Territt [*sic*] is out of the world, isn't it? I own Territt & 2 tracts of 320 acres but the land is of no value is it?"

46. See Darlington, "St. Mark's."

47. See Alice Felt Tyler, *Freedom's Ferment: Phases of American Social History from the Colonial Period to the Outbreak of the Civil War*, p. 78.

48. Letter of Apr. 10, 1853, Clow Papers.

49. Tyler, *Freedom's Ferment*, p. 79.

50. See Dancy's diary, Jon Winfield Scott Dancy Papers, Barker Texas History Center, and Maverick's letter to his wife of Dec. 4, 1856, MFP. Chestnut, *Diary*, p. 214, also referred to her father's friend Thompson as believing in spirit rappings and mediums and noted, "Follies of the wise!"

51. Summer, 1853, entry, Mary's 1850–57 diary, MFP.

52. Richardson, Wallace, and Anderson, *Texas* (1970 ed.), p. 143.

53. *Journals of the House of Representatives of the State of Texas, Fifth Legislature, Regular Session*, pp. 35, 50. The journals report that Maverick switched his place on the Judiciary Committee with another representative on the Internal Improvements Committee, but later reports of proceedings show that Maverick remained on the Judiciary Committee as well. (See proceedings of Jan. 4, 1854).

54. Greer's transcript of the company's minutes shows that on Sept. 5, 1853, Maverick and Gen. R. B. Campbell were delegated to write a report squashing the "malicious rumors" circulating concerning the awarding of the contract to Jones and Devine in April. Jones resigned as president when given the contract, but Devine apparently remained as director.

55. Letter of Jan. 9, 1854; Richardson, Wallace, and Anderson, *Texas* (1970 ed.), p. 143.

56. See letter of Feb. 17, 1854, James Milam to Maverick, MFP.

57. Letter of Dec. 11, 1853, MFP. This is one of the few letters from Mary to her husband that survives.

58. Ibid. Mary's mention of "the Bloomer costume" shows that she was well-informed despite her frontier situation, as Amelia Bloomer had only introduced the costume in 1851.

59. Letter of Dec. 4, 1856, MFP.

60. An agreement of Dec. 13, 1858, between Maverick and James, in Box 2F9, Business Papers, MFP, reads, "To cure all difficulty about the conflicting claims of the undersigned in regard to Devil's River Locations and particularly, the

site of Fort Hudson: we the undersigned do hereby agree to go halves in the ownership and profits of all surveys made on Fort Hudson and within five miles of said Fort."

61. See Stanley's letter of July 24, 1850; Lytle's of Sept. 30, 1850; Powers' of Jan. 13, 1851; Cunningham's of Sept. 22, 1851; and the May, 1853, letter of "A friend to justice," all in MFP.

62. Letter of May 15, 1854, MFP.

63. May, 1854, diary entry, Mary's 1850–57 diary, MFP.

64. Ibid., undated diary entries of 1854.

CHAPTER 12, A "RESPECTABLE AND RATHER VENERABLE SENATOR"

1. Stephen Oates, ed. *Rip Ford's Texas*, pp. 208–209.

2. James P. Shenton, *Robert John Walker: A Politician from Jackson to Lincoln*, pp. 129–31.

3. See Greer, "Antebellum History," pp. 56, 121–22.

4. Oates, *Rip Ford's Texas*, pp. 209–10.

5. Greer, "Antebellum History," p. 9.

6. See William Van Wyck's letter of Nov. 12, 1852, to Maverick, MFP.

7. See newspaper clipping of Nov. 9, 1852, and Van Wyck's letters of Mar. 1 and May 2, 1853, in family correspondence, MFP.

8. The Texas lands purchased by Samuel for his grandchildren and held in trust by his son were not affected.

9. Letter of Oct. 23, 1854, MFP.

10. Letters of Apr. 9, 1854, and Jan. [no specific date, 1855], Clow Papers.

11. Letter of Jan. 25, 1855, MFP.

12. Richardson, Wallace, and Anderson, *Texas* (1970 edition), pp. 144–45.

13. See Virginia Noel, "The Know-Nothing Party in San Antonio," typescript, Barker Texas History Center, p. 13.

14. Ibid.; newspaper clipping of letter of July 11, 1855, Box 2F6; MFP; San Antonio *Ledger*, July 21, 1855.

15. San Antonio *Ledger*, July 21, 1855.

16. Ibid., July 7, 1855.

17. See report in Clarksville *Northern Standard*, June 23, 1855.

18. See San Antonio *Ledger*, July 21, 1855; Bobby D. Weaver, *Castro's Colony: Empresario Development in Texas, 1842–1865*, p. 130. Maverick was one of a number of speculators buying land from colony members, and he helped them perfect their titles in the legislature.

19. Richardson, Wallace, and Anderson, *Texas* (1970 ed.), p. 145.

20. *Journal of the Senate of the State of Texas, Sixth Legislature*, pp. 106–109.

21. Nothing came of the call. See J. Fred Rippy, "Border Troubles along the Rio Grande," *Southwestern Historical Quarterly* 23, no. 1 (July, 1919): 100–103.

22. *State Gazette Appendix of the Sixth Legislature,* p. 24.

23. Green, *Memoirs,* p. 116.

24. *State Gazette Appendix of the Sixth Legislature,* p. 26.

25. *Journal of the . . . Sixth Legislature,* pp. 462–63. Maverick also chaired another joint select committee considering a bill for the relief of Ben Milam's heirs. On Dec. 7, the twentieth anniversary of Milam's death, Maverick presented a report favoring the heirs' claims and stating that "the people of Texas own [Milam's] memory a debt of gratitude which can never be discharged."

26. *State Gazette Appendix of the Sixth Legislature,* pp. 52–53.

27. Ibid., p. 96.

28. Gammel, vol. IV, Sixth Legislature, p. 71.

29. When Jack and Jinny were left at Tiltonia, both made requests of Maverick concerning marriage partners. Jack had asked for permission by John Graham's letter from Matagorda on Nov. 25, 1849, to marry a girl named Elizabeth at Matagorda, and Jinny had requested by Samuel Worcester's letter from Matagorda about a month later that Maverick buy her husband, Ben, who was about to be sold by a neighbor. These letters are in MFP, and there is no indication that Maverick acted on them.

30. Letter of Feb. 11, 1856, MFP.

31. Letter of Jan. 2, 1855, MFP.

32. See his brother's "Reminiscences of Sam Maverick Related to His Daughter Mrs. Emily Maverick Miller, 1923," MFP. Dennison was from New England, and during his sojourn at the University of Vermont, Lewis spent much time with the Dennison family. Sam and Mary Maverick disapproved, fearing that the family with its unmarried daughters was interested in Lewis because of reports the Dennisons had heard concerning the Mavericks' wealth.

33. Letter of Dec. 7, 1857, from Maverick to his wife when Lewis was considering changing schools, MFP.

34. Green, *Memoirs,* p. 117.

35. Letter of Aug. 10, 1856, MFP.

36. Letters of July 16, 21, 1854, MFP.

37. Letter of July 16, 1854, MFP.

38. *State Gazette Appendix of the Sixth Legislature, Adjourned Session,* p. 9.

39. Ibid., pp. 222, 235–36.

40. Greer, "Antebellum History," pp. 86–87.

41. See letter from Toutant to Maverick in Green, *Memoirs,* p. 126.

42. See Mary's letter to Lewis of Aug. 10, 1856, and Maverick's letter of Sept. 30, 1856, to Mary, MFP.

43. Letter of Oct. 18, 1856, Clow Papers.

44. Letter of Sept. 30, 1856, MFP.

45. Greer, "Antebellum History," pp. 88–89.

46. Letter of Oct. 18, 1856, Clow Papers.

47. Letter of Nov. 15, 1856, MFP.
48. Greer, "Antebellum History," pp. 91–92, 122.
49. Letter of Nov. 27, 1856, MFP.
50. Letter of Dec. 19, 1856, MFP.

CHAPTER 13, LOVE, HONOR, AND DUTY

1. Letter of Nov. 27, 1856, MFP.
2. Letter of Aug. 31, 1856, MFP.
3. Letter of Dec. 14, 1856, Clow Papers.
4. Undated 1856 entry; Jan. 1, 1857, entry, Mary's 1850–57 diary, MFP.
5. Undated 1856 entry, in ibid; letter of Aug. 23, 1857, MFP.
6. Letter of Aug. 10, 1856, MFP.
7. See Sublett's letter of Feb. 18, 1857, MFP.
8. San Antonio *Ledger*, Feb. 28, 1857.
9. Letter of May 28, 1857, MFP.
10. Letter of Aug. 9, 1857, to Lewis, MFP. Rusk had recently been widowed, and this has been given as a cause of his suicide.
11. See Mary's letter to Lewis of Nov. 11, 1857, MFP.
12. Letter of Nov. 9, 1857, MFP. During this session, Maverick would push through a bill for relief of one of the struggling sisterhood, Mary's Aunt Ann, who had returned to the name Bradley.
13. *Journal of the Senate of the State of Texas, Seventh Biennial Session*, p. 417.
14. Ibid., proceedings of Feb. 10, 1858.
15. *State Gazette Appendix of the Seventh Legislature*, pp. 189–92.
16. Ibid. The resolution did not pass.
17. *Journal of the . . . Seventh Legislature*, pp. 594–95.
18. Letter of June 7, 1857, MFP.
19. See Maverick's letter to Mary of Nov. 9, 1857, MFP.
20. A five-dollar receipt of Oct. 30, 1857, in family correspondence, MFP, is endorsed as follows by the Mavericks' daughter-in-law Jane Maury Maverick: "Dec. 12, 1918. This is a receipt for having Granvill [sic] a slave of S. A. Maverick whipped. Mr. Maverick always refused to whip a slave but when it was necessary the law required it should be done by the sheriff & owner [illegible] the costs. Sam Maverick [the eldest Maverick son] who remembered t[he] circumstance told me."
21. Letter of Nov. 13, 1857, MFP.
22. Letters of Aug. 19 and Nov. 11, 1857, to Lewis, MFP.
23. Letters of Nov. 20 and Dec. 7, 1857, MFP.
24. Letter of May 13, 1858, MFP.
25. Letter of July 4, 1858, MFP.

26. Letter of June 20, 1858, MFP.

27. See 1857 Bexar County tax list, Microfilm Roll 60 (1855–62), Texas State Library Genealogy Section. Maverick seldom held land as an agent for others, but MacKay was an exception.

28. See Mills, "My Story" in Watkins, *One League*, p. 352. Many of Mills' recollections of Maverick are fanciful; he says, for example, that Maverick participated in the Mier expedition and implies that he was a participant in the black bean episode. He also repeats or embroiders a fictitious story about Maverick's cattle empire (see conclusion). However, his comments about Maverick's opposition to secession are in keeping with other sources.

29. Greer, "Antebellum History," pp. 10–11, 114, (directors' minutes of Dec. 21, 1858). It is unclear how much the failed railroad effort cost Maverick financially, but in Nov., 1859, he wrote his wife, "I am still treated with the Rail Rd debt & expect some of our lots levied on in December."

30. See letter from both Mavericks to Lewis, Oct. 28, 29, 1858, MFP.

31. See letter from Paschal dated Mar. 2, 1859, MFP.

32. See Greer, "Antebellum History," Mar. 8, 1859, report of stockholders' meeting.

33. See Mary's letter of Dec. 23, 1858, and her undated fragment written in Nov. or Dec., 1858, as she identifies Lizzie as being thirteen months old, MFP.

34. See Clow's letter of Apr. 6, 1859, in Box 2F9, Maverick Business Papers.

35. The certificates could be used to locate lands within twenty miles of the railroad right-of-way. *Abstract of All Original Texas Land Titles Comprising Grants and Locations to August 31, 1941*, p. 126, shows Maverick laying claim to only one actual tract direct from the failed railroad. He did, however, pick up a number of tracts direct from the Buffalo Bayou and Colorado Railroad Company (pp. 113–14, 510).

36. Letter of May 16, 1859, MFP.

37. Letter of Feb. 1, 1860, MFP.

38. The San Antonio *Herald* of Mar. 4, 1859, reported that Maverick read the Declaration of Texas Independence in a "clear and distinct voice" at the independence day celebration. See Everett, *San Antonio*, p. 79. Navarro's letter, dated July 21, 1859, is included in Box 2F9, Business Papers, MFP.

39. Letter of July 15, 1859, MFP.

40. San Antonio *Ledger*, July 20, 1859.

41. Clarksville *Northern Standard*, Aug. 27, 1859; and Maverick's undated draft of his denial in MFP correspondence.

42. Letter of Feb. 1, 1860, MFP.

43. Wooster, "Early Texas Legislatures" pp. 170, 172.

44. *Journal of the House of Representatives, Eighth Legislature, State of Texas*, p. 49.

45. Ibid., p. 160, shows that Maverick as a member of the Committee on Internal Improvements recommended passage of the bill.

46. *State Gazette Appendix, Containing Debates in the House of Representatives of the Eighth Legislature of the State of Texas,* 30–31.

47. Ibid., pp. 51, 152–53. Maverick indicated that he had previously supported such a bill but had changed his mind.

48. *Journal of the . . . Eighth Legislature,* p. 401.

49. Maverick included the gist of his resolutions in his letter to his wife of Feb. 1, 1860, MFP.

50. *Journal of the . . . Eighth Legislature,* pp. 634–35. A minority report agreeing with Maverick's stand follows the majority report but is signed by only one member, John H. Manly.

51. Caroline Mitchell Remy, "A Study of the Transition of San Antonio from a Frontier to an Urban Community from 1875–1900," M.A. thesis, Trinity University, 1960, p. 55.

52. See excerpt from Frederick Law Olmsted's *A Journey through Texas,* in B. P. Gallaway, ed., *The Dark Corner of the Confederacy: Accounts of Civil War Texas as Told by Contemporaries,* pp. 35–42.

53. Ibid.

54. See Maverick's Bexar County Tax Receipt for 1860, Box 2F19, MFP.

55. See Darlington, "St. Mark's."

56. See Clarksville *Northern Standard,* Oct. 22, 1859, for one such instance.

57. Zenas R. Bliss memoirs, typescript, II, 233, Barker Texas History Center. Quoted by permission of Ben E. Pingenot.

58. Anonymous, undated newspaper clipping in Box 2F6, MFP.

59. See James Day, "Jacob de Cordova's Exploration of Northwest Texas," in Watkins, *One League,* pp. 229–39.

60. See Ralph A. Wooster, "Wealthy Texans, 1860," *Southwestern Historical Quarterly* 71, no. 2 (Oct., 1967): 163–80.

61. Letter of Oct. 12, 1860, MFP.

62. Letter of Dec. 25, 1860, MFP.

CHAPTER 14, LEAVING THE CONSEQUENCES TO GOD

1. *Journal of the House of Representatives of the State of Texas, Extra Session of the Eighth Legislature,* pp. 9, 11, 42, 59–61.

2. See Gallaway, *Dark Corner,* p. 81. Maverick was not a delegate to the convention, although he apparently attended.

3. Figures drawn from Richardson, Wallace, and Anderson, *Texas* (1970 edition), p. 190.

4. See *The War of the Rebellion: A Compilation of the Official Records of the Union and Confederate Armies,* series II, vol. I, 28–29.

5. Ibid., p. 31.

6. Caroline Baldwin Darrow, "David Twiggs' Surrender of U.S. Army Posts in Texas," in Gallaway, *Dark Corner,* pp. 82–88.

7. *The War of the Rebellion,* series I, vol. I (1880), 513.

8. Clarksville *Northern Standard,* Mar. 9, 1861.

9. Maverick in June, 1860, had written to his wife from Austin after losing a land claim case that "the Paschals (my counsel) are very unpopular at this time."

10. Glen E. Lich, *The German Texans,* p. 91.

11. See Darrow's account in Gallaway, *Dark Corner,* pp. 82–88.

12. *Journal of the Adjourned Session, Eighth Legislature,* pp. 126, 133–34.

13. See Maverick's letter of Apr. 8, 1861, to Sam, and of Nov. 10, 1861, to Mary, MFP.

14. See San Antonio *Daily Ledger & Texan* clipping of July 2, 1861, MFP. Mary in her memoirs identifies Lewis' company as the First North Alabama Regiment, but this appears to be a slip, as Lewis himself refers to the First North Carolina volunteers, and he volunteered in North Carolina.

15. See Zenas R. Bliss, typescript, vol. III; and Van Dorn's report in *War of the Rebellion,* series I, vol. I, 572. This latter account refers to a Captain Maverick who was part of a "battalion of infantry raised for the occasion in San Antonio" and under the command of Henry McCulloch. The younger Sam Maverick was not enrolled as a private under McCulloch until May 18, so the reference is probably to the elder Maverick.

16. Bliss, typescript, III, 41.

17. Letter of Dec. 27, 1861, MFP.

18. Letter of Mar. 3, 1862, MFP.

19. Edward King, *Texas: 1874, an Eyewitness Account of Conditions in Post-Reconstruction Texas,* p. 104.

20. Letters to Lewis of Nov. 16, Dec. 1, 1863, MFP.

21. Letter of Nov. 1, 1861, MFP.

22. San Antonio *Daily Ledger & Texan,* June 25, 1861.

23. Minutes of San Antonio City Council meeting, Oct. 9, 1862, Journal C, City Council Minutes, Apr. 1, 1856–Feb. 21, 1870, San Antonio City Hall; *House Journal of the Ninth Legislature, First Called Session of the State of Texas,* pp. 114, 180; Gammel, vol. V, Special Laws of the Extra Session of the Ninth Legislature of the State of Texas, p. 13.

24. Letter of May 9, 1862, MFP.

25. Letter of Nov. 10, 1861, MFP.

26. Letter of Dec. 27, 1861, MFP.

27. See Bruce Catton, *The Civil War,* p. 59.

28. Letter of Dec. 11, 1862, MFP.

29. Note of June 20, 1862, MFP.

30. San Antonio *Semi-Weekly News*, Jan. 5, 1863.

31. See minutes of San Antonio City Council meetings, June–Dec., 1862, and Jan. 5, 1863.

32. Letter of Jan. 7, 1863, MFP.

33. Letter of June 9, 1863, MFP.

34. Mary to Lewis on Feb. 16, 1863: "I have grafted more fine roses the white 'Augusta' one, *dear name*."

35. Letter to Lewis of Feb. 17, 1863, MFP.

36. See Wooten, *Comprehensive History of Texas, 1685–1897*, p. 689, for mention of the younger Maverick's action.

37. Maverick's letter is filed under Feb. 19, 1862, in MFP, but his presence at the extra session and his references to his son's exploits show that the letter was written Feb. 19, 1863.

38. *Journal of the . . . Ninth Legislature, First Called Session*, p. 41.

39. Letter to Mary of Feb. 25, 1863, MFP.

40. Ibid.

41. Registers of Elected and Appointed County and State Officials, 1836–1920, Ledger 2/1-6, pp. 117–20, Texas State Library Archives Section, shows that Maverick was elected chief justice on Oct. 15, 1863, and again on Aug. 1, 1864, and was replaced on Aug. 11, 1865.

42. County Commissioners' Court Records, Bexar County Courthouse Archives.

43. Claude Elliott, "Union Sentiment in Texas," *Southwestern Historical Quarterly* 50, no. 4 (Apr., 1947): 458.

44. Letter of Dec. 13, 1863, MFP.

45. Letter of Feb. 2, 1864, MFP.

46. Ibid.

47. Quoted in Ludwell H. Johnson, *Red River Campaign: Politics and Cotton in the Civil War*, pp. 212–13.

48. Letter of May 1, 1864, MFP.

49. Letter of June 5, 1864, MFP.

50. Letter of Mar. 2, 1864, to Lewis, MFP.

51. Letter of June 18, 1864, MFP.

52. Ford often stopped in to see the Mavericks when in San Antonio. Mary's letter of Feb. 2, 1864, to Lewis: "Col. Ford called in the other day and I gave him a nice carpet haversack."

53. Letter of Aug. 7, 1864, MFP.

54. See Mary's letters to Lewis of Oct. 22, 1864, and Feb. 17, 1863, MFP. Of the money raised from the slaves' supper, Mary wrote, "I value it much as coming from the negroes, and would like the Yankees to get the [newspaper] which notices it."

55. On Feb. 24, 1851, Lizzie Adams Clow wrote Mary, "It must be quite

amusing to those uninterested to observe the movements of the two [San Antonio] societies. . . . I presume you are one of the retired party: and would be quite nobody if it were not for your husband's reputed wealth." On Nov. 27, 1856, Maverick wrote to his wife from New York, "You must make up your mind to be lied against—otherwise how can you be a distinguished member of society?"

56. Letter of Oct. 22, 1864, to Lewis.

57. Letter of Jan. 26, 1865, from M. A. Butts, MFP.

58. Address of May 29, 1865, MFP.

59. Mary to Lewis, Feb. 27, 1864, MFP.

60. See Ralph A. Wooster, "Wealthy Texans, 1870," *Southwestern Historical Quarterly* 74, no. 3 (July, 1970): 24–35.

CHAPTER 15, "THEY THAT WAIT UPON THE LORD"

1. For listing of Maverick slaves, see Maverick's San Antonio tax lists, 1862–64, Box 2F19, Business Papers, MFP.

2. Letter of Sept. 16, 1869, MFP. The San Antonio *Express* of Jan. 18, 1891, reported the death of "Jennie Anderson," "at least 106 years of age." It erroneously reported that she had come from *North* Carolina with Maverick and concluded, "She was much liked by the family to which she belonged, all of whom she served for many years as a nurse." A *Texas Pioneer* clipping of Apr., 1929, included in Maverick's biographical file at the Barker Texas History Center, relates that Jinny's son Jack had been sold to a man in New Orleans, settled in Kansas after emancipation, and died on a visit to his mother in San Antonio.

3. See San Antonio *Express*, Mar. 24, 1869.

4. Thomas McKinney's letter to Lewis Maverick of Sept. 9, 1865, MFP, relates the meeting. (McKinney's letter is not dated by year, but its recipient and contents clearly indicate that it was written the September after the war's end.)

5. See agreement of Oct. 25, 1865, Thomas Jefferson Devine Papers, Barker Texas History Center.

6. Maverick's substance copy of his letter to Bell of Nov. 6 is in MFP.

7. Letter of Jan. 4, 1866, MFP.

8. Letter of Apr. 23, 1865, MFP.

9. See Wooster, "Wealthy Texans, 1870," pp. 24–35.

10. See Houston *Tri-Weekly Telegraph*, July 4, 1866.

11. See Treasurer's Book of Dorcas Society, Archives of St. Mark's, quoted in Darlington, "St. Mark's."

12. Bexar County tax lists, Microfilm Roll 61 (1862–67), Texas State Library Genealogy Section.

13. See Maverick's memo titled "Salt Lake Patents worth $100,000" in Box 2F9, MFP. Also see Walter Prescott Webb's mention of Maverick's 1866 ownership in *The Texas Rangers: A Century of Frontier Defense*, pp. 347, 351. There is no indication that Maverick was involved in the El Paso Salt War that erupted in the late 1860's and continued after his death.

14. Richardson, Wallace, and Anderson, *Texas* (1970 edition), p. 213.

15. San Antonio *Express*, May 30, 1867. The *Express* for Mar. 24, 1869, reported the case still suspended. The standard reference work on federal cases before 1880, the thirty-volume *Federal Cases, 1789-1879*, does not include information on the suit.

16. See William Van Wyck's letter of July 11, MFP.

17. Dallas *Herald*, Feb. 1, 1868.

18. See Maverick's letter to Mary of May 19, 1868, MFP. Maverick mentions meeting with Throckmorton, Coke, and "Hancock," probably John Hancock, a former state legislator and delegate to the 1866 constitutional convention.

19. San Antonio *Express*, Sept. 20, 1868.

20. The apparent original of the bogus letter, dated Feb. 21, 1869, is included in MFP in handwriting unlike Maverick's and with his own notation identifying it as a forgery.

21. Letter of June 21, 1869, in possession of Ellen Maverick Dickson.

22. Ibid.

23. San Antonio *Express*, Sept. 14, 1869. Again, *Federal Cases, 1789-1879* does not include information on the case. Mary Maverick endorsed a letter from her husband during this period by writing "under arrest Austin about Castroville land." The General Index to Deeds for Bexar County shows that Maverick relinquished two tracts in March, 1870, one "by U.S. Court confirmation of Judgmt &c," one "by D. Ct. Decree vesting Title & Patent."

24. Letters of Oct. 6 and 25, 1869, MFP. The latter is misfiled under a speculative date of May 25, 1868, but numerous references in the letter, including one concerning son George, who had just returned to San Antonio from college, have led to my placement of it.

25. Last Will and Testament of S. A. Maverick, transcribed from Bexar County Courthouse Records.

26. Letters of Sept. 27, 1869, and Mar. 10, 1870, MFP.

27. Wooster, "Wealthy Texans, 1870," pp. 24-35.

28. Maverick's 1870 Bexar holdings were 46,237 acres, plus 7,680 jointly owned with G. J. Houston, according to Bexar County tax list, Microfilm Roll 62 (1867-71), Texas State Library Genealogy Section. His name does not appear on out-county lists in the Bexar tax records for that year or the year preceding it. In 1871, Bexar tax lists showed over 248,000 acres in other counties as part of the Maverick estate. Maverick's holdings in Alabama and

South Carolina had never been extensive and most had been sold by his death.

29. For example, Bliss in his reminiscences called him "the largest land-owner in the United States."

30. Bexar County tax list, Microfilm Roll 62. Gustav Schleicher held about seventy thousand acres, John James only about fifty thousand.

31. Wooster, "Wealthy Texans, 1870," p. 30; Webb, *Handbook*, I, 961.

32. Remy, "Transition of San Antonio," p. 55.

33. See notation of son George in Maverick Estate Day Book, MFP.

34. See Green, *Samuel Maverick, Texan*.

35. Ramsdell, *San Antonio* (1976 edition), p. 48.

36. King, *Texas*, pp. 89, 105–107.

37. Genealogy prepared by Ellen Maverick Dickson, Mar., 1987, and in my possession shows that Jane Lewis Maury was the great-great-granddaughter of Thomas Jefferson's teacher James Maury through the line of his oldest son, Matthew Maury, and she was cousin to naval officer and hydrographer Matthew Fontaine Maury, the grandson of James Maury by Matthew's half-brother Richard. Among Albert and Jane's children was New Deal legislator Maury Maverick.

38. Remy, "Transition of San Antonio."

39. Typescript reminiscences of Mary Vance Maverick in the possession of Green family.

40. See "A Big Victory–The Sabriego Land Suit Settled in Favor of the Mavericks," San Antonio *Daily Express*, Jan. 28, 1888.

41. See General Index to Deeds, Bexar County Courthouse.

42. Figures drawn from "Estate of Mary A. Maverick, Deceased. No. 2463," copy of official county court property listing in the possession of Emily Wells.

43. The Texas *State Gazette* of June 19, 1852, reported, "We learn from the *Western Texian* that some hands engaged in digging a trench for a fence on the premises of S. A. Maverick, Esq. at San Antonio, a few days since, discovered thirteen cannon buried in the ground." Workers continued to dig up cannon on the Maverick property, as newspapers contained reports of more cannon being uncovered in 1866 and 1889.

44. See Ramsdell, *San Antonio*; Darlington, "St. Mark's," pp. 98–99; and Rote, "Treasures of St. Mark's." There is some confusion over the third date on the bell, as Richardson says it was 1876. Rote says 1874, and this makes sense as the date of donation.

45. Quoted in Albert Curtis, *Fabulous San Antonio*, p. 231.

46. Richardson, "In Memory." This pamphlet is included in MFP.

47. See Green, *Samuel Maverick, Texan*, p. xiii.

48. See letter of Jan. 30, 1874, to Margaret C. Van Wyck included in Box 2R157, Charles William Ramsdell Papers, Barker Texas History Center. This

letter, cited earlier, contains extensive description of San Antonio as well as family news.

49. See obituary, "Mrs. Mary A. Maverick," San Antonio *Daily Light*, Feb. 24, 1898.

50. The manuscript is included in Green, *Memoirs*, pp. 51-56.

51. See the preface in ibid.

52. Richardson, "In Memory," p. 17.

53. *Daily Light* obituary, Feb. 24, 1898; Darlington, "St. Mark's," p. 91.

CONCLUSION

1. "Women of the Texas Republic and Revolution," typescript, Barker Texas History Center Archives.

2. Mills, excerpt from *My Story* published in Watkins, *One League*, p. 351; Roberts, *Rangers and Sovereignty* (San Antonio: Wood Printing & Engraving Co., 1914), p. 141.

3. J. David Stern quoted in William Safire, *The New Language of American Politics* (New York: Random House, 1968), p. 377.

4. See Remy, "San Antonio," p. 50. Remy speculates that it was son Sam who donated the land for the railroad, since Maverick had died in 1870. However, the bequest was made by Samuel A. Maverick, not Samuel Maverick.

Bibliography

Manuscript and Archival Sources

Anderson, Robert. General Robert Anderson File. Pendleton District Historical and Recreational Commission Archives, Pendleton, South Carolina.

Anderson County Deed Records. County Courthouse, Anderson, South
Carolina.

Audited Civil Service Claims for the Republic. Texas State Library Archives
Section, Austin.

Audited Military Claim Records. Texas State Library Archives Section, Austin.

Bexar County Commissioners' Court Records, 1863–65. County Courthouse,
San Antonio.

Bexar County Deed, Headright, and Will Records. County Courthouse, San
Antonio.

Bexar County Tax Lists. Texas State Library Genealogy Section, Austin.

Bliss, Zenas R. Zenas R. Bliss Papers, Barker Texas History Center, Austin.

Clow, Alice. Alice Clow Papers. Barker Texas History Center, Austin.

Confederate Service Index. Texas State Library Archives Section, Austin.

Cooke, William G. William G. Cooke Family Papers. Barker Texas History
Center, Austin.

Dancy, Jon Winfield Scott. Jon Winfield Scott Dancy Papers. Barker Texas
History Center, Austin.

Darlington, Ella M. "A Brief History of St. Mark's Protestant Episcopal Church
of San Antonio, Texas." M.A. thesis, St. Mary's University, 1947.

Devine, Thomas Jefferson. Thomas Jefferson Devine Papers. Barker Texas
History Center, Austin.

Fenstermaker, A. L. (Bebe). Biographical sketches of Maverick sons Sam and
George, to be published in a forthcoming edition of *The Handbook of Texas*
(Texas State Historical Association).

Garrett, Jill Knight. "A History of Lauderdale County, Alabama." Typescript in Texas State Library Genealogy Section, Austin, copyright 1964 by the author.

Green, William Elton. "Land Settlement in West Texas: Tom Green County, A Case Study, 1874–1903." Ph.D. dissertation, Texas Tech University, 1981.

Greer, Julian P. "The Antebellum History of the San Antonio and Mexican Gulf Rail Road." M.A. thesis, Southwest Texas State University, 1968.

Journals of the City Council of San Antonio, June 1837 to January 1849 and Apr. 1, 1856 to Feb. 21, 1870.

Journals of the Convention of 1836 (originals), Box 2-9/32, Texas State Library Archives Section, Austin.

Lauderdale County Deed Records. County Courthouse, Florence, Alabama.

Libro Registro. Bexar Archives, Barker Texas History Center, Austin.

Maverick, Maury. Maury Maverick Papers. Barker Texas History Center, Austin. Contains limited family history relating to Maury's grandparents, Samuel Augustus and Mary Adams Maverick.

Maverick, Samuel. Samuel Maverick File, Pendleton District Historical and Recreational Commission Archives, Pendleton, South Carolina.

———. Maverick and Van Wyck Family Papers. South Caroliniana Library, University of South Carolina, Columbia. These contain correspondence and land books of the elder Samuel Maverick as well as papers of Samuel Augustus Maverick's nephew Samuel Maverick Van Wyck and his family.

Maverick, Samuel Augustus. Bounty and Donation Land Grant Files for Samuel Augustus Maverick. Original Land Grant Collection, Archives and Records Division, Texas General Land Office, Austin.

———. Samuel Augustus Maverick File. Pendleton District Historical and Recreational Commission Archives, Pendleton, South Carolina.

Maverick, Samuel Augustus and Mary Adams. Maverick family and Maverick-related files. Daughters of the Republic of Texas Library, San Antonio.

———. Maverick Family Papers. Barker Texas History Center, Austin. This collection includes intermittent journals of Samuel Augustus Maverick, 1826–69; diaries of Mary Adams Maverick, 1842–57; Maverick family correspondence, 1825–70; drafts of Mary Adams Maverick's Memoirs; reminiscences of a Maverick son; business papers including land and tax records.

Noel, Virginia. "The Know-Nothing Party in San Antonio." Typescript, Barker Texas History Center Archives.

Pitts, John Bost III. "Speculation in Headright Land Grants in San Antonio from 1837 to 1842," M.A. thesis, Trinity University, 1966.

Ramsdell, Charles W. Charles W. Ramsdell Papers. Barker Texas History Center, Austin.

Remy, Caroline Mitchell. "A Study of the Transition of San Antonio from a Frontier to an Urban Community from 1875–1900." M.A. thesis, Trinity University, 1960.

Rote, Carey. "Treasures of St. Mark's." 1984, manuscript in my possession.

Rusk, Thomas Jefferson. Thomas Jefferson Rusk Papers. Barker Texas History Center, Austin.

Smith, John. John W. Smith File. Daughters of the Republic of Texas Library, San Antonio.

Texas Election Register, 1836–1842. Box 2-1/1, Texas State Library Archives Section.

Texas Public Debt Papers. Box 304-246, Texas State Library Archives Section.

Texas Registers of Elected and Appointed County and State Officials, 1836–1920. Ledger 2/1-6, Texas State Library Archives Section.

Texas Slave Censuses, 1850 and 1860. Microfilm Rolls 297, 298, Barker Texas History Center.

Tuscaloosa County Deed Records and Will Book, 1821–1855. County Courthouse, Tuscaloosa, Alabama.

U.S. Census Records for South Carolina, 1810, 1820, 1830. Texas State Library Genealogy Section, Austin.

PUBLISHED MATERIALS

Abstract of All Original Texas Land Titles Comprising Grants and Locations to August 31, 1941. Austin: General Land Office, 1942.

Alden, John R. *A History of the American Revolution.* New York: Alfred A. Knopf, 1969.

Axtell, James. *The Invasion Within: The Contest of Cultures in Colonial North America.* New York: Oxford University Press, 1985.

Barr, Amelia. *All the Days of My Life: An Autobiography.* New York: D. Appleton and Company, 1913.

Bishop, Curtis. *Lots of Land.* Austin: Steck Company, 1949.

Bonham, Milledge L., Jr. "James Butler Bonham: A Consistent Rebel," *Southwestern Historical Quarterly* 35, no. 2. (Oct., 1931).

Broussard, Ray F. *San Antonio during the Texas Republic.* El Paso: Texas Western Press, 1967.

Castaneda, Carlos E., ed. and trans. *The Mexican Side of the Texas Revolution, 1836, by the Chief Mexican Participants.* Reprint, New York: Arno Press, 1976.

Catton, Bruce. *The Civil War.* New York: American Heritage Press, 1971.

Chabot, Frederick C. *The Alamo: Altar of Texas Liberty.* San Antonio: Naylor Printing Company, 1931.

———. *The Mavericks. On the Occasion of Maury Maverick for Congress.* San Antonio: Privately printed, 1934.

————. *With the Makers of San Antonio: Genealogies of the Early Latin, Anglo-American, and German Families.* San Antonio: Privately printed, 1937.

Chestnut, Mary Boykin. *A Diary from Dixie.* Cambridge: Harvard University Press, 1980 edition.

Clinton, Catherine. *The Plantation Mistress: Woman's World in the Old South.* New York: Pantheon Books, 1982.

Clinton, Matthew. *Tuscaloosa, Alabama: Its Early Days, 1816–1865.* Tuscaloosa: Zonta Club, 1958.

Coulter, Harris L. *Science and Ethics in American Medicine, 1800–1914.* Washington, D.C.: McGrath Publishing Co., 1973.

Curtis, Albert. *Fabulous San Antonio.* San Antonio: Naylor Co., 1955.

Degler, Carl N. *At Odds: Women and the Family in America from the Revolution to the Present.* Oxford: Oxford University Press, 1980.

DeRyee, William. *The Texas Album of the Eighth Legislature.* Austin: Miner, Lambert & Perry, 1860.

Dexter, Franklin. "Student Life at Yale College, 1795–1817," *Proceedings of the American Antiquarian Society* 27 (1917): 318–35.

Eaton, Clement. *A History of the Old South.* New York: MacMillan Company, 1966.

————. *The Growth of Southern Civilization, 1790–1860.* New York: Harper & Brothers, 1961.

Ehrenberg, Hermann. *With Milam and Fannin: Adventures of a German Boy in Texas' Revolution.* Austin: Pemberton Press, 1968.

Eliott, Claude. "Union Sentiment in Texas," *Southwestern Historical Quarterly* 50, no. 4 (April, 1947).

Everett, Donald E. *San Antonio: The Flavor of Its Past, 1845–1898.* San Antonio: Trinity University Press, 1975.

Fehrenbach, T. S. *Lone Star: A History of Texas and the Texans.* New York: Collier Books, 1968.

Field, Joseph E. *Three Years in Texas.* Greenfield, Mass.: Justin Jones, 1836.

Ford, John. *History, Battles and Fall of the Alamo.* San Antonio: Maverick-Clarke Litho Co., 1894.

Frazier, Irvin. *The Family of John Lewis, Pioneer.* San Antonio: Fisher Publications, 1985.

Gabriel, Ralph Henry. *Religion and Learning at Yale: The Church of Christ in the College and University, 1757–1957.* New Haven: Yale University Press, 1958.

Gallaway, B. P., ed. *The Dark Corner of the Confederacy: Accounts of Civil War Texas as Told by Contemporaries.* Dubuque, Iowa: Kendall/Hunt Publishing Company, 1972.

Gammel, H. P. N. *The Laws of Texas, 1822–1897.* Austin: Gammel Book Company, 1898.

Geiser, S. W. Biographical sketch of John Veatch in *Southwestern Historical Quarterly* 46, no. 2 (Oct., 1942): 169–73.

Goetzmann, William H. *Army Exploration in the American West, 1803–1863*. New Haven: Yale University Press, 1959.

Green, Rena Maverick, ed. *Memoirs of Mary A. Maverick*. San Antonio: Alamo Printing Co., 1921.

———. *Samuel Maverick, Texan, 1803–1870: A Collection of Letters, Journals, and Memoirs*. San Antonio: Privately printed, 1952.

Greer, James Kimmins. *Colonel Jack Hays: Texas Frontier Leader and California Builder*. New York: E. P. Dutton & Company, 1952.

Griffin, Inez H., comp. "Marriage and Death Notices from the City Gazette of Charleston 1825," *South Carolina Historical Magazine* 60, no. 2 (April, 1959).

Griffith, Lucille. *History of Alabama, 1540–1900*. Northport, Ala.: Colonial Press, 1962.

Haley, J. Evetts. *Fort Concho and the Texas Frontier*. San Angelo: San Angelo Standard-Times, 1952.

Hill, Edward E. *The Office of Indian Affairs, 1824–1880: Historical Sketches*. New York: Clearwater Publishing Co., 1974.

Hogan, William Ransom. *The Texas Republic: A Social and Economic History*. Austin: University of Texas Press, 1969.

Holcomb, Brent. *South Carolina Marriages, 1688–1799*. Baltimore: Genealogical Publishing Co., 1983.

House, Boyce. *City of Flaming Adventure: The Chronicle of San Antonio*. San Antonio: Naylor Company, 1949.

House Journal of the Ninth Legislature, First Called Session of the State of Texas. Austin, Texas State Library, 1963.

House Journal of the Ninth Legislature Regular Session of the State of Texas. Austin: Texas State Library, 1964.

Humphrey, David C. *Austin: An Illustrated History*. Northridge, Calif.: Windsor Publications, 1985.

Hunter, J. Marvin. "The Mavericks in San Antonio," *Frontier Times* 18 (1940): 107–12.

Jackson, Ronald, Gary Teeples, and David Schaefermeyer, eds. *Index to South Carolina Land Grants 1784–1800*. Bountiful, Utah: Accelerated Indexing Systems, 1977.

Jenkins, John H., ed. *The Papers of the Texas Revolution 1835–1836*, vols. 4 and 9. Austin: Presidial Press, 1973.

Jervey, Elizabeth H. "Marriage and Death Notices from the City Gazette of Charleston, S.C.," *South Carolina Historical and Genealogical Magazine* 45, no. 3 (July, 1944).

Johnson, Ludwell H. *Red River Campaign: Politics and Cotton in the Civil War*. Baltimore: Johns Hopkins University Press, 1958.

Johnson, William R. *Schooled Lawyers: A Study in the Clash of Professional Cultures*. New York: New York University Press, 1978.

Jones, Kathleen Paul, and Pauline Jones Gandrud. *Alabama Records*. Easly, S.C.: Southern Historical Press, 1980?

Journal of the Adjourned Session, Eighth Legislature. Austin: John Marshall, 1861.

Journal of the House of Representatives, Eighth Legislature, State of Texas. Austin: Marshall & Co., 1860.

Journal of the House of Representatives of the State of Texas, Extra Session of the Eighth Legislature. Austin: John Marshall, 1861.

Journal of the House of Representatives of the State of Texas: Fourth Legislature. Austin: State Gazette Office, 1852.

Journal of the Senate of Texas, Seventh Biennial Session. Austin: John Marshall & Co., 1857.

Journal of the Senate of the State of Texas, Sixth Legislature. Austin: Marshall & Oldham, 1855.

Journal of the Senate of the State of Texas at the Adjourned Session, Sixth Legislature. Austin: Marshall & Oldham, 1856.

Journals of the House of Representatives of the Eighth Congress, Republic of Texas. Houston: Cruger & Moore, 1844.

Journals of the House of Representatives of the State of Texas, Fifth Legislature, Regular Session. Austin: J. W. Hampton, 1853.

Journals of the House of Representatives of the State of Texas: Fourth Legislature, Extra Session. Austin: J. W. Hampton, 1853.

Kemp, Louis W. *The Signers of the Texas Declaration of Independence*. Salado, Tex.: Anson Jones Press, 1944.

Kilgore, Daniel Edmond. *How Did Davy Die?* College Station: Texas A&M University Press, 1978.

King, Edward. *Texas: 1874, an Eyewitness Account of Conditions in Post-Reconstruction Texas*. Houston: Cordovan Press, 1974.

Klosky, Beth Ann. *The Pendleton Legacy*. Columbia, S. Car.: Sandlapper Press, 1971.

Lamar, Howard, ed., *The Reader's Encyclopedia of the American West*. New York: Thomas Y. Crowell Company, 1977.

Lander, Ernest M., Jr. "Ante-Bellum Milling in South Carolina," *South Carolina Historical and Genealogical Magazine* 52, no. 3 (July, 1951).

————."The Reluctant Imperialist: South Carolina, the Rio Grande, and the Mexican War," *Southwestern Historical Quarterly* 78, no. 3 (Jan., 1975): 254–70.

Laurens, Caroline Olivia. "Journal of a Visit to Greenville from Charleston in the Summer of 1825," *South Carolina Historical Magazine* 72, no. 4 (Oct., 1971).

Ledbetter, Billy D. "The Election of Louis T. Wigfall to the United States Senate, 1859: A Reevaluation." *Southwestern Historical Quarterly* 77, no. 2 (Oct., 1973): 241–54.

Leland, Isabella G. *Charleston: Crossroads of History*. Woodland Hills, Calif.: Windsor Publications, 1980.

Lich, Glen E. *The German Texans*. San Antonio: University of Texas Institute of Texan Cultures, 1981.

Lucas, Rev. Silas Emmett, Jr. *Marriage and Death Notices from Pendleton (S.C.) Messenger 1807–1851*. Easley, S. Car.: Southern Historical Press, 1977.

McCorvey, Thomas. *Alabama Historical Sketches*. Charlottesville: University of Virginia Press, 1960.

Maverick, James Slayden. *Maverick Ancestors of the Maverick Family of Texas*. San Antonio: Privately printed, 1937.

Meusebach, John O. *Answer to Interrogatories in Case No. 396, Mary C. Pascal et al vs. Theodore Evan, District Court of McCulloch County, Texas, November Term, 1893*. Reprint, Austin: Pemberton Press, 1964.

Miller, Thomas Lloyd. *Bounty and Donation Land Grants of Texas, 1835–1888*. Austin: University of Texas Press, 1967.

Moore, Harriet Brown. *St. Mark's Church, 1859–1943*. San Antonio, 1944.

Murry, Ellen N. "Promise in a Lonely Land," *Texas Libraries* 45, no. 4 (Winter, 1984).

Myers, John. *The Alamo*. Lincoln: University of Nebraska Press, 1973.

Neighbours, Kenneth F. *Robert Simpson Neighbors and the Texas Frontier*. Waco: Texian Press, 1975.

Nielsen, George, ed. "Lydia Ann McHenry and Revolutionary Texas," *Southwestern Historical Quarterly* 74, no. 3 (Jan., 1971).

Norton, Barbara. "A Sketch of St. Paul's Church, Pendleton," *South Carolina Historical Magazine* 63, no. 1.

Nye, Russell B. *The Cultural Life of the New Nation, 1776–1830*. New York: Harper & Row, 1960.

Oates, Stephen, ed. *Rip Ford's Texas*. Austin: University of Texas Press, 1963.

Official Journal of the Senate of the State of Texas at the Adjourned Session, Sixth Legislature. Austin: Marshall & Oldham, 1856.

Pancake, John S. *The Destructive War: The British Campaign in the Carolinas, 1780–1782*. Tuscaloosa: University of Alabama Press, 1985.

Pendleton District and Anderson County, South Carolina Wills, Estates, Inventories, Tax Returns and Census Records. Easley, S. Car.: Southern Historical Press, 1980.

Pierce, Gerald S. *Texas under Arms: The Camps, Posts, Forts, and Military Towns of the Republic of Texas, 1836–1846*. Austin: Encino Press, 1969.

Pierson, Marion John Bennett. *Louisiana Soldiers in the War of 1812*. Baton Rouge: Louisiana Genealogical and Historical Society, 1963.

Pool, William. *A Historical Atlas of Texas*. Austin: Encino Press, 1975.

Ramsdell, Charles. *San Antonio: A Historical and Pictorial Guide.* Austin: University of Texas Press, 1959 and 1976 editions.

Remy, Caroline. "Hispanic-Mexican San Antonio: 1836–1861," *Southwestern Historical Quarterly* 71, no. 4 (April, 1968).

Richardson, Rupert N., Ernest Wallace, and Adrian N. Anderson. *Texas: The Lone Star State.* Englewood Cliffs, N.J.: Prentice-Hall, 1970 and 1981.

Richardson, Walter R. *In Memory of Mrs. Mary A. Maverick.* New York: Knickerbocker Press, 1898.

Rippy, J. Fred. "Border Troubles along the Rio Grande," *Southwestern Historical Quarterly* 23, no. 1 (July, 1919): 100–103.

Roller, David C., and Robert W. Twyman. *The Encyclopedia of Southern History.* Baton Rouge: Louisiana State University Press, 1979.

Royall, Anne. *Letters from Alabama on Various Subjects.* Washington: N.p., 1839.

Salley, A. S., Jr., ed. *Journal of the Commissioners of the Navy of South Carolina, Oct. 9, 1776–March 1, 1779.* Columbia, S. Car.: State Company, 1912.

San Antonio Bicentennial Heritage Committee. *San Antonio in the Eighteenth Century.* San Antonio: Clarke Printing Co., 1976.

Schmitz, Joseph William. *Texas Culture, 1836–1846: In the Days of the Republic.* San Antonio: Naylor Company, 1960.

Schroeder, John H. *Mr. Polk's War: American Opposition and Dissent, 1846–1848.* Madison: University of Wisconsin Press, 1973.

Seguin, Juan. *Personal Memoirs of John N. Seguin from the Year 1834 to the Retreat of General Woll from the City of San Antonio in 1842.* San Antonio: Ledger Book and Job Office, 1858.

Sexton, Irwin, and Kathryn Sexton. *Samuel A. Maverick.* San Antonio: Naylor Company, 1964.

Shenton, James P. *Robert John Walker: A Politician from Jackson to Lincoln.* New York: Columbia University Press, 1961.

Simmons, Marc. *New Mexico: A Bicentennial History.* New York: W. W. Norton & Company, 1977.

Simpson, Harold B. *Frontier Forts of Texas.* Waco: Texian Press, 1966.

Smithwick, Noah. *The Evolution of a State: Recollections of Old Texas Days.* Austin: University of Texas Press, 1984.

Stapp, William Preston. *The Prisoners of Perote.* Austin: University of Texas Press, 1977.

State Gazette Appendix Containing Debates in the House of Representatives of the Eighth Legislature of the State of Texas. Austin: John Marshall & Co., 1860.

State Gazette Appendix of the Sixth Legislature. Austin: Marshall & Oldham, 1855.

State Gazette Appendix of the Sixth Legislature, Adjourned Session. Austin: Marshall & Oldham, 1856.

State Gazette Appendix of the Seventh Legislature. Austin: Marshall & Co., 1858.

Sutherland, John. *The Fall of the Alamo*. San Antonio: Naylor Company, 1936.

Thompson, Waddy. *Recollections of Mexico*. New York: Wiley and Putnam, 1846.

Tinkle, Lon. *Thirteen Days to Glory: The Siege of the Alamo*. New York: McGraw-Hill Book Company, 1958.

Tuscaloosa Genealogical Society. *Pioneers of Tuscaloosa County, Alabama prior to 1830*. Tuscaloosa, 1981.

Tyler, Alice Felt. *Freedom's Ferment: Phases of American Social History from the Colonial Period to the Outbreak of the Civil War*. New York: Harper & Row, 1944.

Vandiver, Louise. *Traditions and History of Anderson County*. Atlanta, Ga.: Ruralist Press, 1928.

Vedder, Edwin. *Records of St. Paul's Episcopal Church of Pendleton, South Carolina*. Greenville, S. Car.: A Press, 1982.

The War of the Rebellion: A Compilation of the Official Records of the Union and Confederate Armies. Washington, D.C.: Government Printing Office. Series I, vol. I, 1880; series II, vol. I, 1894.

Watkins, Sue, ed. *One League to Each Wind: Accounts of Early Surveying in Texas*. Austin: Von Boeckmann-Jones, 1964.

Weaver, Bobby D. *Castro's Colony: Empresario Development in Texas, 1842–1865*. College Station: Texas A&M University Press, 1985.

Webb, Walter Prescott. *The Texas Rangers: A Century of Frontier Defense*. Austin: University of Texas Press, 1965 edition.

————, ed. *Handbook of Texas*. Austin: Texas State Historical Association, 1952.

Webber, Mabel L., ed. "Death Notices from the South Carolina and American General Gazette, and Its Continuation the Royal Gazette, May 1766–June 1782," *South Carolina Historical and Genealogical Magazine* 17, no. 1 (Jan., 1916).

————. "Register of St. Andrew's Parish, Berkeley County, South Carolina, 1719–1774," *South Carolina Historical and Genealogical Magazine* 14, no. 1.

Weems, John Edward. *Dream of Empire: A Human History of the Republic of Texas, 1836–1846*. New York: Simon & Schuster, 1971.

Weland, Leonie Rummel, and Houston Wade. *An Early History of Fayette County*. LaGrange, Tex.: LaGrange Journal, 1936.

White, Gifford, ed. *The 1840 Census of the Republic of Texas*. Austin: Pemberton Press, 1966.

Williams, Amelia. "A Critical Study of the Siege of the Alamo and of the Personnel of Its Defenders," *Southwestern Historical Quarterly* 37, nos. 1–4 (July, 1933–Apr., 1934): 1–44, 79–115, 157–84, 237–312.

Wilson, Clyde N., ed. *The Papers of John C. Calhoun*. Columbia: University of South Carolina Press, 1959–87 (vols. X and XI, 1977 and 1978).

Winkler, E. W., ed. "The Bexar and Dawson Prisoners," *Texas Historical Association Quarterly* 13, no. 4 (Apr., 1910).

Winkler, William, ed. *Journal of the Secession Convention of Texas, 1861*. Austin Printing Company, 1912.

Wooster, Ralph A. "Membership in Early Texas Legislatures, 1850–1860," *Southwestern Historical Quarterly* 69, no. 2 (Oct., 1965): 163–73.

———. "Wealthy Texans, 1860," *Southwestern Historical Quarterly* 71, no. 2 (Oct., 1967): 163–80.

———. "Wealthy Texans, 1870," *Southwestern Historical Quarterly* 74, no. 3 (July, 1970): 24–35.

Wooten, Dudley G. *A Comprehensive History of Texas, 1685–1897*. Dallas: William G. Scarff, 1898.

Wright, Louis B. *South Carolina: A Bicentennial History*. New York: W. W. Norton & Company, 1976.

Yoakum, Henderson K. *History of Texas from Its First Settlement in 1685 to Its Annexation to the United States in 1836*. New York: Redfield, 1856.

Newspapers

Selected editions of the following nineteenth-century newspapers were consulted:

Courier, Charleston, S. Car.

Messenger, Pendleton, S. Car.

Miller's Weekly Messenger, Pendleton, S. Car.

National Pilot, New Haven, Conn.

Selected issues of the following Texas newspapers from Barker Texas History Center files were consulted:

Dallas Herald

Express, San Antonio

Northern Standard, Clarksville

San Antonio Ledger

San Antonio Semi-Weekly News

Telegraph & Texas Register, Houston

Texas State Gazette, Austin

Index

Turn Your Eyes Toward Texas was composed into type on a Compugraphic digital phototypesetter in eleven point Goudy Old Style with two points of spacing between the lines. Goudy Old Style was also selected for display. The book was designed by Jim Billingsley, typeset by Metricomp, Inc., printed offset by Thomson-Shore, Inc., and bound by John H. Dekker & Sons. The paper on which the book is printed bears acid-free characteristics for an effective life of at least three hundred years.

Texas A&M University Press

COLLEGE STATION